W9-DBX-364

More
WORDS
that make
a difference

ROBERT
GREENMAN

CAROL
GREENMAN

LEVENGER
PRESS

Published by
Levenger Press
420 South Congress Avenue
Delray Beach, Florida 33445-4696 USA
www.Levengerpress.com

©2007 Robert Greenman and Carol Greenman. All rights reserved.
First Edition

Library of Congress Cataloging-in-Publication Data

Greenman, Robert.
  More words that make a difference / Robert Greenman, Carol Greenman. --
1st ed.
     p. cm.
  Includes bibliographical references and index.
  ISBN-13: 978-1-929154-28-9
  1. Vocabulary. 2. English language--Glossaries, vocabularies, etc. 3.
American newspapers--Language. I. Greenman, Carol, 1940- II. Title.
  PE1449.G669 2007
  428.1--dc22
                         2007015437

To our grandchildren

Rebecca

Gabriel

Emma

Noah

Zoe

For what are all our contrivings,
And the wisdom of our books,
When compared with your caresses,
And the gladness of your looks?

–Henry Wadsworth Longfellow

"An author's writing desk is something infinitely higher than a pulpit."

–James Russell Lowell

Contents

Introduction

For the past 150 years, *The Atlantic Monthly* has chronicled, commented on, evaluated and influenced American culture. It has dealt with the major issues of American life and countless small ones, having perhaps a greater effect on American thought than any other magazine.

Its founders brought it into existence specifically as a platform from which to speak out against slavery and support the Abolitionist cause in the 1850s, as well as to lift American writing from its position as England's poor cousin. It was influential in both respects, but in an even larger sense, it facilitated the development of American thinking.

We chose *The Atlantic* to illustrate the use of words worth using because of the richness of its subject matter and vocabulary, the quality of its writing, and the magazine's central place in American journalism and thought. No matter how extensive your vocabulary, you are bound to meet new words here that you will find invaluable aids to thinking and communicating. You may also encounter many with which you are familiar but rarely if ever think of employing, something these *Atlantic* passages may spur you to do.

While each passage contains a vocabulary-enhancing word, each is here because it is good reading in and of itself. Step into the woods at raiment, into Manhattan at palisade, or among a pod of dolphins at vanguard. Meet Einstein at accede, Lincoln at fleece, Dickens at florid.

Each passage appears word for word as it did in the original article, including words that were hyphenated at the time but are no longer. Any brackets were in the original passage. For the sake of consistency, double quotation marks are used throughout the book, although from July 1910 through June 1942 single quotation marks were used to save space on the magazine page. And in a few cases, commas have been added or removed for clarity.

To gather the passages and words for this book, we examined every nonfiction article in *The Atlantic Monthly* from its initial issue in November 1857 through December 2005. (We omitted fiction because it did not lend itself to brief, self-contained passages that make interesting reading in themselves, or to passages whose context illuminates the meaning of a word the way nonfiction does.)

As unfamiliar as some of these words may seem, especially if they appeared in *Atlantic* passages more than a century ago, none are obsolete. All of them occur in contemporary books and periodicals; all are words for our times. Many will eventually help you to express a thought, describe a feeling or convey an observation. Encountering a word here is only the beginning. New words settle and ferment. You meet them later in other reading. And one day they emerge — during a conversation, while writing a speech, a letter, a story, a poem, an article, an essay, a paper, an email. That's when you know a word is yours.

Creating this book has been a deeply personal encounter for us, and one of the richest experiences of our lives. Reading through 148 years of *The Atlantic* imbued us with a sense of America at its most thoughtful and engaging, and working among *The Atlantic's* remarkable staff allowed us to absorb the atmosphere of this venerated yet still vibrant magazine. We hope that the passages in this book will fill you, too, with the spirit of *The Atlantic*.

Robert and Carol Greenman

Index
of
More WORDS that make a difference

Pronunciation Key

The pronunciations in this edition of *More Words That Make A Difference* are presented in a form called respelling, adopted from the *NBC Handbook of Pronunciation*, the bible of pronunciation for radio and television announcers. (The pronunciations of the words themselves, however, are not necessarily those given in the *NBC Handbook*.) If some of the pronunciations sound a bit strange or stilted when you say them aloud, that's because they are not supposed to be spoken as independent units but as they would sound in conversational speech. Try them that way and they will sound natural.

Most pronunciations will be obvious at first glance. The following key will be helpful, however, in distinguishing the way the vowel sounds and several consonant sounds are respelled. Stress the syllables that are printed in uppercase letters.

This sound...	*...is respelled like this*
art	ahrt
date	dayt
fall	fawl
hat	hat
face	fays
server	SER ver
heat	heet
above	uh BUHV
show	shoh
root	roo:t
hour	OW er
rouge	roo:zh
phone	fone
then	th:en
thin	thin
try	trigh
put	poot

If a pronunciation differs from the one you've been using or hearing, check your dictionary; for the purposes of this book, we have provided only one pronunciation per word, but it's quite possible that the pronunciation you're familiar with is equally acceptable. Dictionaries do not attempt to dictate correctness in pronunciation; rather, they indicate how educated speakers pronounce words. For that reason, dictionaries provide alternate pronunciations for thousands of words. For example, the pronunciation for inexplicable in this book is given as *in EKS pli kuh buhl*. However, *in eks PLI kuh buhl* is just as commonly heard among educated speakers and will also be found in the dictionary.

The words
and
their passages

acclamation

A man writes the best he can about what moves him deeply. Once his writing gets published as a book, he loses control over it. Time and the human family do what they want to with it. It may have periods of wide reading and acclamation, other periods of condemnation, decline, neglect; then a complete fade-out — or maybe a revival. And what revives in later years is often what was neglected when new. This happens. In literature and other arts — it happens.

Chicago Poems

Carl Sandburg   March 1942

see page 7

abasement   *uh BAYS mint*
a lowering in value or esteem

Evolution makes its appeal to reason, but its acceptance does not mean the abasement, let alone the denial, of emotion, faith, and religion, those great springs of the higher human attitudes and activities.

Vernon Kellogg   April 1924

abate   *uh BAYT*
to diminish or lessen

As the uncritically positive and unabashedly patriotic approach that for so long characterized the teaching of American history in the public schools has abated, the emphasis has steadily shifted to the problems and failures of the past. The saga of the glories of the old West has thus given way to a saga of exploitation and greed. Pride in conquering the wilderness has yielded to the shame of despoiling the land and dispossessing the indigenous peoples. What seems to have happened is that a laudably corrective trend has predominated to such an extent that the emphasis seems somehow reversed, and parents complain that they scarcely recognize the history their children are taught.

Douglas L. Wilson   November 1992

abnegate   *AB nuh gayt*
to give up or renounce; deny; reject; abandon ("abnegation" is the noun)

Early in its history photography was dismissed as a lesser art, or as no art at all. A photograph, critics said, was just a record of the external moment — a critique that the medium has never entirely escaped. Well into this century photographers found themselves apologetic about their work, and many were drawn to the abnegation of pictorialism. The Pictorialists produced blurred, symbolic, "poetic" prints in an effort to be painterly.

Kenneth Brower   May 1998

abound   *uh BOWND*
to be plentiful

Birds, as Messiaen never tired of saying, were earth's first musicians, and to his ears the best. People have been mimicking birds in music since the dawn of time. Certainly the Western canon, from Rameau, Vivaldi, and Bach on to Wagner, Strauss, and Stravinsky, abounds with owls, nightingales, cuckoos, and larks, evoked in picturesque but simplistic approximations. Until Messiaen the challenge of catching the complexities of contour and timbre of any but the plainest birdsongs went unattempted.

Matthew Gurewitsch   March 1997

absolutism   *AB suh loo: ti zuhm*
government by one all-powerful ruler; despotism ("absolutist" is the adjective)

Taking full advantage of Russia's absolutist traditions, Joseph Stalin followed in the footsteps of Ivan the Terrible and Peter the Great and set about strengthening the state, enacting programs of industrialization and agricultural collectivization: he enslaved vast segments of his population to build industries, mine the earth, and gather crops. Under his direction the state pillaged its citizens, dispossessing them of land, factories, homes, and personal wealth, murdering them by the millions in purges designed to crush potential resistance.

Jeffrey Tayler   May 2001

abut   *uh BUHT*
to touch at one end or one side of something; lie adjacent ("abutting" is the adjective)

In 1968 California built what are believed to be the first noise barriers along modern federal highways. Walls were erected on Highway 101 in San Francisco and Interstate 680 north of San Jose to shield abutting residential neighborhoods from the sound of heavy traffic. Within four years the federal government followed California's lead, adopting regulations requiring that whenever a state builds, expands, or realigns a federally funded highway, an attempt be made to curtail excessive noise that would otherwise be inflicted on sensitive neighbors, such as schools, hospitals, and residential areas.

Philip Langdon   August 1997

abysmal   *uh BIZ muhl*
extremely or hopelessly bad

When CBS, NBC, and ABC dominated the airwaves, their blanket coverage of presidential speeches, political conventions, and presidential debates sometimes left little else to watch on TV. But as channels have proliferated, it has become much easier to avoid exposure to politics altogether. Whereas President Richard Nixon got an average rating of 50 for his televised addresses to the nation, President Clinton averaged only about 30 in his first term. Political conventions, which once received more TV coverage than the Summer Olympics, have been relegated to an hour per night and draw abysmal ratings. In sum, young people today have never known a time when most citizens paid attention to major political events. As a result, most of them have yet to get into the habit of voting.

Martin P. Wattenberg   October 1998

accede   *ak SEED*
to give in; agree to

Typical of Einstein is the story of the popular lecture he was finally prevailed upon to give, for it shows his incapability of behavior that was not genuine. He had been asked many times to speak to a certain audience, but had always begged off on the basis that he had nothing to say. Finally, however, the pressure became so great that he was forced to accede. Came the evening of the lecture, and amidst applause Dr. Einstein was led to the front of the stage and introduced. For a few moments he looked out at the audience, tongue-tied and silent. Finally he could stand it no longer and, smiling sheepishly, said, "I find that I have nothing to say," and returned to his seat.

George R. Harrison   June 1955

acclamation   *a kluh MAY shuhn*
enthusiastic approval; loud applause

A man writes the best he can about what moves him deeply. Once his writing gets published as a book, he loses control over it. Time and the human family do what they want to with it. It may have periods of wide reading and acclamation, other periods of condemnation, decline, neglect; then a complete fade-out — or maybe a revival. And what revives in later years is often what was neglected when new. This happens. In literature and other arts — it happens.

Carl Sandburg   March 1942

accoutrements   *uh KOO: truh mints*
furnishings, equipment or accessories that lend identification to someone

Sherlock Holmes stories have been translated into fifty-six languages, including

Esperanto and shorthand. There have been at least 264 movies, 630 radio plays, thirty-two stage plays, twenty-five TV shows, and fifteen burlesques featuring the detective, as well as a ballet, a musical and an oratorio. So familiar is Holmes that he is instantly recognized by his accoutrements alone — the deerstalker cap, inverness cape, and curved pipe — even by people who have never read a word of the stories.

Cait Murphy   March 1987

❋ Having Sherlock Holmes wear a deerstalker hat was not the idea of the author, Arthur Conan Doyle, but of Sidney Paget, whose drawings in *The Strand Magazine*, beginning in 1891, illustrated many of the Holmes stories. Doyle did not mention a hat of any kind until after it had appeared in a Paget drawing, and then described it only as an "ear-flapped travelling cap." Paget chose the deerstalker because he owned one and liked it.The magazine's editors hired Paget by mistake; they meant to hire his brother Walter, whose drawings in *Robinson Crusoe* and *Treasure Island* had attracted them. Ironically, Sidney used Walter as the model for Holmes, depicting not the "thin razor-like face with a great hawks-bill of a nose, and two small eyes, set close together on either side of it" that Doyle imagined, but a handsome man whose appearance Doyle found agreeable because he appealed to his "lady readers." Paget gave Holmes the inverness cape, too, but a later illustrator, Frederick Dorr Steele, gave Holmes the curved pipe in 1903, an idea he took from photographs of the actor William Gillette, who played Holmes on the English and American stage from 1889 to 1935. When Gillette found that he could not hold a straight pipe between his teeth, speak, and use his hands at the same time, he adopted a meerschaum. Photos of Gillette onstage with this curved pipe led Steele to add it to the Holmes image.

accrue   *uh KROO:*
to gain by increment; accumulate

When Lyndon Johnson assumed the presidency, after the assassination of John F. Kennedy, in November of 1963, he knew that in order to accrue political capital he would initially need to champion goals and policies that Kennedy had already been pursuing. Not long before his death Kennedy had scrawled the word "poverty" on a piece of paper and circled it multiple times; this note fell into the hands of his brother Robert and became a symbolic justification for Johnson's declaration of the War on Poverty, early in 1964.

Robert Dallek   June 2003

acme   *AK mee*
the highest point; peak

The acme, the climax, of Coolidge's remoteness and reserve, of his asocial quality, is indisputably his utter disregard of conversation as mankind in general practices it. There are men who cannot talk even when they wish to. Coolidge can talk freely enough, but talk for talk's sake means nothing to him. If he wants to get information, he will pelt you with a string of questions for half an hour on end. Then he has done with you, and you may go. The ordinary small talk of the world, its trivial gossip, drifts by him, slips over him, like the idle wind. He stands silent, apart, absorbed in his thoughts, and wonders how people can chatter so, and why they should.

Gamaliel Bradford   January 1930

acquiesce   *a kwee ES*
to agree or consent quietly, but without enthusiasm; to agree to tacitly

I can remember when Balzac's novels were kept on the top shelf, though now they are freely given out in many public libraries. It was, in my opinion, a loss that they were so long reserved. I acquiesced in the reservation, however, since it was demanded by a considerable number of intelligent people. I do not think they are good food for children, even now. The same principle can be, and should be, applied in public museums of art. If the public demands that the Discobolus should be relegated to an attic because it is unclothed, very well, let it go there. Let me have the key to the attic when I wish it. If the statue is really good and pure, as thousands of good people believe, it will, by and by, be brought down to the main hall.

Contributors' Club: Edward S. Holden   August 1901

✳ William Dean Howells, *The Atlantic's* third editor, launched the Contributors' Club in the January 1877 issue of *The Atlantic*. Looking for material that was offbeat, informal and mildly provocative, in an era when writers might prefer not putting their names to it, Howells invited new authors and regular contributors to submit short pieces that would appear unsigned. Encouraging "all writers who have minds upon any ethical or aesthetic subject briefly to free them here," he cautioned against "personal spite," but welcomed "the expression of intellectual grudges of every sort." They responded with musings, memories, prejudices and predilections — and, sometimes, more strongly expressed feelings and opinions than they might have felt comfortable with had the writing not been anonymous. The feature lasted 65 years, ending in 1942, during Edward Weeks's editorship.

acrid   *A krid*
sharp or biting to the taste or smell; irritating to the eyes or nose

A chain of cities unreels in my memory like a roll of archival film. I rewind to Ankara, Turkey, in the mid-seventies: An acrid pall shrouds the minarets. The city has some of the worst air pollution on Earth. Each room of our large house has an electrostatic air-cleaner; an army of plastic woodgrained boxes tries mightily to zap particulates before they reach our soft American lungs. But this brown haze is winter coal smoke. In the spring the stars blink and wheel high over the Balgat hills, pristine and clear in the thin, dry Anatolian air.

Michael Benson   July/August 2002

acrimonious   *a kri MOH nee uhs*
caustic, stinging or bitter in words or behavior

The appearance of Walt Whitman's *Leaves of Grass* in a new edition has revived a discussion always imminent when the name of this writer is brought forward, and always more or less acrimonious. Some persons even imagine it obligatory upon them to deny him all merit of poetic endowment, so violent is their revolt against the offensiveness which Mr. Whitman has chosen to make a central and integral point of his literary method. Such critics stultify themselves by the coarseness of view (and sometimes of expression) with which they meet the grossness they condemn. If they can see nothing in this book except indecency and bombastic truisms, the inference must be that their sensibilities are not delicate enough to recognize the fresh, strong, healthy presentation of common things in a way that revivifies them, the generous aspiration, the fine sympathy with man and nature, the buoyant belief in immortality, which are no less characteristic of the author than his mistaken boldness in displaying the carnal side of existence, and his particularity in describing disease or loathsome decay.

George Parsons Lathrop   January 1882

actuary   *AK choo ai ree*
a person who compiles statistical tables of mortality and estimates from them the rates of insurance premiums ("actuarial" is the adjective)

"I'm going to enjoy the time I've got left," Johnson told friends when he left Washington in January, 1969, a worn old man at sixty, consumed by the bitter, often violent, five years of his presidency. He had never doubted that he could have won the 1968 election against Richard Nixon if he had chosen to run for another term. But in 1967 he launched a secret actuarial study on his life expectancy, supplying personal histories of all the males in the recent Johnson line, himself included. "The men in the Johnson family have a history of dying young," he told me at his ranch in the summer of 1971. "My daddy was only sixty-two when he died, and I figured that with my history of heart trouble I'd never live through another four years. The

American people had enough of Presidents dying in office." The prediction handed to Johnson was that he would die at the age of sixty-four. He did.

Leo Janos   July 1973

acumen   *A kyuh min*
quickness to perceive and understand a situation

I have just returned from Hannibal, Missouri, and I should like to report that it is a success. It is a success beyond anything Mark Twain ever dreamed of for the Paige typesetting machine, and it is my guess that Twain had the business acumen to see that this would one day be so and invested heavily in Hannibal real estate — else how do you account for the Mark Twain Chinchilla Ranch and Mark Twain Frozen Custard? It seems obvious to me that the genius of Mark Twain has been enormously underestimated; a man who could foresee frozen custard was an American Nostradamus; can you buy Thoreau Balsam Pillows at Concord, or Emily Dickinson African Violets at Amherst?

Charles Boewe   March 1953

> ✳ Believing the Paige typesetting machine would transform the publishing industry and make him a millionaire, Mark Twain invested hundreds of thousands of dollars with its inventor, James W. Paige, between 1880 and 1894. It was, indeed, brilliantly conceived and constructed, and superior to the Merganthaler company's Linotype machine then currently in use. At the peak of its development, one person at the keyboard could not only set type as fast as ten or more hand compositors, but perform other complex tasks thought undoable by a machine up till then, including justifying lines and setting syllables as well as letters. But with 18,000 parts performing operations as sophisticated as any machine yet invented, it frequently broke down. In addition, Paige's refusal to stop refining and redesigning it so it could be marketed made the Linotype, by default, the choice of the nation's newspapers. The Paige debacle, as well as the failure of his publishing company, put Twain deeply in debt, which he paid off through lecture tours around the world and across America.

acute   *uh KYOO:T*
sharply or keenly sensitive

Toulouse-Lautrec is an artist with a reputation for debauchery. Yet look at his drawings and paintings, and where do you see the results of debauchery? There is nothing loose, careless, or feeble in them. The drawing is sensitive and tense; the compositions are thought out, the work of a great artist with acute observation.

Jacob Epstein   November 1940

addle   *A duhl*
to make or become confused; muddle

My introduction to Bellagio came through a visit to its Gallery of Fine Art, which announced a show of twenty-six paintings from The Phillips Collection, in Washington, D.C., including works by Monet, Matisse, Bonnard, and Picasso. It is a mark of the way Las Vegas addles the brain that after paying a $12 admission fee I more than half expected the paintings to be forgeries.

Richard Todd   February 2001

ad infinitum   *AD in fuh NIGH tuhm*
endlessly; forever; without limit: Latin, to infinity

THE VANISHING AMERICAN OUTHOUSE *by Ronald S. Barlow. Viking Studio, 142 pages, $19.95.* The outhouse, backhouse, privy, loo, with similar titles ad infinitum, was once ubiquitous, there being no substitute for it. It deserves commemoration.

Phoebe-Lou Adams   August 2000

✳ Between 1952 and 2000, Phoebe-Lou Adams (1918-2001) reviewed close to 4,000 books for *The Atlantic* under four editors in chief. Asked how she chose from among the hundreds that arrived each month at *The Atlantic*, she said: "I turn them over, I riffle the pages, I smell the glue, and then I consider the reputation of the publishing house and the author's reputation, if any. Many books by unknown authors turn out to be wonderful."

admixture   *ad MIKS chuhr*
a compound formed by mixing

In place of our largely degenerated olfactory sense, ants appear to have the most exquisite sense of smell, apparently combined and fused with a sense of touch through an intimate admixture of these sense organs on the antennae, to give a sort of "contact odor" sensation of which we can have little conception.

Caryl P. Haskins   March 1946

admonition   *ad muh NI shuhn*
a cautionary reminder

I who am blind can give one hint to those who see — one admonition to those who would make full use of the gift of sight: Use your eyes as if tomorrow you would be stricken blind. And the same method can be applied to the other senses. Hear the music of voices, the song of a bird, the mighty strains of an orchestra, as if you would be stricken deaf tomorrow. Touch each object you want to touch as if tomorrow your tactile sense would fail. Smell the perfume of flowers, taste with relish each morsel, as if tomorrow you could never smell and taste again. Make the most of every sense; glory in all the facets of pleasure and beauty which the world reveals to you through the several means of contact which Nature provides. But of all the senses, I am sure that sight must be the most delightful.

Helen Keller   January 1933

ad nauseam   *ad NAW zee uhm*
to a disgusting or ridiculous degree: Latin, to sickness

It's now an axiom of the U.S. foreign-policy establishment that economic, technological, and demographic changes are making East Asia the world's most dynamic arena, a driving force — increasingly the dominant force — in the international economy. The Pacific Century, we are told ad nauseam, has dawned.

Benjamin Schwarz   June 1996

adroit   *uh DROIT*
skillful, physically or mentally

One of the greatest problems confronting the deans of Harvard, Yale, and Princeton is that of undergraduate aviators. At Princeton, the students are no longer allowed to have airplanes. At Yale and Harvard, undergraduate flying clubs flourish under very lukewarm official approval. In both communities, the clubs have become exceedingly popular. Their members are adroit and expert aviators, but, for the most part, lamentable scholars. The academic mortality of members of the flying clubs far outruns that of the pedestrian students; and naturally enough, for their members spend so much of their time at the airports that they soon leave their studies far in arrears.

William I. Nichols   October 1929

✳ Harvard, Yale and Princeton are all Ivy League institutions. The term Ivy League appeared in print for the first time in October 1937 when Stanley Woodward, a *New York Herald Tribune* sports editor, used it in a column. The day before he had heard Caswell Adams, a sportswriter, complain, "Oh, they're just Ivy League," when he was assigned to cover a Columbia-Pennsylvania football game. Caswell, who preferred covering powerhouse teams, was referring to the interscholastic athletic league composed of Brown, Columbia, Cornell, Dartmouth, Harvard, the University of Pennsylvania, Princeton and Yale. Although the term caught on quickly, Ivy League was not used as the official term for the colleges' association until February 1954.

adulterate   *uh DUHL tuh rayt*
to make impure by adding inferior or unsuitable ingredients

> The cost and vast consumption of coffee and tea have made the inducements to adulterate them very great. The most harmless form is the selling of coffee grounds and old tea-leaves for fresh coffee and tea. There is no security in buying coffee ready-ground; and we always look at the neat little packages of it in the grocers' windows with a shudder. Beans and peas we have certainly tasted in ground coffee. The most fashionable adulteration, and one even openly vaunted as economical and increasing the richness of the beverage, is with the root of the wild endive, or chicory. Roasted and ground, it closely resembles coffee. It contains, however, none of the virtues of the latter, and has nothing to recommend it but its cheapness.
>
> David William Cheever   January 1859

adumbrate   *uh DUHM brayt*
to foreshadow in a vague way; suggest beforehand; prefigure

> It is not impossible to adumbrate the general nature of the catastrophe which threatens mankind if war-making goes on.
>
> H. G. Wells   January 1919

adventitious   *ad ven TI shuhs*
added from outside; arriving from another source; added by chance; not inherent

> Yet the principal duty of the novelist is to get himself read, as the principal duty of the playwright is to get himself acted before a considerable audience. Otherwise his support becomes artificial — fellowships, grants-in-aid, publishers' advances, and writers' conferences. But in accepting these well-meant yet adventitious supports, the novelist loses living touch with a potential public in a manner that would have horrified Dickens and puzzled Henry James.
>
> Howard Mumford Jones   October 1966

adventurism   *ad VEN chuh ri zuhm*
defiance or disregard of accepted standards of behavior

> Ovid expends many lines in his *Art of Love* warning men against underestimating the ladies' amorous adventurism. In Dante's *Inferno* the circle of hell for sins of the flesh is populated in great part by women. It is the lust of a mother (not, say, an uncle) that so tortures Shakespeare's Hamlet ("Frailty, thy name is woman"), a girl's sexual fickleness that takes out the hero in *Troilus and Cressida*, a queen's love for an ass that brings down the house in *A Midsummer Night's Dream*. The greatest adulterers in the

Western canon — Emma Bovary, Anna Karenina, Molly Bloom, Carmen — have, in fact, been adulteresses. Each had a faithful husband at home.

Cristina Nehring   July/August 2005

reckless intervention by one nation in the affairs of another

While U.S. policy-makers ponder who and how to help, Soviet adventurism in Afghanistan has mired Russian tanks and troops in a struggle that alarms Pakistan and China — and intensifies the suffering of an already desperate land.

The *Atlantic* Editors   May 1980

aesthetic   *es THE tik*
relating to beauty

Plaster, like almost everything else, reached its aesthetic zenith during the Renaissance. Exacting craftsmen filled magnificent rooms with moldings, reliefs, and other ornaments, achieving a degree of interior decoration seldom aspired to nowadays beyond the city limits of Las Vegas. When Michaelangelo sprawled on his back for four years beneath the ceiling of the Sistine Chapel, it was onto wet plaster (*fresco* means "fresh," the condition in which the surface to be frescoed must be) that he painted his astonishing vision.

David Owen   May 1987

affinity   *uh FIN uh tee*
a natural attraction toward, or liking for, something

There is abundant evidence that in the most trying hours of his presidency Lincoln sought out Shakespeare's plays as a source of strength and consolation. Don E. Fehrenbacher relates this affinity for Shakespeare to Lincoln's keen sense of his role and ultimate responsibility in the carnage of the Civil War. "To some indeterminable extent and in some intuitive ways, Lincoln seems to have assimilated the substance of the plays into his own experience and deepening sense of tragedy."

Douglas L. Wilson   January 1991

afford   *uh FAWRD*
to provide; furnish

If it were not for the mists and fogs which come rolling in from the river, Chelsea would be an ideal place of residence. One never tires of the Thames, for the river has made London, and to watch the tide ebb and flow affords one the most delightful exercise. George Eliot lived in Chelsea, and Carlyle, and Rossetti, and Wilde, and Whistler.

A. Edward Newton   July 1926

aficionado   *uh fish uh NAH doh*
a devoted follower of a sport, art or other interest; enthusiast; fan

The novel's scandal-tinted history and its subject — the affair between a middle-aged sexual pervert and a twelve-year-old girl — inevitably conjure up expectations of pornography. But there is not a single obscene term in *Lolita*, and aficionados of erotica are likely to find it a dud.

Charles J. Rolo   September 1958

✳ Borrowed from Spanish, aficionado first appeared in English around 1845, when it meant a bullfighting devotee. Ernest Hemingway used it in that sense in *Death in the Afternoon*, a book about bullfighting published in 1932, but the book's popularity lifted the word into mainstream English as a general term for enthusiast.

agglomeration   *uh glah muh RAY shuhn*
a jumbled heap; mass

I was forty-five years old before I discovered the city of my dreams. In Hong Kong there is agglomeration beyond my fondest imaginings. The Kowloon district claims a population density four times that of New York City. You could hardly fail to find a soul mate here. Probably you're standing on his or her foot and have just received a swift soul-mate elbow in the ribs.

P. J. O'Rourke   October 2002

aggrandize   *uh GRAN dighz*
to make greater, more powerful or richer ("aggrandizement" is the noun)

I have tried to understand what brought about the abuses of power that came to a head in Watergate. Knowing all that I now know, I think I can discern three principal contributory ingredients. One was Richard Nixon's own distrustful style, a compound of his personal insecurity and his reaction to the reality of bitter attack. A second was the amoral alacrity to do his bidding of a politically inexperienced, organization-minded staff obsessively driven by the compulsion to win. A third was the aggrandizement of presidential power and the tendencies toward its abuse that had already been set in motion before Nixon took office.

Elliot Richardson   March 1976

aggregate   *A gruh git*
a group of distinct parts considered as a whole; all together

The development of brand advertising, coinciding roughly with the introduction of the telegraph, the rise of the department store, and urbanization, hastened the nationalization of the United States. By helping to create aggregate demand, advertising quickened the shift to mass production. The branding of mass-produced goods helped to usurp the primacy of local markets. National advertisements for these products, running among the stories in new national magazines, impelled the nation to coalesce around shared customs, creating what the historian Roland Marchand has termed "a 'community of discourse,' an integrative common language shared by an otherwise diverse audience."

Randall Rothenberg   June 1997

agitate   *A ji tayt*
to keep a political or other topic perpetually under discussion, so as to impress it on the public mind

To be told that we ought not to agitate the question of Slavery, when it is that which is forever agitating us, is like telling a man with the fever and ague on him to stop shaking and he will be cured.

James Russell Lowell   October 1860

agog   *uh GAHG*
in a state of eager excitement, anticipation or interest

In Modesto I heard that a canning factory was to open the next morning to preserve a large shipment of peaches, the first of the season. The town was agog with the news. I was on hand at 7:30, half an hour early, but so were several thousand others, both men and women. A full crew had already been picked. The bindlestiffs were congregating about the fruit centres to rush the farms at the first sign of a ripening crop. In Fresno, the raisin town, their bedrolls were hanging by the hundreds all around the railroad station and the local water tank.

Robert Whitcomb   May 1931

❋ The Great Depression of the 1930s saw tens of thousands of jobless men and women leave their homes for a wandering life, earning money from temporary menial work by panhandling, or by asking for food at back doors. They were hobos, traveling by foot or hopping freight trains, and carrying their worldly possessions in their bindle, or bedroll. Bindlestiffs they were called, stiff being a synonym for tramp. Groups of hobos gathered near railroad yards in encampments called jungles, or slept in cheap hotels called flophouses. While the words bindlestiff and hobo originated in the late 1880s, the hobo life in America goes at least as far back as the end of the Civil War, when thousands of former soldiers took up that way of life instead of returning home. The origin of *hobo* is unknown.

agrarian   *uh GRA ree in*
characteristic of farmers or their way of life

Whether to encourage domestic manufacturing or to retain the nation's agrarian character was the subject of intense debate in the early decades of the republic. In the end, Jefferson's agrarian vision did not prevail.

Michael J. Sandel   March 1996

✳ "Cultivators of the earth are the most valuable citizens," Thomas Jefferson wrote in 1775 to John Jay, who later became the first chief justice of the United States. "They are the most vigorous, the most independent, the most virtuous, and they are tied to their country and wedded to its liberty and interests by the most lasting bonds."

allegorical   *a luh GAW ruh kuhl*
representing something else symbolically

In 1900, for the Universal Exposition in Paris, a statue of a beautiful woman was commissioned to preside over a majestic archway at the entrance. Christened La Parisienne, she epitomized the spirit of the city at that moment, glorying in its powers of invention, eager for the future. To that end the sculptor dressed her not in classical drapery, as befits an allegorical figure, but in the latest fashion, especially designed for her by Paquin, one of the leading couturiers of the time.

Holly Brubach   March 1986

all-encompassing   *awl in KUHM puh sing*
overwhelming; enveloping

I passed the first two weeks in the United States in New York riding subways up and down Manhattan, getting used to their sounds — a more all-encompassing noise than any I had ever encountered in the confusion of shouts and vehicles in India — and going on rapidly climbing elevators to the tops of huge buildings, including the Empire State.

Ved Mehta   July 1957

✳ Ved Mehta (b. 1934) has been blind since the age of 3, when he contracted cerebrospinal meningitis. He left India alone at 15 after being admitted to the Arkansas School for the Blind, graduated from Harvard with an M.A., and was a staff writer at *The New Yorker* from 1961 to 1994. He has written more than two dozen books, among them an 11-volume memoir, *Continents of Exile*.

alliteration   *uh li tuh RAY shuhn*

the repetition, for its effect in a phrase or poem, of the same sound in two or more neighboring words, usually at the beginning of words

There is no evidence that "road rage" or an aggressive-driving "epidemic" is anything but a media invention, inspired primarily by something as simple as a powerful alliteration: road rage. The term was presumably based on "roid rage," referring to sudden violent activity by people on steroids. The term, and the alleged epidemic, were quickly popularized by lobbying groups, politicians, opportunistic therapists, publicity-seeking safety agencies, and the U.S. Department of Transportation.

Michael Fumento   August 1998

❋ After the mariner slays the albatross in Samuel Taylor Coleridge's *Rime of the Ancient Mariner*, and just before his ship is becalmed, dooming all the crew but himself to thirst and starvation, the mariner tells us, quite alliteratively:

> The fair breeze blew, the white foam flew
> The furrow followed free
> We were the first that ever burst
> Into that silent sea.

alluring   *uh LOO: ring*

charmingly or subtly attractive; enchanting

The early twilight of a Sunday evening in Hamilton, Bermuda, is an alluring time. There is just enough of whispering breeze, fragrance of flowers, and sense of repose to raise one's thoughts heavenward; and just enough amateur piano music to keep him reminded of the other place.

Mark Twain   January 1879

amalgam   *uh MAL guhm*

a combination or mixture of diverse elements; a blend

If Saddam's regime had been merely a tyranny, perhaps the Iraqis would have risen up at the start of the war, as we hoped. But the ideology of the Baath Party was formulated by intellectuals who studied in Paris in the 1930s. They combined a deep admiration for Nazi ideas with a respect for Leninist party structure. Saddam himself especially idolized Stalin, and the regime he established was an Arab amalgam of the most brutal twentieth-century totalitarianisms, with an Islamic element added in the final decade. As events in Iraq unfold, we need to remember that every segment of Iraqi society has been profoundly affected by that regime.

David Brooks   June 2003

Edinburgh is a city of pure drama. It sits on a natural terrain of ridges, hills, ravines, and stupendous rocks as sharp-edged as a piece of crumpled steel. An amalgam of light and shadow, brightness and gray mist, it joins two separate parts: an Old Town, whose craggy skyline is one of the most dramatic in the world, and a New Town, an eighteenth-century concept of fine residences that is Europe's largest stretch of Georgian houses.

Frances Koltun   August 1975

ambiguous   *am BI gyoo: is*
having two or more possible meanings; indefinite; vague

Virtually everything having to do with the Bible is more complicated, more ambiguous and open to debate, than most Christians and Jews — even educated church and synagogue members — are aware of. To put it another way, too many people give too many easy answers to questions about the Bible.

Barry Hoberman   February 1985

ameliorate   *uh MEEL yuh rayt*
to make more tolerable or less severe

The Depression was not really overcome by the New Deal. Its effects were ameliorated, its burdens shifted, its ravages cloaked over, and that kept people going until the world itself was changed drastically by war.

Garry Wills   April 1994

to make or become better; improve

Twenty years ago Daniel Webster said that Dickens had already done more to ameliorate the condition of the English poor than all the statesmen Great Britain had sent into Parliament. During the unceasing demands upon his time and thought, he found opportunities of visiting personally those haunts of suffering in London which needed the keen eye and sympathetic heart to bring them before the public for relief. Whoever has accompanied him on his midnight walks into the cheap lodging-houses provided for London's lowest poor cannot have failed to learn lessons never to be forgotten.

James T. Fields   August 1870

amplitude   *AM pluh too:d*
abundance; fullness

Philosophers and psychologists, who agree in so little, yet agree in this: that the prime mental needs of human beings are association and vocabulary. Mother

Goose establishes for babies, who come so naked into the world, association with environment and with the past, and she has an amplitude of vocabulary that all the younger writers of our time might envy.

Henderson Daingerfield Norman   January 1931

analgesic   *a nuhl JEE zik*
a pain-killing drug

> Q. When you take an aspirin or some other remedy for pain, how does it know what part of your body to go to?

> A. The principal according to which analgesics locate pain is very similar to the more familiar itch-scratch response. For example, if your foot itches, you don't scratch your nose. Similarly, pain-killing medications rush to where they're needed and nowhere else. It's just one of those things.

Fred Catapano   March 1989

analogous   *uh NA luh guhs*
similar or comparable in certain respects

> Lytton Strachey came to birth as an author at a lucky moment. In 1918, when he made his first attempt, biography, with its new liberties, was a form that offered great attractions. To a writer like himself, who had wished to write poetry or plays but was doubtful of his creative power, biography seemed to offer a promising alternative. For at last it was possible to tell the truth about the dead; and the Victorian age was rich in remarkable figures, many of whom had been grossly deformed by the effigies that had been plastered over them. To recreate them, to show them as they really were, was a task that called for gifts analogous to the poet's or the novelist's, yet did not ask that inventive power in which he found himself lacking.

Virginia Woolf   April 1939

anarchism   *A nuhr ki zuhm*
a political philosphy opposed to all forms of government; resistance to organized government

> The way to make anarchism grow in this country is to refuse to allow organization and collective bargaining. Absentee ownership in a factory should not exempt stockholders from all interest in the lives of their laborers.

Lorin F. Deland   April 1912

ancien régime   *ahn SYEN ray ZHEEM*
the social and political system of France before the Revolution of 1789; any
former system: French, old regime

Thomas Jefferson served as the American Minister to France from 1785 to late in 1789, and thus witnessed the last crisis of the ancien régime. He was in Paris for the opening of the Estates General (May 5, 1789) and for the fall of the Bastille (July 14). In letters to divers correspondents he evinced growing and confident enthusiasm for the burgeoning revolution. To James Madison: "The revolution of France has gone on with the most unexampled success hitherto...." To Thomas Paine: "The National Assembly [showed] a coolness, wisdom, and resolution to set fire the four corners of the kingdom and to perish with it themselves rather than to relinquish an iota from their plan of total change. . . ." To Paine again: "The king, queen and national assembly are removed to Paris. The mobs and murders under which [the revolutionaries] dress this fact are like the rags in which religion robes the true god." No mere observer of the revolution, Jefferson is believed to have played a part in formulating the Declaration of the Rights of Man and of the Citizen, adopted by the National Assembly, the revolutionary heir to the Estates General, on August 26, 1789.

Conor Cruise O'Brien   October 1996

anemic   *uh NEE mik*
lacking vitality; weak; pale; lifeless (symptoms of anemia, a condition caused
by a shortage of hemoglobin): Greek, a, without + haima, *blood*

Spontaneous and deeply individualistic, the Lindy is the ultimate American dance. For this reason it was slow to catch on abroad. The Continent somehow just didn't suit swing, observed the veteran *New York Times* European correspondent Frederick Birchall, in 1939: "Away from home it becomes pallid and anemic," he wrote.

Robert P. Crease   February 1986

* ✳ The Lindy Hop (the dance's full name) originated in Harlem's Savoy Ballroom in the late 1920s and was named for Charles Lindbergh, whose solo flight from New Jersey to France in 1927 had made him a national hero. "Shorty George" Snowden, a professional dancer at the ballroom, is said to have coined the dance's name when a reporter, having seen him break away from his partner during a swing dance to do some fancy steps, asked him what it was called and he replied, "the Lindy Hop." Lindbergh's nickname may have occurred to Snowden because he associated his acrobatics, when he broke away from his partner during a dance, with Lindbergh's flying.

animadversion   *a nuh mad VER zhuhn*

an observation, remark or commentary that is usually based on careful analysis and impartial judgment

Lawyers who appeal from a lower court to a higher court are engaged in criticizing the judge who was responsible for an unsatisfactory decision. The appeal judges are paid by the state to act as critics of their brethren in the court below. In view of this machinery through which the courts are subjected to the animadversion of professional critics, it would be a hardy or a very foolish man who would assert that criticism of the courts should not be indulged in by laymen.

George W. Alger   November 1911

animus   *A nuh muhs*

a feeling of strong ill will; hatred; animosity

"Oh, I would never discuss critics," Gielgud said. "They can never say the right thing for you no matter how much they praise you. If they don't like you, you think they have a personal animus against you, so that I've always been very embarrassed by knowing them, though I've had quite a number among my friends. I never feel I can talk quite freely with them; sometimes I think that they may be prejudiced, either in my favor or against me, for the very fact that I know them, off the stage."

R. S. Stewart   April 1965

annals   *A nuhlz*

a narrative of events written year by year; historical records

This town of Boston has a history. It is not an accident, not a windmill, or a railroad station, or cross-roads tavern, or an army-barracks, grown up by time and luck to a place of wealth, but a seat of humanity, of men of principle, obeying a sentiment and marching loyally whither that should lead them; so that its annals are great historical lines, inextricably national, part of the history of political liberty. I do not speak with any fondness, but the language of coldest history, when I say that Boston commands attention as the town which was appointed in the destiny of nations to lead the civilization of North America.

Ralph Waldo Emerson   January 1892

annihilate   *uh NIGH uh layt*

to destroy; eradicate; wipe out ("annihilation" is the noun)

With the development of science we have reached, or have almost reached, a point at which fighting, unless ended, will mean the eventual annihilation of the human race; at any rate, the disappearance of our present civilization.

Sisley Huddleston   February 1925

anodyne   *A nuh dighn*
soothing to the mind or feelings

Jazz as a state of mind, is symptom, not malady. Jazz, in the guise of music, is both anodyne and stimulant to the afflicted. To the immune, it is an irritant. The term jazz, as applied to music, is rather elastic. It embraces not only the noisy-noisome sort, the jumble-jungle kind, but a type that refines upon and meliorates the racy stuff of wilder species with matter of a distinctly and engagingly musical nature. Good jazz is a composite, the happy union of seemingly incompatible elements. Good jazz is the latest phase of American popular music. It is the upshot of a transformation which started some twenty years ago, and culminated in something unique, unmatched in any other part of the world.

Carl Engel   August 1922

anomaly   *uh NAH muh lee*
a deviation from the ordinary; a departure from the general rule; an abnormality

Wise men of every name and nation, whether poets, philosophers, statesmen, or divines, have been trying to explain the puzzles of human condition, since the world began. For three thousand years, at least, they have been at this problem, and it is far enough from being solved yet. Its anomalies seem to have been expressly contrived by Nature to elude our curiosity and defy our cunning.

Edmund Quincy   December 1857

antagonism   *an TA guh ni zuhm*
opposition, as with two conflicting forces

When Lincoln was asked to make "a few appropriate remarks" at the dedication of the soldiers' cemetery on the battlefield at Gettysburg, it was inevitable that his thoughts should go back to the Founding Fathers, then forward, into the far reach of time, and that he should plead for increased devotion to the ideals the nation's sons were dying for, so that government of the people, by the people, for the people might not perish from the earth. A nearer realization of the American dream became the aim of Lincoln's life. Yet he was no mere dreamer. He realized that the struggle for human freedom is eternal; he had no illusions of its ending in his lifetime or in ours. He understood that the antagonisms between man's better nature and his selfishness endure, and that it would be the fate of every generation of Americans to defend democracy from its enemies of greed, intolerance, and despotism.

Benjamin B. Thomas   February 1954

antebellum   *an tee BE luhm*
before the war; specifically, before the American Civil War

When I was a boy, I read in my grandfather's library what, I dare say, is the most curious book every published in our country. It was a big volume, bound in sheep, and it was called *Cotton is King and Pro-Slavery Arguments*. It was the slave-owners' campaign book in the long antebellum controversy. Its fundamental proposition was that the South had a monopoly of cotton culture, and therefore, a sure foundation of perpetual wealth. The argument was that cotton-culture was possible only by the labor of slaves, and, therefore, slavery had an economic justification.

Walter Hines Page (under the pseudonym of Nicholas Worth)   July 1906

antics   *AN tiks*
playful, silly or ludicrous behavior

If a man desires to be president of these United States he must make himself in public as near the common man as he can — indulge in the theatricalism of Roosevelt, be photographed wearing a Shriner's turban like Harding, or with a pitchfork or chaps like Coolidge, however remote such antics may be from his nature.

James Truslow Adams   November 1927

antipathy   *an TI puh thee*
strong dislike; hostile feelings; aversion

Many Americans have chosen to live in suburbia out of a historic antipathy for life in the city and particularly a fear of the underclass that has come to dwell there. They would sooner move to the dark side of the moon than consider city life.

James Howard Kunstler   September 1996

apace   *uh PAYS*
at a fast pace; rapidly; swiftly

Most states do not license and properly control real-estate brokers, and building codes are nonexistent, inadequate, or honored in the breach, all of which come to the same thing. The same weakness appears in regulating billboards. Local legislation to control them is generally feeble and the destruction or blotting out of scenery by indiscriminate outdoor advertisers goes on apace.

Robert Moses   December 1950

apathy *A puh thee*
a lack of interest in, concern or feeling about something; indifference

Other American cities have taller buildings than New Orleans, more people, greater bank deposits, a larger trade, and many more superior items of that miscellany known as "progress." It may even be granted — although this is a violent assumption and statistically insupportable — that other cities rival New Orleans in the beauty and beguiling charm of their women. But only one other city — San Francisco — is its equal in cuisine. None other is its master in the art of political corruption, whose forms and patterns in New Orleans rival those of its tropical foliage; none other has an electorate whose political apathy so closely verges upon complete paralysis.

David L. Cohn   April 1940

aphrodisiac *a fruh DEE zee ak*
a drug or other substance believed to arouse or increase sexual desire: from Aphrodite, *the Greek goddess of love, beauty and sexual rapture*

North American farmed elk produce 100 tons a year of blood-rich immature "velvet" antler, cut from bulls' heads annually in June and sold mostly by the Asian medicine trade, which markets it as a general tonic and an aphrodisiac — by some estimates a $3 billion industry worldwide.

Hal Herring   June 2000

apocalyptic *uh pah kuh LIP tik*
portending widespread ruin or ultimate doom

In the sensitive world of classical music a lot of people are convinced that the sky is falling. Newspaper articles describe the classical-music business in apocalyptic terms. Sales of classical CDs have slowed, strikes have closed down orchestras in Philadelphia, Atlanta, San Francisco, and Portland for weeks and months, and the number of music critics has declined (is this bad?). Legendary music managers, those gnomes of 57th Street, have shut their offices, and the public still hates modern music. It's not clear, though, whether classical music has already collided with the iceberg or is still steaming toward a fatal encounter.

David Schiff   August 1997

apologia *a puh LOH jee uh*
a formal defense or justification of a position; an opinion or actions

There is a large literature of Western scholarship today that now looks like little more than an apologia for Maoism and its many crimes. The 1959-1961 famine, which extinguished some 25 million lives in the name of the Great Leap Forward, was for decades roundly denied by some American China experts, who, taking their cue from Orwellian Chinese-government propaganda, argued that hunger had been stamped out in China.

Lynn Chu   October 1990

apoplectic   *a puh PLEK tik*
so infuriated or incensed as to seem near collapse; having a fit of anger: from apoplexy, *a medical term synonymous with stroke or hemorrhage*

When I was in grade school, a classmate took an electric barber's razor and shaved some little rectangles on his head — parking spaces for his Matchbox cars. His mother was apoplectic, but the parking lot was his to keep until his hair grew back.

David Owen   October 1986

apostasy   *uh PAHS tuh see*
abandonment of one's faith, party, principles or cause

The late Robert Keable, whose apostasy was a shock to many readers of his early books, returned before his death to the Christian faith. Like many of his fellow countrymen and ours, as well as many Frenchmen and Germans, when he began to examine the historical basis of Christianity he discovered it to be, as he thought, unsound. Thereupon he abandoned the ship as unseaworthy, scuttled by the pirates of higher criticism. Later, observing her still afloat, he boarded her again in the hope of discovering some treasure overlooked. He found things in better shape than he had expected. The old vessel seemed worth saving, after all. Penetrating deep into the hold, he satisfied himself that the pumps were functioning, and then gallantly offered to man a pump handle. Thus he resumed his station in the Ship of the Church.

Elizabeth Case   February 1929

apothegm   *A puh thuhm*
a short, pointed and instructive saying; maxim

Rabbinical literature is full of apothegms that express the positive passion of the teachers of Israel for the soil, the air, the water, the physical being of the national land. "Whosoever walks four cubits in Palestine is assured of the world to come." "It is better to dwell in a Palestine desert than to live in a land of plenty abroad." "To live in the land of Israel outweighs all the commands of the Torah." "The air of Palestine makes men wise."

H. Sacher   July 1919

apotheosis *uh pah thee OH sis*
a raising to the level of the divine; the perfect essence of a thing; ideal: Greek,
apo, *from* + theos, *god*

The tardy apotheoses of Richard Wagner, Walt Whitman, and Claude Monet, have demonstrated that in music, poetry, and painting, the discords of one generation may be the harmonies of the next. What if it should be true of other things than music, poetry, and painting? What if it should be true all along the line? Why not take the broader view, when it is at least every whit as plausible as the narrower view?

Alvan F. Sanborn   October 1906

I had to stop everything when I took my first bite of gelato, the Italian version of ice cream. Although I was in front of the Palazzo Vecchio, in Florence, and surrounded by some of the most famous sculptures in the world, I could concentrate only on what tasted like the biggest, ripest, most richly flavored peach imaginable. It made the ice creams I had had before seem chalky. Each flavor I went back to try — apricot, blueberry, fig, melon — also seemed like the apotheosis of the fruit.

Corby Kummer   August 1984

apparition *a puh RI shuhn*
an unusual or unexpected sight; a ghostly figure

One night during the week we played Indianapolis I saw a man in a gray uniform crouching behind a counter on the stage. I got angry, thinking he was a stagehand who'd been caught on stage when the curtain went up. But when I walked out he'd disappeared. Later, when I described the apparition to the backstage crew fellers, they told me that my description fitted exactly a man who had fallen to his death from the flies about a year before.

Ethel Waters   March 1951

appellation *a puh LAY shuhn*
a name or title that describes or identifies a person or thing

To begin with, the name *mocking-bird* is a heavy load for any bird to bear. Unmusical as it is, the worst feature of such an appellation is the idea of flippancy and ill-breeding that it conveys. To "mock" is to imitate with an ill-natured purpose, to jeer at, to ridicule; it was for mocking that bad children were made food for bears. Such a name carries with it a shadow of something repellant, and no poet can ever rescue it, as a name, from its meaning and its eight harsh consonants. It would indeed require some centuries of romantic and charming associations to make of it a name by which to conjure, as in the case of the nightingale. The bird, with almost any other name than mocking-bird, would fare much better at the hands of artists and poets, and might hope, if birds may hope at all, finally to gain the meed of praise it so richly deserves.

Maurice Thompson   November 1884

appreciable   *uh PREE shuh buhl*
perceptible; measureable; noticeable

The peculiar cry of the New York milkman is the first that breaks the stillness of early morning. It has long been a puzzle to investigators how this fiendish yell originated, and why that most innocuous and pacifying of marketables, milk, should be announced with a war-whoop to which that of the blanketed Arapahoe of the plains is but as the bleat of a spring lamb. The shriek of the New York milkman has no appreciable connection with the word "milk." The rural visitor who hears it for the first time in the rosy morn plunges out from his bedclothes and rushes to the window, expectant of one of those sanguinary hand-to-hand conflicts about which he has been so long reading in the New York papers.

Charles Dawson Shanly   February 1870

❋ The cries of New York City's multiude of street vendors were brought to an end in 1908, at least legally, by police commissioner Theodore Bingham's noise suppression law. Commenting on the edict, *The Sun*, a New York newspaper, pointed out that each type of vendor had a distinctive cry and that "a quaint gamut has been wiped off the map of modern musical chaos." There was the hot, buttered corn cry, and the strawberries cry, and the charcoal cry. There were separate cries for vegetables, bananas, roasted peanuts, brooms and brushes, shoelaces and suspenders, oysters and fish, soap fat, pots and pans, honey, firewood and glassware. There were cries for window repair, chimney cleaning, umbrella fixing, knife sharpening and chair mending, and for buying rags and old clothes. "The assignment to obscurity of these nerve-destroying elements is a boon to many who welcome the city's progressive tenets and its resultant quietude," said *The Sun*, "and in another decade the extinction will have become a memory."

approbation   *a proh BAY shuhn*
authoritative approval or recognition; praise

As has often been the case with innovators, glory came to Mahler only after he had departed the scene. In his own time, two continents hailed him as a conductor and artistic director who revitalized operatic and symphonic concerts in Vienna and New York. Yet this approbation could not make up for the recognition he craved as a composer but failed to receive.

Arthur W. Hepner   November 1976

appropriate *uh PROH pree ayt*
to take possession of or make use of exclusively for oneself

The most striking difference between Roman family life and our own is the awesome power of the Roman father, the *paterfamilias*. He could disown his child at birth, with no reason given; in that case it would be exposed for any passerby to appropriate and raise, most probably as a slave.

Bernard Knox   May 1987

apt *apt*
appropriate; fitting

Some food writers think of balsamic vinegar as soy sauce without the salt, a comparison I don't find particularly apt. The primary tastes of soy sauce are salt, ferment, and then sweetness. The primary tastes of balsamic vinegar are the sweetness of fruit, the acidity of vinegar, and herbal notes if it has aged in wood.

Corby Kummer   September 1994

arable *A ruh buhl*
capable of producing crops; fit for plowing: as opposed to pasture or woodland

Fifty years ago, thirty years ago, vast tracts of arable land were open to every person arriving on our shores, under the Preemption Act, or later, the Homestead Act. A good farm of one hundred and sixty acres could be had at the minimum price of $1.25 an acre, or for merely the fees of registration. Under these circumstances it was a very simple matter to dispose of a large immigration. To-day there is not a good farm within the limits of the United States which is to be had under either of these acts.

Francis A. Walker   June 1896

✻ Between the 19th and 21st centuries, "today" has appeared as one word, two words and with a hyphen, although in the 19th century it was almost exclusively hyphenated and never two words. *The Atlantic* hyphenated it until at least 1937. The magazine's 1921 usage guide, *Text, Type, and Style*, says: "Contrary to the practice of many offices, *Atlantic* usage still requires the hyphen in *to-day, to-night, to-morrow.* This practice is more or less traditional, and it is not altogether clear why these words do not stand on the same footing as 'yesterday.'"

arboreal *ahr BAW ree uhl*
living in trees

A coati-mundi is a tropical, arboreal raccoon of sorts, with a long, ever-wriggling snout, sharp teeth, eyes that twinkle with humor, and clawed paws which are more skillful than many a fingered hand.

William Beebe   February 1920

arch   *ahrch*
cunningly or good-naturedly mischievous ("archly" is the adverb)

Three posthumous cheers for the honorable John M. Woolsey, the district-court judge who decided that James Joyce's *Ulysses* was not pornographic esoterica but fit reading matter for Americans. Interestingly, Woolsey rested his argument for lifting the ban on *Ulysses* on an idea that Joyce himself had archly toyed with in the pages of *Portrait of the Artist as a Young Man.* There Stephen Daedalus makes the distinction between what he calls "kinetic" and "static" art. The former, he declares, is "improper" art that excites desire or loathing; the latter, genuine art that holds the imagination in contemplative thrall by depicting "the most satisfying relations of the sensible." *Ulysses*, Judge Woolsey opined, did not amount to a call for lustful action but led to mere meditative pleasure. Joyce's novel was, Woolsey concluded, a "sincere and honest book," a "very powerful commentary on the inner lives of men and women."

Lee Siegel   February 1997

ardor   *AR duhr*
passion; emotional warmth; enthusiasm; eagerness

Nobody is more deadening than a teacher who pursues day after day the same routine, until his pupils sit down at their desks without curiosity and get up from them with delight. No profession requires more long-continued and unfading ardor. A teacher without enthusiasm is as discouraging as a flat tire.

Claude M. Fuess   October 1932

arrant   *A rint*
out-and-out; thoroughgoing: always used to emphasize disapproval

Looking back across the graves of more than a million brave men who, on one side or the other, laid down their lives in the struggle for mastery which began in Washington in the winter of 1860-61, the recollection of the flippancy and air of lightness and almost sportiveness with which it was entered upon fills me with amazement. How great things were trifled with as if they were playthings, and great stakes were played for almost as boys play for pennies, I could not now, in the lurid light of subsequent events, ever be made to believe, had not my own eyes been the witness. Much that happened would have been impossible but for the impenetrable veil which shut out the future. What seemed to us then arrant nonsense, and scarcely to be recalled now, after thirty years, with a sober face, was in truth the manifestation of a spirit which finally made possible Andersonville, Gettysburg, and the assassination of Lincoln.

Henry Laurens Dawes   August 1893

arrogate   *A ruh gayt*
to claim, or assume as a right, something to which one is not entitled

With history before us, it is no treason to question the infallibility of a court; for courts are never wiser or more venerable than the men composing them, and a decision that reverses precedent cannot arrogate to itself any immunity from reversal. Truth is the only unrepealable thing.

James Russell Lowell   October 1860

articulate   *ahr TI kyoo layt*
to express clearly; to arrange in a connected sequence

Put any company of people together with freedom for conversation, and a rapid self-distribution takes place into sets and pairs. The best are accused of exclusiveness. It would be more true to say, they separate as oil from water, as children from old people, without love or hatred in the matter, each seeking his like; and any interference with the affinities would produce constraint and suffocation. All conversation is a magnetic experiment. I know that my friend can talk eloquently; you know that he cannot articulate a sentence: we have seen him in different company.

Ralph Waldo Emerson   December 1857

artifice   *AHR tuh fis*
an artful device or strategem; false or insincere behavior

Gay men know about role-playing. Most of us become adept at artifice early on. We learn, often before we know that we are learning, how to hide many of our deepest desires, even from ourselves. Coming out almost always sparks an inner struggle between sincerity and duplicity — a fight to find and claim whatever is real inside us.

Michael Joseph Gross   August 2000

artless   *AHRT lis*
simple; innocent; inexperienced

Patience is largely the by-product of sympathy, and cannot be long maintained unless a teacher recalls his own boyhood and artless approaches to knowledge.

Claude M. Fuess   October 1932

ascetic   *uh SE tik*
pertaining to a life of strict self-denial and meditation for religious purposes

There is a certain limit in the style of living, beyond which a man, however wealthy, should not go. In olden times there were daimyos, noted for their wisdom, who, while not sparing in obtaining the very best they could obtain of swords and other weapons, or in giving education to their retainers, or for other purposes of state, themselves led an almost ascetic life, and the teachings of those men are not forgotten today. Some of the most delightful men one meets in Japan are those who take poverty as a matter of course, and devote their lives to some scholarly pursuit. You will find that, in spite of the bareness of their houses, these men often possess a precious library such as only a scholar can bring together. "What! Bend my knees to money or for money?" I have heard a man of this class say. "No, thank you. This life of independence is enough for me."

Kakichi Mitsukuri   March 1898

> ✳ Daimyos (the word means private land) were wealthy samurai who ruled extensive areas of Japan between the 10th and 19th centuries. Above them was the shogun, Japan's military ruler, whose office was more powerful than the emperor's. When the shogunate was abolished in 1867 and the emperor restored to full power, the daimyos were reduced to operating as governors, and in 1871 the government retired them with pensions.

ascribe   *uh SKRYB*
to attribute credit

While the makers of Trivial Pursuit have sought, in new editions of the game, to correct obvious mistakes — for example, the words "Oh, brave new world that has such people in it," are now ascribed to William Shakespeare rather than to Aldous Huxley — the clean-up effort is far from complete.

Cullen Murphy   September 1984

asinine   *A suh nighn*
utterly foolish

As we get along in life most of us lose the inclination to be constantly engaged in fighting strenuously for the progress of even the most praiseworthy causes. The desire wanes of benefiting your fellow man, while encountering in so doing not merely his indifference, but his hostility; of urging him to show himself rational while his proclivities are violently asinine.

Thomas R. Lounsbury   May 1907

askance   *uh SKANS*
with disapproval or distrust

Recognized the world over as the greatest sculptor now living, Rodin is still eyed askance by the representatives of official art in his own country, and has not yet been honored with an election to the Academie des Beaux-Arts.

Alvan F. Sanborn   July 1909

askew   *uh SKYOO:*
crooked; out of line; awry

After wriggling away from the guide, my wife and I walked to the front gate of the old U.S. Embassy. This is the gate everyone has seen in the heartwrenching pictures, with Vietnamese trying to claw their way into the embassy on the day before Saigon fell. The embassy looks as if nothing has been touched since then. The upper prongs of the gate are still slightly askew from all the hands that pulled on them.

James Fallows   December 1988

asperity   *uh SPE ruh tee*
ill temper; irritability

The absence of people from his pictures has been particularly galling to New York reviewers; Adams's depopulated landscapes strike many urbanites as misanthropic and cold. "There is a person in every one of my photographs," I once heard Adams tell my father with asperity. At first I did not get it, and then I did: on Ansel Adams's starkest granite wall, in his emptiest desert landscape, a person is always present, and that person is Adams himself.

Kenneth Brower   July/August 2002

aspersion   *uh SPER zhuhn*
damaging or disparaging remarks; false and injurious charges; unjust insinuations

It is rather the habit just now to cast aspersion upon the sapsucker. The ancient accusation stands, of course, that as he drives his precise rings around the bole and branch and takes his fill of the tree's blood he is an active — if not, indeed, an immediate — menace to its life. Some are saying in addition that it is not food alone he seeks in his methodical rounds, but drink, and strong drink at that; so strong sometimes that he staggers in his flight to find a place where he may sleep off its effects. But these indictments leave me cold. The sapsucker has killed no tree of mine, and never yet has he made one the scene of a debauch. I rather wish he might; the morality of most birds falls little, if at all, short of monotony.

William Preston Beazell   October 1926

assail   *uh SAYL*
to attack verbally with argument, criticism or ridicule

Attempting to define a political opponent as something less than presidential is a hallowed American tradition. Two centuries ago, in attacks that echo in Republican characterizations of John Kerry, Federalist opponents assailed Thomas Jefferson with what amounted to the charge that he — a free-thinking deist who sympathized with the French Revolution — was in fact a godless Francophile bent on destroying the institution of marriage. Andrew Jackson's marriage to a woman he wrongly believed to be divorced, Grover Cleveland's illegitimate child, and Teddy Roosevelt's alleged drunkenness were all pushed by opponents during nasty presidential campaigns.

Joshua Green   June 2004

astringent   *uh STRIN jint*
severe; stern; caustic

Rilke's diaries and letters, lively with tales of self-dislike and depression, seem to out-Kafka Kafka himself. Still, biographers should beware of making too much of these highly polished introspections. Rilke conceived of writing as a form of prayer, as Kafka did, and he made astringent self-examination a ritualistic prelude to work.

Lee Siegel   April 1996

atavism   *A tuh vi suhm*
a trait characteristic of a remote ancestor ("atavistic" is the adjective)

Japanese food is varied and flavorful, and when accompanied by mounds of rice it can even seem filling. But for us it lacked staying power, because it had so little fat. A week or two after arrival we suddenly grasped what was wrong when we passed one of Tokyo's countless McDonald's outlets and, overcome by atavistic cravings, turned back and rushed in. We ate Big Macs and drank milkshakes, felt the grease on our lips and fingers, and carried a full feeling with us the rest of the day.

James Fallows   November 1986

Some atavistic fear or urge, older than time, leads women to slander mice by believing that they harbor a lascivious desire to run up the female leg.

Dean Acheson   March 1965

atelier   *A tuhl yay*
an artist's studio

Having gone to Paris to spend a winter in professional studies, I made an earnest application by letter to Delacroix to be admitted as a pupil to his *atelier*. In reply, he invited me to visit him at his rooms the next day at four, to talk with him about my studies, proffering any counsel in his gift, but assuring me that it was impossible for him to receive me into his studio, as he could not work in the room with another, and his strength and occupations did not permit him to have a school apart, as he once had.

William James Stillman   December 1863

atomize   *A tuh myz*
to separate into many parts or fragments ("atomized" is the adjective)

Sixty percent or more of all households with television watched the first televised addresses of Presidents Nixon, Carter, and Reagan, in the days before cable's ascendancy. George Bush never even broke 40 percent except with one speech — during the Gulf War. In this environment it becomes far more difficult for a President to mobilize the nation. The once all-powerful national megaphone of the presidency competes with many amplified voices in a diverse, atomized culture.

Steven Stark   April 1993

attendant   *uh TEN duhnt*
accompanying or following as a result

In addition to designing and developing Chicago's lakefront (specifically the magnificent Lake Shore Drive and its attendant system of parks), Daniel H. Burnham (1846-1912) led the design teams that built a large number of the canonical structures of American architecture — including New York's Flatiron Building, famously depicted in photographs by Alfred Stieglitz and Edward Steichen.

Benjamin Schwarz   June 2003

audacious   *aw DAY shuhs*
bold; daring; confident

The four men arrived by U-boat and landed on a deserted beach near Amagansett, Long Island, in the midnight darkness on Saturday, June 13, 1942, a mere six months after Japan's attack on Pearl Harbor. They had close to $80,000 (equivalent to nearly a million dollars today) in cash, four boxes of explosives, and a mission that had been planned at the highest levels of the Third Reich — namely, to halt production at key American manufacturing plants, create railroad bottlenecks, disrupt communication lines, and cripple New York City's water-supply system. The mission, audacious in means and scope, had the potential to seriously impede America's military buildup, and perhaps even to affect the outcome of the war.

Gary Cohen   February 2002

augment   *awg MENT*
to add; increase ("augmentation" is the noun)

We meet to-day under happy omens to our ancient society, to the commonwealth of letters, to the country, and to mankind. No good citizen but shares the wonderful prosperity of the Federal Union. The heart still beats with the public pulse of joy, that the country has withstood the rude trial which threatened its existence, and thrills with the vast augmentation of strength which it draws from this proof. The storm which has been resisted is a crown of honor and a pledge of strength to the ship. We may be well contented with our fair inheritance.

Ralph Waldo Emerson   January 1868

august   *aw GUHST*
inspiring reverence and admiration; impressing the emotions or imagination as magnificent; majestic

The Southern army will be fighting for Jefferson Davis, or at most for the liberty of self-misgovernment, while we go forth in the defence of principles which alone make government august and civil society possible. It is the very life of the nation that is at stake.

James Russell Lowell   June 1861

auspicious   *aw SPI shuhs*
of good omen; boding well for the future

In days of old, seers entered a trance state and then informed anxious seekers what kind of mood the gods were in, and whether this was an auspicious time to begin a journey, get married, or start a war.

Harvey Cox   March 1999

austere   *aw STEER*
severe in manner or appearance ("austerely" is the adverb)

There is something austerely impersonal, as though emotionally tentative, in Auden's readings. One hears it in the way he adheres so strictly — at times almost woodenly — to the meter of the verses. Quite often he will come to a full stop even at the end of an enjambed line — one in which the punctuation and syntax do not call for so much as a pause.

Wen Stephenson   April 2000

autarky   *AW tahr kee*
a national policy of economic self-sufficiency, to the exclusion of imports
("autarkic" is the adjective)

In its efforts to ensure the distribution of power in its favor and at the expense of actual or potential rivals, a state will "nationalize" — that is, pursue autarkic policies, practicing capitalism only within its borders or among countries in a trading bloc. This circumscribes both production factors and markets, and thereby fragments an international economy.

Benjamin Schwarz   June 1996

authoritarian   *aw thah ri TA ree in*
exercising complete or almost complete control over the personal freedom of others; undemocratic and dictatorial

The first thing for us to realize about modern China is that beneath the veneer of westernization and the hopeful developments of our lifetime, the Chinese political tradition still remains authoritarian. The most cursory glance at Chinese history shows that from the earliest period the ruler was above the people, their father and not their representative. The ruler intervened between mankind below and the forces of heaven above. On behalf of the people he performed ritual observances, and the proper performance of those rites maintained the harmony between man and nature. When this harmony failed, as when drought or flood upset the agrarian economy, the emperor not only performed sacrifices but took full responsibility before his people for all natural calamities.

John K. Fairbank   September 1946

autochthon   *aw TAHK thahn*
an original inhabitant of a country: Greek, sprung from the land itself

The quiet manner in which Hamilton laid entirely aside, far remote from sight or memory of himself or others, the fact that he was not sprung of old American stock, was not an autochthon of the North American colonies, is only one among several evidences of a peculiar trait in his character. In just the same way, his writings indicate that he neither spoke nor apparently thought at all of his social origin. Who he was, what he might be expected to be according to the principles of descent and heredity, were questions which he so tranquilly ignored that the few persons who ventured to ask or to answer them did so covertly, and whispering among themselves. He simply stepped into a position among those who were socially and intellectually the best and foremost people; and in doing so did not seem to be challenging a right, but only to be appearing where he naturally belonged. What he, in this easy and careless fashion, took for granted was granted, at once and by everybody. No one ever doubted that he belonged where he placed himself.

Charles Creighton Hazewell   January 1887

autodidact *aw toh DIGH dakt*

a self-educated person

Kierkegaard, whose name in Old Danish means "churchyard" (with all the familiar connotations of "graveyard"), was born in Copenhagen in 1813. He was the youngest of seven children born to Michael Pederson Kierkegaard and his second wife and quondam servant, Anne Sørensdatter Lund. In thousands of pages of personal jottings Kierkegaard did not mention his mother once, and yet his journals swim with notes about his autodidact father. By all accounts Kierkegaard's melancholic, pious, and indisputably brilliant father left an unusually deep impression on him. Some would call it a scar.

Gordon D. Marino July 1993

avarice *A vuh ris*

excessive desire for wealth; greed

Sing a song of sixpence a pocket full of rye,
Four and twenty blackbirds baked in a pie.
When the pie was opened the birds began to sing,
And wasn't that a dainty dish to set before a king?

The king was in his counting-house, counting out his money.
The queen was in the parlor, eating bread and honey.
The maid was in the garden, hanging out the clothes,
When by came a blackbird and pecked off her nose!

Passing over the vulgar ostentation of the first few lines and the intimation of the atrocious cuisine which would leave the birds so underdone, we find put forth for the amusement of the young an account of avarice and gluttony in high places. In neither king nor queen is there any suggestion of social responsibility, and the phrase "*his* money" is deliberately misleading. While the monarch gloats over extorted pelf, no doubt wrung from horny-handed peasants, and his degenerate consort pampers heself in greedy sloth, the worker, upon whose efforts their cleanliness and health depend, is foully mutilated by what was most probably an escaped victim of their bizarre appetites and barbaric cookery. And yet they manifest no concern!

Bergen Evans December 1934

❋ Bergen Evans (1904-1978) taught at Northwestern University from 1932 to 1974, where his Introduction to Literature class, with upwards of 500 students, was the school's most popular course. His *Dictionary of Contemporary American Usage* (1957), which he co-authored with his sister, Cornelia Evans Goodhue, remains a standard guide for writers. Other Evans passages in this book in which he analyzes nursery rhymes (with tongue in cheek) appear under delectation, engender, obviate and sullen.

avatar   *A vuh tahr*
the embodiment on earth of a god, ideal, quality or concept

Flush with celebrity as London's leading "aesthete," Wilde arrived in New York in January of 1882 for a triumphal tour of the United States; he is said to have announced to Customs officials, "I have nothing to declare except my genius." Thus genius became not merely a synonym for exalted intellectual power but a performed role. With his ostentatious clothing, his green carnations, his witty epigrams, and his flair for publicity, Wilde became the avatar of self-proclaimed genius.

Marjorie Garber   December 2002

✳ An epigram is a witty or wise statement with a clever twist in thought. Among the epigrams of Oscar Wilde (1856-1900):

"There is only one thing in the world worse than being talked about, and that is not being talked about."

"I can resist everything except temptation."

"Experience is the name everyone gives to their mistakes."

avenue   *A vuh noo:*
a path toward something or somewhere

The epistemological question "How do we know what we know?" is tough enough to answer in the natural sciences, where there is at least an agreed-upon scientific method. It is notoriously harder to answer when the subject is our collective past. There are biases and clouded motives to contend with of an especially insidious kind. Very often there is little in the way of unequivocal information. And there is no single avenue of approach.

Cullen Murphy   August 1995

aversion   *uh VER zhuhn*
a fixed dislike of something, accompanied by avoidance

The aversion with which men of the world — bankers, lawyers and manufacturers — often regard a teacher is due to their detection in him of a dogmatism and complacency unconsciously created in him by daily contact with inferior minds. It is easy for a first-class brain to become annoyed at sluggishness or unresponsiveness in others; but a teacher must learn to forget his own endowments and to put himself in the place of his pupils.

Claude M. Fuess   October 1932

avocation   *a voh KAY shuhn*
an activity engaged in for the enjoyment of it, in addition to one's regular work;
a hobby

A handful of musicians — the Perlmans and Pavarottis — can make in one night what the average orchestral player earns in a year. Several thousand others — either freelancers (known as "gig pigs") putting together a living with pickup groups, teaching, and commercial work, or the musicians in the country's twenty-seven full-time orchestras — support themselves as musicians, earning incomes that place them in the middle-class professions. For everyone else the choice is between keeping your day job and leaving music as an avocation, and living a monastic existence playing in subways and on street corners.

David Schiff   August 1997

avowal   *uh VOW uhl*
an open acknowledgment

Much that was suppressed in the young people of my generation found a frank avowal in the *Leaves of Grass*; feelings and affection for each other, which we had been ashamed of, thoughts which we had hidden as unutterable, we found printed in its pages, discovering that they were not, as we believed, the thoughts and feelings of young, guilty, half-crazy goblins, but portions of the Kingdom of Truth and the sane experience of mankind. It was above all Walt Whitman's rejoicing in his flesh and blood, — "there is so much of me," he sang, "and all so luscious," — his delight in his own body and the bodies of his friends, which seemed a revelation and gave the *Leaves of Grass* so strong a hold upon a generation born of puritans who had ignored, or treated as shameful, those habitations of the spirit.

Logan Pearsall Smith   November 1937

awry   *uh RIGH*
away from the expected direction; amiss; wrong

Two speeches that Richard Nixon never gave surfaced not long ago in the National Archives. One was the text of the grim public statement Nixon would have made had the 1969 moon landing gone awry, stranding two astronauts on the lunar surface. The second was the speech that Nixon would have given in August of 1974 had he decided not to resign the presidency: "We must not let this office be destroyed or let it fall such easy prey to those who would exult in the breaking of the President that the game becomes a national habit."

Cullen Murphy   July 2000

bankrupt

The onion is the pride and joy of Bermuda. It is her jewel, her
gem of gems. In her conversation, her pulpit, her literature, it is
her most frequent and eloquent figure. In Bermudian metaphor
it stands for perfection,— perfection absolute. The Bermudian
weeping over the departed exhausts praise when he says,
"He was an onion!" The Bermudian extolling the
living hero bankrupts applause when he says,
"He is an onion!" The Bermudian setting his son
upon the stage of life to dare and do for himself
climaxes all counsel, supplication, admonition,
comprehends all ambition, when he says, "Be an onion!"

Mark Twain   December 1877

see page 47

backslide   *BAK slighd*
to fall away from an attainment already reached ("backslider" is the noun)

> The Ayatollah told his young followers that the war with Iraq was a holy crusade of the true faith against corrupted backsliders. He reminded them that they had struck down the Shah and humbled the mighty United States, and he claimed that the Iraqis would suffer the same fate.

David Evans and Richard Campany   November 1984

backwater   *BAK waw ter*
an isolated, secluded or backward place

> Ancient university towns are wonderfully alike. Göttingen is like Cambridge in England or New Haven in America: very provincial, not on the way to anywhere — no one comes to these backwaters except for the company of professors. And the professors are sure that this is the center of the world. There is an inscription in the Ratskeller in Göttingen which reads: *Extra Gottingam non est vita* (Outside Göttingen there is no life). This epigram, or should I call it epitaph, is not taken as seriously by the undergraduates as by the professors.

Jacob Bronowski   December 1973

badinage   *BA duh nij*
playful, teasing talk; banter

> William James corresponded with many people of many sorts. Sometimes he communicated by postcards, or short notes; at others he wrote copious letters. Whether he was compressing his correspondence into the briefest messages, or allowing it to

expand into letters of friendly badinage and extended comment, he was incapable of writing a half page that was not characteristic, free, and vivid.

Henry James Jr.   July 1920

bait   *bayt*
to tease or goad, so as to provoke a reaction

Children are merciless — as much in what they expect as in what they offer. Not only will they bait unmercifully a schoolmaster who lacks the power to discipline them, but they lavish the most fantastic and unreasonable adorations. The utmost bond of lover and mistress is less than the comprehension a boy expects from a schoolmaster whom he has singled out for worship.

James Hilton   July 1938

baleful   *BAIL fuhl*
threatening; menacing; ominous

To sensibilities shaped by the past fifty years, the emerging media landscape seems not just chaotic but baleful. Common sense would suggest that as the vast village green of the broadcast era is chopped up into tiny plots, divisions in the culture will only multiply. If everyone tunes in to a different channel, and discourse happens only among like minds, is there any hope for social and political cohesion? Oh, for a cozy living room with one screen and Walter Cronkite signing off with his author-itative, unifying "That's the way it is."

William Powers   January/February 2005

Balkanization   *bawl kin uh ZAY shuhn*
the breaking up of a large area or group into smaller units: originally, the breaking up of the Balkan Peninsula in the late 19th and early 20th centuries into smaller, often mutually hostile units

Cable penetration is slowly bringing about the Balkanization of the American tele-vision audience. That audience, roughly identical to the U.S. population at large, is gradually declining its independence from three-network cultural hegemony and reconstituting itself into dozens of smaller but more cleanly defined "taste culture" viewing groups. Whereas once CBS, NBC, and ABC were the Sears, the Montgomery Ward, and the K-Mart in a shopping center without boutiques, now the industry offers viewers opportunities for more personalized services.

David Marc   November 1984

balm   *bahm*

something that soothes, heals or comforts

Haunted by the ghosts of the doughboys he had led into World War I, Woodrow Wilson in his second term lost his capacity for pragmatic accommodation in his fight for the League of Nations, which was to him the only redemption for their sacrifice and the only balm for his guilt. Refusing to compromise with the Senate, Wilson broke his health campaigning for the League; and then the Senate, in his words, "broke the heart of the world" by rejecting it.

Jack Beatty   September 2003

✳ Doughboy, best known as the nickname for all American combat troops in World War I, was earlier applied to the infantryman in the Mexican War (1846-48) and the Civil War (1861-65). The word's origin is unknown, although there are several theories: that baked globs of dough and rice were a frequent meal for infantrymen; that the buttons on infantrymen's uniforms resembled the boiled dumpling, called a doughboy, eaten by soldiers and sailors as far back as the 17th century; that infantrymen in the Mexican War and Civil War polished their white belts with a whitish doughy-looking clay; that the dust stirred up by horses, vehicles and men in the Mexican war covered infantrymen, giving them an adobe look. These so-called adobe boys evolved into doughboys.

bankrupt   *BANK ruhpt*

to exhaust, leaving nothing remaining

The onion is the pride and joy of Bermuda. It is her jewel, her gem of gems. In her conversation, her pulpit, her literature, it is her most frequent and eloquent figure. In Bermudian metaphor it stands for perfection, — perfection absolute. The Bermudian weeping over the departed exhausts praise when he says, "He was an onion!" The Bermudian extolling the living hero bankrupts applause when he says, "He is an onion!" The Bermudian setting his son upon the stage of life to dare and do for himself climaxes all counsel, supplication, admonition, comprehends all ambition, when he says, "Be an onion!"

Mark Twain   December 1877

banter   *BAN tuhr*

teasing or joking in a playful, good-natured way

For Roosevelt to "walk" in public, he had to balance on his locked braces and pretend to be using his legs while he was actually shifting back and forth from his cane to the man (often one of his sons) whose arm he gripped on the other side. The strain always left his suit soaked with sweat, the hand on the cane shaking violently from the effort, the son's arm bruised where his fingers had dug in. And all the while he would be smiling, keeping up pleasant banter, pretending to enjoy himself.

Garry Wills   April 1994

barb *bahrb*
a cutting remark

The annual Saint Patrick's Day breakfast is an old Boston tradition. Held in South Boston on the Sunday after Saint Patrick's Day, the event is an occasion for Massachusetts pols to sling barbs at one another between rounds of local ballads such as "Charlie on the MTA" and "Southie Is My Hometown."

Sridhar Pappu   September 2005

bare-bones *BAIR bohnz*
reduced to the essentials; basic

A short history of the American house since 1950 would have to include a chapter called "Bigger and Better." The Levittown house had two bedrooms, one small bathroom, and an eat-in kitchen; all its rooms were arranged on a concrete slab whose dimensions were twenty-five by thirty feet (an unfinished attic was often converted into additional living space). William Levitt's strategy becomes apparent if one compares his house with earlier designs for modestly priced houses, such as those included in *Homes of Character*, a pattern book published in 1923 by the Boston architect Robert L. Stevenson. The porches, vestibules, entry halls, and dining rooms (or at least dining alcoves) that were standard domestic amenities in the twenties were absent from the Levittown house, which lacked even a basement. It was bare-bones living.

Witold Rybczynski   February 1991

barefaced *BAIR fayst*
shameless; audacious; brazen

One of the duties of an institution devoted to cancer research is the investigation of such "cures" as are not too preposterous, and it is within the knowledge of the writer that not a single one of all those that have been tested has proved of the slightest value. At the worst they have been equivalent to a barefaced robbery; at the best, the product of an ignorant enthusiast; and it cannot be too strongly emphasized that no drug, serum, vaccine, or other preparation is known that will select and destroy the cancer cell without detriment to the normal tissues surrounding it.

William H. Woglom   June 1928

barnstorm   *BAHRN stawrm*

to travel from one small town and rural district to another, performing,
lecturing or campaigning: from the practice of using barns as auditoriums

One thing Roy Rogers remembers vividly about the start of his career is how hungry he was. During his early years as a singer of cowboy ballads, he recalls, "Me and the band were barnstorming in New Mexico, Arizona, and Texas, and we got to Roswell, New Mexico. We didn't have a dime. So we got on a little radio station, and I came up with the idea to talk about our favorite things to eat, thinking maybe some listener would send us something. I said I liked lemon pie, and we got a phone call at the station from a fella who said that if I would sing 'The Swiss Yodel,' his sister would bring a lemon pie to our motor court that night. By golly, I sang 'The Swiss Yodel' better than I ever did, and sure enough, that night a car pulled up and there were not one but two pies! Man, we couldn't wait for them folks to leave so we could eat those pies!"

Jane and Michael Stern   November 1993

base   *bays*

devoid of high values; inferior in quality; lowly

Henry James lost his job as Paris correspondent of the *New York Tribune* because he was too highbrow; then, when *Harper's Weekly* dropped the monthly newsletter he had been assigned to write, James complained, "And yet, I tried to be so Base!"

Thomas Griffith   November 1978

bask   *bask*

to enjoy a warm or pleasant feeling from being in a certain environment
or situation

When you sit down to dinner with your disagreeable relations, or comrades who bask in their rectitude and compassion, you have a civic duty to annoy them.

Wendy Kaminer   September 1997

bas-relief   *bah ruh LEEF*

sculpture in which figures are carved in a flat surface, so that they project only
slightly from the background

Angkor's most spectacular architectural achievement is Angkor Wat. Occupying a square mile of cleared jungle, surrounded by a wide moat it is, according to some, the largest stone monument and the largest religious structure in the world. Virtually every inch of the mellow gray sandstone, inside and out, is carved with bas-reliefs — half a mile of them. The most famous relief, depicting a Hindu mythological scene called the "Churning of the Sea of Milk," is a masterpiece of world art, a superbly balanced composition and a carving of exceptionally high quality.

Jamie James   April 2002

bawdy   *BAW dee*
humorously crude or obscene; risqué

One of the great joys of Nepal is its freshness. Even people who were in the position of being servants and who would have been, in India or other formerly colonial lands, at once servile and distant, were open and forthcoming in Nepal. A man would bring tea and sit to chat; waiters would smile, bring flowers, make bawdy jokes. My driver helped me market, but while helping me, was quite firm about what ingredients to buy for what, changing my menu completely the day I wanted to try cooking in a Nepalese kitchen.

Merry I. White   August 1970

befuddled   *bi FUH duhld*
confused or stupefied

The sapsucker is a greedy fellow, who gets positively drunk on maple juice. I have seen one on a large sugar tree in such a befuddled condition that the best he could do was to cling to the bark and crawl around and around the trunk, while I pursued him till I was even dizzier than he and had to give up the attempt to lay hands on him.

Walter Prichard Eaton   June 1932

✳ The sapsucker is one of 11 birds native to the United States whose common name describes its diet. The others are the acorn woodpecker, Clark's nutcracker, the flycatcher, the gnatcatcher, the grasshopper sparrow, the kingfisher, the nuthatch, the oystercatcher, the snail kite, the sparrow hawk and the worm-eating warbler. (The sandwich tern is not in this category, as it is named for Sandwich, England.)

beggar   *BE guhr*
to make something seem inadequate or useless

Though Sedona, Arizona, was founded in 1902, Zane Grey, the hardworking western novelist, was the first writer to "discover" it, in the 1920s. Landscape on the Arizona scale challenges the resources of human speech; it beggared Grey, who had to resort to stilted terms from the construction industry to describe the mighty cliffs of the Grand Canyon: "Turrets, mesas, domes, parapets, and escarpments gave the appearance of an architectural work of giant hands." To use such language for the vastness of these badlands is to commend the horse in the lingo of the horsefly. There's an old story that a priest and a cowboy arrived together at the canyon's North

Rim and stood silent a while. Finally the priest fell upon his knees and exclaimed, "O Lord, how wonderful are thy works!" The cowboy ruminated, spat, and muttered, "Don't it beat hell?"

Peter Davison   October 1997

✳ Peter Davison (1928-2004) was *The Atlantic*'s poetry editor for more than 30 years. He received some 30,000 poems a year, and although only about 40 of them were published in the magazine, each year he encouraged hundreds of people to continue writing and submitting their work. His own poems appeared in *The Atlantic* from time to time, and 11 books of his poetry were published.

begrudge   *bi GRUHJ*
to give or expend with reluctance

Some "distinguished professors" earn superstar salaries, though their lectures are merely cribs of the books they are writing. They begrudge their students any personal contact, though their presence is supposed to enhance the students' education.

Thomas Griffith   December 1975

beleaguered   *bee LEE guhrd*
surrounded or beset, as with troubles; besieged

Middle-class Americans today feel hard pressed and beleaguered — and they are. Nobody could possibly argue that even a well-above-the-median $50,000 a year in household income will put one on easy street. It's hard to make it on a typical middle-class income today — when paychecks barely keep up with the cost of homes, of college educations, and even of necessities.

Peter G. Peterson   October 1993

bellicose   *BE luh kohs*
eager to fight; hostile in nature; warlike ("bellicosity" is the noun)

Our permanent enemy is the noted bellicosity of human nature. Man, biologically considered, and whatever else he may be in the bargain, is simply the most formidable of all beasts of prey, and, indeed, the only one that preys systematically on its own species. We are once for all adapted to the military *status*. A millennium of peace would not breed the fighting disposition out of our bone and marrow, and a function so ingrained and vital will never consent to die without resistance, and will always find impassioned apologists and idealizers.

William James   December 1904

In 1988 President Ronald Reagan signed an executive order revising the Code of Conduct for POWs. What formerly began with "I am an American fighting man" was changed to the gender-neutral and less bellicose "I am an American."

Charles Mosko   August 1990

bellwether   *BEL we th:uhr*
one that takes the lead or initiative; one that is followed as a leader

Music, especially popular music, has been a cultural bellwether since the end of World War II. Swing, bebop, blues, rock, minimalism, funk, rap: each in its own way has shaped cinema, literature, fashion, television, advertising, and, it sometimes seems, everything else one encounters.

Charles C. Mann   September 2000

✳ The original meaning of bellwether is a male sheep, usually castrated, that carries a bell around its neck and acts as a leader of the flock.

bemuse   *bi MYOO:Z*
to confuse or bewilder

Well before the war every German knew the sound of Hitler's voice from his ranting orations, but the Russians didn't know Stalin's voice until he broadcast for the first time, after the Soviet Union was invaded, in July of 1941. His listeners must have been taken aback by his Georgian accent, just as the Japanese were bemused by their Emperor's lilting court intonation when he broadcast for the first time, after the bombing of Hiroshima, announcing the coming surrender in the memorably meiotic words, "The war situation has developed not necessarily to Japan's advantage."

Geoffrey Wheatcroft   March 2001

✳ *The Oxford Companion to the English Language* defines meiosis, the noun form of the adjective meiotic, as "a kind of understatement that dismisses or belittles, especially by using terms that make something seem less significant than it really is." The word derives from the ancient Greek *meioun*, meaning "to make small."

beneficent   *buh NE fuh sint*
bringing benefit; doing good

The Nobel Prizes perpetuate the memory and wealth of Alfred Bernhard Nobel, a Swedish inventor whose fortune was made by his discovery of dynamite in 1865-1866. As if to counteract the danger of some of his inventions, his will provided as beneficent a series of gifts as could well be imagined.

Edward Weeks   October 1935

benevolent   *buh NE vuh luhnt*
doing or inclined to do good; desiring to help others; kindly

In order to be free to develop ourselves, we must rely on an international police force to take care of international ruffians. Instead of envisioning ourselves in the role of benevolent world cops, we should be turning over our badges to international deputies of peace, who would relieve us of the responsibility of being constantly alerted for trouble. We should be working toward a united world, indivisible, with equal restraints and correspondingly equal liberties for all.

Edgar L. Jones   February 1946

benighted   *bi NIGH tid*
enveloped in intellectual, moral or social darkness

If Haiti is not a victim of imperialism, how can its tragic history be explained? Why has this benighted country experienced since independence a virtually unbroken chain of brutal and corrupt leaders? Why have repeated efforts to encourage democracy and due process — including the U.S. occupation — failed? Why are the vast majority of Haitians illiterate? Why has abuse of power at all levels permeated Haiti's history? Why is the country that was once the richest in the Caribbean now the poorest?

Lawrence E. Harrison   June 1993

benignant   *bi NIG nuhnt*
exerting a good or kindly influence; favorable; beneficial

We have entire faith in the benignant influence of Truth, the sunlight of the moral world, and believe that slavery, like other worn-out systems, will melt gradually before it.

James Russell Lowell   October 1860

beseech   *bee SEECH*
to beg eagerly for ("beseeching" is the adjective)

The longest road in the world is the road that lies between feeling and fact. The road can be made passable only by knowledge. Wishing is just the initial motive force designed to drive one to seek the knowledge of the way. Processions of longing, beseeching human beings through plague-stricken cities, imploring the removal of the curse, effected nothing, until their desires were converted into patient investigation of the causes and cure of plague. The processions were valuable in so far as they incited and stung the lethargic scientific mind into investigation and discovery. Wishing, looked upon as an end in itself, is barren, but it is the initial stage of all progress.

J. Edgar Park   October 1921

bespeak   *bi SPEEK*
to indicate; point to; be the outward expression of ("bespoke" is the past tense)

Religion and the Bible had been important in Lincoln's upbringing but he had known skepticism too. During his campaign for Congress, when pressed to define his faith, he had declared: "That I am not a member of any Christian church is true; but I have never denied the truth of the Scriptures." This is not the same as saying that he accepted the Scriptures fully; and, having trained his mind to demand proof, he had not yet gained that broader understanding of how the incomprehensible may still be true. Yet his very goodness bespoke a latent spirituality, which, if awakened and motivated, might widen his horizon and make his life more purposeful.

Benjamin B. Thomas   February 1954

✤ Lincoln used Biblical metaphors plentifully in his speeches and writing. One of the most enduring is his borrowing from Mark, Chapter 3, verse 25 at the Republican State Convention of 1858, when he was running against Stephen Douglas for the U.S. Senate. Describing the danger of disunion that the United States was facing over the slavery issue, Lincoln said: "A house divided against itself cannot stand. I believe this government cannot endure permanently half slave and half free."

bestir   *bi STER*
to become active; rouse

There is a kind of typical, late November day, when autumn may be said to take its leave of the landscape, when nature shuts the door of the seasons, and turns the lock which is to hold all vegetation fixed and motionless until the spring. It is a dark, cold, silent day. One vast, lead-colored, low-hanging cloud covers the sky, and in the still, raw, yet strangely exhilarating air there is an unmistakable suggestion of snow. If anybody has neglected to bank up his house or to fetch his stock from their mountain pasture, let him bestir himself now, for winter is at hand.

Henry Childs Merwin   November 1905

bête noire   *bet NWAHR*
someone or something especially disliked or avoided

The best airplanes in 1914 were *easier* to fly than the best commercially available today. They were not, however, *safer* to fly. Little was then known of aircraft structural engineering. The machines of that day were flimsy affairs and apt to fall apart in the air. They were so underpowered that the difference between their top speed and the minimum required to sustain flight was not much more than ten miles an hour. The stall was an ever-present menace, and this, with the tailspin which frequently follows it, remains to this day the *bête noire* of the novice pilot.

Malcolm B. Ronald   January 1937

blandishments *BLAN dish mints*
expressions of affection or kindness, and tending to win the heart

There are regular mealtimes on air liners just as there are on boats and trains, and in between times it has been found wiser to keep the wolf at bay with fruit-store blandishments. On the twenty-four hour run between Chicago and Oakland, three meals are served — dinner over Iowa, breakfast over Utah, and lunch over Nevada — and the company takes no chances. It dictates the menus, provides the stewardesses to set the meals up punctually, and, incidentally, it foots the bill.

Francis Vivian Drake   February 1933

blasphemy *BLAS fuh mee*
disrespectful or irreverent speaking of God or sacred things

In the year 1573, the painter Veronese was summoned before the Inquisition to answer a charge of blasphemy. In a painting of the Last Supper he had created an outer scene of worldliness in contrast to the inner scene of solemnity. Among the figures of the outer scene was a dog, and it was the dog that constituted the blasphemy. Ten years earlier the Council of Trent had decided upon the proper iconography for this and other religious scenes: their decision was held to be final, and a dog was not among the items listed. The painter sought to explain the formal considerations which had led to this arrangement. His explanation was disregarded and he was ordered to substitute a Magdalene for the dog or be subjected to whatever penalty the Holy Tribunal might decide to impose. Veronese did not yield (he retained the dog and changed the title of the painting).

Ben Shahn   August 1957

blather *BLA th:uhr*
foolish talk; verbose nonsense

THE HAZARDS OF WALKING *edited by Carol Trueblood and Donna Fenn. Houghton Mifflin,* $3.95. An Army memo on the hazards of walking employs a full page and approximately 260 words, exclusive of letterhead, signature, and such, to instruct personnel to "Look where you're going." It is not the worst of the examples of bureaucratic blather that the editors have assembled.

Phoebe-Lou Adams   January 1983

✳ Herewith, an assortment of colorful words to describe talk one considers nonsense, each of which has its own nuances: balderdash, claptrap, drivel, eyewash, flapdoodle, flummery, gobbledygook, guff, hogwash, jabber, piffle, poppycock, prattle, rigmarole, rot, rubbish, tommyrot, twaddle.

blazon   *BLAY zuhn*
a bright show

> The venerable ex-President of Harvard and a popular moving-picture star died the same day. Dr. Eliot received a decent tribute from the newspapers, but Rudolph Valentino's passing was chronicled with a blazon of headlines and a fullness of detail once reserved for an assassinated President.

> Earnest Elmo Calkins   January 1927

bleak   *bleek*
harsh; grim

> The Greek historian Polybius, of the second century B.C., interpreted what we consider the Golden Age of Athens as the beginning of its decline. To Thucydides, the very security and satisfactory life that the Athenians enjoyed under Pericles blinded them to the bleak forces of human nature that were gradually to be their undoing in the Peloponnesian War.

> Robert D. Kaplan   December 1997

gloomy; dreary

> The writer Barry Lopez has described the Eskimo concept of *perlerorneq*, an extreme wintertime depression that can drive sufferers to run half-naked out of their igloos, screaming into the noonday darkness, and devouring malamute scat. Baseball fans will know this bleak phenomenon by its more common name, the off-season—which, by virtue of a calendrical oddity no one has adequately explained, somehow lasts a little longer every year. The Library of America's indispensable new anthology may just be *perlerorneq*'s only known antidote.

> David Kipen   May 2002

blight   *blight*
a spoiled or ruined environmental condition, especially of an urban area

> A national study of housing abandonment found that the "tipping point" in a neighborhood occurred when just three to six percent of the structures were abandoned. Vacant lots and empty buildings are more than just symptoms of blight — they are also causes of it.

> Witold Rybczynski   October 1995

blue-nose   *BLOO: nohz*
a puritanical person, especially one who tries to impose a strict moral code on others ("blue-nosed" is the adjective)

Here it is at last, Vladimir Nabokov's *Lolita* (Putnam, $5.00) — first issued in 1955 by an unorthodox Paris press after being rejected by a string of American publishers; banned by the French government, presumably out of solicitude for immature English-speaking readers (the ban was later quashed by the French High Court); pronounced unobjectionable by that blue-nosed body, the U. S. Customs office; and heralded by ovations from writers, professors, and critics on both sides of the Atlantic.

Charles J. Rolo   September 1958

✳ Today's blue laws, consisting mostly of regulations banning the Sunday sale of alcoholic beverages or other goods in some states and municipalities, are the remnants of blue laws supposedly enacted to regulate morals and conduct in colonial New England. They were first described by the Reverend Samuel Peters, in *General History of Connecticut,* a 1781 book that historians have debunked as rife with fabrications, such as his being the founder of Yale College. Peters' falsifications, which included dozens of what he called "blue laws," became imbedded in the American mind as later writers took his book as truth and carried them forward. He writes about a clergyman who was punished in 1750 for breaking the Sabbath law by walking too fast from church; and that on the Sabbath it was criminal to make mince pies or for a mother to kiss her infant. Totally untrue. Rabidly pro-British, Peters' intent was to slander Connecticut after he was forced to leave the colonies when the Revolution began. That blue laws are so called because they were printed on blue paper is also not true. No Connecticut laws on blue paper or bound in blue have ever been found.

bogey   *BOH gee*
an evil or mischievous spirit; a hobgoblin

The makers of household appliances say that they have given the modern housewife great amounts of free time, such as her mother and grandmother never had. This, of course, is nonsense. The truth is that mama is freed from the hard work that used to be done by grandma's maid. The free time comes in dribs and drabs, fifteen minutes here, half an hour there. The bogey of the young mother is in believing that she is simply abounding in leisure and so she really ought to cram in a few more activities and be a better wife than ever.

Nora Johnson   June 1961

bonhomie   *bah nuh MEE*
easy good humor; easygoing friendliness; amiability: French, bon, good +
homme, *man ("bonhomous" is the adjective)*

Most politicians are born, whereas Richard Nixon is a made politician. He once remarked to me: "I just can't be a buddy-buddy boy." Natural politicians are buddy-buddy boys by instinct — they are bonhomous fellows, always ready with the smile and the slap on the back. Richard Nixon has never slapped a back in his life, and his smile often seems a difficult muscular exercise. He is so totally non-bonhomous that his small talk, as on that occasion at the Lincoln Memorial, can be agonizingly embarrassing. Nowadays, for the ceremonial and social occasions at which a President is expected to display bonhomie, aides prepare for the President suggested topics of meaningless conversation plus a selection of small jokes.

Stewart Alsop   February 1972

bon mot   *bohn MOH*
a clever or witty remark

No truer American existed than Thoreau. His preference of his country and condition was genuine, and his aversation from English and European manners and tastes almost reached contempt. He listened impatiently to news or bon mots gleaned from London circles; and though he tried to be civil, these anecdotes fatigued him. The men were all imitating each other, and on a small mould. Why can they not live as far apart as possible, and each be a man by himself? What he sought was the most energetic nature; and he wished to go to Oregon, not to London.

Ralph Waldo Emerson   August 1862

✳ Aversation, an obsolete word meaning a turning away from, is the equivalent of today's aversion.

boon   *boo:n*
a welcome and unexpected benefit; advantage

It has been reserved for California, from the plenitude of her capacities, to give to us a truly great boon in her light and delicate wines. Our Pacific sister, from whose generous hand has flowed an uninterrupted stream of golden gifts, has announced the fact that henceforth we are to be a wine-growing people.

Samuel Cony Perkins   May 1864

boondoggle   *BOO:N dah guhl*
a trifling or pointless project financed by public funds

Denver International Airport: a $4 billion ghost field. Until computerized robotic baggage handlers can be made to function properly, the airport's towers, hangars, and shops will lie idle, awaiting the first pulse of commerce. Denver International can scarcely be invoked in the press without being tagged one of the costliest boondoggles ever.

J. E. Lighter   March 1995

✳ Boondoggle was originally a Boy Scout term for a wood or bone ring through which scouts slipped a neckerchief, or for a braided leather lanyard they made from which to hang whistles, compasses and keys. The *Oxford English Dictionary* lists the word's origin as unknown, but there is reason to believe an American scoutmaster, Robert H. Link (d. 1957), coined it. The word acquired its political meaning in 1935, after a *New York Times* article described an investigation into the wasteful spending of government money in New York City during the Depression. It was headlined: "$3,187,000 Relief Is Spent to Teach Jobless to Play." A sub-headline read, "Boon Doggles Made." A city commission learned that the money was spent teaching people on relief pastimes such as ballet and tap dance. One witness said he taught boon doggles, which he described as "gadgets" such as leather belts.

bracing *BRAY sing*
stimulating; invigorating

Geneva is a glaciated Paris. Here the mechanics of banking, diplomacy, and sophisticated bourgeois living have asphyxiated passion. The silvery blue of Lake Leman suggests money and oblivion. Geneva: I think of Calvinism and gray stones and too many jewelry shops. Despite the bracing winds and the swans, Lake Leman seems but another enclosure. The wrought iron, the pollarded trees, the conical hedges, the crystalline dawn haze where Lake Leman meets the Rhone, the Gothic monuments and gabled roofs, the marble fireplaces and the valences in my hotel room — all are exquisite, but it is an austere and hollow beauty. Joseph Conrad called Geneva "the very perfection of mediocrity."

Robert D. Kaplan   January 1999

bravura *bruh VYOO: ruh*
a display of skill and technique

With maturity Cash grew into his voice. To read his obituaries, one might think that his credibility as a singer depended entirely on his credibility as a man. True, he never developed his upper range to the point where he could trust it, and the clear emphasis he gave every single word would have precluded gliding from note to note even if he had been able to. Among the singers of his own generation he lacked the bravura and the sheer lung power of such country Carusos as Elvis Presley, Conway Twitty, Roy Orbison, Ferlin Husky, and the young Waylon Jennings. We tend not to value deep voices as much as we do high, soaring ones, perhaps because the effort involved in producing a low note is less apparent. Something about hearing a singer go low strikes most ears as a trick, a human special effect. The bass singer does the grunt work in doo-wop and rhythm and blues, sometimes literally. There is a style of country music, however, in which a male singer's descent to a virile low note at the end of a phrase, or for the closing chorus, supplies the same payoff as a soul singer's falsetto — one conveys masculine certainty and the other uncontrollable passion, but each signifies a moment of truth. No country singer was better at this than Cash, and few singers in any field of music have been as expressive or as instantly recognizable.

Francis Davis   March 2004

bridle *BRIGH duhl*
to restrain; hold back

If jazz is a reflection of life, as it seems to be, why then has it aroused such antagonism among many people? First, I think, because it challenges complacency. Secondly, because it refuses to be bridled by the accepted and equivocal standards of society. Thirdly, because it is never still; it does not hesitate to press forward on every boundary of the emotions no matter how they may be denied. But most of all it has tried to speak without guile or circumvention to the troubled mind and bewildered heart. As long as doubt and loneliness exist this music will try to speak to them.

Arnold Sundgaard   July 1955

bristle *BRI suhl*
to react with irritation, anger or fear; display temper or indignation
("bristling" is the noun)

I recall a scene the morning after my first fight with Jack Dempsey as one of the strangest I ever experienced. It had me disconcerted, as well as considerably embarrassed. After that bout in the rain in Philadelphia it seemed to me proper to go and pay my respects to Jack. He had been severely punished, and must feel pretty blue after losing the championship. The next afternoon I went to his hotel. He had a suite of rooms, and when I got there Jack was in an inside bedroom. In the outer room were gathered the Dempsey entourage of manager, handlers, trainers, and disappointed followers. They greeted me with an instant bristling of hostility. I was the focus of scowls and angry, sullen glances. Gene Normile was in tears. Jerry the Greek came to me, shook his fist, and mumbled hoarsely, "You can't licka the 'Chump,' you can't licka the 'Chump.'" Jack Dempsey always inspired loyalty, and this was it. They bitterly resented my defeating him.

Gene Tunney   June 1939

broach *brohch*
to bring up for conversation or discussion; introduce

It was in New York that it was first suspected that Charles Dickens would not be likely to approve American slavery; he had also at the Hartford dinner broached the very unpopular subject of an "international copyright law"; and the newspapers began extensively to exhibit that unfriendly feeling toward him which afterward became so violent and even malignant.

George W. Putnam   October 1870

broadside   *BRAWD sighd*
a vigorous or abusive volley of criticism or denunciation: a figurative use of the tactic of simultaneously firing all the guns on one side of a warship

In 1939 the Dancing Masters of America recruited Irene Castle, the doyenne of American ballroom dancing, to deliver a broadside at their annual convention. "Jitterbug dancing is neither graceful nor beautiful," she proclaimed. "One should float to the music." Meanwhile, the Dancing Teachers Business Association warned that Lindy dancing was "a form of hysteria that will prove harmful to the poise of the present generation."

Robert P. Crease   February 1986

❋ Nineteenth-century dance teachers were equally skeptical of the waltz, seeing the waltz's simple steps as a threat to their livelihood. Music critics denounced it for what they considered its crude sound and movement. It was the era's dirty dancing. Originally a rollicking peasant dance whose partners clutched each other joyfully, the waltz was the opposite of the minuet and quadrille, whose hands-only touching typified 17th- and 18th-century social dancing. Queen Victoria, an accomplished ballroom dancer, loved it.

bromide   *BROH mighd*
an unoriginal remark spoken at what seems to be the appropriate moment for it; commonplace or conventional expression; trite saying; platitude

Chances are that more than a few bromides you utter originated with Longfellow. Indeed, they may have originated in one of the more than sixty poems he published in this magazine. "The patter of little feet:" — "The mills of God grind slowly, yet they grind exceeding small," "One, if by land, and two, if by sea," "This is the forest primeval," "Ships that pass in the night," "Shall fold their tents, like the Arabs, / and as silently steal away," are famously his; but so are "Into each life some rain must fall"; "footprints on the sands of time," and "a boy's will is the wind's will," famous thanks to Frost.

Peter Davison   February 2001

❋ Although he did not invent the word bromide, the American humorist Gelett Burgess popularized the word with his 1906 article, "The Sulphitic Theory, or Are You a Bromide?," in which he separates people into the Bromides, who think conventionally, and the Sulphites, who do their own thinking. "The accepted Bromidic belief," he wrote, "is that each of the ordinary acts of life is, and necessarily must be, accompanied by its own especial remark or opinion." Among the examples of bromides Burgess offered were "I don't know much about art, but I know what I like," and "It isn't the money — it's the principle of the thing."

brood   *broo:d*
to hover or loom as if to envelop; hang low

It is nine o'clock upon a summer Sunday morning, in the year sixteen hundred and something. The sun looks down brightly on a little forest settlement, around whose expanding fields the great American wilderness recedes each day, withdrawing its bears and wolves and Indians into an ever remoter distance, — not yet so far but that a stout wooden gate at each end of the village's street indicates that there is something outside which must stay outside, if possible. It would look very busy and thriving in this little place, to-day, but for the Sabbath stillness which broods over everything with almost an excess of calm. Even the smoke ascends more faintly than usual from the chimneys of these abundant log-huts and scanty framed houses, and since three o'clock yesterday afternoon not a stroke of this world's work has been done.

Thomas Wentworth Higginson   September 1863

browbeat   *BROW beet*
to intimidate with harsh words or threats; bully

In the typical case, FBI agents do not initially take a man into custody for questioning, but interview him at his home or place of work. They ask him casually about the offense, not probing too deeply on the first try. The agents do not bully or browbeat the suspect into incriminating himself. They operate on precisely the opposite theory, that the suspect's normal reaction will be to try to exculpate himself. Rarely will the suspect refuse to talk at all, for he fears that this will be taken by the agents as an admission of guilt.

Robert Cipes   September 1966

buffet   *BUH fit*
to struggle against

A birch canoe is the right thing in the right place. Maine's rivers are violently impulsive and spasmodic in their running. Sometimes you have a foamy rapid, sometimes a broad shoal, sometimes a barricade of boulders with gleams of white water springing through or leaping over its rocks. Your boat for voyaging here must be stout enough to buffet the rapid, light enough to skim the shallow, agile enough to vault over, or lithe enough to slip through, the barricade.

Theodore Winthrop   September 1862

bugbear *BUHG bair*
a needless fear; originally, a hobgoblin that devoured naughty children

Oddly enough, the same Americans who do not hesitate to confuse, misuse, duplicate, and miscegenate words remain absurdly conventional about grammar, especially in print. On second thoughts, there is nothing odd about it, for it is part of the same uncertain desire to show off knowledge, fostered in this case by the etiquette of the "Write It Right" books and editorial style sheets. Yet when everybody "knows enough" not to split an infinitive, or makes some similar bugbear equivalent to a knowledge of the mother tongue, it is perhaps time to reconsider what the schools and the books should teach as good English.

Jacques Barzun   January 1946

bullheaded *BOOL hed id*
blindly stubborn

The proper education of an umpire is directed toward the development of three capacities — sharp sight, instant decision, and resolution enough to make the decision stick. Resolute, of course, does not mean bullheaded. A good umpire is not to be intimidated, not even by the bleachers spilling onto the field, roaring; yet if they pull the rule book on him, he has humility enough to reverse a wrong decision gracefully.

Gerald W. Johnson   January 1964

✳ *An umpire* was originally *a numpire*. The original French term for a third party who settles disputes was a *noumpere* (not equal), but through a process called faulty separation, the *n* was transferred to the article that preceded it. Similarly, from the faulty separation of article and noun we have *an adder* from *a nadder, a newt* from *an ewt, an apron* from *a napron, an orange* from *a narange* and *a nickname* from *an eke name* (eke meaning also).

bulwark *BOOL werk*
a powerful defense or safeguard

In our schools we attempt to teach the best literature, to inculcate ideals of good music and sound art. We open museums and establish free libraries. Why? For the simple reason that we believe, and rightly believe, that a knowledge and love of these better things is a bulwark of our civilization.

Walter Prichard Eaton   January 1915

bumble   *BUM buhl*
to blunder; stumble; botch ("bumbler" is the noun)

Only once in modern history has the substance of a presidential candidate's comments in a debate mattered politically. That was in 1976, when the incumbent, Gerald Ford, appeared to say that Poland, then part of the Soviet bloc, was not subject to Communist control. A fair-minded observer could parse what Ford was trying to say — that the free spirit of the Polish people would never be quashed. But the episode fit Ford's image as a bumbler and gave Jimmy Carter a decisive debate "win."

James Fallows   July/August 2004

bumper crop   *BUM puhr crahp*
an exceptionally abundant harvest

When Robert Lowell's *Lord Weary's Castle* appeared, in 1946, it was as welcome as a bumper crop. The sheer gorgeousness and encrusted bookishness of this poetry startled readers used to the plain talk of Robert Frost and William Carlos Williams. The book — the first of his to find a general publisher — won Lowell a Pulitzer Prize at twenty-nine.

Peter Davison   July/August 2003

bumpkin   *BUHMP kin*
an awkward or simple country person; yokel: in this case, with an urban twist

We have seen many a city bumpkin start for a White-Mountain walk in the thinnest of cotton foot-coverings, but we never knew one to try them a second time.

James T. Fields   December 1861

bumptious   *BUHMP shuhs*
crudely or loudly self-assertive; pushy; arrogant ("bumptiousness" is the noun)

The repute of superciliousness which always, and often most unfairly, dogs the steps of the visiting Englishman, in America and Australia alike, does not operate on either side in Australian-American relations, nor does the American share a widespread British dislike of Australian "bumptiousness."

Dixon Wechter   May 1946

bunk   *buhnk*
nonsense: short for bunkum

I do not agree with the dictum of Mr. Henry Ford that "history is bunk." But the historian will be the first to admit that history as set down in a book is not what many people think it is. It is not a record of all the important things that happened during a particular period. It is an arrangement of selected facts, and the historian is responsible for the selection. He may do his best to rid his mind of prejudice. But he has an ineradicable prejudice in favor of intelligibility. He tries to set down the facts in such a way that their relations may be readily understood. They are marshaled in an orderly fashion. Unfortunately that is not the way they happened. So for the sake of an intelligible narrative he must eliminate those happenings that were irrelevant, confusing, and incoherent.

Samuel McChord Crothers   October 1926

   ✳ In 1819, as a Congressional debate on whether to admit Missouri to the union as a slave or a free state was ending, Felix Walker, a congressman from North Carolina, rose to speak. When his colleagues realized the irrelevancy of his speech to the Missouri question and asked him to sit down, he persisted, saying he owed it to his constituents "to make a speech for Buncombe," the county he represented. Repeated in newspapers, buncombe became a synonym for political claptrap. By 1850 it was spelled bunkum, and by 1900 it had been shortened to bunk.

Bunyanesque *buhn yuh NESK*
hugely out of proportion to ordinary human endeavor

Even among other hallowed figures in the pantheon of inventors, Edison is Bunyanesque. What Henry Ford is to the automobile, George Eastman to photography, and Charles Goodyear to rubber, Edison is to not one but several of today's essential technologies.

Kathleen McAuliffe   December 1995

   ✳ In American folklore, Paul Bunyan was a gigantic lumberjack who performed prodigious feats. Although he originated in the oral storytelling of Pennsylvania lumbermen, the character gained national notice after the first published tale about him appeared in the Detroit *News-Tribune* in 1910.

buoyancy *BOI uhn see*
the ability to stay afloat; quick to recover from disappointment or disaster

It was said in the war that although we had not invented an unsinkable ship we had succeeded in producing an unsinkable politician, and, whatever else may be said of Mr. Winston Churchill, it will be conceded that his buoyancy is nothing short of amazing. The two catastrophes of Antwerp and the Dardanelles failed to sink him. He has been several times upon a lee shore, battering himself to pieces — or so it seemed — upon the rocks of various obdurate constituencies. The vessel might seem to be derelict, detached without any hope of salvage or any powerful party political tug to tow it out of danger; and yet, somehow or other, it has always floated away, not merely to the open sea again, but into some prosperous harbor of ministerial office.

Ian Colvin   February 1925

burgeon   *BER jin*
to grow or develop rapidly; expand

Perhaps the lawmakers really couldn't have foreseen in 1909, the year the copyright law was passed, that there ever would be such a universal dispenser of culture as a jukebox. With rare shortsightedness, they passed a special amendment specifically exempting coin-operated music machines from being considered as a public performance. In those days, such machines were no more than novelty gadgets, but they have since burgeoned into big business. Dimes and quarters are being swallowed up in ever-increasing amounts, to the nonlicensed tune of over $500 million annual profit. Yet no matter how often a song is played, its composer and lyricist receive no royalty.

Stanley Green   April 1962

buttonhole   *BUH tuhn hohl*
to hold a person as if by the buttonhole in order to detain in conversation

A jaded American millionaire, trying to get pleasure out of a too long deferred holiday in Europe, is one of the most depressing of pococurantist spectacles. For twenty or thirty years he has been amassing a fortune, with the pluck and energy which we all admire. And here he is set down in Paris or Dresden or Florence, ignorant of the language, the history, the architecture, the ideas of the country. He is a good fellow, but he is homesick, listless, indifferent: he speeds his automobile along some famous Roman road without once kindling at the thought of Cæsar or Napoleon; the Mediterranean means to him Monte Carlo; and nothing in his trip gives him so much real satisfaction as to buttonhole a fellow American and talk to him about the superiority of American hotels. He is taking his holiday too late. He has no longer any oil in his lamp. Curiosity, imagination, sympathy, zest, have been burned out of him in that fierce competitive struggle where his life forces have been spent.

Bliss Perry   September 1903

✳ Pococurante is a character in Voltaire's novel *Candide*. Searching through Europe and America for his beloved Cunegonde, the naïve Candide meets the Venetian noble Signor Pococurante. He is 60 years old, rich, bored, and so hypercritical that he can never be happy with anything, although he has everything. Asked by Candide what master painted two of the pictures in his gallery, he replies,

"They are by Raphael. I bought them at a very high price, merely out of vanity, some years ago. They are said to be the finest paintings in Italy: but they do not please me at all; the colors are dead, the figures not finished, and do not appear with relief enough; the drapery is very bad." Pococurantist has become an adjective meaning indifferent or apathetic — in Bliss Perry's words, "the caring little for things that are worth caring much for."

buttress   *BUH tris*
to support or reinforce; bolster

A parent who respects himself will feel no need to demand or command respect from his child, since he feels no need for the child's respect to buttress his security as a parent or as a person. Secure in himself, he will not feel his authority threatened and will accept it when his child sometimes shows a lack of respect for him, as young children, in particular, are apt to do. The parent's self-respect tells him that such displays arise from immaturity of judgment, which time and experience will eventually correct.

Bruno Bettelheim   November 1985

byword   *BIGH werd*
a person or thing proverbial for some quality

More than a third of the approximately 72,000 Marines who landed on Iwo Jima were killed or wounded. The bravery, too, was shocking. Of the 353 Congressional Medals of Honor awarded during World War II, twenty-seven were given for heroism on Iwo Jima, thirteen of them posthumously. Iwo became a byword for fighting while it was still being fought. The U.S. military had hoped the island could be taken in two weeks. The battle lasted thirty-six days. Japanese resistance was expected to be stubborn. It was ferocious. Only 1,083 of the approximately 21,000 Japanese defenders surrendered or were taken prisoner.

P. J. O'Rourke   June 2004

C

capacious

Never will I allude to the English Language or tongue without exultation.
This is the tongue that spurns laws, as the greatest tongue must. It is the
most capacious vital tongue of all, — full of ease, definiteness, and
power, — full of sustenance, — an enormous treasure house, or ranges of
treasure houses, arsenals, granary, chock full of so many contributions
from the north and from the south, from Scandinavia, from
Greece and Rome — from Spaniards, Italians, and the
French — that its own sturdy home-dated Angles-
bred words have long been outnumbered by the
foreigners whom they lead — which is all good
enough, and indeed must be. America owes
immeasurable respect and love to the past, and to
many ancestries, for many inheritances, — but of all
that America has received from the past from the mothers and fathers of
laws, arts, letters, etc., by far the greatest inheritance is the English
Language — so long in growing — so fitted.

Walt Whitman   April 1904

see page 75

cachinnate   *KA kuh nayt*

to laugh too loudly or too hard ("cachinnation" is the noun)

I woke up with a start. It was quite still outside. For thirty days I had listened to the laughter of wind — sometimes a faint chuckle, then rising to a roar, catching at the sides of the house and shaking the roof, or pouring like a solid stream across the pampa and thrashing the *calafate* bushes as it passed by. Sometimes it would rise until it shrieked with cachinnations of a madman. One could not help thinking that the land was holding its sides in mirth over the jokes it had played on mankind. For this was Patagonia, where only sheep and Englishmen seem at home.

James Terry Duce   September 1937

cad   *kad*

a man who is unprincipled and callous in his relations with women

There is the tale of the lady in Boston. She refused the attentions of a distinguished gentleman, so he took his revenge. He ordered his carriage and pair to stand outside the door of her house all night. In the morning the sober citizens, as they went to their offices, saw coachman and horses still waiting there. The lady lost her reputation. But that evening when the gentleman entered his club, he was cut. He had been a cad.

Gretchen Finletter   May 1947

    ✳ Cad derives ultimately from the 15th-century French *cadet*, younger son. From that came the Scottish *caddie*, an errand boy, in the 18th century, and then, in the 19th century, a golfer's assistant. From these neutral meanings, caddie shrank to cad, and its acquired perjorative senses: in the 1820s, a contemptuous term used by British university students for town boys, and in the 1830s a man of low manners. At the turn of the 20th century it took on its current meaning.

cadaverous   *kuh DA vuh ruhs*
gaunt and haggard; corpselike

I have never known so great a change to take place in any man's appearance as in Mr. Lincoln's during the three years following the day when I first saw him — March 4, 1861. He was never handsome, indeed, but he grew more cadaverous and ungainly month by month. The terrible labor which the war imposed prevented him from taking systematic exercise, and he became constantly more lean and sallow. He had a very dejected appearance, and ugly black rings appeared under his eyes. I well remember how weary and sad he looked at one of the inevitable receptions as he stood near the folding doors where the central corridor empties itself into the East Room.

William A. Croffut   January 1930

cagey   *KAY jee*
careful not to get caught or fooled; sly; tricky

Malaria parasites have spent centuries adapting to life in the human body, and as a result have grown cagey. Unlike human immunodeficiency virus, or HIV, which both infects and is transmitted by human beings, malaria parasites keep their delivery system separate from their food supply — they do not shoot the messenger. The parasites are transmitted to human beings through the saliva of the female mosquito, which is so efficient at this task that it is sometimes described as a flying syringe.

Ellen Ruppel Shell   August 1997

calcified   *KAL suh fighd*
hardened, as into stone; fixed; inflexible

Muhammad ibn Abdul Wahhab was an eighteenth-century Arabian religious leader who led a back-to-the-roots Islamic movement away from the calcified orthodoxy of Ottoman Turkey and the pre-Islamic paganism practiced by some desert tribes. Though almost all Saudis today are nominally Wahhabis, it is the most extreme Wahhabi fundamentalists who have been active in Afghanistan and Pakistan.

Robert D. Kaplan   April 1992

calculus   *KAL kyuh luhs*
a consideration that gets figured into a situation or problem

If Chile were a less developed society, its response to Pinochet's regime could be attributed to a rational, if coldhearted, calculus in which human-rights violations are a necessary price to pay for order and prosperity. But Chileans, too cultured and democratic to face such a decision, are left only with denial: torture and political murder don't happen. This blindness continues in Pinochet's supporters today.

Tina Rosenberg   December 1986

In the weird calculus of Chinese politics — and contrary to the conventional wisdom on Tiananmen — Deng's 1989 crackdown on dissent was as much a rejection of hard-line communism as a return to it.

Trevor Corson   February 2000

> ✱ The economist John Kenneth Galbraith coined the term conventional wisdom in *The Affluent Society* (1958) to describe a belief generally accepted by the public.

calibrate *KA luh brayt*
to plan or devise carefully; to measure with mechanical accuracy

For politicians to succeed, humor must also be carefully calibrated to humanize them, which means that it must almost always be self-deprecating. "Humor has to flow upward," Jon Macks explains. "It's okay to make fun of your boss, but if you're the guy on top, it's not okay to make jokes about people beneath you, because you look mean —which means your jokes have to come at your own expense." John Edwards, needled for his boyish good looks, has succeeded with this ("I know what you're thinking: 'He's even better-looking in person' "); as a candidate and as President, George W. Bush, for whom self-deprecation is hardly an impulse, has also submitted to necessity (quoting Garrison Keillor's crack that "George Bush's lips are where words go to die").

Joshua Green   May 2004

callow *KA loh*
young and inexperienced; immature

I was a callow seventeen-year-old when I first walked into a newspaper city room. I knew almost instantly that I had found my calling, if the calling would have me. There was nothing quite like the amiable, disheveled intensity of a newspaper city room, the kind that existed in many American cities until the efficiency engineers, the interior decorators, and the computers forced themselves into the trade and provided working quarters that could pass for the home offices of an insurance company or a conglomerate devoted to fast foods and corrugated containers.

Robert Manning   December 1976

calumny *KA luhm nee*
a false statement meant to hurt someone's reputation; slander

Among the unwarranted calumnies formerly circulated about Brook Farm was the assertion that a good deal of flirting was carried on there. I have been much with people in my life, — a teacher for some years, a mother with several children, and now a grandmother with hosts of grandchildren, — and I have never seen more truly gentlemanly and gentlewomanly relations between youths and maidens than at Brook Farm.

Ora Gannett Sedgwick   March 1900

✳ The utopian experiment known as Brook Farm was begun in 1841 in West Roxbury, Massachusetts, by George Ripley, a former Unitarian minister, and his wife, Sofia. Transcendentalists like their friends Emerson and Thoreau, they believed that life's deepest truths emerged from insight rather than through logic and experience. They set out to create a place where people would cultivate the land as well as their minds, free from the competitive world. Members paid $500 for a share of stock in Brook Farm, most of them leaving comfortable lives to labor hard for the sake of living in an intellectual communal environment. Lectures, music and discussions were daily events, and the school taught students from the primary grades through high school. Nathaniel Hawthorne lived among Brook Farm's 70 or 80 members for its first several months, but left because he found it difficult to write there (among his tasks was milking the cows). But his stay inspired his novel *The Blithedale Romance*. Because its soil was poor and its farmers inexperienced, Brook Farm had a difficult time supporting itself, and in 1847, after a fire razed an uninsured new building that had cost all its available funds, Brook Farm closed.

camaraderie   *kah muh RA duh ree*
warmth, closeness and goodwill among friends

As we settle back into our private lives, the guard goes up. Reticence has returned. I see it as I travel. I miss the camaraderie, the sharing, the boy picked up as he thumbed his way back from leave, the friendliness which so often led to unburdening. I miss the candor and the heart with which Americans turned to each other while the pressure was on.

Edward Weeks   March 1946

canard   *kuh NAHRD*
a false or unfounded story; fabricated report; a groundless, malicious rumor

Nader estimated that $700 of each car's retail cost proceeded mostly from styling changes, and that most of this should be spent on safety; that some changes would not be more costly, just different. To the industry's argument that "safety doesn't sell," he replied that this was a self-serving, irresponsible canard, which became a self-fulfilled prophecy.

Elizabeth Brenner Drew   October 1966

cant *kant*
insincere or meaningless words spoken by habit; falsely pious talk

The whole culture of Jefferson's youth was, of all things in the world, least likely to make him support slavery or apologize for it. The man who did most to work into his mind ideas of moral and political science was Dr. William Small, a liberal Scotchman; the man who did most to direct his studies in law, and his grappling with social problems, was George Wythe. To both of these Jefferson confessed the deepest debt for their efforts to strengthen his mind and make his footing firm. Now, of all men in this country at that time, these two were least likely to support pro-slavery theories or tolerate pro-slavery cant.

Andrew Dickson Worth   January 1862

capacious *kuh PAY shuhs*
able to contain or hold much; roomy; spacious

Never will I allude to the English Language or tongue without exultation. This is the tongue that spurns laws, as the greatest tongue must. It is the most capacious vital tongue of all, — full of ease, definiteness, and power, — full of sustenance, — an enormous treasure house, or ranges of treasure houses, arsenals, granary, chock full of so many contributions from the north and from the south, from Scandinavia, from Greece and Rome — from Spaniards, Italians, and the French — that its own sturdy home-dated Angles-bred words have long been outnumbered by the foreigners whom they lead — which is all good enough, and indeed must be. America owes immeasurable respect and love to the past, and to many ancestries, for many inheritances, — but of all that America has received from the past from the mothers and fathers of laws, arts, letters, etc., by far the greatest inheritance is the English Language — so long in growing — so fitted.

Walt Whitman   April 1904

capital *KA puh tuhl*
principal; chief

From day to day, the capital facts of human life are hidden from our eyes. Suddenly the mist rolls up, and reveals them, and we think how much good time is gone, that might have been saved, had any hint of these things been shown.

Ralph Waldo Emerson   November 1857

capitulate *kuh PI chuh layt*
to give up; stop resisting; surrender ("capitulation" is the noun)

Like any other subject, Sheikh Mohammed presented his interrogators with a unique problem. The critical hub of a worldwide secret network, he had a potential road map in his head to the whole shadow world of jihad. If he could be made to talk, to reveal even a few secrets, what an intelligence bonanza that would be! Here was a man who lived to further his cause by whatever means, who saw himself as morally, spiritually, and intellectually superior to the entire infidel Western world, a man for whom capitulation meant betraying not just his friends and his cherished cause but his very soul.

Mark Bowden   October 2003

captious   *KAP shuhs*
made only for the sake of argument or faultfinding

I am not much an advocate for travelling, and I observe that men run away to other countries because they are not good in their own, and run back to their own because they pass for nothing in the new places. For the most part, only the light characters travel. Who are you that have no task to keep you at home? I have been quoted as saying captious things about travel; but I mean to do justice. I think there is a restlessness in our people which argues want of character. All educated Americans, first or last, go to Europe, — perhaps because it is their mental home, as the invalid habits of this country might suggest. An eminent teacher of girls said, "The idea of a girl's education is whatever qualifies them for going to Europe." Can we never extract this tape-worm of Europe from the brain of our countrymen?

Ralph Waldo Emerson   September 1860

cardinal   *KAHR duh nuhl*
principal; chief

The cardinal fact about Emily Dickinson is that she was a product of her time and place. Her connection with Amherst was closer than that of any other American author with the spot where his life was passed. She was born of the stock that originally settled the Connecticut Valley. Her mind was shaped by church, school, and college, which in her time expressed with dynamic vigor the intellectual and spiritual energies of the Puritan tradition. It was in her father's house on Main Street that she was able to achieve the seclusion which her nature more and more insistently required as she turned to poetry as her only means of personal fulfillment. It was there that she died.

George F. Whicher   February 1946

careerist   *kuh REER ist*
a person chiefly interested in career advancement, often by unscrupulous means

Kennedy, who fashioned himself after Franklin D. Roosevelt, wanted to make the major foreign-policy decisions in his Administration; he did not want them made by the Secretary of State or by the careerists at the State Department.

Carl Brauer   November 1988

carnage   *KAHR nij*
bloody and extensive slaughter, especially in battle; massacre; bloodshed

The amount of bloodshed in the United States is difficult to comprehend, like the carnage of a shadowy, undeclared civil war. During the past two decades nearly half a million Americans have been murdered, and an additional 2.5 million have been wounded by gunfire — more casualties than the U. S. military has suffered in all the wars of the past 200 years.

Eric Schlosser   September 1997

carp   *kahrp*
to constantly complain or find fault in a petty, nagging way ("carping" is used as an adjective in the first passage)

If it is a true saying that no man is a hero to his valet, it is an even truer one that no author is an object of awe to his secretary, and fortunately so, for her carping criticism may save him from many a blunder. "You said yesterday that man had blue eyes," Deanie tells me caustically. "Now you have made them brown. Which do you really want?"

Frances Parkinson Keyes   September 1950

The President's human frailties are most sharply seen in his relations with the Washington press, the first representatives of the public on the scene. Instead of openness and frankness, with each side aware of the limitations and restraints that should govern all human relations, there is carping and distrust on both sides. The press believes that the President enjoys playing games with it; the President seriously believes that the press dislikes him because he is a Texan, a Southerner, or the inheritor of the Kennedy mantle.

Carroll Kilpatrick   April 1965

carpetbagger   *KAR pit BA guhr*
an opportunistic or exploitive outsider; someone from outside a community whose political influence there is resented

If local people have no lively interest in their place of birth or adoption, how can carpetbaggers who have no roots or attachments be expected to preserve its natural beauties and maintain its traditions? A community must have leadership and conscience to resist the ruthless modern developer. These are commodities no outsider can supply. The most we as public officials can do is to hold the mirror up to nature, point the moral, and hope for the best.

Robert Moses   December 1950

✳ Historically, carpetbaggers were Northerners who sought political and business careers in the southern states after the Civil War. For luggage, many of them carried only a sturdy satchel made of carpet that held all of their belongings, symbolizing to the Southerner the transience of their visit. These Northern interlopers were despised by Southerners as opportunists in a ruined economy, and exploiters of newly-freed slaves whose votes elected them to public office. Most of them, however, were well-intentioned, especially in helping the South to adapt to a new era and former slaves to adjust to freedom. "Carpetbagger" is sometimes used today by opponents of office-seekers in a state that has not been their home.

cartel   *kahr TEL*

an association of independent business organizations formed to establish a monopoly by regulating the production, prices and marketing of goods by its members

Since 1796 the United States has protected domestic sugar against imports. American sugar growers, in part as a reward for large contributions to political campaigns, have long enjoyed a system of quotas and prohibitive tariffs against foreign competition. American consumers paid about three times world prices for sugar in the 1980s, enriching a small cartel of U.S. growers.

Mark Sagoff   June 1997

cartographer   *kahr TAH gruh fer*
a person who makes maps

The most revolutionary changes are changes in man's basic beliefs about himself. Three such revolutions have occurred in Western thought in the past five hundred years — the Copernican, the Darwinian, and the Freudian — and they have successively dealt shattering blows to man's pride. Copernicus dethroned man from the center of the universe. Darwin challenged his sense of divinity by tracing his descent to the animal kingdom. And Sigmund Freud, the first cartographer of the unconscious, punctured his conviction that the conscious mind was master of man's fate. "I belonged," Freud justly said, quoting the poet Hebbel, "to those who have profoundly troubled the sleep of mankind."

Charles J. Rolo   July 1961

cascade   *kas KAYD*
to fall from one level to another, like a series of waterfalls

Niagara Falls is a city of unmatched natural beauty; it is also a tired industrial workhorse, beaten often and with a hard hand. A magnificent river — a strait, really —

connecting Lake Erie to Lake Ontario flows hurriedly north, at a pace of a half-million tons a minute, widening into a smooth expanse near the city before breaking into whitecaps and taking its famous 186-foot plunge. Then it cascades through a gorge of overhung shale and limestone to rapids higher and swifter than anywhere else on the continent.

Michael H. Brown   December 1979

cashier   *ka SHEER*
to dishonorably dismiss from a position of command or trust

The country is now on the eve of an election the importance of which it would be impossible to overrate. Yet a few days, and it will be decided whether the people of the United States shall condemn their own conduct, by cashiering an Administration which they called upon to make war on the rebellious slaveholders of the South, or support that Administration in the strenuous endeavors which it is making to effect the reconstruction of the Republic, and the destruction of Slavery. It is to insult the intelligence and patriotism of the American people to entertain any serious doubt as to the issue of the contest. It can have but one issue, unless the country has lost its senses; — and never has it given better evidence of its sobriety, firmness, and rectitude of purpose than it now daily affords.

Charles Creighton Hazewell   November 1864

castigate   *KA stuh gayt*
to criticize or punish severely, especially by harsh public criticism
("castigation" is the noun)

One of the lowest forms of human life is the professorial bully whose temper is not under control. I have known cases where a sensitive youngster, at the mere preliminary rumble of the tyrant's voice, has shivered with fear. Perhaps there are some types of boys who deserve verbal castigation, just as there are animals that can learn only through a sound beating. But the tongue, always an unruly member, is a dangerous weapon, and a cowardly one when conditions allow the victim no retaliation.

Claude M. Fuess   October 1932

casuistry   *KA zhoo i stree*
subtle but misleading or false reasoning; sophistry

The politician must get his power through votes. So his daily task is the invention of cunning devices for catching voters. The average man is reached more quickly through his prejudices than through his reasoning faculties. Therefore it is that into the ordinary campaigns is carried casuistry rather than argument, passion rather than logic. Therefore it is that the vote-getter seeks to tingle the nerves rather than excite the brain cells.

Samuel P. Orth   July 1907

catchall *KA chahl*
covering a wide variety of items or situations

"Tuna" is a catchall word for seven or eight species of related finfish. There are the Pacific yellowfin tuna, the big-eye tuna, the albacore tuna, the skipjack tuna, the blackfin tuna, the Atlantic yellowfin tuna, the so-called "little tuna" (the bonito and other tunalike smaller fish), and the largest (more than 1400 pounds) and fastest (up to 60 mph) tuna of them all — the Atlantic bluefin.

John N. Cole   December 1976

catchword *KACH werd*
a word or phrase that gains wide public use to the point of becoming a slogan or expression

Descartes's great philosophical monument, "I think, therefore I am," has become a mere schoolboy's catchword for sophomores to startle freshmen with. It has a glitter, it is true, which fascinates the infant philosopher; but we no longer use it as a platform to build upon. It has disappeared from modern philosophy just as the soliloquy has disappeared from modern drama. They are both important solely as facts of history.

Cornelia Throop Geer   June 1919

✳ A catchphrase or catchword can be a cliché (What goes around comes around), an exclamation (No kidding!), a proverb (The early bird catches the worm) or a quotation ("What fools these mortals be").

categorically *ka tuh GAW rik lee*
without exception or qualification; absolute

"Upon what meat doth this, our Caesar, feed, That he is grown so great?" Ignorance prevents anybody from answering categorically, but I would bet a silver dollar against the hole in a doughnut that Caesar did not feed on milk-fed turkey or battery-fed chicken or baby beef or any other form of flesh which, after it is cooked, can be eaten with a spoon as easily as with knife and fork.

J. Frank Dobie   June 1960

catspaw *KATS paw*
a person used as a tool by another to do dangerous, distasteful or unlawful work; dupe

The romance of truffles! The very word itself appears in a halo, an aristocratic halo full of mystery and suggestion. One remembers the hunters who must track their quarry through marshy and treacherous lands, and one cannot forget their confiding catspaw, that desolated pig, created only to be betrayed and robbed of the fungi of his labors. He is one of the pathetic characters of history, born to secret sorrow, victimized by those superior tastes which do not become his lowly station. Born to labor and to suffer, but not to eat. To this day he commands my sympathy; his ghost — lean, bourgeois, reproachful — looks out at me from every marketplace in the world where the truffle proclaims his faithful service.

William Beebe   February 1919

cavil   *KA vuhl*
a trivial objection

Philip Roth's first collection of stories, *Goodbye, Columbus*, showed a remarkable gift of sharp and incisive characterization. One's only cavil was that sometimes the stories seemed to make their points too neatly, and one wondered whether his fine talent might not end by becoming too tight and stereotyped.

William Barrett   July 1962

censure
strong criticism or disapproval; condemnation

Few subjects interest the world as does the marvel of human flight, no prospect is so alluring as "the conquest of the air," and when airmen, greatly daring, cross the wide seas they call forth admiration and wonder at their enterprise and courage, their skill and endurance: yet so narrow is the gulf between amazing success and tragic failure, so far are the determining factors beyond the control of the pilot, that enthusiasm yields to misgiving and even to censure, mingled with increasing skepticism regarding the value of long-distance flights.

Marion Whiteford Ackworth (under the pseudonym of Neon)   January 1928

centripetal   *sen TRI puh tuhl*
moving toward the center: the opposite of centrifugal

The creation of a single self-governing nation from Minnesota to Florida and from Calais to San Diego, containing people from all the jealous and hostile races of Europe, is no small feat for little more than a century. The fact that the greater part of the newer states were first settled by people from the older ones helped, no doubt, in the process, but should not obscure the achievement of forming so elastic and yet so solid a structure. It was accomplished because the plan was federal and each of the forty-eight states could, to a great extent, develop in its own way. Truly, in its influence upon its membership, the American federal system has shown itself centripetal.

A. Lawrence Lowell   May 1936

✳ Calais, Maine, the easternmost city in America, was named for the French seaport of Calais in 1806 out of gratitude for France's assistance to the colonies during the Revolutionary War. Its name was especially appropriate, as the town lies across the river from Dover Hill, in New Brunswick, Canada, and France's Calais lies across the Channel from the white cliffs of England's Dover. But in Maine, Calais is not pronounced *kuh LAY*, the French way: it's *KA luhs*. They were grateful, but they were still Americans.

chafe   *chayf*
to become irritated, annoyed or impatient

Epitaphs for democracy are the fashion of the day. Both Left and Right acclaim the failure of democracy. Those who chafe at governmental intervention are as distrustful of popular institutions as are the romantics who expect from government heaven upon earth.

Felix Frankfurter   November 1930

chagrin   *shuh GRIN*
embarrassment and annoyance caused by failure or disappoinment
("chagrined" is the verb)

Neither was particularly the other's type. They met first at a Gray's Inn dinner, in London in 1918, during the Great War. Roosevelt thought Churchill cocky and condescending. Churchill thought nothing at all of Roosevelt and soon forgot having met him, which chagrined Roosevelt at their next meeting, when they were drawing up the Atlantic Charter, at Argentia in 1941.

Arthur M. Schlesinger Jr.   October 1984

Edison was in many respects a typical Victorian man, with solid midwestern tastes. Like many of his contemporaries, he was sheltered from women in his youth, and he seems to have been genuinely chagrined to discover that his partner in marriage would not be his partner at the laboratory bench. Just over a month after marrying Mary Stilwell, the twenty-four-year-old Edison despaired in a notebook, "My wife Dearly Beloved Cannot invent worth a Damn!!"

Kathleen McAuliffe   December 1995

chameleon   *kuh MEEL yin*
a changeable or inconstant person: from the lizard that can change its color

No one else in modern politics has matched Clinton's ability to speak with equal poise to people at every level of class, education, and sophistication. To skeptics, this is further proof that Clinton is a chameleon. To me, it demonstrates a combination of emotional and intellectual acuity that other people would copy if they could.

James Fallows   March 2003

✳ Because chameleons spend so much time standing statuelike, centuries ago they were reputed to subsist on air only. That is why, when Hamlet is asked by Claudius, the King of Denmark and his father's murderer, "How fares our cousin Hamlet?" he reples, "Excellent, i' faith; of the chamelion's dish: I eat the air, promise-crammed: you cannot feed capons so."

charlatan   *SHAHR luh tin*
a person who claims to have expert knowledge or skill that he or she does not have; quack; fraud

Mencken seemed to think it was inevitable that American democracy would produce as leaders clowns and charlatans who, along with their other disabilities, couldn't speak English.

Philip Roth   December 1971

chary   *CHA ree*
not taking chances; careful; cautious

Record companies are understandably chary of divulging the details of royalty arrangements with composers, which vary considerably from case to case. But the average fee *before* royalties to a composer for a top-ranked Hollywood film is a minimum of $10,000 and in some instances much higher. Henry Mancini, whose *oeuvre* includes *Breakfast at Tiffany's*, *Days of Wine and Roses*, *Charade*, and *Pink Panther*, reportedly gets $50,000 a film.

Herbert Kupferberg   April 1968

chastened   *CHAY suhnd*
made to see and regret the wrongness of one's ways

When Martha the passenger pigeon shut her eyes at the Cincinnati Zoo on September 1, 1914, an entire nation was chastened. Martha was the last of an indigenous American species that just a century earlier had numbered between five billion and nine billion; the ornithologist John James Audubon once recorded seeing a flock pass overhead that literally blackened the sky for hours. The birds' utter and unnatural extinction, in such a brief period, must rank as one of history's greatest crimes against nature. Like the Native American, the passenger pigeon was a victim of ruthless expansionism — the birds were killed for food and sport and the protection of nascent corn crops, but mostly, it seems, they were killed because they were an easy target. After her death Martha's carcass was frozen and shipped to Washington, D.C.; there it was stuffed and put on display at the Smithsonian Institution.

Richard Rubin   December 1997

chattel *CHA tuhl*
a movable item of personal property

Fortune has become indifferent to me, except as fortune might allow me to despise fortune and to live simply in some beautiful place. I have cut off all artificial society, reducing it to the limits of sincere friendship or intellectual sympathy. Instead of collecting pictures and books, as I had a tendency to do in the early 1890's, I have distributed my few possessions, eschewed chattels of every kind, a fixed residence, servants, carriages, or anything that would pin me down materially or engulf me in engagements.

George Santayana   December 1948

cheeky *CHEE kee*
disrespectfully bold; impudent

Federal wildlife-protection laws go back to the end of the past century, when a famous poacher named Ed Howell slaughtered bison in Yellowstone National Park with impunity because no statute forbade it; public outrage at Howell's cheeky remarks to the newspapers pushed Congress into passing the Yellowstone Park Protection Act of 1894.

Charles C. Mann and Mark L. Plummer   January 1992

chestnut *CHES nuht*
an anecdote or musical piece that is often repeated, frequently to the point of staleness

Every profession, every job, has its sound bites. "Easy reading, hard writing" is a chestnut from the writing trade.

Jack Beatty   June 1995

chicanery *shi KAY nuh ree*
the use of clever but tricky talk or action to deceive or evade

A hundred years ago the American Forest was being plundered on a scale we now find inconceivable. Millions of acres were acquired by the railroads and timber interests through political chicanery and outright fraud.

Paul Brooks   February 1967

chimera *kuh MI ruh*
an impossible or foolish fancy ("chimerical" is the adjective)

It would be chimerical to hope that the new frontiers established by the peace treaties can definitely ensure European stability. It was a good thing to eliminate most of the injustices that apparently cause the World War, but new injustices have been created and their effect will make itself increasingly felt in international relations.

William Martin   January 1929

churlish *CHER lish*
boorish; rude; harshly inconsiderate; grossly ill-mannered ("churlishness" is the noun)

Stepping onto the rapidly descending escalator at the Belorusskaya Station in the Moscow metro is like going over Niagara Falls without a barrel: you jump on, and far, far below, at stairs' end, you discern a sour-faced attendant sitting in her booth, like a boulder you are destined to slam into at falls' bottom. "Male passenger in the black hat!" she barks over the PA system. "Take that box off the railing! Metro regulations forbid the placing of objects on the railing! Yes, YOU! TAKE THAT BOX OFF THE RAILING!" The PA system is old; her voice screeches. Even after the passenger has removed the offending box, the attendant continues her tiresome litany, as if lecturing a brood of impudent schoolchildren for the thousandth time: "Passengers! When stepping off the escalator move QUICKLY to prevent obstructions! Do NOT tarry! Step to the RIGHT to allow those who wish to move ahead free passage on the LEFT!" To descend into the Moscow metro is to grapple with the frustration, rancor, and churlishness that beleaguer Muscovites to this day.

Jeffrey Tayler   February 1998

cicerone *SI suh roh nee*
a tour guide; specifically, one who conducts sightseers through places of interest: from Cicero, the Roman orator, supposedly in reference to his learning and eloquence

Traveling in Egypt a few months before his fall, Nikita Khrushchev more than once proudly described himself as "still a peasant." So his official cicerone on the trip, Gamal Abdel Nasser's confidante Mohamed Heikal, who had accompanied him on the boat trip from the Crimea to Alexandria, was taken aback when Khrushchev complained that Heikal had described him as such in a newspaper article. How could he object? "But you wrote that I was like a peasant from a story by Dostoyevsky — why didn't you say peasant from Tolstoy?" came the indignant reply.

Perry Anderson   April 2003

cipher   *SIGH fuhr*
a code

In 1787, while serving as the U.S. ambassador in Paris, Thomas Jefferson sent a report to James Madison on the volatile situation in pre-Revolutionary France. "These views are said to gain upon the nation," he wrote. "The 1647 678.914 for 411.454 is 979.996.607.935 of all 789. The 404 is 474.872. And an 223 435.918 of some sort is not impossible." The message was diplomatically sensitive, and to keep its contents private Jefferson had resorted to using a secret cipher that he knew only Madison could unlock. (Decrypted, the message read, "These views are said to gain upon the nation. The king's passion for drink is divesting him of all respect. The queen is detested. And an explosion of some sort is not impossible.")

Toby Lester   March 2001

circumspect   *SER kuhm spekt*
careful to consider all related circumstances and possible consequences before
acting, judging or deciding; cautious ("circumspection" is the noun)

We may be grateful that our Founding Fathers were a mixed lot. The idealist Jefferson, Lockean in his optimism, and the radical Calvinist James Madison, whose circumspection about the virtues and vices of both the rules and the ruled gave us the balance of our Constitution and our insurance against totalitarian democracy, were fortunately both among our Founding Fathers. They agreed in their common passion for civil rights and religious liberty.

Reinhold Niebuhr   August 1962

civility   *si VI luh tee*
behavior proper to a society of civilized people

The one power that has legs long enough and strong enough to cross the Potomac offers itself at this hour; the one strong enough to bring all the civility up to the height of that which is best prays now at the door of Congress for leave to move. Emancipation is the demand of civilization. That is a principle; everything else is an intrigue. This is a progressive policy, — puts the whole people in healthy, productive, amiable position, — puts every man in the South in just and natural relations with every man in the North, laborer with laborer.

Ralph Waldo Emerson   April 1862

clairvoyance   *klair VOI uhns*
the supposed power to see things that cannot be seen or known by the senses

Irrationality must come close to being the largest single vested interest in the world. It has a dozen service stations in every town. There are twenty-five thousand practicing astrologers in America who disseminate their lore through a hundred daily columns, fifteen monthly and two annual publications. (This does not include the half-dozen "confidential" news letters that keep business executives consistently misinformed about the future.) It is even said that there is a movement on foot to have a Federal astrologer appointed as an officer of the government, and considering the official recognition given to other forms of clairvoyance, the movement may succeed.

Bergen Evans   April 1946

clamor   KLA mer
a loud outcry of appeal, complaint or opposition; uproar

In the eighties and nineties the business office of the newspaper swallowed, without gulping, advertising of fortune tellers, astrologers, healers, or traveling quack doctors, and in some cases fairly reputable city newspapers took "personals" which were thinly disguised advertisements for prostitutes. This kind of local advertising aroused no public clamor. A few preachers fidgeted. A few "holier than thou" agitators scowled, but in the eighties and nineties that was about the extent of the public indignation over fraudulent advertising.

William Allen White   November 1939

claptrap   KLAP trap
pretentious, insincere or empty language intended to get applause

Ayn Rand, author of that weird best seller of 1943, *The Fountainhead*, has now produced a novel of over half a million words which might mildly be described as execrable claptrap; but which, I suspect, is going to rival the huge sale of its predecessor. *Atlas Shrugged* (Random House, $6.95) is the gospel according to Ayn Rand dressed up in fictional trappings which set a record for solemn grotesquerie.

Charles J. Rolo   November 1957

cocky   KAH kee
self-confident in a pushy or swaggering way ("cockily" is the adverb)

Bugs was designed by Charles Thorson at the request of the animator Ben "Bugs" Hardaway (and labeled "Bugs' bunny"), and his personality as a Brooklyn wiseacre cockily demanding "What's up, Doc?" was the creation of Tex Avery (who also invented the wild, nonrealistic Warner Brothers animation style).

Lloyd Rose   December 1984

cocooned   *kuh KOO:ND*
securely enclosed

How much of China does the foreigner get to see? Only about a hundred cities are open to outsiders; vast areas the size of American states are effectively off limits. Visitors usually travel around countryside and cities in tour buses, cocooned with their own kind, directed by young, cheerful and bright English-speaking guides.

Thomas Griffith   January 1981

codify   *KA duh figh*
to arrange in systematic order

The American form of government is a natural outgrowth of the Hanoverian British system, as simplified by Puritans and codified by lawyers. It tends toward legalities because the lawyers made it; it tends to protect minorities because the Puritans feared the effects of suppression by the majority. The struggle to maintain the equality of thirteen colonies has perpetuated itself in forty-nine constitutions, one national and the rest governing each of the states. There are forty-nine sets of laws; forty-nine governments; forty-nine political systems. Nobody knows how to operate such a machine except the lawyers who made it, continue it, and run it.

George E. Sokolsky   March 1933

Italians have codified which sauce goes with which pasta, and the code allows for a good deal of exchange. Luigi Veronelli gives a short outline in *The Pasta Book*, which was recently published here. In the broadest terms, long shapes go with tomato sauce and short shapes go with meat and vegetable sauces.

Corby Kummer   July 1986

coerce   *koh ERS*
to force or compel to do something ("coercive" is the adjective)

All régimes of authority have been established by armed bands who, by force or intrigue or both, have seized the coercive machinery of the state. This power they have used to imprison, terrorize, exile, or kill all who might be disposed to dissent, and to extirpate all organs of representation — such as elections, a free press, and voluntary assembly — through which dissent might be encouraged.

Walter Lippmann   December 1936

coeval   *koh EE vuhl*
existing during the same period of time; contemporary

The privilege of the countryman is the culture of the land, the laying out of grounds and gardens, the orchard, and the forest. The Rosaceous tribe in botany, including the apple, pear, peach and cherry, are coeval with man. The apple is our national fruit. In October, the country is covered with its ornamental harvests. The American sun paints itself in these glowing balls amid the green leaves, the social fruit, in which Nature has deposited every possible flavor; whole zones and climates she has concentrated into apples.

Ralph Waldo Emerson   November 1904

coextensive   *koh ik STEN siv*
having the same extent in time or boundaries

The fact that the belief in immortality is coextensive with the human race does not, unfortunately, prove that the belief is well founded, but it does prove that the desire for a life beyond this life is universal, and that, in turn, may be used to show that individualism is one of the most fundamental human traits, since the desire for immortality is an expression of the human protest against the scheme of nature which takes so little account of man and his demands.

Joseph Wood Krutch   December 1927

coherent   *koh HEER int*
sticking together as one entity; logically connected

It is not to be expected that a new civilization should be as coherent as an old civilization; and it would be surprising, indeed, if New York were either materially, intellectually, or morally as coherent as Paris, which is so thoroughly organic that it has not so much as a vermiform appendix, so to say, to spare. Formlessness is a reproach only when it is a finality, the end of a devolution instead of the first stage of an evolution.

Alvan F. Sanborn   October 1906

coin   *koin*
to invent a new word or phrase

Consider a future device for individual use, which is a sort of mechanized private file and library. It needs a name, and, to coin one at random, "memex" will do. A memex is a device in which an individual stores all his books, records, and communications, and which is mechanized so that it may be consulted with exceeding speed and flexibility. It is an enlarged intimate supplement to his memory.

Vannevar Bush   July 1945

> ✳ In "As We May Think," the *Atlantic* article that this passage is from, Vannevar Bush (1890-1974) envisioned the modern computer. After

directing the U.S. Office of Scientific Research and Development during the Second World War, where thousands of scientists worked on projects devoted to weaponry, Bush turned his attention to creating a machine that would make a virtually infinite amount of information accessible to everyone. He had already built the first computer in 1928, a room-size machine called the differential analyzer that was devoted to solving differential equations that had practical wartime applications. But as the war was ending, he envisioned a keyboard-controlled desk-size device for everyone. It would store and retrieve unlimited information, any part of which could be retrieved instantly, and show it on a screen.

collocation   *kah luh KAY shuhn*
the association between two words that are typically or frequently used together

As there are prejudices which begin in verbal misunderstandings, so there are those which are nourished by the accidental collocation of words. A noun is known by the adjectives it keeps. When we hear of dull conservatism, rabid radicalism, selfish culture, timid piety, smug respectability, we receive unfavorable impressions. We do not always stop to consider that all that is objectionable really inheres in the qualifying words. In a well-regulated mind, after every such verbal turn there should be a call to change partners. Let every noun take a new adjective, and every verb a new adverb.

Samuel McChord Crothers   May 1904

❋ Collocations are of huge interest to teachers of English as a second language. The more collocations their students know, the more natural and correct their speech. While native speakers use collocations almost without thinking, learners of English must search for the associated words to find the right ones, despite knowing the concept they are trying to convey. When the right words are not accessible, they create combinations such as a *bull in a Chinese shop, My lips are glued, I'm going to remove a hot shower* and *I wouldn't want to be in his pants.* Native speakers of English would almost certainly assume the second half of each of the following pairs of collocations the instant before they heard it or read it:

bohemian lifestyle	hermetically sealed
bright idea	standing ovation
expensive tastes	standard procedure

colloquialism   *kuh LOH kwee uh li zuhm*
a word or phrase typical of ordinary conversation rather than formal speech

Young Saudi technocrats, on the first meeting, do not seem like their Wahhabi grand-fathers. They wear business suits; they have come back from USC and UCLA easy-going and likeable with their American colloquialisms and their passion for college football. But in Riyadh, religious police still patrol, enforcing the five-times-a-day call to prayer, rapping on the shutters of shopkeepers who are tardy in closing for prayer.

George Jerome Goodman (under the pseudonym of Adam Smith)   December 1978

coloration   *kuh luh RAY shuhn*
the characteristic quality or appearance of something

The severely grieving Robert Kennedy found a piece of notepaper on which his brother, during the last Cabinet meeting he had conducted, had scribbled the word *poverty* several times and circled it; he framed it and kept it in his office at the Justice Department. By the time Lyndon Johnson assumed the presidency, fighting poverty had taken on the coloration of having been John F. Kennedy's last wish.

Nicholas Lemann   December 1988

comminuted   *KAH mi noo: tid*
broken up into small, fine particles

The seventeenth-century theologian, Archbishop James Ussher of Armagh, Ireland, concluded from his study of sacred texts that the world was founded precisely in the year 4004 B.C. But even people who were not fundamentalists of Ussher's arithmetic stripe suffered comminuted fractures of belief when, in the nineteenth century, Charles Darwin and evolutionary science opened up appalling vistas of time.

Justin Kaplan   October 1973

commodious   *kuh MOH dee uhs*
spacious; roomy

Science has made or is making the world over for us. It has built us a new house,— built it over our heads while we were yet living in the old, and the con-fusion and disruption and the wiping-out of the old features and the old associa-tions, have been, and still are, a sore trial — a much finer, more spacious and commodious house, with endless improvements and convenience, but new, new, all bright and hard and unfamiliar, with the spirit of newness; not yet home, not yet a part of our lives, not yet sacred to memory and affection. The question now is: Can we live as worthy and contented lives there as our fathers and grandfathers did in their ruder, humbler dwelling-place?

John Burroughs   September 1912

compass   *KUHM puhs*
range; extent

The bee and the ant, in a few particulars, show wonderful sagacity; but remove them from the narrow compass of their instincts, and all their wisdom is at an end.

Leonard Augustus Jones   May 1860

complicity   *kuhm PLI suh tee*
partnership in wrongdoing; acting as an accomplice

If it has not been proved that tobacco is guilty of causing cancer of the lung, it has certainly been shown to have been on the scene of the crime. The American Cancer Society, along with a growing body of professional and scientific opinion, has taken this position: Although the complicity of the cigarette in the present prevalence of cancer of the lung has not been proved to the satisfaction of everyone, yet the weight of evidence against it is so serious as to demand of stewards of the public welfare that they make the evidence known to all.

Charles S. Cameron, M.D.   January 1956

comport   *kuhm PAWRT*
to agree or accord with

It has often been alleged, and with considerable strength of assertion, that poets are not well suited for married life; that the very constitution of their minds pre-disposes them to disappointment and discontent if they commit the imprudence of matrimony; and that, as a matter of fact, the married poets have very generally been unhappy family men. Their intellectual subtilty, their ideal aspirations, we are told, will not comport with the commonplace conditions of conjugal life; they dream of goddesses, and they find their spouses to be not goddesses, but women, — and sometimes very ordinary women, too.

William M. Rossetti   January 1881

composite   *kuhm PAH zit*
made up of various parts

Fontane turned out novels at an enviable clip, averaging almost a book a year for the last two decades of his life. By the end of this run he had become the finest German novelist of his era, an exemplar for the young Thomas Mann and a keen observer of city life whose composite portrait of Berlin ranks with Dickens's portrait of London, Balzac's of Paris, and Dostoevski's of St. Petersburg.

Dennis Drabelle   October 2000

✳ Theodor Fontane (1819-1898) was a journalist, poet, editor and drama critic before turning his attention to writing novels at the age of 57.

compunction *kuhm PUNK shuhn*
a slight uneasiness or regret about the rightness of an action; sting of conscience

> Though I had not come a-hunting, and felt some compunctions about accompanying the hunters, I wished to see a moose near at hand, and was not sorry to learn how the Indian managed to kill one.
>
> Henry David Thoreau   June 1858

concession *kuhn SE shuhn*
an act of granting, yielding or compromising, usually reluctantly

> Occasionally one hears some well-meaning person say of another, apparently in praise, that he is "never willing to compromise." It is a mere truism to say that, in politics, there has to be one continual compromise. Of course now and then questions arise upon which a compromise is inadmissible. There could be no compromise with secession, and there was none. There should be no avoidable compromise about any great moral question. But only a very few great reforms or great measures of any kind can be carried through without concession. No student of American history needs to be reminded that the Constitution itself is a bundle of compromises, and was adopted only because of this fact, and that the same thing is true of the Emancipation Proclamation.
>
> Theodore Roosevelt   August 1894

conciliate *kuhn SI lee ayt*
to win over from a state of distrust or hostility by soothing and pacifying means; placate

> Liberal indulgence toward the Soviet Union is thought to have threatened our very survival. According to foreign-policy hard-liners like Richard Pipes, of Harvard, we cannot conciliate the Soviets, nor should we try to. The danger of nuclear war will recede only when the Soviet Union transforms itself from a totalitarian state into a freer and more democratic one.
>
> Robert B. Reich   May 1985

condign *kuhn DIGHN*
deserved; suitable: said especially of punishment for wrongdoing ("condignly" is the adverb)

> If the Nixon White House escapes the legal consequences of its illegal behavior, why

will future Presidents and their associates not suppose themselves entitled to do what the Nixon White House has done? Only condign punishment will restore popular faith in the presidency and deter future Presidents from illegal conduct — so long, as least, as Watergate remains a vivid memory.

Arthur M. Schlesinger Jr.   November 1973

The time is long past when Alexander Pope was identified with his least impressive verse, and having been the eighteenth century's supreme English poet, was adjudged in the nineteenth no poet at all. So precipitous a fall has been condignly discredited, so inverted a fate has been dazzlingly revised.

Louis Kronenberger   May 1969

✳ Memorable lines from Alexander Pope — "A little learning is a dangerous thing." "To err is human, to forgive divine." "As all looks yellow to the jaundiced eye." "For fools rush in where angels fear to tread." "Blessed is he who expects nothing, for he shall never be disappointed." "Hope springs eternal in the human breast." "Just as the tree's inclined, the twig is bent." "Damn with faint praise." "Eternal sunshine of the spotless mind!"

conducive   *kuhn DOO: suhv*
contributing or leading to

In Buddhism, there is no such thing as belief in a body of dogma which must be taken on faith, such as belief in a Supreme Being, a creator of the universe, the reality of an immortal soul, a personal savior, or archangels who are supposed to carry out the will of the Supreme Deity. Buddhism begins as a search for truth. The Buddha taught that we should believe only that which is true in the light of our own experience, that which conforms to reason and is conducive to the highest good and welfare of all beings. Men must rely on themselves.

Bhikkhu U Thittila   February 1958

conduit   *KAHN doo: it*
any channel or means through which something is passed on

Nixon's Administration has made systematic efforts to cow the networks and destroy the credibility of the press, including television news. There is no inconsistency, however, if one understands that in Nixon's view television ideally should serve only as a carrier, a mechanical means of electronically transmitting his picture and words directly to the voters. It is this concept of television-as-conduit that has won Nixon's praise, not television as a form of electronic journalism. The moment that television analyzes his words, qualifies his remarks, or renders news judgments, it becomes part of the "press," and a political target.

David Wise   April 1973

confidante   *KAHN fuh dahnt*
a close, trusted friend or associate to whom one confides intimate matters or secrets

All wives and most secretaries expect to be dumped on now and then, not just as confidantes to whom frustrations can be reported but as surrogates on whom they can be vented.

Elizabeth Janeway   December 1973

conflagration   *kahn fluh GRAY shuhn*
a large, destructive fire

The unconquerable determination of the typical Chicago man has been repeatedly shown, but most grandly in the rebuilding of the city after its well-nigh total destruction by fire, twenty years ago. A conflagration which destroyed the business centre and swept over an area of more than three square miles, annihilated property of the value of two hundred million dollars, and rendered a hundred thousand people homeless seemed a calamity from which the city could not recover. But its people, their immediate needs supplied by the world's generosity, began the work of reconstruction while the embers were glowing, and carried it to such swift completion that within three years buildings were erected of greater capacity than those burned, and of more than twice their value.

Edward Gay Mason   July 1892

conflate   *kuhn FLAYT*
to fuse into one entity; merge; blend

In justifying war against Iraq, the Administration suggested ties between a mortal adversary (al-Qaeda) and what was at worst a worrisome future adversary (Saddam) — ties whose existence nearly every knowledgeable observer has called into question. Furthermore, the Administration conflated the dangers posed by terrorists with those posed by tyrants, and said that the same sort of pre-emptive measures must be applied to both.

Benjamin Schwarz   April 2004

confute   *kuhn FYOO:T*
to prove a person or statement to be in error or false; to overcome by argument or proof

"I always wanted to be historical, from almost a baby on," wrote the late Gertrude Stein; and she confuted the moralists who say that those whose goal is glory are doomed to be disillusioned with its fruits. When fame finally came to her in her late fifties, she never ceased to revel in it.

Charles J. Rolo   March 1957

The most exciting new book to come from abroad is Edith Sitwell's *Song of the Cold* (Vanguard). It is full of surprises for those critics who had pigeonholed her work as gorgeously irresponsible and hermetically "l'art pour l'art." She confutes her classifiers by writing movingly about such immediate social problems as the war and the atom bomb.

Peter Viereck   October 1949

congeal   *kuhn JEEL*
to solidify or thicken; coagulate; jell

It used to be that acquiring a country of one's own was a career option open to virtually any tribal warlord. World governance has since congealed into about two hundred nation-states, with new ones coming on the market very infrequently. (The last big yard sale occurred after the collapse of the Soviet Union.)

Cullen Murphy   November 2002

congeries   *kuhn JI reez*
a collection of parts in one mass; an aggregation

As the great French historian Fernand Braudel pointed out in his last major work, *The Identity of France* (1986), it was the railroad that made France into one nation and one culture. It had previously been a congeries of self-contained regions, held together only politically.

Peter F. Drucker   October 1999

conifer   *KAH nuh fuhr*
a tree or shrub, most often an evergreen, that bears cones

The redwood is one of the few conifers that sprout from the stump and roots, and it declares itself willing to begin immediately to repair the damage of the lumberman and also that of the forest-burner. As soon as a redwood is cut down or burned it sends up a crowd of eager, hopeful shoots, which, if allowed to grow, would in a few decades attain a height of a hundred feet, and the strongest of them would finally become giants as great as the original tree.

John Muir   August 1897

conjecture   *kuhn JEK cher*
to make an inference or judgment based on incomplete evidence; guess

Before the memorable work of Newton some of the great Continental painters of the Renaissance had formed theories of light and color based upon the mixture of pigments; and a few of them naturally attempted to account for the blue color of the sky. Leonardo da Vinci, who had devoted much attention to the composition of colors in his extensive artistic designs, conjectured that the blue color of the sky was the result of the mixing of the white sunlight reflected from the upper layers of the atmosphere with the intense blackness of space.

Thomas Jefferson Jackson See   January 1904

conjure up   *KAHN jer uhp*
to bring into existence as if by magic

Dubrovnik is, of course, unique — the most complete and perfectly walled city to be found on any coast. Standing out over the water with its battlements and towers, the compact old city is like a dazzling series of magnificent stage sets conjured up to bring the past to life. Indeed, a dozen plays and operas are staged in its squares and on its castle walls during the summer festival.

Scott Corbett   December 1966

connive   *kuh NIGHV*
to scheme in an underhanded way

In Preston Sturges's classic comedy *The Lady Eve*, Barbara Stanwyck connives to attract the attention of Henry Fonda, an oblivious bachelor millionaire and fellow passenger on an ocean cruise. After watching other female contenders demurely drop their handkerchiefs in front of his table at dinner or try sweetly to engage him in conversation, neither to any avail, the resourceful Stanwyck sticks out her foot and trips him.

Holly Brubach   May 1986

connoisseur   *kah nuh SER*
a person who has expert knowledge and taste in some field, especially the arts

No reasonable theory will every be able to explain how or why it was that so many Dutchmen were painters, and all during one, or at the most two, human generations. It is not enough to say that hard-won national independence made them take up their brushes. In seventeenth-century Holland the number of artists was entirely incredible; and down to today, connoisseurs of painting with some pretension to knowledge often have the experience of entering a picture gallery to find some beautiful painting of supreme handling and technical merit by a Dutchman whose name they never remember having heard before.

Sacheverell Sitwell   April 1954

consequential   *kahn suh KWEN shuhl*
significant; meaningful

By now virtually anything can be insured. Dolly Parton, Jennifer Lopez, Tina Turner, Betty Grable, Fred Astaire — the insurance industry has been involved in underwriting economically consequential body parts for all of these people. Surgeons insure their hands, soccer players their feet, chefs their taste buds. And there is plenty of room to grow in this direction, toward the insuring of ever more ineffable competencies. Could Roger Ebert take out insurance against the sudden loss of critical faculties? Or Donald Rumsfeld against a catastrophic lapse in judgment?

Cullen Murphy   January/February 2004

consign   *kuhn SIGHN*
to assign to an undesirable place or position

Orchestras usually consign any Gershwin to pops concerts.

David Schiff   October 1998

constellation   *kahn stuh LAY shuhn*
a group of related objects or concepts

Elloris Cooper, the supervisor of adult reading programs for Mississippi's Hinds Community College, says, "There's a whole constellation of things poor people face that make potential adult learners hard to reach, hard to recruit, and even harder to keep in programs, beginning with transportation to classes and child care for young mothers."

Jonathan Maslow   August 1990

constituency   *kuhn STI choo: uhn see*
a group of people with common objectives or views, and therefore sometimes appealed to for support

The only thing that has ever saved wilderness, a single acre of it, is a constituency — people who have come, who have seen, who care about wildness, fight for it, vote for it.

Kenneth Brower   July/August 2002

constraint   *kuhn STRAYNT*
something that restricts, limits or regulates

The freedom of universities from market constraints is precisely what allowed them in the past to nurture the kind of open-ended basic research that led to some of the most important (and least expected) discoveries in history.

Eyal Press and Jennifer Washburn   March 2000

construct   *KAHN strukt*
an idea or theory, especially a complex one, formed from a number of
simpler elements

Those who think that armed conflicts among the European states are now out of the question, that the two world wars burned all the war out of Europe, are projecting unwarranted optimism onto the future. The theories of peace that implicitly undergird this optimism are notably shallow constructs. They stand up to neither logical nor historical analysis. You would not want to bet the farm on their prophetic accuracy.

John J. Mearsheimer   August 1990

construe   *kuhn STROO:*
to give an explanation or interpretation to something whose meaning is not clear

I have no wish to play down the relevance of madness to poetry. In England the two have long been allied, never more fruitfully than in the age of the French Revolution, when the roster of mad poets carried many of the illustrious names of the day: Christopher Smart, William Collins, William Cowper, and, most illustrious of all, William Blake. In the last twenty years American poetry and madness have entered into an alliance closer still. Madness can be construed, and is by some poets, as the regular and inescapable concomitant of the reach beyond reality; and sanity is construed as the dullness of those who refrain from reaching.

Peter Davison   January 1965

consummation   *kahn suh MAY shuhn*
a fulfillment or outcome

Pinocchio is as firmly rooted in Italian culture as Alice is in the English. He looks back to Dante and *Orlando Furioso*, forward to Pirandello and Federico Fellini. He is a descendant and an ancestor. He emerges from a log of wood and becomes a "*ragazzo per bene*" (a real boy). He faces death by fire, by hanging, and by drowning, and achieves at last the human condition, the unification of the flesh with the spirit. The consummation was no more than that which his author asked for his country.

Martha Bacon   April 1970

contemplative *kuhn TEM pluh tiv*
given to thinking deeply; meditative

Of all forms of sport, angling is the most esoteric. Well does Walton call it the contemplative man's recreation. The angler is not only contemplative himself, but he is the cause of contemplation in other men. To a super-contemplator, sitting on a breezy hilltop, he is the subject of curious speculation. There he is in a superlatively damp place, surrounded by pestering mosquitoes, waiting for an accident that may not happen. Nothing that he can do seems to accelerate the crisis. No tempting variety of bait can ensure success against the procrastination of the slow, unwilling trout. Nor does he know that the trout is here. This may be his day out. Wherein is the joy of this long trial and predatory patience? Why should a man spend the best part of a spring day dangling an unavailing hook over an unresponsive pool? Where is the sport? To such a question the cheerful angler, returning with an empty basket, deigns no reply. He has the inner satisfaction that comes from an eventless day well spent.

Samuel McChord Crothers   October 1926

contested *kuhn TEST id*
controversial; disputed

No one, it seems, has ever been neutral or aloof about Jane Austen. From the time of her death, at the age of forty-one, in 1817, possibly from either Addison's or Hodgkin's disease, she has been a contested figure. Her beloved sister Cassandra destroyed many of her letters and made excisions in others, prompting biographers to suspect that she was trying to suppress evidence either of some deep depression or of unseemly malice or spleen.

Lee Siegel   January 1998

contingency *kuhn TIN jin see*
an event that may possibly occur in the future

No man pretends that under the Constitution there is any possibility of interference with the domestic relations of the individual States; no party has ever remotely hinted at any such interference; but what the Republicans affirm is, that in every contingency where the Constitution can be construed in favor of freedom, it ought to be and shall be so construed. It is idle to talk of sectionalism, abolitionism, and hostility to the laws. The principles of liberty and humanity cannot, by virtue of their very nature, be sectional, any more than light and heat.

James Russell Lowell   October 1860

continuum   *kuhn TIN yoo: uhm*
a series of elements flowing into each other

Mass communication creates a continuum of small talk, gossip, news, jokes, celebrities, commercials. It makes us aware of life-styles and concerns that are not our own, exposes us to advertising meant for others. Without it, Walter Mondale's "Where's the beef?" would have been impossible. Mass communication, and the industries that came into being in tandem with it, can be irritating, distasteful, and worse, but they account for the sense that we all have that "America" is a nation-wide phenomenon.

Cullen Murphy   July 1992

contraband   *KAHN truh band*
smuggled

It has been thought necessary to stimulate the enforcement of liquor laws by offering large rewards to informers. Thus, in Ohio, half the fine imposed goes to the informer, whenever a house of ill fame is convicted of selling liquor. In South Carolina, twenty cents on every gallon of confiscated liquor is paid to the informer, and any sheriff or trial justice who seizes contraband liquor is paid half its value. Laws like these excite intense animosities, and necessitate other laws for the protection of informers. They have been effective, however, in some instances.

Charles W. Eliot   February 1897

contrivance   *kuhn TRIGH vins*
an invention; mechanical device

A league of nations, to be worth the name, must be a league of national *souls*. A mere combination of political machinery, effected by joining up the official governments of all nations, would obviously be a useless contrivance. Unless a unitary soul inspired its workings, it would not work at all.

L. P. Jacks   February 1923

controvert   *KAN truh vert*
to argue against; contradict; deny; dispute

Writers on landscape-gardening — whose imaginations seldom stray beyond the dressed grounds of a nobleman's estate, and whose "Nature" is a sort of queen-like personage, arrayed in Eastern splendor and magnificence — declare that trees of a certain form only will harmonize with certain styles of architecture; that round-headed trees, for example, are more proper for Gothic forms of architecture, and pyramidal trees for Grecian forms. I shall not enumerate the reasons given for this opinion, nor attempt to controvert it. Suffice it to say, that Accident — who is the best artist in real landscape, and who can exhibit among her works more beautiful pictures than Art ever yet executed or imagined — pays no regard to any such rules.

Wilson Flagg   June 1868

contumacy   *KAHN too: muh see*
stubborn refusal to submit to authority; insubordination; disobedience

An unfit clerk holding his place undisturbed is as noxious an influence, in his way, as a smallpox patient. The infection of his laziness or contumacy spreads among his fellow clerks, who suspect that some hidden and unwholesome power, loosely described by the cant term "pull," is at work in his interest. Outside censors of the merit system find in his case fresh proof either of the impotence of the civil-service law to keep poor material out, or of its use as a bulwark by the undeserving when they have once got in.

Francis E. Leupp   February 1914

contumely   *KAHN too: muh lee*
insulting or contemptuous treatment or language; scorn

It has become fashionable among the so-called literary sophisticates of our day to speak with contumely of the Rev. Dr. Thomas Bowdler (1754-1825). Bowdler, it will be recalled, was the editor who sought to save no less a treasure than the poetry of William Shakespeare from falling into public desuetude by causing to be published, in 1818, an edition of the bard's plays in which, as Bowdler explained, "those words and expressions are omitted which cannot with propriety be read aloud in a family."

Robert Bingham   July 1968

✳ Thomas Bowdler's *Family Shakespeare*, first published in London in 1818, was actually preceded by an 1807 book of Shakespeare's expurgated plays edited entirely — and anonymously — by his sister Henrietta, a prominent and proper London lady. Taking credit publicly would have revealed that she understood the obscenity, raciness and blasphemy in Shakespeare well enough to remove it. In her lifetime few people knew that Henrietta had edited all of the 1807 *Family Shakespeare* and most of the 1818 and later editions of the book. Among the many other Shakespeare expurgators, both in England and America, was John W. S. Hows, of Columbia University. In 1849, he out-Bowdlerized the Bowdlers by cutting *Othello's* last two acts and adding four years to Juliet Capulet's thirteen. Another American, Thomas Bulfinch, of Boston, had Lady Macbeth look at her hand and say, "Out, crimson spot!"

conundrum   *kuh NUHN druhm*
a puzzling question or problem

For years nailing down the date and location of the origin of chess was stymied by an archaeological conundrum. Experts had long believed that chess was invented in Asia in the sixth century, but this conclusion was cast into doubt by the discovery, in 1932, of a set of ivory chess pieces in a grave in Italy dating back to the third century. Six decades passed before radiocarbon dating established that the chess pieces were probably of tenth-century manufacture, reviving the original theory. How the pieces found their way into that third-century grave remains a mystery.

Cullen Murphy   September 2000

conversant   *kuhn VER suhnt*
familiar or acquainted with something, as from study or experience

More than half of the 1.7 million Sardinians are conversant in the Sardinian language, limba sarda. This is not an Italian dialect but a distinct Romance tongue with a strong basis in Latin, even if Dante's crude assessment was that Sardinian is to Latin as monkeys are to men.

Patricia Corbett   May 1994

converse   *KAHN vers*
the opposite ("conversely" is the adverb)

Orville Prescott, long the powerful daily reviewer for *The New York Times*, was a perfect critic for me. I knew that his liking a book meant that I would hate it, and conversely, when he said he hated a book, it was a good augury for my reading. He rarely missed my aim. When he described *Lolita* as dull and boring, I knew I would find it fascinating and thrilling.

Herbert Gold   June 1970

convivial   *kuhn VI vee uhl*
sociable; jovial; festive

Closemouthed and closeminded to boot, sitting aloof and glum in the midst of convivial dinner parties at my home, Hopper reminded me of one of his favorite subjects for painting: a Victorian mansion stranded beside a railroad track. He radiated the looming ugliness and the paradoxical, lost dignity of such structures.

Alexander Eliot   December 1979

convoluted   *KAHN vuh loo: tid*
extremely involved; intricate; complicated

In *Bleak House* the wearisome and convoluted case of *Jarndyce M. Jarndyce* eventually exhausts all the resources of the contending parties in the sheer costs of the suit.

Christopher Hitchens   December 2003

convulsive   *kuhn VUHL suhv*
characterized by great disturbance, agitation or agony

An attractive sinner is better material for biography than a dull saint. But the life of even the most obscure and insignificant wastrel may be made to seem significant by a biographer who understands the convulsive drama of the human soul.

Claude M. Fuess   January 1932

cordial   *KAWR juhl*
warm and friendly ("cordiality" is the noun)

There was little cordiality, during the administration of John Quincy Adams, between the occupants of the Capitol and of the Executive Mansion, or, as it has been called since the occupation of Washington by the British, the White House. The interior of the building was then burned, and the exterior walls were so blackened by the smoke that they were painted white to conceal the marks of the conflagration.

Ben Perley Poore   March 1880

> ✳ Actually, the White House was white from the start. In 1798, during its construction, the exterior was whitewashed to protect its sandstone walls from frost damage. After the War of 1812, when it was burned by the British, the building was indeed painted white to cover its scorched walls, but as early as 1811 people were calling it the White House. In 1901, Theodore Roosevelt officially proclaimed it such and had "The White House" engraved on his presidential stationery.

corollary   *KAH ruh le ree*
something that follows as a natural result or consequence

Since the expansion of college enrollment after World War II, colleges have generally proclaimed their belief in need-blind admissions — that is, they say that family wealth should not be a factor in judging students' applications. The corollary has been need-based aid — offering loans, grants, and scholarships to ensure that anyone the college admits can afford to attend.

James Fallows   November 2003

America's great contributions to structural architecture are the skeleton steel frame, on which are hung the walls and floors; the high-speed elevator, a necessary corollary; and the development of reënforced concrete — a new element in architecture, by the way, the youngest of the family of which the elder brothers are the post, the lintel, the arch, and the truss.

Thomas E. Tallmadge   August 1925

corporeal   *kawr PAW ree uhl*
physical, not spiritual; of a material nature; tangible

Some thinkers have postulated that living beings might not need to have solid bodies — that intelligence could exist as pure thought, as patterns of magnetism within the burning fury of a star, or in other strange genres. For the moment, however, the only kind of life that we know exists is corporeal and carbon-based.

Gregg Easterbrook   August 1988

corrugations   *kah ruh GAY shuhnz*
regular ridges, grooves, wrinkles or folds, like those in corrugated cardboard or iron

The western margin of this continent is built of a succession of mountain chains folded in broad corrugations, like waves of stone upon whose seaward base beat the mild small breakers of the Pacific.

Clarence King   May 1871

countenance   *KOWN tuh nins*
to look upon approvingly or with toleration

Gandhi's successes throughout his career depended upon a combination of deep religious conviction and astute political insight. He was immovable when he was certain that one of his many moral principles was involved. He was flexible whenever there was negotiation within the limits of his principles. When his followers got out of hand and practiced violence that he could not countenance, he would punish himself by a fast. And as his devoted adherents imagined him becoming daily more emaciated and risking death on account of their misbehavior, they inevitably repented and, like naughty children, promised not to do it again.

Bertrand Russell   September 1951

counterintuitive   *kown tuhr in TOO: uh tiv*
not in accordance with what would naturally be assumed or expected; contrary to what common sense would indicate

While the spread of democracy across Europe has great potential benefits for human rights, it will not guarantee peaceful relations among the states of post-Cold War Europe. Most Americans will find this argument counterintuitive. They see the United States as fundamentally peace-loving, and they ascribe this peacefulness to its democratic character. From this they generalize that democracies are more peaceful than authoritarian states, which leads them to conclude that the complete democratization of Europe would largely eliminate the threat of war. This view of international politics is likely to be repudiated by the events of coming years.

John J. Mearsheimer   August 1990

counterpart   *KOWN tuhr pahrt*
a person or thing that corresponds to or closely resembles another

Every week *The Times of India* publishes several hundred carefully categorized matrimonial ads. These are mostly organized by community, caste, language, or religion, though new categories have recently crept in: "Doctors," "Working Girls," "Defence" (referring to army families). These ads, with their own vocabulary and shorthand, are the Indian counterpart to the personals found in Western newspapers and magazines (although certain progressive Indian magazines carry Indian versions of those as well). Usually the ads and responses are handled by parents — proof that the arranged marriage is alive and well in India. I have found in speaking with numerous couples whose marriages were arranged that although family compatibility is the starting point for such matches, most of the couples end up falling in love. For a number of reasons arranged marriages have a very high rate of success. One reason, Indians often joke, is that a traditional wedding lasts three to seven days. Most people can handle only one such ceremony in a lifetime.

Chitra Divakaruni   March 2000

counterpoint   *KOWN tuhr point*
a contrasting but parallel element, item or theme

In the aftermath of President Sadat's assassination, the manifest indifference of most Egyptians provided a curious counterpoint to worldwide expressions of shock and grief.

Jennifer Seymour Whitaker   January 1982

coup   *koo:*
a brilliant success resulting from a highly successful move or plan

When Stanley found Livingstone in Central Africa it was considered quite a coup. But when you think about it, how many people named Livingstone were living in Central Africa in 1871?

Ken Burnhardt   November 1955

coup de grace   *koo: duh GRAHS*
death blow, usually one that follows the wounding of the victim: French, stroke of mercy

My father, a Royal Navy commander, was on board H.M.S. Jamaica when it helped to deal the coup de grace to the Nazi warship Scharnhorst on December 26, 1943 — a more solid day's work than any I have ever done.

Christopher Hitchens   April 2002

cow   *kow*
to make timid and submissive by filling with fear; intimidate

It was with Nixon's blessing that Spiro Agnew launched his celebrated attack on network news analysts. Nixon's Administration has made systematic efforts to cow the networks and destroy the credibility of the press, including television news.

David Wise   April 1973

❈ During the congressional campaign of 1970, Spiro T. Agnew, Richard Nixon's vice president, asked White House speechwriter William Safire to give him some attention-getting speeches scolding politicians and critics in the media who were against the Administration's policies in Vietnam. Safire created speeches with alliterative phrases that practically jumped by themselves into soundbites and reporters' notebooks. Agnew charged the Administration's critics in the U.S. Senate with being "hopeless, hysterical hypochondriacs of history," "vicars of vacillation," "pussilanimous pussyfooters" and "nattering nabobs of negativism."

coxcomb   *KAHKS kohm*
a foolish, conceited, showy man, vain of his accomplishments, appearance or dress

In each generation there have been men of fashion who have mistaken themselves for gentlemen. They are uninteresting enough while in the flesh, but after a generation or two they become very quaint and curious, when considered as specimens. Each generation imagines that it has discovered a new variety, and invents a name for it. The dude, the swell, the dandy, the fop, the spark, the macaroni, the blade, the popinjay, the coxcomb, — these are butterflies of different summers. There is here endless variation, but no advancement. One fashion comes after another, but we cannot call it better.

Samuel McChord Crothers   May 1898

coy   *koi*
playfully or slyly unwilling to reveal information or make a statement

Mary Baker Eddy was nobody's fool. She wanted her Church to be accepted by society, and she knew, having been raised as a Congregationalist, that the surest way to earn the enmity of the Christian world was to set herself up as a holy figure. But she could be coy in defining herself. She wrote to the New York Herald in 1895, "'Am I the second Christ?' Even the question shocks me. What I am is for God to declare in His infinite mercy. As it is, I claim nothing more than what I am, the Discoverer and Founder of Christian Science, and the blessing it has been to mankind which eternity enfolds."

Caroline Fraser   April 1995

craggy   *KRA gee*
steep and rugged or rocky, like a mountain or shoreline ("cragginess" is the noun)

Iceberg tourism is one of the few new growth industries in Newfoundland, an island still reeling from the collapse of the cod fishery a decade ago. Icebergs are becoming to Newfoundland what wines are to Napa Valley: tourists can be overheard talking about individual specimens in precise yet lofty terms, discussing the cragginess of towers and the sapphire radiance of blue streaks as if comparing rare vintages.

Wayne Curtis   March 2002

crank   *krangk*
an unbalanced person who is overzealous in the advocacy of a private cause; a person with odd, stubborn notions

A discriminating critic of Canadian life deplores the scarcity of cranks in his native land — not because the crank is in himself so precious a national possession, but because he is symptomatic of the tolerance for differences of opinion which is the very essence of an expanding intellectual and spiritual life.

Cornelia James Cannon   September 1925

creditable   *KRE di tuh buhl*
deserving credit or praise

Bouillabaisse, despite the long name, is a dish that anyone can make with a minimum of ingredients and utensils. The catch is that "anyone" is supposed to live somewhere along the French or Italian Riviera, where fishermen troll for fish that have only vague counterparts in North American waters and that only occasionally appear, imported, in U.S. markets — fish like rascasse and grondin. It is more than possible, though, to make a creditable bouillabaisse-inspired soup in this country.

Corby Kummer   September 1997

crucible   *KROO: suh buhl*
a severe test or trial: literally, a vessel made to endure great heat, used for melting ores or metals

Theodore Roosevelt articulated the unspoken American linguistic-melting-pot theory when he boomed, "We have room for but one language here, and that is the English language, for we intend to see that the crucible turns our people out as Americans, of American nationality, and not as dwellers in a polyglot boarding house." And: "We must have but one flag. We must also have but one language. That must be the language of the Declaration of Independence, of Washington's Farewell address, of Lincoln's Gettysburg speech and second inaugural."

Robert D. King   April 1997

crusty   *KRUS tee*
rough or harsh in manner or speech; short-tempered

The House became notorious in this century as a gerontocracy, a place where nothing mattered so much as length of service and obedience to unwritten rules of behavior. "If you want to get along, go along" was the motto of Sam Rayburn, the crusty Texas Democrat who was speaker between 1940 and 1961 (except for four years when the Republicans controlled the House), a man who drank bourbon and branch water and smoked stogies and was married to the House. New members were expected to be quiet and respectful of their elders. As Rayburn often said, "Anyone could be elected once by accident. Beginning with the second term, it's worth paying attention."

Sanford J. Ungar   July 1977

❋ Today a stogie means any cheap cigar, but beginning in the late 1740s it was a long and thin, coarse black cigar made in Conestoga, Pennsylvania. It was originally called a stoga, after the Conestoga-made wagons, whose drivers smoked them. Branch water is a term in the American South for water from a stream, or plain water as distinguished from soda water.

crux   *kruhks*
the essential point or feature

Very clearly the crux of the Klan problem in Indiana is the Catholic Church. The Klan is feeding on a revival of anti-Catholic feeling and renewed circulation of Catholic goblin stories. Men actually join the Klan because they believe that a magnificent home (a million-dollar palace, is the term usually used) is being built in Washington, D.C., to house the Pope, and that the Vatican is soon to be moved to the American capital!

Lowell Mellett   November 1923

crystallize   *KRIS tuh lighz*
to give a fixed, definite and usually permanent form to

Until well into the last quarter of the nineteenth century Syracuse was the principal source of salt supply for the entire United States. Not only was the industry the basis of most of the early local fortunes, but pressure from those interested in salt making crystallized the demand for the Erie Canal, completed in 1825, which proved to be the greatest single factor in the remarkable development and prosperity of the Empire State.

E. Alexander Powell   August 1938

cul-de-sac   *KUHL duh sak*
a passage with no outlet except by the entrance; a dead end street with a turn-around at the closed end; blind alley: French, bottom of a sack

As I sat alongside the pilot in a Border Patrol helicopter, he relentlessly tracked a limping Mexican man and two Mexican women carrying string shopping bags, flushing them from a housing development where they attempted to hide, pinning them in a cul-de-sac as a van roared through the streets to apprehend them. The drama and terror of such a moment, or of the nighttime chases on foot through back alleys, seemed lost on the patrolmen — and on their quarry, as well. Each was doing his job; they would probably meet again, in the same way.

James Fallows   November 1983

cumbersome   *KUHM buhr suhm*
hard to handle or deal with because of size, weight or many parts; unwieldy

Democracy is the most intricate and cumbersome of political systems, and the minimal prerequisite for its effective operation is the existence of an adequate cadre of an educated elite. One of the least forgivable sins of the South Africans is that the literacy rate among blacks is only 55 percent, and that no more than a handful of blacks have been allowed to advance educationally beyond the rudimentary level. Indeed, blacks seem to have been discouraged from attaining the advanced educations that might help them play effective roles in government.

George W. Ball   October 1977

cupidity *kyoo: PI duh tee*
extreme desire for material wealth; greed; avarice

A racket can never exist in any area where the law is enforced. A racketeer thrives on the cupidity of politicians and the weakness of law enforcement agencies. There are ample laws on the statute books of every state to make racketeering difficult, if not impossible, should the police and other law enforcement authorities wish to end the practice. It is, therefore, an axiom that if a racket exists officials are lax.

George E. Sokolsky   September 1938

curmudgeon *ker MUH jin*
someone who finds fault where others do not; a grouch

Whatever happened to standards? This has been a consistent refrain of social observers and literary critics down through the ages, and although some of these people are professional curmudgeons, it's hard to argue that they don't have a point.

Cullen Murphy   December 2003

currency *KUH ruhn see*
common acceptance

It was a Scottish politican and patriot named Andrew Fletcher of Saltoun who first gave currency to the sentiment that "if a man were permitted to make all the ballads, he need not care who should make the laws of a nation." Fletcher of Saltoun died in 1716, predeceasing by some years the advent of the Beatles, the Animals, the Beachboys, the Cliff Dwellers, and various other modern ballad makers, who could conceivably have given him second thoughts on the matter.

Herbert Kupferberg   November 1964

curry favor *KUH ree FAY vuhr*
to seek to win favor by flattery or attention; ingratiate

No one who has not lived in New York can imagine the despotic power which Tammany Hall exercises there. No citizen is too humble to be beneath its notice; no citizen is too rich or too powerful to be safe from its interference. There is not a man living in New York, however independent his character, who would not think twice before doing an act likely to offend Tammany, — or the city government, for they are one and the same thing. People outside of New York would be astonished if they knew what eminent citizens of that town, Republican as well as Democratic, what respectable and wealthy corporations, curry favor with Tammany by keeping their hands off in city politics, by downright contributions of money, and in various other ways. In many assembly districts the Republican party organization is a sort of annex to Tammany; many of the Republican inspectors of election are in the pay of Tammany. Rich and respectable Republicans in the city refrain from vigorous warfare against Tammany, because they do not want to be harassed in respect to their real estate, their shops, their railroads, their factories, their tax returns.

Henry Childs Merwin   February 1894

✳ Tammany, New York City's Democratic Party organization from 1789 to 1970, was named after a Delaware Indian chief known for his wisdom and integrity, and was originally called the Society of St. Tammany. The organization's headquarters became known as Tammany Hall around 1810 and its leaders controlled New York City politics during the 19th and into the 20th century. Its most famous leader was the notorious William Tweed, known as Boss Tweed. From 1859 to 1872 he controlled New York City politics, even deciding the Democratic candidates for mayor and New York State governor. Documentary evidence of Tweed's corruption in *The New York Times*, and satirical cartoons by Thomas Nast in *Harper's Weekly* magazine, hastened Tweed's undoing. He was tried on a variety of charges and died in jail in 1878.

cursory   *KER suh ree*
performed with haste and little attention to detail

Any cursory glance at the journals of Europe must convince even the most heedless American that tides of hatred, mixed with envy, are rising against us in the world, which bode no good either for us or for the peace of nations. The development of sufficient social intelligence and moral imagination to control the vast and intricate economic relationships that modern inventions have made possible and inevitable is an urgent duty which the entire world faces, but of all nations it is most urgent for us; for our nation, which is economically most powerful, is also politically most inept. We are a land of industrial experts and political novices whose limitations are the more dangerous for being so little understood among us.

Reinhold Niebuhr   June 1926

curt   *kert*
brief to the point of rudeness

Francis Jeffrey, famous in the early nineteenth century as the editor of the influential *Edinburgh Review*, is now remembered — if he is remembered at all — as the critic who began his review of Wordsworth's *Excursion* with the curt announcement: "This will not do."

James Atlas   August 1981

droll

Sojourner stayed several days with us, a welcome guest. Her conversation was so strong, simple, shrewd, and with such a droll flavoring of humor, that the Professor was wont to say of an evening, "Come, I am dull, can't you get Sojourner up here to talk a little?" She would come up into the parlor, and sit among pictures and ornaments, in her simple stuff gown, with her heavy travelling shoes, the central object of attention both to parents and children, always ready to talk or to sing, and putting into the common flow of conversation the keen edge of some shrewd remark.

Harriet Beecher Stowe   April 1863

see page 141

dark horse   *dahrk hawrs*
an almost unknown contestant, regarded by few as a likely winner

In fifteen years or so of farm forays I have watched potatoes come and go in the gourmet revival of heirloom everything. Novelty candy stripes and blue or purple potatoes appear one season and vanish the next, as growers learn which kinds best suit their soil and cooks realize that color seldom indicates better flavor. Chefs discover that the secret of the best puree they ever tasted was not the Ratte variety that Parisian chefs swear by but the equal weight of butter whipped in before serving. In my experiments dark-horse varieties have often turned out to taste far better than touted ones. As always, variety counts less than climate and the care the farmer takes.

Corby Kummer   September 2002

dastardly   *DA stuhrd lee*
showing mean, despicable and sneaky cowardice

Senator Goldwater had earned a "trigger-happy" label in 1964 for recommending the use of American bombers in Vietnam, but Administration spokesmen rationalized the bombing in 1965 by dramatic references to the Viet Cong's dastardly "sneak attack"— implying that enemy troops should attack only in broad daylight after a fair warning. Apparently our spokesmen had forgotten our schoolboy pride in George Washington's "sneak attack" on the British after he and his rebel forces stole across the Delaware River.

George McGovern   January 1967

debase   *di BAYS*
to lower in value, quality or significance; cheapen

In the intense competition for higher television ratings or more record sales, many good people working at great and honorable companies have **debased** themselves by conveying images of extreme violence, sexual promiscuity, and vulgarity into our children's minds. By extension they have debased us all. And they have defended their behavior by waving the First Amendment as if it were some kind of constitutional hall pass, whereby the right to speak freely justifies any and all behavior exercised under that right, no matter who is hurt.

Joseph Lieberman   July 1998

debauchery   *di BAW chuh ree*
extreme indulgence in sensual pleasures; dissipation

Byron must have been aware that his compulsive, exorbitant sex life was the enemy of his grander ambitions as a radical. Not only did his **debauchery**, alcoholic as well as carnal, consume an inordinate amount of his time, but it exacted a tremendous toll on his health.

Christopher Hitchens   October 2002

✱ After Lord Byron's last mistress, the Countess Teresa Guiccioli, published a memoir in 1868 describing Byron's former wife, Annabella Milbanke, as a narrow-minded, cold-hearted and prudish woman who ensnared Byron in a dreary, year-long marriage that caused him to flee her and England, Harriet Beecher Stowe responded with a September 1869 article in *The Atlantic* defending her late friend. Stowe had spent an entire day several years earlier listening to Milbanke describe her life with Byron, who died at 36 in 1824 — his numerous affairs, verbal abuse, emotional cruelty and "a secret adulterous intrigue with a blood relation, so near in consanguinity that discovery must have been utter ruin and expulsion from civilized society." What Lady Byron told Stowe, she had told no one else since her separation 44 years before, although Byron's promiscuity was as famous as his poetry, and an affair with his half-sister, Augusta Leigh, was widely rumored.

decadent   *DE kuh dint*
self-indulgent to a degree indicating a decline or decay of values, taste or morals

The sociologist of leisure should note the exacting — I go so far as to call it **decadent** — care the picnickers at Tanglewood take with the lunches they eat on the lawns. As I watched the bright big baskets disgorge their contents (the baked ham, the skinned chicken parts, the redolent cheese, the pert pots of mustard, the wine, the two-tone grapes, the French bread, the cunning little cakes), I thought of the small, dark, dented green lunch bucket my father carried to his job every day (the baloney sandwich, the bruised pear, the burnt cookies, the tepid coffee in the leaky

Thermos) and I felt inexpressibly sad. One cannot, as perhaps you too have discovered, take a holiday from the deposits of one's past which define one's character, and a striking thing about travel is how unexpectedly new surroundings can ambush the heart with old memories.

Jack Beatty   May 1993

decidedly   *duh SIGH did lee*
definitely; beyond doubt

The Magic Mountain is a very German book, and that might be the reason foreign critics very much underestimated its universal appeal. A Swedish critic, member of the Swedish Academy, with a decisive voice in the Nobel Prize Awards, told me in public, and very decidedly, that nobody would dare to venture a translation of this book in a foreign language, as it was absolutely unsuited to such a purpose. That was a false prophesy. *The Magic Mountain* has been translated into all the European languages, and, so far as I can judge, no other of my books has had an equal success — I may say with pride that this is especially the case in America.

Thomas Mann   January 1953

decimate   *DE suh mayt*
to destroy a large part of

Columbus is now vilified as a Eurocentric genocidal maniac who, in addition to decimating the native population of the Americas, was also responsible for destroying their ecology and bringing to this part of the world the most atrocious of all economic systems, namely, capitalism. Had Columbus foreseen even a portion of all the sins he would be held accountable for five centuries later, he might never have bothered to discover America.

Arthur M. Schlesinger Jr.   September 1992

✳ Decimate originally meant to select by lot one tenth of a group and kill them, or to take a tenth part of, as by a tax. Later it meant, more generally, to kill a portion of, and that is how it is used today, almost exclusively. No other word by itself means to kill or remove a large number of but not all.

declivity   *di KLI vi tee*
a downward slope

A subcommittee of the International Federation of Associations of Anatomists has developed a new worldwide anatomical lexicon. Although the term "Adam's apple" will surely survive for a time in Anglophone usage, the preferred designation is now "the laryngeal prominence." The declivity between a woman's breasts, which doctors themselves have often referred to as cleavage, will now officially be called "the inter-mammary sulcus." The term may never catch on, but it probably won't be long before some cybersquatter pays his $35 for intermammarysulcus.com.

Cullen Murphy   February 2000

decree   *duh KREE*
to order, decide or ordain officially and authoritatively

Thirty years ago almost every critic in England exploded with laughter over the poetry of Tennyson. Yet his poetry has exactly the same characteristics now that it had then; and Tennyson has gone up to his place among English poets. It is not "Blackwood," nor any quarterly review or monthly magazine (except, of course, the "North American" and the "Atlantic"), which can decree or deny fame.

George William Curtis   December 1863

de facto   *di FAK toh*
in actual fact though not as a result of law: Latin, from the fact

A person can't function in American society without regularly using a Social Security number, which has become a de facto national ID number — and which, as such, is the key to all sorts of private information.

Toby Lester   March 2001

defang   *dee FANG*
to make harmless; remove the fighting ability of

Most of the Arab states are troubled about a policy that has defanged the Iraqi mil-itary. Although that military threatened their security, it also provided protection against non-Arab Iran, whose size, population, and military-economic potential make it the region's natural hegemon. For this reason Iraq's wealthy neighbors, including Kuwait, lent the Iraqi dictator vast sums to finance his war with Iran in the 1980s.

Alan Tonelson   June 1993

deference   *DE fuh rins*
courteous or respectful regard for another ("deferential" is the adjective)

My acquaintance with Theodore Roosevelt began back in the eighties. At that time I was editor of a weekly paper in New York, and we had some correspondence on social and literary subjects. Everything he said was interesting, very much to the point; and — what was very flattering to me, from a man of his strong convictions — he was most deferential in considering my opinions, especially on literary matters. I found afterwards that this attitude was largely due to his having read two sonnets of mine, 'Theocritus' and 'Maurice de Guérin,' which he did not pretend to understand. Even at that time, when the mists that obscure the future of every young man were just beginning to part and to show the landscape to him, he seemed to find time to read almost everything.

Maurice Francis Egan   May 1919

defray   *di FRAY*
to pay or furnish the money for

In 1843 a government board of inquiry estimated that a quarter to a third of all money on deposit in British banks was earmarked to defray funeral expenses.

William Rathje   September 1985

degenerate   *duh JE nuh rayt*
to decline in quality; fall to an inferior or undesirable state ("degenerative" is the adjective)

In 1747 Samuel Johnson issued a plan for a new dictionary of the English language. It was supported by the most distinguished printers of the day and was dedicated to the model of all correctness, Philip Dormer Stanhope, Fourth Earl of Chesterfield. Such a book, it was felt, was urgently needed to "fix" the language, to arrest its "corruption" and "decay," a degenerative process which, then as now, was attributed to the influence of "the vulgar" and which, then as now, it was a mark of superiority and elegance to decry. And Mr. Johnson seemed the man to write it. He had an enormous knowledge of Latin, deep piety, and dogmatic convictions.

Bergen Evans   March 1960

✳ Although Samuel Johnson's intent when he began his dictionary was to "fix" the language by including the words that would be a permanent part of it and leaving out those that should wither and die, he gradually changed his mind as his dictionary work progressed. He came to realize that the English language was inexorably changeable and ever evolving. In the introduction to his dictionary (1755), he wrote: "Those who have been persuaded to think well of my design will require that I should fix our language, and put a stop to those alterations which time and chance have hitherto been suffered to make in it without opposition. With this consequence I will confess that I flattered myself for a while; but now begin to fear that I have indulged expectation which neither reason nor experience can justify."

degrade   *di GRAYD*
to lower in estimation; bring into dishonor or contempt; humiliate
("degradation" is the noun)

> In the college seminar I teach on sports and culture, nothing infuriates the female students more than the degradation of women that is associated with male sports: bikini-clad ring girls at boxing matches, inanely grinning cheerleaders at basketball and football games, victory-circle girls at auto races.

> Scott Stossel   June 2001

dejected   *dee JEK tid*
low in spirits; downcast; disheartened ("dejectedly" is the adverb)

> I have myself watched and pitied the too evident ennui of my cat, poor little beast of prey, deprived in a mouseless home of the supreme pleasures of the hunt; fed until dinner ceases to be a coveted enjoyment; housed, cushioned, combed, caressed, and forced to bear upon her pretty shoulders the burden of a wearisome opulence, — or what represents opulence to a pussy. I have seen Agrippina listlessly moving from chair to chair, and from sofa to sofa, in a vain attempt to nap; looking for a few languid minutes out of the window with the air of a great lady sadly bored at the play; and then turning dejectedly back into the room whose attractions she had long since exhausted. Her expressive eyes lifted to mine betrayed her discontent; the lassitude of an irksome luxury unnerved her graceful limbs; if she could have spoken, it would have been to complain with Charles Lamb of that "dumb, soporifical good-for-nothingness" which clogs the wheels of life.

> Agnes Repplier   June 1893

de jure   *di JOO ree*
by legal establishment; according to law: Latin, of law

> In the early days of the foundation of Israel, while the United States maintained a certain distance, the Soviet Union granted immediate *de jure* recognition and support, and arms sent from a Soviet satellite, Czechoslovakia, saved the infant state of Israel from defeat and death in its first weeks of life.

> Bernard Lewis   September 1990

delectation   *dee lek TAY shuhn*
delight; entertainment: before the 18th century, denoting all kinds of pleasure, from sensual to spiritual; today restricted to lighter pleasures and used somewhat humorously

Goosie, goosie gander, whither shall I wander?
Upstairs and downstairs and in my lady's chamber.
There I met an old man who wouldn't say his prayers —
I took him by the left leg and threw him downstairs.

Here we see, held up for the **delectation** of the young, a representation of someone, apparently a member of the leisured classes, wandering about a house in a state of dangerous aimlessness and indolence, boldly disregarding all privacy. In the course of this peregrination he chances upon an elderly man upon whom he attempts to force his own religious practices and, not meeting with immediate and slavish acquiescence, proceeds to employ brutal violence.

Bergen Evans   December 1934

✳ See also **avarice**, **engender**, **obviate** and **sullen** for other passages in which Bergen Evans provides his tongue-in-cheek analyses of nursery rhymes.

delineate   *di LI nee ayt*
to portray in words; describe

Dickens with his transcendent memory chronicled in his mind whatever of interest met his eye or reached his ear, any time or anywhere. Speaking of memory one day, he said the memory of children was prodigious; it was a mistake to fancy children ever forgot anything. When he was **delineating** the character of Mrs. Pipchin, he had in his mind an old lodging-house keeper in an English watering-place where he was living with his father and mother when he was but two years old. After the book was written he sent it to his sister, who wrote back at once: "Good heavens! what does this mean? you have painted our lodging-house keeper, and you were but two years old at that time!" Characters and incidents crowded the chambers of his brain, all ready for use when occasion required. No subject of human interest was ever indifferent to him, and never a day went by that did not afford him some suggestion to be utilized in the future.

James T. Fields   August 1870

deliquesce   *de li KWES*
to melt away

I have known several very genteel idiots whose whole vocabulary had **deliquesced** into some half dozen expressions. All things fell into one of two great categories, — *fast* or *slow*. Man's chief end was to be a *brick*. When the great calamities of life overtook their friends, these last were spoken of as *being a good deal cut up*. Nine-tenths of human existence were summed up in the single word, *bore*.

Oliver Wendell Holmes   September 1858

deluge *DEL yoo:j*
to overwhelm with a large quantity or amount; flood

Spring came on with a rush in the swamp; everything flaunted rich greenery. By the 3d of April it was like June. Still there were not many birds, until one day they deluged the forest. It was as if a sudden tide had borne them up from the south. At daybreak I heard their chattering and twittering, their whistling, their warbling, a very pandemonium of early throat-swellings and syrinx-shaking; above them all the voice of an ivory-bill, a clarion call to his mate and a challenge to me. Very few are the naturalists who have studied the ivory-billed woodpecker (*Campephilus principalis*) in its native haunts.

Maurice Thompson   April 1896

✻ John Milton (1608-1674) coined the word pandemonium from the Greek *pan* (all) and *daimon* (demon). It was the name he gave to the capital city of Hell, the site of Satan's palace, in his epic poem *Paradise Lost.*

delusive *di LOO: suhv*
misleading; imaginary; false

To the old-fashioned psychologist the mind was a well-ordered city, with the streets well paved and lighted and the limits of each ward well defined. Reason was the Lord Mayor, and the various mental faculties formed the Board of Aldermen. If there were any recalcitrant citizens they were promptly jailed. But it is so no longer. The mind is revealed to us in a state of perpetual insurgency. It is nature in a state of eruption. Instincts, desires, inchoate tendencies, lawless appetites, contend for the chance for expression. It is the realm of chaos and old night, with here and there a gleam of delusive sham rationality. For the more rational we are in our own eyes, the more we are in error.

Samuel McChord Crothers   May 1928

demagogue *DE muh gahg*
an unprincipled person who obtains power and popularity by arousing the emotions, passions and prejudices of the populace

We must realize that it is very hard to save a civilization when its hour has come to fall beneath the power of demagogues. For the demagogue has been the greatest strangler of civilizations. Both Greek and Roman civilizations fell at the hands of this loathsome creature who brought from Macaulay the remark that "in every century the vilest examples of human nature have been among demagogues."

José Ortega Y Gasset   April 1941

demeanor   *duh MEE nuhr*
outward behavior; conduct

On visiting England for the first time in 1872, I was offered a letter to Carlyle, and declined it. Like all of this generation, I had been under some personal obligations to him for his early writings, — though in my case this debt was trifling compared with that due to Emerson, — but his Latter Day Pamphlets and his reported utterances on American affairs had taken away all special desire to meet him, besides the ungraciousness said to mark his demeanor toward visitors from the United States. Yet when I was once fairly launched in that fascinating world of London society where the American sees, as Willis used to say, whole shelves of his library walking about in coats and gowns, this disinclination rapidly softened. And when Mr. Froude kindly offered to take me with him on one of his afternoon visits to Carlyle, and further proposed that I should join them in their habitual walk through the parks, it was not in human nature — or at least in American nature — to resist.

Thomas Wentworth Higginson   October 1861

demur   *di MER*
to make objection, especially on the grounds of scruples; take exception; object

In 1977 Ronny Zamora, a fifteen-year-old, shot and killed the eighty-two-year-old woman who lived next door to him in Florida. Not guilty, pleaded his lawyer, Ellis Rubin, by reason of the boy's having watched too much television. From watching television Ronny had become dangerously inured to violence. Suffering from what Rubin called "television intoxication," he could no longer tell right from wrong. "If you judge Ronny Zamora guilty," Rubin argued, "television will be an accessory." The jury demurred: Ronny was convicted of first-degree murder.

Scott Stossel   May 1997

demure   *di MYOOR*
modest; reserved: sometimes affectedly so ("demureness" is the noun)

Women in Kerala will look one in the eye; there is little of that socially conditioned demureness one finds in the rest of India.

Akash Kapur   September 1998

denigrate   *DE nuh grayt*
to criticize in a derogatory manner; to represent as lacking in importance or value; belittle

Twenty years ago feminists made the mistake of denigrating homemaking and volunteer work. It's hard to imagine how else they might have made their case. Still, the feminist attack on volunteering was simplistic and ill-informed. Feminists might have paid attention to the historical experiences of middle-class African-American women combining paid work, volunteering, and family life. They might have paid attention to the critical role played by the volunteer tradition in the nineteenth-century feminist movement. Women's sense of their maternal responsibilities at home and in the wider world was at the core of their shared social conscience, which feminists ignored at their peril.

Wendy Kaminer   October 1993

denizen   *DEN uh zin*
a person or creature who is thoroughly a part of a place; a dweller

Unlike other major world capitals, Washington is a one-industry town. Little is there to distract its denizens from the single-minded practice of politics and the pursuit of power. The city offers only sporadic imports from the lively arts. The pulsations of big commerce and high finance all come from New York, as does the leadership of the everpresent communications media. There is not much big money and not much social glamour, nor is there much of the yeasty interplay of ethnic groupings or neighborhoods that characterizes other big cities. The social life is merely the after-sundown extension of the day's business — politics and government.

Robert Manning   December 1971

deplore   *duh PLAWR*
to express strong disapproval of; regard as scandalous; lament

A university law school professor recently deplored, in conversation with me, the meager vocabulary, feeble style, and paucity of ideas characteristic of the 'picked' students to whom his first professional courses were addressed. How could it be otherwise. The art of expression develops where there is something to say; but the preparatory school curriculum, and, most of all, the English course, disdains any content such as would give the pupil something to say, and, instead, devotes itself, as consistently as it can, to a 'discipline,' which bleaches out all subjects to a uniform deadly pallor.

Abraham Flexner   April 1917

depose   *di POHZ*
to remove from office or power

Suppose we receive an alien message that is deciphered as warm greetings and petitions for peace. How could we know whether the sentiments were genuine or pretense? Whether the noble government that had sent them a thousand years before had been deposed by warlike fanatics? Furthermore, there is no reason to assume that any other planet would have cohesive single governments whose word would be bond. Earth doesn't. An extraterrestrial emissary approaching our world would have grave difficulty just figuring out whom to deal with.

Gregg Easterbrook   August 1988

depreciate   *di PREE shee ayt*
to attribute less value to; belittle

The artistic sense of Chicago partakes of the spirit of the town, in that it persists in spite of all contumely. It is the fashion to depreciate it, to laugh at all pretensions to achievement on any save commercial lines, and to berate the city generally whenever it is mentioned. To all this Chicago turns a broad, good-humored smile, and tramps on through her mud, indifferent and besmeared. She has no time to pause; she is too busy and absorbed even to clean her streets; that which would be a disgrace to another city is only an incident with her. She is so confident of her destiny that she takes no note of mistakes, is not irritated at her failures nor depressed at her shortcomings. On the contrary, she is amused at herself, — at her exaggerations, her absurdities. But she knows, after all, that she is not understood. She knows that deep in her heart is an ideal, and it is the knowledge of this ideal which is responsible for the excessive civic pride noticeable in those who live within her limits. It is the belief in this ideal which inspires confidence in her ultimate artistic expression.

Elia W. Peattie   December 1899

depredation   *de pruh DAY shuhn*
the act of robbing, plundering or laying waste

The treasures of China's past that foreigners most want to see are somehow a reproach to the bleak, utilitarian Communist mentality. A vindictiveness toward the past has to account for the terrible destruction of the recent Cultural Revolution, whose yet uncounted depredations may match those of invading armies.

Thomas Griffith   January 1981

derogatory   *duh RAH guh taw ree*
disparaging; belittling

Twenty years ago, in student days (Paris, GI Bill), I was writing a first novel when the editor of a little magazine asked me to review a new book by Nelson Algren. I read it with rage. I thought it trivial, windy, derogatory of the human species; it violated the principles I had learned from Aristotle and the Columbia College humanities program; I savaged the book in a hot, merciless, young-man's review. The book was *The Man With the Golden Arm*, and I have never forgotten it. The characters are still vivid and touching, the prose is heated, urban-weird, with disturbing rhythms. Years later I realized why I couldn't put the book out of my mind: *I had been moved by it.* True, it violated my principles, but my principles were wrong. I was writing a first book by principle, and Algren had written a book from his chaotic feelings. With all its crudities, the book has a mythic power.

Herbert Gold   June 1970

descant   *de SKANT*
to talk or write at length; discourse on

Whenever you hear ponderous statements about the moral values of football, when someone descants upon self-control and chivalry through sport, when you hear it said that sport is useful for the building of character — laugh.

John R. Tunis   January 1932

desiccated   *DE si kay tid*
dried up; empty of spirit, spontaneity or vitality

In *Middlemarch* the desiccated pedant Casaubon wastes his life, and the life of another, in a futile search for "the Key to all Mythologies."

Christopher Hitchens   December 2003

desideratum   *di si duh RAH tuhm*
something desired as a necessity

The great artificial capital of the country is Washington, and a more artificial one could not well be imagined. Without trade, or commerce, or manufactures, or even that great desideratum of American existence, a "live" newspaper, it has been built up simply by the continual expansion of the government and the steady increase of the office-holding class. Without its political population Washington would cease to exist.

Arthur George Sedgwick   December 1877

despoil   *di SPOIL*
to strip of value; plunder

What despoils wilderness, as any student of that despoliation knows, is not back-packers, campers, and fishermen but miners, logging companies, oil drillers, and the like. Wilderness is spoiled not by love but by greed.

Kenneth Brower   July/August 2002

despondent   *di SPON dint*
dejected; depressed; disheartened; without hope ("despondency" is the noun)

William Wordsworth, the longest-lived of his storied generation of English Romantics, appraised the dire effects of the aging process on those in his line of work in a couplet that has since come to have a proverbial ring: "We Poets in our youth begin in gladness; / But thereof come in the end despondency and madness." That sounds gloomy beyond the call of duty. Still, it succinctly lays out one plausible hypothesis for the high incidence of burnout among poets of a certain age.

David Barber   June 1996

desultory   *DE suhl taw ree*
jumping from one thing to another in an aimless way; unmethodical; random

Variety, which in limitations is wholesome in literary as well as in physical diet, creates dyspepsia when it is excessive, and when the literary viands are badly cooked and badly served the evil is increased. The mind loses the power of discrimination, the taste is lowered, and the appetite becomes diseased. The effect of this scrappy, desultory reading is bad enough when the hashed compound selected is tolerably good. It becomes a very serious matter when the reading itself is vapid, frivolous, or bad.

Charles Dudley Warner   June 1890

determinism   *de TER mi ni zuhm*
the theory that human behavior arises not from free will but is the result of biological, psychological and environmental causes ("deterministic" is the adjective)

It is too deterministic to say that people are programmed for violence, like some aggressive species of ants. But the archaeological evidence shows that men — and often women as well — have been fighting wars for at least 5,000 years. Organized conflict emerged independently in cultures that had little or no contact with one another. It appears to have been as frequent among the inhabitants of pre-conquest North and South America as in Europe, Asia, and Africa.

John Lewis Gaddis   April 1999

detriment   *DE truh mint*
loss; damage; injury or disadvantage

The problems we have created for the Indians continue to defy solution because we do not know their history or their true nature. To our detriment, we do not know what they might be able to teach us about conservation, the rearing of children, psychosomatic medicine, and the attainment of harmonious and ordered lives. And we fail utterly to appreciate how knowledge of our mistakes in our treatment of the Indians might now help us in our relations with other peoples in the world.

Alvin M. Josephy Jr.   June 1970

devolve   *di VAHLV*
to fall upon as a duty or responsibility

As the offices of courtship devolve entirely upon the males, it is the more necessary that they should be possessed of conspicuous attractions; but as the task of sitting upon the nest devolves upon the female, she requires more of that protection which arises from the conformity of her plumage with the general hue of the objects that surround her nest.

Wilson Flagg   August 1858

to change gradually for the worse

From 1929 to 1953 Stalin transformed Russia into the Soviet Union largely through the labor-camp system of Siberia and the fear it generated in his subject population. Speaking out became pointless suicide; language devolved too often into a series of besotted grunts. For many the only remaining escape from the lie of sovietism was descent into an alcoholic stupor, wordless and sullen, repeated over and over again until the cognitive functions withered, the liver gave out, and death arrived as a relief.

Jeffrey Tayler   April 1997

dextrous   *DEK struhs*
showing mental skill

There was nothing in all Douglas's powerful effort that appealed to the higher instincts of human nature, while Lincoln always touched sympathetic chords. Lincoln's speech excited and sustained the enthusiasm of his audience to the end. When he had finished, two stalwart young farmers rushed on the platform, and, in spite of his remonstrances, seized and put him on their shoulders and carried him in that uncomfortable posture for a considerable distance. It was really a ludicrous sight to see the grotesque figure holding frantically to the heads of his supporters, with his legs dangling from their shoulders and his pantaloons pulled up so as to expose his underwear almost to his knees. Douglas made dextrous use of this incident in his next speech, expressing sincere regret that, against his wish, he had used up his old friend Lincoln so completely that he had to be carried off the stage.

Henry Villard   February 1904

diadem   *DIGH uh dem*
a crown or crowning ornament

Europeans coming to New York City for the first time are ecstatic about the view of lower Manhattan in the early morning from a great liner as it passes through upper New York Bay; mid-Manhattan seen from the Triborough Bridge at sundown; the jeweled diadem spread before the jet flyer at night; the clean gossamer cobwebs of its suspension bridges; the successive bustle and tomblike silences of its streets; the fantastic daring, imagination, and aspiration of its builders.

Robert Moses   January 1962

diaspora   *digh A spuh ruh*
the spreading or dispersion of people from one original place; originally, the Jews living outside of biblical Israel or the modern state of Israel, or the places outside Israel where they have lived

From its birth, in the 1920s, commercial country music was never simply a rural genre. It was the soundtrack for one of this century's great diasporas: the flow of rural white southerners into America's cities. Country softened the traumas of that move. Right through the sixties, songs like "The Streets of Baltimore" mirrored the rural southerner's feelings about his displacement, from elation ("Her heart was filled with laughter / When she saw those city lights / She said the prettiest place on earth is Baltimore at night") to defeat ("Now I'm a-goin' back on that same train / That brought me here before / While my baby walks the streets of Baltimore"). If the narrator didn't stick it out, his cousins probably did, and raised families, and left their roots behind.

Tony Scherman   August 1996

diatribe   *DIGH ugh trighb*
a bitter, abusive criticism or denunciation

HOCUS POCUS *by Kurt Vonnegut. Putnam, $21.95.* This novel consists of Mr. Vonnegut's diatribe against what he considers wrong with American society and the human race, which turns out to be practically everything.

Phoebe-Lou Adams   October 1990

dichotomy   *digh KAH tuh mee*
a division into two sharply distinguished or opposed parts

We are so used to thinking of spirituality as withdrawal from the world and human affairs that it is hard to think of it as political. Spirituality is personal and private, we assume, while politics is public. But such a dichotomy drastically diminishes spirituality, construing it as a relationship to God without implications for one's relationship to the surrounding world.

Glenn Tinder   December 1989

Dickensian   *di KEN zee uhn*

resembling conditions and features described by Charles Dickens in his novels,
especially with regard to poor social and economic conditions

In spite of the Dickensian reputation that outlives them, orphanages, which began
to proliferate in this country in the mid-1800s, represented a significant social
reform for their time, just as the group homes and residential treatment centers that
took their place are now seen as reforms.

Mary-Lou Weisman   July 1994

dictates   *DIK tayts*

guiding principles or rules

Chess-players say that after the first few moves they are not conscious of any further
activity of their own minds, but play the game according to the dictates of a subconscious master, a wholly different personality, who comes avidly to the fore and
takes command of the intricate tactics. It is as if a puppet, a small Robot in the brain,
were acting for them: while the game is in progress, he works with super-brilliancy
and activity; when it is over, he disappears instantly from the conscious mind. Many
creative minds admit the same thing — it seems that it is not conscious thought or
will-power which produces the poem, novel, or play which delights the world, but
the workings of an independent creator, who hides within the brain.

Contributors' Club: Elizabeth H. Russell   August 1923

dictum   *DIK tuhm*

an authoritative pronouncement

Gertrude Stein helped Hemingway discover not only what he was seeing, and how
to communicate the sight, but what to look for. It was she who explained that he
must look at his material, and at each new experience, as certain painters —
Cézanne, in particular — looked at their own compositions. His own subsequent
dictums on writing are often variations and extensions of what she had either told
him or permitted him to learn.

Charles A. Fenton   May 1954

didactic   *digh DAK tik*

intended to be instructive; moralistic ("didacticism" is the noun)

Stevenson's avowed aim in *Treasure Island* was to write a story for boys — "No
need of psychology or fine writing," he said. Many readers, including James,
praised the novel. Probably no one at the time, including Stevenson himself, recognized his most significant accomplishment. With the tap of Pew's cane and a few

choruses of yo-ho-ho, he liberated children's writing from the heavy chains of Victorian didacticism.

Margot Livesey   November 1994

diffident   *DI fuh dint*
hesitant in asserting or expressing oneself

The English may be diffident with each other, but a lively sense of hospitality and innate politeness lead them easily enough into conversation with strangers.

Ken W. Purdy   February 1963

diffusion   *di FYOO: zhuhn*
the spread of elements of a culture or language from one region or people to another; wide and general distribution; dissemination

Bilingualism, about which reams of paper have been wasted in Puerto Rico, is merely a theory — and not a very good theory. No people anywhere is bilingual in the complete sense of the word. No nationality has grown up with the knowledge acquired from childhood of two languages. None of the Puerto Ricans speak English habitually or as the mother tongue. English is an alien and foreign thing, with no local roots and no tradition. To bring about its diffusion, it has been necessary to make it the official vehicle of expression and decree its use in the schools.

Richard Pattee   September 1944

dim   *dim*
not bright intellectually

In 1885 Edith Jones married the charming but dim Edward Wharton. As was the custom in that far-off time, Edith went to the bridal bed a virgin. Whether or not she was still a virgin the next day is moot. We do know that whatever happened so traumatized her that that was that: no more sex. The marriage itself was not too bad (both of them liked animals).

Gore Vidal   February 1978

din   *din*
a loud, continuous noise; confused clamor or uproar

Along Broadway, the cries of the itinerant venders and tradesmen are seldom to be heard; for it is not in the great business thoroughfares that these industrials ply their vocations; and even if they did, their voices would be lost in the dominant din of that clashing, rattling, shrieking, thundering thoroughfare.

Charles Dawson Shanly   February 1870

disaffected   *dis uh FEK tid*
feeling separate or alienated; resentful and rebellious against authority

Fifteen families of Columbine victims have filed lawsuits against Jefferson County, and several of those suits claim that lives could have been saved if the police had entered the school sooner. The consensus among law-enforcement authorities across the country is that Columbine was handled by the book — but that the book should be rewritten. The traditional police response was designed for dealing with trapped bank robbers, angry husbands, or disgruntled employees — not with disaffected teenagers running through a school killing as many people as possible.

Timothy Harper   October 2000

disapprobation   *dis a pruh BAY shuhn*
an expression of strong moral or social disapproval

There were growls of disapprobation from novel-readers, that Hester Prynne and the Rev. Mr. Dimmesdale were subjected to cruel punishments unknown to the jurisprudence of fiction, — that the author was an inquisitor who put his victims on the rack, — and that neither amusement nor delight resulted from seeing the contortions and hearing the groans of these martyrs of sin; but the fact was no less plain that Hawthorne had for once compelled the most superficial lovers of romance to submit themselves to the magic of his genius.

Edwin Percy Whipple   May 1860

✳ When Nathaniel Hawthorne finished writing *The Scarlet Letter*, he read it to his wife, Sophia, over two evenings. In *The Atlantic* of April 1871, a few months after she died, Thomas Wentworth Higginson related the story Mrs. Hawthorne told him, years after her husband's death, about how he prefaced the reading by telling her that he did not think the book worth very much but that she might as well hear it. On the second evening, "the concentrated excitement had grown so great that she could scarcely bear it," Higginson wrote. "At last it grew unendurable; and in the midst of the scene, near the end of the book, where Arthur Dimmesdale meets Hester and her child in the forest, Mrs. Hawthorne fell from her low stool upon the floor, pressed her hands upon her ears and said she could hear no more. Hawthorne put down the manuscript and looked at her in perfect amazement. 'Do you really feel it so much?' he said. 'Then there must be something in it.' He prevailed on her to rise and to hear the few remaining chapters of the romance."

discern   *di SERN*
to perceive or recognize as distinct or different

Readers of Homer who are themselves writers or men of war nearly always reject the idea of a single authorship. Samuel Butler and Robert Graves discern in the *Odyssey* a woman's hand unraveling the ancient web of heroic action. John Cowper Powys states that the two poems "had different authors or originals" and that there is "an historic gap of three or four hundred years between them." T.E. Lawrence characterized the poet of the *Odyssey* as a "great if uncritical reader of the *Iliad*" and guessed that he was not much of a practical soldier. We seem to be dealing with contrasting qualities of mind.

George Steiner   August 1961

discomfited   *dis KUHM fi tid*
to have one's plans thrown into upset; confused or frustrated

The hazards faced by those attempting to shoot close-up video footage of tornadoes cannot be overstated. Tornadoes can form suddenly and with little warning, and photographers who turn down the wrong road at the wrong time can find themselves discomfited by 200-mph winds containing jagged bits of automobiles, sheets of razor-sharp aluminum siding, and lancelike sections of splintered fence posts.

Wayne Curtis   October 2001

disconcerting   *dis kuhn SERT ing*
disturbing the composure or calm of

New York's disconcerting sky-scrapers are vastly picturesque, and even grandiose in certain lights. On winter afternoons, when the dusk comes early, their myriad lamps afford a spectacle which outclasses in brilliancy the grandest electric displays of the greatest world's fairs. Athwart the moonlit or starlit sky, their soaring masses stand forth black and ominous, like the donjon keeps of colossal castles; and, under these conditions, the lower end of Manhattan, where they most abound, might pass for the Mont St. Michel of the New World.

Alvan F. Sanborn   October 1906

＊ The term skyscraper originated in the 18th century as the topmost sail on a ship. In the 19th century it was also a tall horse, a very tall man, a high hat, a high fly ball in baseball, or a tall story.

disconsolate   *dis KAHN suh lit*
so unhappy that nothing will comfort; cheerless; gloomy ("disconsolately" is the adverb)

Everyone knows the story, so popular with success magazines, of the old man who bravely turns his business over to the younger generation and goes off, freed at last to live his own life. Soon he is back again to haunt the arena of his former triumphs, pottering about disconsolately, a jealous or wistful critic of his successor's policies. If some turn of events gives him a chance to "muscle in," he is soon ensconced again in the old swivel chair, radiating authority and action.

Earnest Elmo Calkins   May 1933

discordant   *dis KAWR dint*
not in harmony; conflicting; clashing

Were the question raised, "What benefits will the world enjoy under a League of Nations?" would it not be enough to answer, "It will be better *governed*," all other benefits, which would doubtless be many, being dependent upon and derivative from this? In place of the discordant relationships between nations now existing, the League will substitute harmonious government under international law. What other object, we are tempted to ask, could the League conceivably have?

L. P. Jacks   February 1923

discrepancy   *dis KRE puhn see*
inconsistency; variance

Scribner has recently reissued in hardcover Ernest Hemingway's four major works — *The Sun Also Rises*, *A Farewell to Arms*, *For Whom the Bell Tolls*, and *The Old Man and the Sea* — and I made my way through them again, mesmerized by Hemingway's genius as a storyteller and alarmed by the vicissitudes of his prose. The discrepancy between eloquence and maudlin self-indulgence was often visible on a single page; I never knew when he would soar and when he would lapse into the fabled macho pose that has proved so irresistible to parody.

James Atlas   October 1983

❋ Parody, a work of literature, music or art that imitates another work to ridicule it or just to be funny, is one of many arts-related words that originated in ancient Greece, where most Western art forms were developed. Others are anachronism, anthology, archetype, biography, catharsis, comedy, elegy, epic, euphemism, hubris, irony, lyric, metaphor, mime, mythology, poetics, rhetoric, sarcasm, symbolism and tragedy.

discursive   *dis KER siv*
wandering from one topic to another; digressive

William James and his wife have been a part of my life ever since my husband — we were then engaged — was a Harvard student in 1879. Mr. James was at that time an instructor in physiology, and well do I remember my husband's talk of his extraordinary personality, or the discursive quality of his mind, and more especially how it would dart off from the subject matter of his lectures and discuss for the full hour some philosophical question far afield.

Elizabeth Glendower Evans   September 1929

disembowel   *dis im BOW uhl*
to take out the entrails of; rip open

The strength of the ostrich is prodigious; he can disembowel a horse or kick through a sheet of corrugated iron. To an unprotected man in the open an infuriated ostrich is as dangerous as the lion. Many have lost their lives through ignorance of his strength, his speed, and his implacable ferocity.

William Charles Scully   March 1918

✳ Theodore Roosevelt's response to Scully's assertions appears in the passage for expedient.

disenfranchise   *dis in FRAN chighz*
to deprive of the right to vote ("disfranchised" is an older, alternate form of the adjective)

What sort of philosophy is that which says, "John is a fool; Jane is a genius; nevertheless, John, being a man, shall learn, lead, make laws, make money; Jane, being a woman, shall be ignorant, dependent, disfranchised, underpaid."

Thomas Wentworth Higginson   February 1859

disequilibrium   *dis ee kwuh LI bree uhm*
the absence or destruction of equilibrium; a throwing out of balance

The rich see opportunities to work and invest in situations where great disequilibriums —imbalances or openings in the economy created by new circumstances — exist. Something, usually a new technology, has opened up opportunities to jump to new products with very different capabilities or to new processes with much higher levels of productivity. This was as true for John D. Rockefeller as it is for Bill Gates. For both of them lifetime savings constituted a small fraction of total wealth. Carefully saving money and investing in normal equilibrium situations can make one comfortable in old age but never really wealthy.

Lester C. Thurow   June 1999

disgruntled   *dis GRUN tuhld*
in a state of moody discontent; peevishly dissatisfied; displeased

In most of our cities there is a prevalent, provincial feeling that looks with disdain and disfavor upon the hiring of teachers from other towns. This sentiment makes of our schools semi-eleemosynary institutions, whose principal function is to give employment to the daughters and sons of the place. The bane of this in-and-in breeding is felt in every large city. So acute is the feeling that, if the superintendent goes abroad for a few alien teachers, he is decried as disloyal, and he is fortunate if the disgruntled ones fail in organizing a foolish opposition to his well-meant endeavor to infuse new life into his schools. There are instances on record where a determined parent has set out to elect a school board so that her daughter might be appointed a teacher, though she was lacking both in spirit and knowledge.

Samuel P. Orth   March 1909

❊ Eleemosynary means the giving and receiving of alms. The word derives from the Latin *eleemosyna*, alms.

dishabille   *dis uh BEEL*
dressed carelessly or negligently; disheveled

There are those who indite elegant notes to comparative strangers, but, probably upon the principle that familiarity breeds or should breed contempt, send the most villainous scrawls to their intimate friends and those of their own household. They are akin to the numerous wives, who, reserving not only silks and satins, but neatness and courtesy, for company, are always in dishabille in their husbands' houses.

Adams Sherman Hill   June 1858

disinterested   *dis IN tris tid*
without selfish motives when considering an issue; fair-minded

The men who create power make an indispensable contribution to the nation's greatness, but the men who question power make a contribution just as indispensable, especially when that questioning is disinterested, for they determine whether we use power or power uses us. Our national strength matters; but the spirit which informs and controls our strength matters just as much.

John Fitzgerald Kennedy   February 1964

❊ Less than a month before his assassination on November 22, 1963, President Kennedy spoke at Amherst College in honor of Robert Frost, who had died in January of that year. Frost had read his poem, "The Gift Outright," at President Kennedy's inauguration in 1961. Kennedy's speech was published a few months later in *The Atlantic*. Another passage from President Kennedy's speech appears in this book at touchstone.

disjunction *dis JUHNGK shuhn*
a condition of being disconnected; separation

Is there not something supremely childlike about both Napoleon and Hitler? Just as the child in the dawn of his life cannot make a distinction between an object and himself, so the conqueror cannot understand why there should be any disjunction between himself and what he wants. When a disjunction appears, both the child and the conqueror express their frustration by fits of temper. Such fits are described by Tolstoy as characteristic of Napoleon and are described by contemporaries as characteristic of Hitler.

Clifton Fadiman   May 1942

dismissive *dis MI siv*
rejecting as beneath consideration; contemptuous; disdainful

The Between Boyfriends Book describes men in a manner so dismissive and callous that had a man written such a book about women, the cries of misogyny would be deafening.

Caitlin Flanagan   December 2003

disparage *dis PA rij*
to speak slightingly of; deny as having worth; belittle ("disparagement" is the noun)

A lively negative review tends to stay in the mind. The language of disparagement is simply more vivid than the language of praise. Henry James's description of Russian novels as "large, loose baggy monsters" is worth pages of his panegyrics to George Eliot and Balzac.

James Atlas   August 1981

dispassionate *dis PA shuh nit*
unaffected by emotion or bias; impartial; calm; cool ("dispassionately" is the adverb)

Children, particularly those younger than ten, can put up with more family discord without being distressed than most adults realize. Arguments and disputes, even heated ones, can be overheard and observed by children dispassionately. They can be quite objective about such controversies and even discuss them humorously among themselves. Anger and frustration are emotions with which they are very familiar, and watching such feelings being openly expressed by their elders may even be reassuring.

Graham B. Blaine Jr., M.D.   March 1963

dispensation   *dis pen SAY shuhn*
a release or exemption from an obligation or rule

A cigar commercial on TV is granting a special dispensation to smokers: you don't have to inhale it to enjoy it, says the announcer. His words bring relief to anyone who ever inhaled, inadvertently, a nickel cigar and felt, thereupon, as if he had been kicked in the chest by a horse.

Charles W. Morton   September 1964

disposed   *dis POHZD*
to be inclined; of a mind to

Like the man who said he knew the earth was flat because it had looked flat to him in all the places he had ever visited, each generation is disposed to regard its main assumptions as self-evident when in fact they have merely been adopted uncritically.

Walter Lippman   October 1936

disputatious   *dis pyoo: TAY shuhs*
inclined to argue or disagree; contentious

We find it human to enjoy likenesses rather than unlikenesses. Our clubs, associations, churches, societies, are founded on the basis of like-mindedness. We narrow our personal lives by surrendering to this preference and spending our free time with those who are socially, economically, and intellectually of our own kind. When we meet one of the audacious ones of the earth who have ignored such distinctions and known all manner of men, we have a momentary pang of envy and then, all too easily, slip back into a studied avoidance of the disputatious.

Cornelia James Cannon   September 1925

disquisition   *dis kwuh ZI shuhn*
a formal or academic discussion of or inquiry into a subject; dissertation

I don't suppose my hands ever trembled more than they did in opening a letter — four onionskin pages, airmailed from Paris — that Mary McCarthy wrote to me on March 23, 1973. "Thank you for sending me your honors thesis," she began, "which I have been rather slow to read." I had sent this 152-page disquisition on her work at the urging of my adviser and with, as one biographer says in telling the story, "the innocence of the very young." I was twenty-one.

Thomas Mallon   November 2002

✳ Onionskin is a thin, strong, lightweight translucent paper with a glossy finish used especially for making carbon copies.

disseminate   *di SE mi nayt*
to distribute widely; spread abroad

As stock ownership expands, so does education by mutual funds, banks, brokerage firms, journalists, and scholars. Research is far better today than it was in the past, and it is easily disseminated on the Internet. Seventy years ago few investors understood that excessive trading undermines profits, that stock-price fluctuations tend to cancel themselves out over time, making stocks less risky than they might appear at first glance, and that it is extremely difficult to outperform the market averages. American investors have learned to buy and hold.

James K. Glassman and Kevin A. Hassett   September 1999

distance   *DIS tins*
to socially or emotionally separate oneself from others

Ten years ago, when *Sunday in the Park With George* was new, Sondheim was frequently likened to the painter Georges Seurat, the show's protagonist, whose immersion in his canvases distanced him from the other characters in much the same way that Sondheim has increasingly distanced himself from Broadway audiences.

Francis Davis   March 1995

doctrinaire   *dahk truh NAIR*
stubbornly adhering to principles or beliefs regardless of practical considerations

The vast majority of the American people do not want another war, with all its incredible horrors of atomic and biological attack. Neither do the Russian people, who have already endured so much. But corrupted by power or blinded by national pride and doctrinaire beliefs, our leaders and theirs may refuse to make those sacrifices of national independence and armed strength that are the true costs of peace. Of one thing we can be sure. If the UN is not strengthened in time to avert war, a long night of ignorance and brutality will descend upon our ingenious species.

Cord Meyer Jr.   October 1947

doddering   *DAH duh ring*
shaky; tottering; feeble

Twenty-six states do not require so much as a license to drive, while only seventeen out of the forty-eight states require any instruction or demonstration of fitness; and in most of these seventeen states anyone, from a doddering old man to a sixteen-year-old girl who can back a car around twice in the same half hour without maiming the teacher, is entitled to a license.

Seth K. Humphrey   December 1931

doggerel *DAW guh ruhl*
trivial, awkward, often comic verse characterized by a monotonous rhythm;
any trivial or bad poetry

Naturally, when I pick up a newspaper these days, the first place I turn to isn't sports, or arts, or the business of business, or the op-eds. I immediately turn to the obituaries. The old doggerel with which many mature readers may be acquainted has become my mantra.

> I wake up each morning and gather my wits,
> I pick up the paper and read the obits.
> If my name is not in it, I know I'm not dead,
> So I eat a good breakfast and go back to bed.

Studs Terkel   October 2001

dogma *DAWG muh*
a set of unquestioned assertions or attitudes, religious or otherwise; doctrine

In spite of the brilliance of Southern Agrarian poets like Allen Tate, John Crowe Ransom, John Peale Bishop, and Robert Penn Warren, none of them has ever won a Pulitzer Prize for poetry. The heroic refusal by the judges to recognize persistent merit however great is almost enough to make even a Yankee share the slightly paranoid Southern literary dogma that New York's control of the business side of literature is used to discriminate against Southern writers.

Arthur Mizener   July 1957

✳ Robert Penn Warren won the Pulitzer Prize for poetry in 1958 and 1979.

dolt *dohlt*
a dull, stupid person

A number of years ago Mort Walker, the cartoonist, gave me a pencil sketch of one of his *Beetle Bailey* comic strips. It shows the character Plato, the strip's intellectual, talking to Zero, the strip's dolt. They are putting some of Plato's books on a shelf, and Zero asks if Plato has read them all. Yes, mostly, Plato says. What's in them?, Zero wonders. Plato replies, "All the knowledge of the past on which we can base our actions in the future." And Zero asks, "What if some of the pages get stuck together?"

Cullen Murphy   July/August 2003

doomsayer *DOO:M say er*
a prophet of doom, especially one of political or economic disaster

The doomsayers who see in television the death of literacy sound very much like the nineteenth-century critics who thought that photography would be the end of painting. But television and radio are now the principal means for disseminating political information to a large public. Consequently, it is increasingly important for people to know how to listen critically and how to evaluate spoken arguments.

Geoffrey Nunberg   December 1983

doppelgänger   *DAH puhl gayng ger*
a ghostly double of a living person: German, doppel, *double* + ganger, *goer*

Graham Greene once wrote a celebrated essay about a *doppelgänger* who cared enough to haunt and shadow him, even to masquerade as him. This "other" Greene appeared to have anterior knowledge of the movements of his model, sometimes showing up to grant an interview or fill a seat in a restaurant, so that Greene himself, when he arrived in some old haunt or new locale, would be asked why he had returned so soon.

Christopher Hitchens   March 2005

dovetail   *DUHV tayl*
to fit together closely or harmoniously

Western communism's first break with Moscow was made by the Italians in the 1970s, under Enrico Berlinguer, who invented Eurocommunism — a liberal, free-flying Marxism designed to dovetail with capitalism.

David Lawday   August 1990

dramatis personae   *DRAH muh tis per SOH nee*
the characters in a play, or a list of them

In the diurnal drama of a major city it is often the minor players in the long list of dramatis personae that provide the spectator with the most entertainment. Dickens knew it and proved it. Of all the characters in his novels, we enjoy most and remember best the obscure eccentrics, not his heroes, heroines, and villains.

John Shand   September 1946

droll   *drohl*
oddly amusingly; offbeat

Sojourner stayed several days with us, a welcome guest. Her conversation was so strong, simple, shrewd, and with such a droll flavoring of humor, that the Professor was wont to say of an evening, "Come, I am dull, can't you get Sojourner up here to talk a little?" She would come up into the parlor, and sit among pictures and ornaments, in her simple stuff gown, with her heavy travelling shoes, the central object of attention both to parents and children, always ready to talk or to sing, and putting into the common flow of conversation the keen edge of some shrewd remark.

Harriet Beecher Stowe   April 1863

✳ Sojourner Truth (1797-1883) was born into slavery as Isabella Baumfree, near Kingston, New York, and escaped from the last of five masters in 1826, a year before New York outlawed slavery. As a free woman she worked as a domestic servant until 1843, when a vision inspired her to become an itinerant preacher. At first she adopted only one name, Sojourner. Later, when she was told she had to have a second name, she chose Truth, as a sign of her religious mission. Although illiterate, she was an eloquent speaker, riveting her audiences at anti-slavery meetings and church services in free states with accounts of her life as a slave and her views on slavery and women's rights. Harriet Beecher Stowe considered her the most magnetic person she had ever met, a "great warm soul," and was among many who felt privileged to have her stay in their home.

drone   *drohn*

a continuous and monotonous humming or buzzing

I woke recently, in the unfamiliar and unfurnished silence of a new apartment, into a hyperawareness of the music around me. Without recourse to radio, tapes, CDs, or television, I suddenly found myself aware of — no, *listening* to — a sort of secondhand music emanating from the machines and appliances nearby. My alarm clock woke me that morning, as it does every working day, on a distinctly musical note (B natural, to be precise). I shuffled sleepily to the refrigerator, which kept up a stoic hum (B-flat) as I reached into its guts for a frozen bagel. The bagel I subjected to the resolute drone (E) of the microwave, which concluded its efforts with a *ding!* (the B-flat an octave above the refrigerator hum) just as my teakettle began to whistle (A). Later that morning my subway train pulled me into town with a weary whine (F), and the office elevator deposited me on my floor with a relieved *bleep* (C-sharp). I entered the code (C) of the security system with a staccato flourish and was at work.

Toby Lester   April 1997

dross   *drawss*

waste matter; worthless stuff

Aspiring, toward the end of my nonage, to the black robes of a dramatic critic, I took counsel with an ancient whose service went back to the days of Our American Cousin, asking him what qualities were chiefly demanded by the craft. "The main idea," he told me frankly, "is to be interesting, to write a good story. All else is dross.

Of course, I am not against accuracy, fairness, information, learning. If you want to read Lessing and Freytag, Hazlitt and Brunetière, go read them: they will do you no harm. It is also useful to know something about Shakespeare. But unless you can make people *read* your criticisms, you may as well shut up your shop. And the only way to make them read you is to give them something exciting."

H. L. Mencken   March 1914

dullard   *DUH luhrd*
a person who is not very bright; a dolt

King George III., whose virtues would have shone radiantly in a narrow sphere and a lowly station, was a conscientious dullard, with so little intellect that there was no room for him to wander in his mind, and there was no need of his going far to wander out of it. He was the prime cause and mover of American independence.

Andrew Preston Peabody   September 1888

dunderhead   *DUHN der hed*
a stupid or foolish person; blockhead; numbskull ("dunderheaded" is the adjective)

After my first term at school, I settled down — it seemed for life — in a dunces' class, under a dunce master. Before long, I had reached a state of dunderheaded despair, out of the depths of which I could not rise. I could, for instance, pass no examination, since, in order for me to do my best, or even tolerably well at anything, I had then — as I have today — to be congratulated very warmly and at frequent intervals upon my performance.

Sir Osbert Sitwell   April 1946

dupe   *doo:p*
a deception or trick

I find men victims of illusion in all parts of life. Children, youths, adults, and old men, all are led by one bawble or another. Yoganidra, the goddess of illusion, Proteus, or Momus, or Gylfi's Mocking,— for the Power has many names, — is stronger than the Titans, stronger than Apollo. The toys, to be sure, are various, and are graduated in refinement to the quality of the dupe. The intellectual man requires a fine bait; the sots are easily amused. But everybody is drugged with his own dream, and the pageant marches at all hours, with music and banner and badge.

Ralph Waldo Emerson   November 1857

duplicity   *doo: PLI suh tee*
falseness; deception

In this kingdom of illusions we grope eagerly for stays and foundations. There is none but a strict and faithful dealing at home, and a severe barring out of all duplicity and illusion there. Whatever games are played with us, we must play no games with ourselves, but deal in our privacy with the last honesty and truth. I look upon the simple and childish virtues of veracity and honesty as the root of all that is sublime in character. Speak as you think, be what you are, pay your debts of all kinds.

Ralph Waldo Emerson   November 1857

epigone

Every successful modern play (aesthetically successful, that is) reinvents the theater. For a while the theater, rescued from intellectual disgrace, can exist again, but then the avant-garde, having defined a new reality onstage, repeats itself, or the imitators and epigones take over, and soon someone has to come up with a new definition of theater. Beckett, it turns out, devised the perfect title not only for his play but also for twentieth-century drama: *Endgame*.

David Denby   January 1985

see page 158

éclat *ay KLAH*

brilliant or conspicuous success; great acclamation or applause; renown

If the sin of self-quotation can be pardoned, this is how I described the young Mencken in my introduction to his posthumously published journalistic memoir, *My Life as Author and Editor*: "He was a force of nature, brushing aside all objects animal and mineral in his headlong rush to the éclat that surely awaited him. He seized each day, shook it to within an inch of its life, then gaily went on to the next."

Jonathan Yardley   December 2002

eddy *E dee*

a drift or tendency that is counter to or separate from a main current

Some people welcome poetry anthologies, for they shorten the task of choosing what to read. I dislike them, in general, preferring to make choices for myself. (I've got to confess, moreover, that I don't even much like reading poems in magazines. I prefer the open waters of a *Collected Poems*, or the eddies of a slim volume, by a single author, where I hope for the excitement of hauling out a slippery, glittering catch.)

Peter Davison   June 1998

edict *EE dikt*

an official public order issued by an authority and having the force of law; decree

Like any authoritarian state, the People's Republic of China has the power to enforce its edicts and protect official ideology by absolute control of education and all regular mass media. A vast supplementary network of village radio receivers and loudspeakers, housetop megaphone recasts, and door-to-door agents of oral propaganda carries official news, slogans, rousing songs, and propaganda skits to the illiterate in remote rural areas.

Harriet C. Mills   December 1959

efface   *uh FAYS*
to rub out; erase

He lived his last years imprisoned by age, and now that the iron gates of life are opened, his spirit soars to the liberty he lived for. Nothing survives — not marble nor gilded monuments at Westminster Abbey, not even pyramids enclosing pharaohs. Only legend remains, and Sir Winston's legend is as secure as that of any hero who fought and triumphed over evil. His fame will last when records are effaced, till legends become fables, and fables histories.

Lady Diana Cooper   March 1965

to make oneself inconspicuous; withdraw from notice

It is a good thing to accustom a child early to be alone. It is during the long glorious hours of solitary play that he does his hardest thinking. For him as for us the world may be too much with him. If we could but learn merely to supply him the incentive in the form of book or garden or personal suggestion, and then leave the leaven to work. If we elders could but have a little more faith in nature, a little more strength to efface ourselves and let our children alone. Here is an element of education that all the text-books seem to have overlooked. If we could but learn — well, some day we shall, perhaps.

Robert M. Gay   August 1912

effect   *uh FEKT*
to bring about; accomplish; cause

In 1818, Illinois, then having a population of about forty-five thousand, was admitted into the Union. The State was formed out of that territory which by the Ordinance of 1787 was dedicated to freedom; but there was a strong party in the State who wished for the introduction of slavery, and in order to effect this it was necessary to call a convention to amend the Constitution. On this arose a desperate contest between the two principles, and it ended in the triumph of freedom. Among those opposed to the introduction of slavery were Morris Birkbeck, Governor Coles, David Blackwell, Judge Lockwood, and Daniel P. Cook. It was a fitting memorial of the latter, that the County of Cook, containing the great commercial city of Chicago, should bear his name. The names of the pro-slavery leaders we will leave to oblivion.

Thomas Curtis Clarke   May 1861

effervescence   *e fuhr VE suhns*
high spirits; liveliness

Morocco has a lot of capitals. First in history is Fez, first in size and riches is Casablanca, first in politics is Rabat, and first in effervescence and beauty is Marrakesh.

Keith Williams   January 1965

effete   *e FEET*
depleted of vitality; lacking force of character or moral stamina; worn out; decadent

How can any noble literature germinate where young men are habitually taught that there is no such thing as originality, and that nothing remains for us in this effete epoch of history but the mere recombining of thoughts which sprang first from braver brains?

Thomas Wentworth Higginson   January 1870

efflorescence   *e flaw RE sins*
flowering; blooming

When I sat down to write the first paper I sent to *The Atlantic Monthly*, I felt somewhat as a maiden of more than mature efflorescence may be supposed to feel as she paces down the broad aisle, in her bridal veil and with her wreath of orange-blossoms. I had written little of late years. I was at that time older than Goldsmith was when he died; and Goldsmith, as Dr. Johnson said, was a plant that flowered late. A new generation had grown up since I had written the verses by which, if remembered at all, I was best known. I honestly feared that I might prove the superfluous veteran who has no business behind the footlights. I can as honestly say that it turned out otherwise; I was most kindly welcomed.

Oliver Wendell Holmes   January 1883

✳ Oliver Wendell Holmes's poems, essays and articles appeared in *The Atlantic* from the magazine's first issue, in November 1857, until he died at age 85 in 1894. His best-known poem, "Old Ironsides," appeared in the *Boston Daily Advertiser* in 1830 as a plea not to scrap the fighting ship *U.S.S. Constitution*, and saved it. It was Holmes who suggested *The Atlantic Monthly* as the magazine's name.

eidolon   *igh DOH luhn*
an idealized image of someone or something: Greek, eidolon, *an image*

Every living author has a projection of himself, a sort of eidolon, that goes about in near and remote places making friends or enemies for him among persons who never lay eyes upon the writer in the flesh. When he dies, this phantasmal personality fades away, and the author lives only in the impression created by his own literature. It is only then that the world begins to perceive what manner of man the poet, the novelist, or the historian really was. Not until he is dead, and perhaps some long time dead, is it possible for the public to take his exact measure.

Thomas Bailey Aldrich   December 1902

eldritch *EL drich*

weird; eerie

Out of the shadows of the past comes another memory, the picture of that strange old Salem homestead which has been made known to fame as the House of the Seven Gables. Some alterations have done away with two of the gables, but the old house is otherwise unchanged. In the days of my childhood its mistress was a lonely woman, about whom hung the mystery of one whose solitude is peopled by the weird visions that opium brings. We regarded her with something of awe, and I have wondered, in later days, what strange and eldritch beings walked with her about those shadowy rooms, or flitted noiselessly up and down the fine old staircase.

Eleanor Putnam   February 1886

elegy *E luh jee*

a poem or song of lament and praise for one who is dead

Death places his icy democratic hand on kings, heroes, and paupers, and now the free world and the enslaved will register with mourning or contempt the passing of Winston Churchill. Stones will be graven, elegies voiced from platforms and pulpits, the muffled drums will roll, the arms will be reversed, the hatchments put up, the last post sounded.

Lady Diana Cooper   March 1965

> ⁂ During World War II, the phrase "the free world," as used by the United States and its allies, referred to those countries not under the domination of Germany or Japan. Between World War II and the fall of Communism in the Soviet Union and its satellite countries, "the free world" was a phrase Western democracies used to describe the non-Communist nations.

elucidate *i LOO: suh dayt*

to make clear; throw light upon; explain

All our best English literature is shot through and through with Biblical quotations, maxims, metaphors, characters, allusions; the one book with which a reader needs to have familiar acquaintance is the English Bible. It is ridiculous for any one to undertake to teach English literature who does not know his Bible at least as well as he knows his Shakespeare. On the pages he is undertaking to elucidate he will meet the Bible five times where he will meet Shakespeare once.

Walter Prichard Eaton   January 1915

elude   *i LOO:D*
to avoid or escape through quickness and cunning; evade

In 1896 Congress appropriated funds for construction of the first federal penitentiary, to be located on more than 1,500 acres in rural Kansas, a few miles from the Army base at Fort Leavenworth. The new prison was built by the convicts who would soon occupy it. In the eighty-eight years since it opened, only one prisoner has ever escaped from Leavenworth and eluded recapture.

Eric Schlosser   September 1994

emanate   *E muh nayt*
to come forth from a source; issue ("emanation" is the noun)

It is the tendency of all creeds, opinions, and political dogmas that have once defined themselves in institutions to become inoperative. The vital and formative principle, which was active during the process of crystallization into sects, or schools of thought, or governments, ceases to act; and what was once a living emanation of the Eternal Mind, organically operative in history, becomes the dead formula on men's lips and the dry topic of the annalist.

James Russell Lowell   October 1860

embattled   *im BA tuhld*
under attack

Did they grow Gold of Ophir in your old home garden? Robert Fortune found that rose on his first journey to China in 1843. Disguising himself as a coolie to enter the forbidden city of Soochow, haggling endlessly with polite, bowing, wily growers, fighting off river pirates from his embattled junk, he got for us our forsythias, white wisterias, camellias, chrysanthemums, pompon daisies, peonies, autumns anemones, and this burning-hearted rose.

Donald Culross Peattie   June 1953

✿ The forsythia was named in honor of William Forsyth (1737-1804), a much admired British botanist. Other flowers named for people include:

begonia	Michel Bégon (1638-1710), governor of Canada and French patron of botany
camellia	George Josef Kamel (1661-1706), Moravian Jesuit missionary
dahlia	Anders Dahl (1751-1789), Swedish botanist
freesia	F. H. T. Freese (d. 1876), German physician
fuchsia	Leonard Fuchs (1501-1566), German botanist
gardenia	Alexander Garden (1730-1791), Scottish-American botanist
magnolia	Pierre Magnol (1638-1715), French botanist
poinsettia	Joel Roberts Poinsett (1779-1851), U.S. minister to Mexico
wisteria	Casper Wistar (1761-1818), American anatomist
zinnia	Johann Gottfried Zinn (1727-1759), German botanist

embodiment   *em BAH dee muhnt*
the concrete expression of an idea

About a hundred years ago saddles were elevated from cowhands' working tools to dream objects that signified the frontier. Thanks to the romantic image of the West created by mythmakers as varied as Teddy Roosevelt, Buffalo Bill Cody, and the railroad magnate Fred Harvey, and also to a spate of pop-culture frontier heroes in books and weekly magazines, cowpunchers began to see themselves — and their gear — as the embodiment of freedom, independence, and adventure. Saddle shops, which had grown up throughout the West wherever the cattle business went, issued catalogues showing saddles far more handsome than any working ranch hand needed. The catalogues came to be known in the cowboy fraternity as bunkhouse bibles, and were studied and memorized by men for whom their contents were fantasies.

Jane and Michael Stern   July 1998

embroil   *im BROYL*
to involve or entangle in conflict or difficulties

The issue of homosexuality has arrived at the forefront of America's political consciousness. The nation is embroiled in debate over the acceptance of openly gay soldiers in the U.S. military. It confronts a growing number of cases in the courts over the legal rights of gay people with respect to marriage, adoption, insurance, and inheritance. It has seen referenda opposing gay rights reach the ballot in two states and become enacted in one of them — Colorado, where local ordinances banning discrimination against homosexuals were repealed. The issue of homosexuality has always been volatile, and it is sure to continue to inflame political passions.

Chandler Burr   March 1993

emendation   *ee muhn DAY shuhn*
a correction or change to a text

In 1849, the discovery by Mr. Payne Collier of a copy of the Works of Shakspeare, known as the folio of 1632, with manuscript notes and emendations of the same or nearly the same date, created a great and general interest in the world of letters. The marginal notes were said to be in a handwriting not much later than the period when the volume came from the press; and Shakspearian scholars and students of Shakspeare, and the far more numerous class, lovers of Shakspeare, learned and unlearned, received with respectful eagerness a version of his text claiming a date so near to the lifetime of the master that it was impossible to resist the impression that the alterations came to the world with only less weight of authority than if they had been undoubtedly his own.

Frances Anne Kemble   September 1860

emolument   *i MAHL yoo muhnt*
payment received for work; remuneration; compensation

In the quaint little bow-windowed office at 186, Strand, Dickens and the publishers worked out their arrangements. From a letter of February 10, 1836, to Catherine Hogarth, soon to become his wife, we learn that Chapman and Hall "have made me an offer of £14 *a month* to write and edit a new publication they contemplate, entirely by myself; to be edited monthly and each number to contain four woodcuts. I am to make my estimate and calculation, and to give them a decisive answer on Friday morning. The work will be no joke, but the emolument is too tempting to resist."

Clifton Fadiman   December 1949

✻ What Dickens wrote for Chapman and Hall's magazine was *The Pickwick Papers*, his first full-length work of fiction, published as a monthly serial between April 1836 and November 1837 under the pseudonym Boz. Out of 1,000 copies of the first installment, about 50 were sold. The second part sold even fewer. It wasn't until the fifth part, when the character of Sam Weller entered the story, that sales leaped to the tens of thousands. Part Fifteen sold 40,000 copies. The story was published as a book in 1837; Dickens was 25.

empiricism   *em PI ruh si zuhm*
the view that all knowledge is derived from experience rather than reason

For many, the urge to believe in transcendental existence and immortality is overpowering. Transcendentalism, especially when reinforced by religious faith, is psychically full and rich; it feels somehow right. By comparison, empiricism seems sterile and inadequate. In the quest for ultimate meaning the transcendentalist route is much easier to follow. That is why, even as empiricism is winning the mind, transcendentalism continues to win the heart.

Edward O. Wilson   April 1998

enamored   *e NA muhrd*
captivated; in love with

Betterton was the son of a cook in the service of Charles I. He went on the stage in 1659, when he was twenty-four years old and first played Hamlet two years after his debut. His Ophelia was the charming Mistress Sanderson, of whom he was known to be enamored, and the town was as much interested in the real as the mimic lovers. They were married shortly after, and the young Hamlet found in his Ophelia a sweet and devoted wife. She is said to have been the first woman who appeared on the public stage.

Abby Sage   June 1869

> ✳ In 17th-century England, mistress was the honorable title for an unmarried woman. Miss was applied to a man's mistress or a prostitute, a meaning that held into the late 19th century.

encomium   *en KOH mee uhm*
a formal expression of high praise

It is the dismissive review that we remember, the clever deflation, the impudent reappraisal of an honored name — not Dr. Johnson's encomium to Pope, but his observation of *Paradise Lost* that "no one ever wished it longer."

James Atlas   August 1981

enduring   *in DOOR ing*
lasting

Forty-nine years ago an out-of-work Connecticut man named David Nelson Mullany cut holes in a hard plastic orb of Coty perfume packaging with the intention of creating a marketable ball for kids that wouldn't break windows and would curve easily. Neither he nor his thirteen-year-old son, David, who helped him experiment with different designs, could have foreseen that their creation would become one of the most enduring toys in American history.

Lee Green   June 2002

> ✳ When David Mullany asked his son what they should name the plastic ball with the holes in it, his son repled "whiffle," for the slang word whiff, meaning strike out. But he suggested they spell it without the h. "If we ever have to make a sign for over the door," he explained, "that's one less letter we'll have to pay for."

enervate *E ner vayt*

to weaken or destroy the strength or vitality of ("enervated" is the adjective)

In my first article I told you how Dore and I came to the desert island of Floreana in the Galapagos, having resolved to turn our backs forever upon civilization and establish for ourselves a solitude in the far Pacific. This spot is ideally suited to our purposes. We enjoy a tropical climate which is warm enough to enable us to go entirely without clothes, like the original Adam and Eve in the first earthly paradise, and at the same time cool enough, because of the constant trade winds, to keep us from becoming sluggish and enervated.

Friedrich Ritter   November 1931

enfant terrible *ahn fahn te REE bluh*

one whose behavior, work or thinking disturbs others and mocks conventional opinion: French, an unmanageable, mischievous child

The reason we got along so well in the house was because of our mutually organic — meaning the organs were functioning but not much else — natures when off parade. The home was to Dylan, more especially, a private sanctum where for once he was not compelled, by himself admittedly, to put on an act, to be amusing, to perpetuate the myth of the *enfant terrible* — one of the most damaging myths, and a curse to grow out of.

Caitlin Thomas   June 1957

✴ When Dylan Thomas (1914-1953) died, a tribute by Edith Sitwell appeared in the February 1954 *Atlantic* in which she described a supper with Thomas and his wife, Caitlin, after a poetry reading in London. "Their mutual love was most touching to see," she wrote. "He looked across the table at his young wife, with her bright sparkling hair that seemed to hold all the color of a spring day, her wild-rose cheeks and dancing blue eyes, and exclaimed to me, 'Isn't she beautiful! *Isn't she beautiful!* From the first moment I saw her, she has been the only one. There never has been, there never will be, anyone but her.'"

engender *en JEN der*

to bring about; cause; produce

> Georgie Porgie, pudding and pie,
> Kissed the girls and made them cry.
> When the boys came out to play,
> Georgie Porgie ran away.

An interesting illustration of the state of affairs all too prevalent under the bourgeois sex morality. Here, instead of innocent and natural love play, we see the attitude engendered by the parental teaching of shame. Georgie, though from his cognomen we may assume him to be somewhat heavy and phlegmatic, is possessed of normal instincts and emotions. When, however, he proceeds to allow these their natural expression, the girls, warped by a perverse morality, pretend pain instead of plea-sure. This, of course, has its effect upon Georgie, who, finding his natural feelings inhibited, becomes introverted and shuns the society of his playmates.

Bergen Evans   December 1934

✳ See also avarice, delectation, obviate and sullen for other passages in which Bergen Evans provides his tongue-in-cheek analyses of nursery rhymes.

engross   *in GROHS*
to absorb or engage the whole attention of ("engrossing" is the adjective)

The sudden death of Calvin Coolidge brought out rather pathetically the emptiness of his last days. He went early to his office, but there was nothing to do. He went home again, and there was nothing to do. He went down and watched the handy man shovel coal on the furnace. He was sixty years old and apparently had no engrossing interest.

Earnest Elmo Calkins   May 1933

enjoin   *en JOIN*
to direct or order to do something with authority and emphasis; prohibit; forbid

The ancient Hippocratic Oath enjoins physicians to "neither give a deadly drug to anybody if asked for it, nor make a suggestion to this effect." The oath was written at a time when physicians commonly provided euthanasia and assisted suicide for ailments ranging from foot infections and gallstones to cancer and senility. Indeed, the Hippocratic Oath represented the *minority* view in a debate within the ancient Greek medical community over the ethics of euthanasia.

Ezekiel Emanuel   March 1997

en masse   *ahn MAS*
in a group; all together

Perhaps the most amazing phenomenon at Wimbledon is the tea hour. Promptly at half-past four every afternoon there is a sudden buzz and rising in the stands much like the seventh-inning stretching at an American baseball game. This is the Children's Hour, and the children are going to have tea. "Silence, please," calls the umpire from his chair, but the buzz and hum continues like the noise in an apiary, until half the seats are empty. They pour out en masse to the tea garden in the rear, where black-frocked odalisques of the Messrs. Lyons lean over them asking the discreet question which is heard throughout the British Empire: — "India or China, please?"

John R. Tunis   September 1937

✳ The term odalisques seems too strong a word to describe the whole-some-looking, primly-dressed waitresses employed by J. Lyons & Co., which operated hundreds of tea shops and restaurants in England from 1894 until 1974. While an odalisque is defined in the *Oxford English Dictionary* originally as "a female slave or concubine in a harem, esp. in the seraglio of the Sultan of Turkey," and later as "an exotic, sexually attractive woman," Lyons waitresses were uniformed more like today's hotel housekeepers, in black dresses with white apron fronts, white collars and cuffs, and a small cap. A Lyons wait-ress was officially known as a Nippy, a word derived from her quick service — and an entry in the *OED*, defined as "a waitress."

ennui   *ahn WEE*
weariness and dissatisfaction resulting from inactivity or lack of interest in present surroundings; boredom

One of Ireland's countless gifts to English letters, Oscar Wilde was born in Dublin in 1854 (two years before Bernard Shaw, eleven before W. B. Yeats, and twenty-eight before James Joyce; has any other city ever produced such a crop within the space of three decades?). From Trinity College, Dublin, he proceeded to Oxford and a bril-liant English debut. After graduating he was at loose ends, going to "the Hicks-Beachs' in Hampshire, to kill time and pheasants and the *ennui* of not having set the world quite on fire as yet," but he hadn't long to wait.

Geoffrey Wheatcroft   May 2003

enormity   *i NAWR muh tee*
great wickedness; a monstrous offense or evil

The enormity of the Bolshevist threat looms up on us; it rocks the foundations of the world.

Herbert Wilton Stanley   March 1919

entertain   *en tuhr TAYN*
to allow oneself to think about; have in mind; consider; contemplate

It had not been Santayana's intention to publish *The Last Puritan* during his lifetime. But when his publishers got wind of the fact that the manuscript was nearly ready by the summer of 1934, they naturally clamored for the right to publish it as soon as possible. Santayana could not make up his mind what to do. He never for a moment entertained the idea that the book might become a howling success; his only concern was to keep it on as high a level as possible, so that his friends would not think that he had made a mistake in turning novelist for a season. I remember his saying to me: "I don't care a hang what the general public think of the book, as long as my friends — both personal and in the spirit — don't feel that I was foolish to attempt such a thing at all."

Daniel Cory   May 1944

entrepôt   *AHN truh poh*
a commercial center

By Indian standards Calcutta is young, dating back to the arrival of the British, in the seventeenth century. From then until independence the city was an abode of great wealth and sophistication, a regional entrepôt and a locus of power, and home to an educated elite. It was Partition, in which the majority-Muslim territory to the east broke away from India and became East Pakistan (later Bangladesh), that sent millions of refugees into Calcutta and gave it a reputation for poverty. Ever since, predictions of collapse, implosion, and urban Armageddon have been made about it, but Calcutta goes on.

Jeffrey Tayler   November 1999

envisage   *en VI zij*
to conceive an image or a picture of as a future possibility

No world government of the character envisaged by Professor Einstein could function unless it possessed the power to exercise complete control over the armaments of each constituent state, and unless every nation was willing to open up every inch of its territory and every one of its laboratories and factories to a continuing international inspection.

Sumner Welles   January 1946

epigone   *E puh gohn*
a second-rate imitator or follower, especially of an important writer, artist, musician or philosopher

Every successful modern play (aesthetically successful, that is) reinvents the theater. For a while the theater, rescued from intellectual disgrace, can exist again, but then the avant-garde, having defined a new reality onstage, repeats itself, or the imitators and epigones take over, and soon someone has to come up with a new definition of theater. Beckett, it turns out, devised the perfect title not only for his play but also for twentieth-century drama: *Endgame*.

David Denby   January 1985

epigraph   *E puh graf*
a brief quotation at the beginning of a book

Ann Sexton in *All My Pretty Ones* (Houghton Mifflin, $3.00 cloth; $1.50 paperback) cannot be accused of a lack of seriousness. As her epigraph she quotes Kafka: "the books we need are the kind that act upon us like a misfortune.... A book should serve as the ax for the frozen sea within us."

Peter Davison   November 1962

epistemology   *uh pis tuh MAH luh jee*
the study of the nature, sources and limits of knowledge ("epistemological" is the adjective)

The principles of the open society are admirably put forth in the Declaration of Independence. But the Declaration states, "We hold these truths to be self-evident," whereas the principles of the open society are anything but self-evident; they need to be established by convincing arguments. There is a strong epistemological argument, elaborated by Karl Popper, in favor of the open society: Our understanding is inherently imperfect; the ultimate truth, the perfect design for society, is beyond our reach. We must therefore content ourselves with the next best thing — a form of social organization that falls short of perfection but holds itself open to improvement. That is the concept of the open society: a society open to improvement.

George Soros   January 1998

equilibrium   *ee kwuh LI bree uhm*
the condition of equal balance between opposing forces

Sake to an American seems little more than spring water, but the Japanese, whose wits are more delicately poised than our own, lose their equilibrium more easily, and *sake* drunk in cumulative sips represents to them infinitesimal gradations between sober-sidedness and that spontaneous exhilaration which for one hour at least makes a man a hero to himself, transforms a chance gathering into a brotherhood, and metamorphoses this stable world into the unsubstantial fairy place of the poet's dream.

Ellery Sedgwick   October 1930

equitable   *E kwuh tuh buhl*
even-handed; fair

A mathematician friend of mine remarked the other day that his daughter, aged eight, had just stumbled without his teaching onto the fact that some numbers are prime numbers — those, like 11 or 19 or 83 or 1023, that cannot be divided by any other integer (except, trivially, by 1). "She called them 'unfair' numbers," he said.

"And when I asked her why they were unfair, she told me, 'Because there's no way to share them out evenly.'" What delighted him most was not her charming turn of phrase nor her equitable turn of mind (seventeen peppermints to give to her friends?) but — as a mathematician — the knowledge that the child had experienced a moment of pure scientific perception. She had discovered for herself something of the way things are.

Horace Freeland Judson   April 1980

erstwhile   *ERST wighl*
once, but no longer; former

Shall I bemoan the fate of the poor little sons of the erstwhile rich, whose fathers have suddenly lost their incomes and can no longer be drawn upon *ad libitum* for runabouts, outboard motors, imported skis, and tuxedos? Or shall I pity the fathers who (like me) cannot get to Bermuda for their March golf?

Walter Prichard Eaton   June 1932

esoterica   *e suh TE ri kuh*
knowledge intended for, or understood by, only a small group or inner circle

In preparing *Foucault's Pendulum*, Eco assembled a library of some 1,500 volumes on black magic, astrology, alchemy, and mysticism. He has stuffed as much of his library of esoterica as would fit between the covers of *Foucault's Pendulum*, including a list of 720 variations in the Hebrew name of God, the mathematical dimensions of the Egyptian pyramids, the prophecies of Nostradamus, the "Protocols of the Elders of Zion," and the rituals of the Brazilian macumba.

Alexander Stille   November 1989

etiology   *ee tee AH luh jee*
the cause or origin of something

About 300 children fell ill with stomach cramps and hallucinations and then lost their hair in the Ukrainian city of Chernovtsy in the autumn of 1988. According to *Moscow News*, the illness triggered an exodus from the city, in which parents, desperate to send their offspring to safety, "stormed the railway station, besieged the airport, and battled to get a seat on a bus." In all, 40,000 children were sent away. Whatever its etiology, the affliction known in the USSR today as the "chemical disease" has not disappeared.

Gabriel Schoenfeld   December 1990

etymology   *e tuh MAH luh jee*
the origin and development of a word: Greek, etymon, *word*

In the old days, there was some fun in compiling a dictionary. You had some space for the play of fancy, some scope for the exercise of taste. Having to give the etymology, let us suppose, of 'cribbage,' you looked at the word hard for a while, and noted that, except for two letters, it was exactly like 'cabbage'; and so you wrote on one slip of paper, 'CABBAGE: possibly derived from *cribbage, q.v.*'; and went on to the next word. So far as I can see, the world was just as well off and you were much happier than you could possibly have been if you had, as nowadays, thought it necessary to trace cribbage to the Arabic and cabbage to the Bengalese.

Robert M. Gay   October 1920

euphoria   *yoo: FAW ree uh*
a feeling of well-being or high spirits ("euphoric" is the adjective)

Fifty-one years old, Lincoln was at the peak of his political career, with momentum that would soon sweep him to the nomination of the national party and then to the White House. Yet to the convention audience Lincoln didn't seem **euphoric**, or triumphant, or even pleased. On the contrary, said a man named Johnson, observing from the convention floor, "I then thought him one of the most diffident and worst plagued men I ever saw."

Joshua Wolf Shenk   October 2005

evidence   *E vuh dins*
to indicate; show

To most birds a nest is a comparatively flimsy, temporary affair, used but a few weeks and abandoned forever. But American eagles, mated for life, use the same nest year after year. It is the center of their existence. Few creatures evidence so great an attraction for home. During wartime years one pair stubbornly clung to its nesting tree even though it stood in the middle of a practice bombing range. The Great Eyrie, near Vermilion, Ohio, was occupied for thirty-six years without a break.

Edwin Way Teale   November 1957

✳ Eyrie is a variant spelling of aerie, the nest of an eagle or other bird of prey built on a high place. It can also describe a penthouse or a house located on a cliff or mountainside. While etymologists have suggested varying derivations of aerie, the *Oxford English Dictionary* says it probably derives either from a Latin word meaning "a spot of level ground or an open place," or from the Latin *atrium*, a court or the central hall of a house. Eyrie is a variant spelling based on an incorrect theory in the 17th century that the word derived from egg.

evince   *ee VINS*
to show plainly; indicate or be evidence of

Archaeological evidence indicates that bands of modern and archaic people some-times lived near each other for thousands of years. Yet no remnants of warfare have been found. The cave paintings of Europe, some of which date from the period when modern people were replacing Neanderthals, evince plenty of violence against animals but not against other people.

Steve Olson   April 2001

exalt   *ig ZAWLT*
to raise in value or excellence; praise highly ("exaltation"is the noun)

The paradox underlying all of Kipling's work, whether it be his letters, his poetry, or his stories, is a horror of democracy combined with an exaltation of the common man. He always ostensibly preferred the grunt or the ranker to the officer, the hum-ble colonial servant to the viceroy, the stoker and the sailor to the admiral.

Christopher Hitchens   June 2002

excoriate   *eks KAW ree ayt*
denounce harshly

Most of those who write about American history can be divided into two camps. Those who follow the orthodox line tend toward the panegyric, celebrating America's past, while revisionists excoriate it and condemn its exploitation of minorities and women. Neither approach leads to a subtle understanding of history.

Benjamin Schwarz   March 1997

excrescence   *ek SKRE suhns*
a growth that sticks out from the body of a human, animal or plant

The chief fact of a moose's person is that pair of strange excrescences, his horns. Like fronds of tree-fern, like great corals or sea-fans, these great palmated plates of bone lift themselves from his head, grand, useless, clumsy.

Theodore Winthrop   November 1862

exculpate   *EKS kuhl payt*
to free from blame; prove innocent of guilt or fault

Some Kennedy aides have always insisted that Johnson misread JFK's plans for Vietnam. They say that Kennedy had begun to rethink the U.S. presence in Indochina, and was reluctant to increase it. Johnson's defenders have tended to see this argument as wishful thinking by those who seek to exculpate JFK from what happened in Vietnam while laying all the blame on LBJ.

Robert Dallek   June 2003

exigency   *EK suh jin see*
an urgent or pressing need

There is no department of literature more fascinating to the general reader than biography. When a well-known character himself relates the story of his life, the interest is greatly increased. But when through his correspondence we obtain unpremeditated glimpses of his heart or the development of his career, we reach a mine that yields profit not only of interest, but sometimes of incalculable historic value. The exigencies of the rapid life of this century are rendering these sources of historic record more and more rare. Johnson said, "We travel no more; we only arrive at places." Thus we of the nineteenth century may say in turn, "We correspond no more; we only telegraph."

Samuel Green Wheeler Benjamin   January 1888

ex nihilo   *eks NIGH uh loh*
from or out of nothing

Glittering St. Petersburg! Peter the Great's new capital on the flat marshlands of the Gulf of Finland, known informally as Petersburg and fondly as Peter, created *ex nihilo* by imperial fiat in 1703, was the Czar's "window on Europe," under the protection of his patron saint. The proud beauty of this baroque "Venice of the North" was mirrored in the waters of the vast Baltic, the broad Neva, and threading canals. The city was the north's de facto Paris, too, an intellectual and cultural magnet where the language of those who mattered was French.

Matthew Gurewitsch   April 1998

ex officio   *eks uh FI shee oh*
by virtue of one's position: Latin, from office

The Lord Chief Justice of England is *ex officio* the chief coroner of the realm, an office he has held since time immemorial. There is therefore to an English mind something fitting in the idea that the inquiry into the death of President Kennedy, in its scope and importance the greatest inquest that has ever been held, should have been presided over by the Chief Justice of the United States.

Lord Patrick Devlin   March 1965

ex parte   *eks PAHR tee*
in the interest of one side only; partisan; biased

Feminism has been content with demanding the right to vote, to practice politics and hold public office, as men do, and to enter commerce, finance, the learned professions, and the trades, on equal terms with men, and to share men's social privileges and immunities on equal terms. Its contention is that women are able to do as well with all these activities as men can do, and that the opportunity to engage in them is theirs by natural right. This thesis is wholly sound. Every objection I ever heard raised against it has impressed me as *ex parte* and specious — in a word, as disingenuous.

Albert Jay Nock   November 1931

expatiate   *eks PAY shee ayt*
to speak or write in great detail; elaborate or enlarge upon

Walter Bagehot, who used to figure at Crabb Robinson's famous breakfasts, expatiates on Robinson's chin, "a chin of excessive length and portentous power of extension." The old gentleman "made very able use of the chin at a conversational crisis." "Just at the point of the story he pushed it out and then very slowly drew it in again, so that you always knew when to laugh."

Leon H. Vincent   June 1898

expedient   *ik SPEE dee uhnt*
something contrived to meet an urgent need; stratagem

In Mr. Scully's interesting article on the life of the African ostrich, he states that, as regards "the habits of the wild birds, nearly every extant account bristles with inaccuracies." In the next paragraph, he states that "to an unprotected man in the open an infuriated ostrich is as dangerous as a lion." This sentence is itself a "bristling inaccuracy." If, when assailed by the ostrich, the man stands erect, he is in great danger. But by the simple expedient of lying down, he escapes all danger. In such case, the bird may step on him, or sit on him; his clothes will be rumpled and his feelings injured; but he will suffer no bodily harm. I know various men — including Mr. William Beebe — who have had this experience. Does Mr. Scully imagine that an infuriated lion will merely sit on a man who lies down?

Theodore Roosevelt   June 1918

❖ Theodore Roosevelt, who studied and hunted wildlife in Africa after his presidency ended in 1909, is responding to William Charles Scully, whose article, "The Life of the African Ostrich," appeared in *The Atlantic*'s March 1918 issue. Scully's statements appear in this book in the passage for disembowel.

expendable   *ek SPEN duh buhl*

worth sacrificing under certain circumstances; not essential

Interdiction has led law-enforcement officials into an unwitting symbiotic relationship with drug traffickers. The smugglers understand Washington's need to see a steadily rising number of arrests and confiscations. As a result, a smuggler sends into the country not less cocaine but more — divided among several boats, one of which the smuggler considers expendable.

James Lieber   January 1986

exponential   *eks puh NEN shuhl*

increasing by extraordinary proportions ("exponentially" is the adverb)

Advances in molecular biology and imaging techniques have made the brain more accessible than ever before, and basic knowledge is growing exponentially.

Joseph Alper   December 1983

ex post facto   *eks pohst FAK toh*

done or made afterward; retroactive: Latin, from what is done afterward

Shaw appears to many people, especially to women, as a cynic, because he nonchalantly proceeds in the firm belief that, whereas people imagine that their actions and feelings are directed by moral systems, by religious systems, by codes of honor and conventions of conduct which lie outside the real human will, as a matter of fact these conventions do not supply them with their motives but merely serve as very plausible *ex post facto* excuses for their conduct.

Archibald Henderson   February 1909

expostulate   *eks PAHS chuh layt*

to reason earnestly with someone in an effort to dissuade or correct

Every editor, whether of magazines or books, is aware of the sharp divergence in taste which exists between readers now in their thirties and those who are now in their sixties. This divergence is relayed to me in many forms: in letters from our older readers who have been shocked by an *Atlantic* short story; in comments after a lecture by those who who have been bewildered by modern poetry; or in the words of my late mother, who, after struggling through one of the stronger modern novels, expostulated: "I just don't see why I should be expected to hold my nose over an open sewer and pay an author five dollars for the privilege."

Edward Weeks   November 1963

expurgate   *EKS per gayt*
to remove from a book or other work passages considered obscene or otherwise
objectionable; expunge

> Some years ago Frank O'Connor and I agreed on a system. Since we had no intention whatever of restricting students' choice of subject or language, and no desire to expurgate or bowdlerize while reading their stuff aloud for discussion, but at the same time had to deal with these young girls of an age our daughters might have been, we announced that any stuff so strong that it would embarrass us to read it aloud could be read by its own author.

Wallace Stegner   March 1965

extemporize   *eks TEM puh righz*
to compose, speak or perform without preparation; improvise

> Dancing as an art, we may be sure, cannot die out but will always be undergoing a re-birth. Not merely as an art but also as a social custom, it perpetually emerges afresh from the soul of the people. Less than a century ago the polka thus arose, extemporized by the Bohemian servant girl, Anna Slezakova, out of her own head for the joy of her own heart, and only rendered a permanent form, apt for the world-wide popularity, by the accident that it was observed and noted down by an artist.

Havelock Ellis   February 1914

extenuation   *ek sten yoo AY shuhn*
a partial excuse that helps to lessen the seriousness of an act

> New York may not plead its youthfulness forever in extenuation of its vagaries, of course; but it may plead its youthfulness legitimately for some time longer. It is still, whatever airs of manhood it may assume, in the awkward "high-water pants" age of its career, and it is folly to denominate such a callow youth as this an utter reprobate because he displays a tendency to sow wild oats. At his age it is his privilege, if not his function, to be "fresh."

Alvan F. Sanborn   October 1906

> ✳ Fresh, meaning impudent or saucy, comes from the German *frech*, and originated in America in the middle of the 19th century through German-speaking immigrants.

extirpate   *EK ster payt*
to destroy utterly, as though pulled up by the roots; exterminate

A memory which reaches back a quarter of a century wistfully recalls the concept of One World. In those more innocent days it was possible to hope that once the fascists were extirpated, men everywhere would recognize their common humanity and join forces to further their mutual interests. The will to believe, inflated under the pressure of war, blinded Americans, among others, to the intractable problems of the future.

Oscar Handlin   September 1967

extrapolate   *eks TRA puh layt*
to infer unknown information from what is already known ("extrapolated" is the adjective)

The body dimensions of the original Barbie doll were such that if she were life size, the critical measurements would be 38-18-34. But in 1998 Mattel introduced a revised doll, Really Rad Barbie, whose unofficial extrapolated dimensions were 36-24-34, a modest step toward a different ideal.

Cullen Murphy   December 2003

extrude   *eks TROO:D*
to push or force out; expel

Lobstermen realize that producing offspring is a big commitment for a female lobster — up to twenty months of pregnancy and tens of thousands of eggs. At first the eggs develop inside her body, and she may wait for as long as a year after copulation to extrude them. Then she finds a secluded spot, rolls over onto her back, squirts the eggs onto the underside of her tail, and carries them around for another nine to eleven months. When they finally hatch and become larvae, she releases them into the ocean currents.

Trevor Corson   April 2002

exultation   *eks uhl TAY shuhn*
great rejoicing; triumphant joy

On the evening of the 4th of July, 1776, the Declaration of Independence was unanimously adopted by twelve colonies, the delegation from New York still remaining unable to act. But the acquiescence of that colony was so generally counted upon that there was no drawback to the exultation of the people. All over the country the Declaration was received with bonfires, with the ringing of bells and the firing of guns, and with torchlight processions. Now that the great question was settled there was a general feeling of relief. "The people," said Samuel Adams, "seem to recognize this resolution as though it were a decree promulgated from heaven." On the 9th of July it was formally adopted by New York, and the soldiers there threw down the leaden statue of George III on the Bowling Green, and cast it into bullets. Thus, after eleven years of irritation, and after such calm and temperate discussion as befitted a free and noble people, the Americans had at last entered upon the only course that could preserve their self-respect, and guarantee them in the great part which they had to play in the drama of civilization.

John Fiske   November 1888

F

flout

Literary history and all history is a record of the power of minorities, and of minorities of one. Every book is written with a constant secret reference to the few intelligent persons whom the writer believes to exist in the million. The artist has always the masters in his eye, though he affect to flout them. Michel Angelo is thinking of  Da Vinci, and Raffaelle is thinking of Michel Angelo. Tennyson would give his fame for a verdict in his favor from Wordsworth.

Ralph Waldo Emerson   January 1868

see page 180

facile *FA suhl*
done with ease; effortless

To read Mr. Henry James, Jr., is to experience a light but continuous gratification of mind. It is to be intellectually *tickled*, provided one is capable of such an exercise. It is to take a pleasure so simple and facile that it seems only one step removed from physical content in the lavish cleverness of an almost incessantly witty writer, — a pleasure enhanced, no doubt, by a lurking sense that one must be a little clever one's self in order to keep pace with such dazzling mental agility.

Harriet Waters Preston   February 1879

faction *FAK shuhn*
a group of people inside an organization working against other such groups or against the main body; clique ("factional" is the adjective; "factionalize" is the verb)

Today the idea that a President and his Vice President could hail from competing parties is wholly alien. But the Founders had inadvertently made it rather easy for this to happen. When the Constitution was drafted, the two-party system had not yet emerged, and no one especially wanted parties to arise at all. In fact, most of the political theorists on whom the Founders drew had equated party division with factional strife; republics died when leaders factionalized, culminating in the despotic rule of Caesars or Cromwells.

Bruce Ackerman and David Fontana   March 2004

factitious *fak TI shuhs*
lacking authenticity or genuineness; artificial; contrived

For many non-Scots "Scotland" immediately conjures up the Highlands, Rob Roy,

Braveheart, kilts, and bagpipes — images that have nothing to do with most Scottish people for most of the country's history. Not only is this imagery largely factitious and foolish in itself, but the numerous tartans sold to every gullible American tourist named McSomething are the inventions of astute Victorian businessmen.

Geoffrey Wheatcroft   November 1999

fait accompli   *FAY ta kahm PLEE*
something already done, making opposition useless: French, an accomplished fact

Every time Hitler's actions embroiled Italy more deeply in a war that it was not ready to fight, Mussolini privately seethed; but he never had the courage to object or to opt out, until finally it was too late and Germany had become Italy's master. "Hitler always faces me with a fait accompli," the Duce complained. He approved the ill-conceived invasion of Greece in an attempt to impress his rival: "This time I will pay him back with the same coin. He will learn from the papers that I have occupied Greece. Thus the balance will be re-established." The resulting debacle eventually required German intervention, only confirming Italy's subservience.

Francis X. Rocca   July 2000

fallow   *FA loh*
plowed and left unplanted for a season or more; uncultivated; not in use; inactive

Through the range and the quality of Longfellow's life-work he was enabled to perform a spiritual service for his countrymen. He was to become a national, rather than a merely provincial figure. In our imaginations, indeed, he lingers as a lovely flowering of all that was most fair in the New England temperament and training, in that long blossoming season which began with Emerson's Nature and ended — no one knows just when or how — within a decade or two after the close of the Civil War. There is but too much truth in Mr. Oliver Herford's witty description of the present-day New England as the abandoned farm of literature. Apparently the soil must lie fallow for a while, or someone must plough deeper than our melancholy short-story writers seem to go. But when the old orchard was bearing, what bloom and fruitage were hers!

Bliss Perry   March 1907

familiar   *fuh MIL yuhr*
a close friend or associate

When I began to write these pages, before breakfast, the little fig tree outside my window was rejoicing in the early morning light. It is a special familiar of my work, a young tree that has never yet borne fruit.

Donald Culross Peattie   September 1939

farce *fars*
something absurd or ludicrously insincere, as an obvious pretense; a sham;
a mockery

Los Angeles affects to be "dry." There is no affectation about San Francisco: it is, frankly, "wet," and the liquor is of the best. Prohibition there, as elsewhere, is an empty word; and, between the vintages of France and the excellent wine of the country, prohibition officers have no difficulty in making ends meet and, indeed, lap over. Have we not, now, reason to believe that this tragic and expensive farce will soon be ended?

A. Edward Newton   January 1934

farrago *fuh RAH goh*
a confused mixture; jumble

Joseph Conrad traveled 1,100 miles up the Congo River to find the heart of darkness; I was sure I had seen it at mile one. I stood on the rusty, urine-stained deck of a cargo barge watching Kinshasa, the capital of Zaire, recede into a humid gray haze. The city that from Brazzaville had looked so prosperous, with its skyscrapers and dock cranes, turned out up close to be a farrago of squalor and raucous mayhem: troops of beggars limping on pretzeled legs clogged the multilane Boulevard du 30 Juin; fires smoldered in refuse heaps alive with the ulcerous, emaciated bodies of those too weak to beg; silver Mercedes rocketed through the rubble, scattering crowds, carrying their owners to hush-hush diamond deals in posh Gombe. And outside the confines of the modern district, in the old Cité and beyond, gangs of youths armed with guns and knives patrolled slums four million strong. Someone must have gone mad here to let all this happen: if present-day Kinshasa wasn't Kurtz's "Inner Station," I didn't know what was.

Jeffrey Tayler   September 1996

fastness *FAST nis*
a secure or fortified place; stronghold

With its jagged mountains, chasms choked with thorn and cactus, and fierce-browed people, Mani little resembles the rest of mainland Greece. There is reason for this: Maniots are descended not from the renowned Hellenes but from their rivals, the grim and martial Spartans. When Greek territory began suffering barbarian incursions in the third century, some Spartans fled to the stony fastnesses of the peninsula to the south, and there they remained, isolated and determined to fend off intruders.

Jeffrey Tayler   January 1998

fealty   *FEE uhl tee*
an obligation of loyalty and duty toward a person or idea: Latin, fidelis, *faithful*

> Reagan's stubborn fealty to principles conveyed an image of strength. Bush's willingness to compromise on everything except abortion and taxes conveys an image of calculation, religious conservatives and affluent suburbanites being the core constituencies in the GOP coalition.
>
> William Schneider   January 1990

febrile   *FE bruhl*
caused by fever

> Like all medical interventions, vaccination entails some risk, although the extent and gravity of potential side effects are matters of debate. For example, febrile seizures occur in roughly one in 10,000 children — perhaps 1,000 a year in the United States — who receive the current whooping-cough vaccine. Such seizures rarely, if ever, lead to permanent brain damage, however, and in any case febrile seizures are triggered just as easily by a run-of-the-mill infection as by a vaccine.
>
> Arthur Allen   September 2002

feign   *fayn*
to disguise one's sentiments; put on an appearance of; pretend

> Children, no matter how much they may feign indifference and lack of concern regarding their parents' separation, cannot ever emerge from divorce completely unscathed.
>
> Graham B. Blaine Jr., M.D.   March 1963

felicity   *fuh LI suh tee*
an appropriate or pleasing manner or style of expression

> In that good book *The Summing Up*, Somerset Maugham says that in his opinion Colette writes better than any other living French author, that the felicity of her style convinced him she was that freak, a born writer, able to express herself easily, without crossings-out and painful rewriting — but that when he asked her if this were so, she told him that she often spent a day on half a page.
>
> Monica Stirling   July 1946

ferret   *FE rit*
to search out; bring to light: ferrets are weasel-like animals trained to enter the burrows of rats and rabbits and drive them to the surface

Style, I think, is inseparable from personality. The works of Shakespeare are, of course, the supreme instance. Facts regarding his life, incredible as has been the industry in ferreting them out, are few enough. But the plays are there and the sonnets are there, the sympathies and prejudices, the loves and hates are there. However obscure the circumstance, the manner of the man who wrote them could not be clearer had Titian drawn his portrait.

Ellery Sedgwick   November 1947

fervid   *FER vid*
intensely impassioned; glowing

When war with Mexico began, during Lincoln's campaign for Congress, a fervid martial spirit swept the prairies; and if he harbored any feelings that his country might be wrong he had kept them to himself. By the time he reached Washington, the fighting had stopped. But peace terms were yet to be agreed on, and he found that his fellow Whigs in Congress, looking to the election of 1848, were intent upon making political capital by accusing President Polk of bringing on an unjust war against a feeble neighbor.

Benjamin B. Thomas   February 1954

fetter   *FE tuhr*
to hold in check; restrain; confine

Society is far less satisfactory to us women, who have enjoyed, compared with you, so few of its goods, so many of its evils. Inevitably, therefore, we look upon society as an ill-fitting form which distorts the truth, deforms the mind, fetters the will. Inevitably we look upon societies as conspiracies and conglomerations which sink the private brother, whom many of us have reason to respect, and inflate in his stead a monstrous male, loud of voice, hard of fist, childishly intent upon ruling the floor of the earth with chalk marks, going through mystic rites and enjoying the dubious pleasures of power and dominion, while we, "his women," are firmly locked in the private house within.

Virginia Woolf   June 1938

fiat   *FEE it*
a command that creates something as if without further effort; an
authoritative order

The transformation of Japan was slow. It required detailed interference in the day-to-day workings of Japanese life. U.S. occupation officials supervised what was taught in Japanese classrooms. Douglas MacArthur's assistants not only rewrote the labor laws but wrote the constitution itself. They broke up big estates and reallocated the land. Carrying out this transformation required an effort comparable to the

New Deal. American lawyers, economists, engineers, and administrators by the thousands spent years developing and executing reform plans. Transformation did not happen by fiat. It won't in Iraq either.

James Fallows   November 2002

In his "Author's Introduction" to *Democracy in America*, Tocqueville showed how democracy evolved in the West not through the kind of moral fiat we are trying to impose throughout the world but as an organic outgrowth of development.

Robert D. Kaplan   December 1997

fiefdom   *FEEF duhm*
something over which one dominant person or group exercises control: originally, the estate or domain of a feudal lord

Factories in China are like little fiefdoms, providing workers with the full plate of social services — housing, day care, schools, medical care — and monitoring workers on a scale that in America would amount to a mass invasion of privacy.

Lynn Chu   October 1990

figurehead   *FI gyer hed*
a person in a position of authority who nevertheless has no power

In the twentieth century Woodrow Wilson, Calvin Coolidge, Franklin Delano Roosevelt, and Dwight D. Eisenhower all, to one degree or another, held back the full truth about medical difficulties that could have jeopardized their hold on the Oval Office. Wilson suffered a paralyzing stroke in 1919 that made him merely a figurehead during the last year and a half of his term.

Robert Dallek   December 2002

filch   *filch*
to steal something of little value at an opportune moment

The building of Chicago has been a much more difficult thing than those who traverse its streets to-day can appreciate; for it rests on a sandy slough, where the lake once rocked; its buildings are erected on piles, its streets have been elevated, and miles upon miles of its substructure are composed of practically solid masonry. Hundreds of acres have been filched from the lake, which, jealous of the theft, batters at the sea wall and undermines the esplanades. But in spite of all this, boulevards skirt the lake, intersect the city, and pass about it in a vernal belt from park to park.

Elia W. Peattie   December 1899

filigree   *FIL uh gree*
a delicate, lacelike ornamental work of intertwined wire threads of gold, silver or copper

> The gentle, beautiful chain of hills which encircle Florence smile cheerfully in the sunshine, clapping their hands and skipping like lambs, if little hills ever did make such a demonstration. These environs of the town are like a frame of golden **filigree**, almost too fantastic a one for so shadowy and sombre a city. The green hill-sides and plains are sown thickly with palaces and villas glancing whitely through silvery forests of olive and myrtle; while the distant Apennines, like guardian giants, lift their icy shields in the distance.
>
> John Lothrop Motley   November 1857

fillip   *FI luhp*
something extra that stimulates, livens up or enhances

> A novel or a play without a lawyer in it is rare and unconventional. Wills have to be made, criminals to be tracked, and family secrets to be ferreted out or locked up in the incommunicable bosom of the legal adviser. Somewhere or other in its development the literary worker finds a **fillip** for his story, if not a basis for all of it, in the tangles and mysteries of jurisprudence.
>
> William Henry Rideing   April 1883

finite   *FIGH night*
having an eventual end; limited ("finiteness" is the noun)

> Sondheim's songs and shows have not simply peeled away the sentimentality of Broadway but have tried to delineate some enduring artistic and moral truths. Into a militantly cheerful musical tradition he frequently introduces a whiff of death — not the weepy, sentimentalized tragedy of disease-of-the-week TV movies but a sense of the **finiteness** of life. Sondheim likes to remind us (and, one imagines, himself) that we are not immortal and that life is a matter not of finding a dream at the end of a rainbow or living happily ever after but of doing the best with the time we've got.
>
> Stephen Holden   December 1984

firmament   *FUHR muh mint*
the sky, and all that is within it

> In the Milky Way, where we live, there are at least 100 billion suns. Within range of current detection instruments are 10 billion other galaxies, many larger than our own. Beyond them may lie a gigantic number of galactic islands — perhaps an

infinite number, and corresponding to that, an infinity of suns. Intuition would seem to demand that in such a vast firmament many hearts would beat.

Gregg Easterbrook   August 1988

fixation   *fik SAY shuhn*
an arrest in development at a certain stage of life

It is true of many novelists, perhaps of most novelists except first-rate ones, that they can make the childhood of imagined characters more real than their maturity. The probable reason is that the novelists' own childhood was more real to them than maturity — that minor fiction is frequently a form of infantile fixation.

Bernard DeVoto   January 1940

flag   *flag*
to fall off in energy, activity or interest; slacken

Divas come and go. Maria Callas is forever. That, at any rate, is how it looks now, more than two decades after her death, at fifty-three, in her lonely Paris apartment. Though her glory years at La Scala, Covent Garden, the Opéra, and the Met lie some forty years back, sales of her recordings have never flagged.

Matthew Gurewitsch   April 1999

flaunt   *flawnt*
to display conspicuously; show off

The saddlemakers of Sheridan, Wyoming, carve leather with finesse on the order of skills like gunmetal engraving and scrimshaw. The saddles they produce are majestic creations — fantastic to see, wondrous to touch, and delicious to smell. One could ride in them all day, rope big steers off them, winter with them in Montana's Judith Basin, and they would stay strong for years. But they are more than durable; they are bas-reliefs in leather, flaunting fields of flowers, curling vines, and leaves that run deep into the surface of the honey-colored hide.

Jane and Michael Stern   July 1998

fleece   *flees*
to strip of money or property by fraud; swindle

A man of science in the employ of the Government went to Mr. Lincoln, in 1863, to tell him how the large contractors were debauching our politicians and fleecing the Government. Mr. Lincoln heard his story, but at its end surprised the visitor by saying, "Mr. —, I know all that and a good deal more, but to stop this thieving would stop the war."

John Graham Brooks   February 1904

flirt *flert*
to deal with playfully or carelessly; to make a risky approach to

Log driving was a profession that was dangerous to life and limb, not just some of the time, but every minute. From the moment he began to break out the frozen roll-ways till the day, sometimes six months later, that the drive was safe in the booms hundreds of miles downriver, the riverman was flirting with death a dozen times a day. The heavy, slippery logs that he had to roll, pry, and lift would fly back at him and knock him literally to kingdom come, or he himself would slip and a whole roll-way would pass over him, leaving not enough to bury.

Robert E. Pike   July 1963

florid *FLAW rid*
excessively showy; elaborate

When in the mood for humorous characterization, Dickens's hilarity was most amazing. To hear him tell a ghost story with a very florid imitation of a very pallid ghost, or hear him sing an old-time stage song, such as he used to enjoy in his youth at a cheap London theatre, to see him imitate a lion in a menagerie-cage, or the clown in a pantomime when he flops and folds himself up like a jack-knife, or to join with him in some mirthful game of his own composing, was to become acquainted with one of the most delightful and original companions in the world.

James T. Fields   August 1870

flounder *FLOWN duhr*
to struggle or plunge about in a stumbling manner; to proceed clumsily or helplessly ("floundering" is the adjective)

In the 1830s and 1840s Horace Mann struggled to rescue the floundering American school system and persuade a divided public of the need to educate children more thoroughly. As secretary of the Massachusetts Board of Education, Mann firmly staked out a position against maximum local control of the schools — an undertaking as controversial then as it is now. He undercut hiring prerogatives by proposing statewide standards for teachers, and infringed on curriculum-setting power by pushing for uniformity in textbooks. His influence soon extended across the country. Various state legislatures stepped up the pace of educational reform, passing laws whose effects were to increase drastically the number of children in school, the length of time they spent there, and the cost and quality of the instruction they received.

Michael J. Barrett   November 1990

flout *flowt*
to openly disregard by rejecting, defying or ignoring

Literary history and all history is a record of the power of minorities, and of minorities of one. Every book is written with a constant secret reference to the few intelligent persons whom the writer believes to exist in the million. The artist has always the masters in his eye, though he affect to flout them. Michel Angelo is thinking of Da Vinci, and Raffaelle is thinking of Michel Angelo. Tennyson would give his fame for a verdict in his favor from Wordsworth.

Ralph Waldo Emerson   January 1868

flummox *FLUH miks*
to confuse; perplex; confound; bewilder

Beans flummox cooks, even those who know them to be a nutritional godsend and stock bags of them in the pantry. There the beans stay, waiting for the intended pot of chili or soup to be made, growing ever dustier. Beans are daunting. For years I stopped reading recipes after the words "Soak beans overnight." What starch, no matter how admirable nutritionally, is worth all that advanced planning?

Corby Kummer   April 1992

flush *fluhsh*
a state of freshness or vigor

We are a business people who know nothing about the intricacies of politics, especially international politics, and in the flush of youthful pride we make no calculations of the reactions to our attitudes in the minds of others.

Reinhold Niebuhr   May 1930

foist *foist*
to impose something unwanted upon another by coercion or trickery

Ironically, few people expected anything but failure for a two-hour news program in 1952, when Sylvester L. ("Pat") Weaver, Jr., then the head of the network, foisted *Today* on his dubious colleagues. Richard A. R. Pinkham, the show's first executive producer, now chairman of the executive committee at Ted Bates, the advertising agency, recalls: "People said, '7 a.m. No one will watch.' And no one did, during that first year. The show cost about $2 million, and it barely got renewed for the first thirteen weeks of 1953. Then one morning, a production assistant who was a sort of gopher for us showed me a man with a chimp in the casting room. I said, 'Sure, put him on tomorrow.' The assistant said, 'No, every day.' And we did. We put J. Fred Muggs on every day. That monkey saved the show."

Raymond A. Sokolov   August 1974

Our so-called Structural Impediments Initiative with Japan forced that country to let Toys R Us and other big commercial chains compete with mom-and-pop stores. Must we foist our dreariest institutions on the rest of the world?

Jonathan Schlefer   March 1998

font *fahnt*
a source of abundance

Four key factors set Messiaen's music apart. First is his Catholicism, a faith he claimed to have been simply born with (though his parents were nonbelievers), which to him was an inexhaustible font of metaphysical ideas. Second, his idiosyncratic notion of color. Third, his iconoclastic approach to rhythm. Fourth, his use of meticulously transcribed birdsong, from which he spun fantasias of bizarre brilliance. In various ways each of these wellsprings of inspiration put Messiaen in what he termed "eternal conflict" with the public at large.

Matthew Gurewitsch   March 1997

foolhardy *FOO:L hahr dee*
daring but lacking judgment; unwisely bold; rash; reckless

Little wars with the foolhardy use of weapons of mass destruction could lead to a great war; and if tempers rise, we shall need to curb the trigger-happy fools among us.

Vannevar Bush   February 1956

> ✳ The term "weapons of mass destruction" was first used not about nuclear, biological or chemical weapons, but about conventional aerial bombing. On December 28, 1937, as the Spanish Civil War was under way and a wider war was looming, the *London Times* wrote: "Who can think without horror of what another widespread war would mean waged as it would be with all the new weapons of mass destruction?"

fop *fahp*
a vain, affected man who is preoccupied with his clothes, appearance or manners; dandy

Historians have observed that this country long defined its politics by sex far more than did other industrialized nations. Electoral politics in the nineteenth century — an all-male activity — was closely linked with cultural ideas about masculinity. With its rallies, shop talk, and fraternity, politics then was something akin to sports today. Manhood was frequently an issue. In 1840 the supporters of William Henry Harrison, a war hero, began an American tradition by attacking the incumbent Martin Van Buren as a fop. "Little Van — the used-up man" his enemies called him, noting that Van Buren favored ruffled shirts and had achieved a new level of effeminacy because he enjoyed taking baths. A victim of his own propaganda, the sixty-eight-year-old Harrison refused to wear a coat to his chilly inauguration in March, caught pneumonia, and died a manly death a month later.

Steven Stark   July 1996

foray   *FAW ray*
a raid or brief invasion

What is called military glory is a fitful and uncertain thing. Time and the newspapers play strange tricks with reputations, and of a hundred officers whose names appear with honor in this morning's despatches ninety may never be mentioned again till it is time to write their epitaphs. Who, for instance, can recite the names of the successive cavalry commanders who have ridden on their bold forays through Virginia, since the war began? All must give place to the latest Kautz or Sheridan, who has eclipsed without excelling them all. Yet each is as brave and as faithful to-day, no doubt, as when he too glittered for his hour before all men's gaze, and the obscurer duty may be the more substantial honor.

Thomas Wentworth Higginson   September 1864

forbidding   *fawr BI ding*
constituting a prohibition or strong reason against; rendering impossible or undesirable ("forbiddingly" is the adverb)

Getting a man to the moon is a very expensive proposition, but given the funds, it is not a forbiddingly hard problem to solve.

Franklin A. Lindsay   August 1963

forensic   *fuh REN zik*
the application of a specialized field of knowledge, such as medicine or accounting, to legal matters, as in the investigation of a crime

On *The New Detectives*, a TV show about forensic scientists to which I am addicted, a substance called luminol often comes into play. If luminol is sprayed on a crime scene and subjected to ultraviolet light, invisible bloodstains become visible.

Phyllis Rose   April 2002

forgo   *fawr GOH*
to do without; give up

Inveighing against the employment of political action by Negro citizens is asking them to forgo an instrument which is the very backbone of a democratic society, one that is used for everything from cutting a curbstone to, say, fixing the rate of interstate natural gas. They cannot be expected to acquiesce.

Roy Wilkins   March 1958

forte   *FAWR tay*
something in which a person excels; strong point

Because of the great proportion of the total carrying capacity required for fuel in long flights, the airplane, as applied to practical carrying purposes, is to-day, and must inevitably remain, essentially a short-range vehicle. Its forte is high speed and unprecedented freedom of movement; its weakness, relatively limited range of independent operation.

Lieutenant Commander Bruce G. Leighton   November 1927

fortissimo   *fawr TI suh moh*
very loud

In the second act of *Don Carlo*, the princess Eboli offers to entertain the ladies of the court with a song. She takes up the mandolin, and as she begins strumming, the entire orchestra, brass and woodwinds included, strikes up the opening bars of the "Song of the Veil," *fortissimo*. This is a lot of sound for Eboli to be getting out of one small mandolin.

Holly Brubach   November 1983

founder   *FOWN der*
to sink; break down; collapse; fail

I once heard a woman passenger ask the master what would happen if our ship struck the iceberg then in view. "Madam," he replied, "the berg would go sailing on as if nothing had happened." All the harm any liner could do to an iceberg would be to displace a few tons of ice. Though no one can say with certainty how such fine vessels as the Naronic (White Star Line) and the Huronic (Allan Line) went a-missing, yet in nautical circles it is taken for granted that both vessels foundered after collision with icebergs. Both were bound to the United States during the ice-season, and their course necessitated their cutting across the ice-track. I can conscientiously say that in all the time I have followed the sea in liners, I have never been with a master who did not slow down in fog when crossing the ice-regions.

Charles Terry Delaney   May 1910

The most audacious forgery of the 1990s was a collection of letters, notes, and other jottings in the hand, it was believed, of President John F. Kennedy, which revealed that JFK had had an affair with Marilyn Monroe and had paid her mother $600,000 in hush money. The documents foundered on a shoal of counter-evidence, such as the use of ZIP codes before they had been introduced.

Cullen Murphy December 2004

frangible *FRAN juh buhl*

capable of being broken; breakable; fragile

By the time you read this, I am almost sure, the advent of the stereophonic disc will have been heralded. And our glowingly blissful decade of the adaptation to LP will have come to a nervous end, with the presentment of something as significantly newer than LP as LP was newer than the old, fast, frangible, and noisy shellac record.

John M. Conly March 1958

fraternity *fruh TER nuh tee*

a group of people with the same occupation or interests

After the 1964 conventions Walter Cronkite of CBS made a speech in which he came right out and said, "I heartily believe that in 1968 the political parties ought to ban television from the floor of the convention hall." He was for televising the convention, of course, but he thought television's aggressive and gadgety presence on the floor itself "makes a mockery of the fact that this is a convention of delegates who are supposed to be listening to the speeches and tending to some sort of business." This was heresy to a large segment of the television news fraternity, but Jack Gould, the influential television critic of the *New York Times*, rushed to Cronkite's support, writing: "For any viewer who survived the long summer nights of TV's competitive frenzy and the cathode calisthenics on the convention floor, Mr. Cronkite's stature has achieved heroic proportions."

Charles McDowell Jr. July 1968

freight *frayt*

associations attached to something, often burdensomely

Esperanto was devised ninety-nine years ago in Warsaw, by Dr. L. L. Zamenhof, who is usually identified in the movement's literature as a "Polish oculist." His goal was to create a language so simple and logical that anyone could learn it, and so neutral in its political and cultural connotations that it could be used as everybody's second language, removing nationalistic freight attached to English, French, German, and other dominant tongues.

James Fallows December 1986

❊ What follows is a sampling of Esperanto words and an Esperanto translation of the frequent query of weary travelers.

akvo	water	*ino*	female
amiko	friend	*knabo*	boy
atendi	to wait	*malamiko*	enemy
bela	beautiful	*okupata*	busy
blinda	blind	*patro*	father
chio	everything	*porko*	pig
chiu	everybody	*prapatro*	forefather
danki	to thank	*rozo*	rose
dio	God	*sola*	alone
esperi	to hope	*timi*	fear
friti	fry	*urbo*	city
helpi	aid	*voyo*	road

"Good evening. Can you tell me where we might find accommodations for tonight?"

"Bonan vesperon. Chu vi bonvolus diri al mi, kie ni povos trovi loghlokon por chinokte?"

frequent   *FREE kwint*
to visit often

Hampstead is certainly one of the loveliest parts of London; a century ago it was a not too remote village much frequented by authors and artists in search of quiet and fresh air. Every inch calls to mind some pleasing memory: there once stood a famous tavern, The Upper Flask, patronized by Pope and Steele and celebrated by Richardson in *Clarissa Harlowe*. To this corner Johnson came with Goldsmith; and to that, Lamb and Coleridge, Keats and Leigh Hunt. It was to Jack Straw's Castle that Dickens invited his future biographer, John Forster, to "come for a red-hot chop and a good glass of wine," and it was from the tea gardens of The Spaniards that Mrs. Bardell was unsuspectingly conducted to Fleet Prison, there to meet and be released by Mr. Pickwick.

A. Edward Newton   July 1926

fresco   *FRES koh*
a painting made with water-based paints on a wall or ceiling whose plaster is not quite dry, so that the colors sink in and become more durable

Michelangelo experienced no qualms when Perugino's frescoes were wiped from the wall of the Sistine Chapel to make place for his *Last Judgment*, having been in the habit of referring to Perugino as a man without any sort of talent. Of Raphael he wrote in a letter, "All that he knows of art he learned from me." El Greco said of Michelangelo, "He was a good Italian and a good man, but he simply could not paint."

Lee Simonson   May 1946

frieze _freez_

a sculptured or richly ornamented band around a building or indoor space

In his _Age of Reason_, Thomas Paine listed Confucius with Jesus and the Greek philosophers as the world's great moral teachers. A figure of Confucius in flowing sleeves joins Moses, Hammurabi, and Solon among the lawgivers in the marble frieze encircling the Supreme Court's hearing room in Washington, D.C.

Charlotte Allen   April 1999

frivolous _FRI vuh luhs_

of little value or importance; trivial; silly ("frivolity" is the noun)

St. Paul's, outside and inside, is the ugliest building of any pretension that I ever saw. A large inclosed space is always impressive; and the effect thus produced is all of which St. Paul's can boast. Its forms are without beauty, its lines without meaning; its round windows are ridiculous. Its outside is not only ugly in form, a huge piece of frivolity, but its discoloration by the black deposit from the London atmosphere, and the after-peeling-off of this in patches, give it a most unpleasant look, like that of a great black mangy dog.

Richard Grant White   February 1879

fructify _FRUK tuh figh_

to bear fruit or make fruitful

It is nearly twenty years since _Ulysses_ appeared, a book which was greeted variously as the end of the novel and as the beginning of a new prose literature. _Ulysses_, with all its genius, has done extraordinarily little to fructify or to influence prose fiction.

Edwin Muir   April 1940

fulsome _FOOL suhm_

offensively overdone; excessively or insincerely lavish

Food went abroad while Romanians suffered rationing and hunger. Energy went abroad while Romanians in chilly apartments lived by the light of forty-watt bulbs. Gasoline grew scarce, and horse carts, which had always been part of the rural scene, became vehicles of national purpose. The country's single television channel carried hour after hour of fulsome attention to Ceausescu, his wife, Elena (a harpy who served as his chief adviser and full partner in bad governance), and their supposed achievements. But in the cool blue glare on the other side of the TV screens people hated as well as feared the reigning couple. When the wave of revolutions broke across Eastern

Europe, in 1989, Nicolae Ceausescu achieved distinction as the sole Communist leader who was not only deposed but, along with his wife, promptly executed.

David Quammen   July/August 2003

✳ In classical mythology, the harpies were hideous winged monsters, with the heads and breasts of starved-looking women and the talons of a bird of prey, who plundered food and anything else they could carry away. Harpy evolved into the word for a greedy, predatory person or a shrewish woman.

functionary   *FUHNK shuh nai ree*
a minor official, especially one with trivial duties; bureaucrat

We are persuaded that the election of Mr. Lincoln will do more than anything else to appease the excitement of the country. He has proved both his ability and his integrity; he has had experience enough in public affairs to make him a statesman, and not enough to make him a politician. That he has not had more will be no objection to him in the eyes of those who have seen the administration of the experienced public functionary whose term of office is just drawing to a close. He represents a party who know that true policy is gradual in its advances, that it is conditional and not absolute, that it must deal with facts and not with sentiments, but who know also that it is wiser to stamp out evil in the spark than to wait till there is no help but in fighting fire with fire. They are the only conservative party, because they are the only one based on an enduring principle, the only one that is not willing to pawn tomorrow for the means to gamble with to-day. They have no hostility to the South, but a determined one to doctrines of whose ruinous tendency every day more and more convinces them.

James Russell Lowell   October 1860

fusillade   *FYOO: suh lahd*
a simultaneous and continuous attack, as of many firearms; a barrage

The outstanding symptom of the Anglo-German ailment is a fusillade of almost identical charges. All the schemes and ambitions the anti-Germans in England impute to Germany, the anti-British in Germany impute to England. Every suspicion that is entertained in London about the Kaiser is entertained in Berlin about King Edward. Great Britain sends a squadron to visit the Baltic, and multitudes of Germans look upon its advent as scarcely less than a declaration of war. Germany increases her navy, and the British Teutophobes at once warn their countrymen to prepare for a German invasion.

Sydney Brooks   May 1910

G

glean

The dump was our poetry and our history. We took it home with us by the wagonload, bringing back into town the things the town had used and thrown away. Some little part of what we gathered, mainly bottles, we managed to bring back  to usefulness, but most of our gleanings we left lying around barn or attic or cellar until in some renewed fury of spring cleanup our families carted them off to the dump again, to be rescued and briefly treasured by some other boy with schemes for making them useful.

Wallace Stegner   October 1959

see page 193

gadfly *GAD fligh*
a person who persistently criticizes in order to rouse people from complacency and provoke them to action: so called because of certain species of flies whose bites give livestock no peace

> Over the past twenty-five years Joe Clark has become a self-taught expert on closed captions and a gadfly to the captioning industry. As he watches, he collects examples of bad captioning, including misspellings, inconsistencies, awkward placement on the screen, and miscuing, and distributes them to a listserve he runs, to regulatory agencies, and to captioning companies themselves — efforts for which he receives no remuneration.
>
> Michael Erard   September 2001

galaxy *GA lik see*
a brilliant array or assemblage

> For a country that has celebrated its uniqueness as the land of freedom and the refuge of the oppressed, and in recent decades has acclaimed the feats of "freedom fighters" around the world, the United States has done little to recognize and honor some of its native-born fighters for freedom — slave rebels and fugitives in the antebellum South who risked their lives to escape oppression. Their absence from the galaxy of American heroes is easy to explain. The nation founded on the proposition that "all men are created equal" was based on the most enormous of human inequalities, and for many decades the prevailing interpretation of slavery in our history books reflected the racial views of the slaveowners.
>
> Leon F. Litwack   November 1999

garlanded *GAHR luhn did*
wreathed; decorated

In any attempt at truth, perhaps nothing can be more subjective, impressionist, Pirandellian, than one's memories of a bygone era. The associations are so many, so garlanded with nostalgia, so cankered with ego; the corroborations so few. The mind "lets go a thousand things"; even worse, it hangs on, raggedly, crookedly, to a thousand others; and when what we happen to confront is the confluence of many minds, or many volumes of memoirs, even fairly recent history can become astigmatic and blurred.

Louis Kronenberger   January 1966

garrulous *GA ruh luhs*
excessively talkative; given to chattering away

I once knew a man who could bear a physical infirmity without growing garrulous about it. But he hardly counts as an exception to the general rule. He had lockjaw. What, indeed, is the solace in suffering if one may not talk about it and command respectful attention from one's able-bodied and commonplace friends?

Roger Lewis   December 1927

gawp *gawp*
to stare open-mouthed; gaze in astonishment; gawk; gape

The Aztec capital of Tenochtitlan dazzled Hernan Cortes in 1519; it was bigger than Paris, Europe's greatest metropolis. The Spaniards gawped like hayseeds at the wide streets, ornately carved buildings, and markets bright with goods from hundreds of miles away. They had never before seen a city with botanical gardens, for the excellent reason that none existed in Europe. The same novelty attended the force of a thousand men that kept the crowded streets immaculate. (Streets that weren't ankle-deep in sewage! The conquistadors had never heard of such a thing.)

Charles C. Mann   March 2002

germane *jer MAYN*
closely connected; relevant; pertinent

The world opens up before the young writer as a grand and glorious adventure in feeling and in understanding. Nothing human is unimportant to him. Everything that he sees is germane to his purpose. Every word that he hears uttered is of potential use to him. Every mood, every passing fancy, every trivial thought, can have its meaning and its place in the store of experiences which he accumulates. The opportunities are enormous, endless.

James T. Farrell   September 1938

germinate   *JER muh nayt*
to begin to sprout or grow; to come into existence

Poems are peculiar plants, and nobody knows much about what makes them **germinate**. As W. H. Auden once wrote of the poet in this magazine, "Whatever his future life as a wage-earner, a citizen, a family man may be, to the end of his days his life as a poet will be without anticipation. He will never be able to say: 'Tomorrow I will write a poem and, thanks to my training and experience, I already know I shall do a good job.' In the eyes of others a man is a poet if he has written one good poem. In his own he is only a poet at the moment when he is making his last revision to a new poem. The moment before, he was still only a potential poet: the moment after, he is a man who has ceased to write poetry, perhaps for ever."

Peter Davison   January 1966

gesticulate   *jes TI kyoo layt*
to make motions with the hands or arms; gesture ("gesticulation" is the noun)

A foreigner may talk his way from Lombardy to the Abruzzi by **gesticulation**. By gesture he can ask his road to any French post office or find a Tyrolean path to the nearest inn, but in Japan gesture will not guide you to the first crossroad. Before the unspoken word a Japanese is helpless, and, with every wish in the world to assist the stranger, the simplest and most natural inquiry by head or hand falls, I was about to say, on deaf eyes.

Ellery Sedgwick   August 1936

glean   *gleen*
to gather bit by bit ("gleanings" is the noun)

The dump was our poetry and our history. We took it home with us by the wagonload, bringing back into town the things the town had used and thrown away. Some little part of what we gathered, mainly bottles, we managed to bring back to usefulness, but most of our **gleanings** we left lying around barn or attic or cellar until in some renewed fury of spring cleanup our families carted them off to the dump again, to be rescued and briefly treasured by some other boy with schemes for making them useful.

Wallace Stegner   October 1959

glib   *glib*
speaking fluently but with little thought or knowledge ("glibly" is the adverb)

They who are talking so **glibly** of the likelihood of a war for any cause between Japan and the United States can have no conception of the force or universality of the profound regard in which the Western Republic is everywhere held in that empire.

Arthur May Knapp   January 1910

glut *gluht*

an excessive supply or amount

Even in the complex society of to-day the function of the press differs little from what it was when the first American newspaper, *Publick Occurrences*, appeared on September 25, 1690. Benjamin Harris, the publisher, said in his first and only issue: "It is designed, that the Countrey shall be furnished once a moneth (or if any Glut of Occurrences happen, oftener,) with an account of such considerable things as have arrived unto our Notice."

Herbert Brucker   August 1935

gossamer *GAH suh mer*

the fine film of cobwebs often seen floating in the air or caught on bushes or grass; a soft, sheer, gauzy fabric: hence, anything thin or insubstantial

A young Southerner, Reynolds Price, has written an exceptionally fine first novel, "A LONG AND HAPPY LIFE" (Atheneum, $3.95), and, all told, Mr. Price looks like one of the most promising talents to have emerged for some time. Mr. Price's opening did put me off; the writing seemed lush, and I feared that this might turn into a light trifle of Southern sweet talk and honeysuckle. But very quickly it became clear that this was no purveyor of gossamer sensibility but a very sure and adult writer with a firm grip on his materials.

William Barrett   April 1962

gothic *GAH thik*

a literary style characterized by gloom, terror, mystery, violence and an interest in the supernatural

We don't normally think of Chekhov as a gothic writer, but we shouldn't neglect the ghost in "The Black Monk" or the frightful escalations of "Murder" and "In the Hollow." The extraordinary sadistic sequence of "Ward Number Six," with the brutal payoff of the doctor's being confined to the asylum, is one from which even O. Henry might have shrunk; and it is one of Chekhov's very best things.

Philip Hensher   January 2002

grandiloquence *gran DI luh kwins*

speech that is lofty in tone, often to the point of being pompous or bombastic ("grandiloquently" is the adverb)

It is a measure of the growth of consumerism that one of the things that immediately dates a house of the 1920s is how little storage space it has. In the 1920s a bedroom cupboard three feet wide was considered sufficient; today most bedrooms have a wall-to-wall closet, and master bedrooms are incomplete if they do not have an extended walk-in closet, often grandiloquently called a dressing room. There may be fewer people in the American house of the nineties, but there are a lot more things.

Witold Rybczynski   February 1991

grandiose   *GRAN dee ohs*
trying to seem very important; pompous and showy; affectedly grand

Previous to 1893 there was not a single class of building in which we excelled or equalled contemporary work of the mother countries, although there is a tradition that back in the forties European architects visited this country to study our penal institutions, which had advanced a step or two beyond the Bastille and the Old Bailey. To-day there is hardly a single class of structure in which an excellent claim cannot be advanced for either our supremacy or our equality. In the skyscraping office-building class, the Woolworth Tower not only is supreme, but is one of the great architectural creations of all time. In monumental architecture the serene beauty of the Lincoln Memorial in Washington surely shames the florid extravagance of its grandiose rival, the Memorial to Victor Emmanuel in Rome.

Thomas E. Tallmadge   August 1925

granitic   *gruh NI tik*
like granite in hardness; inflexible

Tchaikovsky: Symphony No. 6 in B Minor, "Pathetique." Otto Klemperer conducting Philharmonia Orchestra; Angel S-35787 (stereo) and 35787. To find Klemperer conducting the *Pathetique* is a little like finding Ulanova dancing at the Folies Bergère. Nothing could be further removed from the usual sphere of interest of this granitic and uncompromising exponent of Beethoven and Brahms at their most monumental.

Herbert Kupferberg   March 1963

grapple   *GRA puhl*
to attempt to cope or deal with; to wrestle with

Whitman grappled with a central paradox: America strives to be great and powerful as a nation so that it can bring about the full flowering of individuals. "Political democracy, as it exists and practically works in America, with all its threatening evils, supplies a training school for making first-class men," he declared. "It is life's gymnasium, not of good only, but of all." Americans, he continued, are or should be "freedom's athletes," filled with "brave delight," audacious aims, and restless hopes.

David Brooks   May 2003

grievous   *GREE vis*

bringing great trouble or hurt as a consequence; lamentable ("grievously" is the adverb)

Like the Brutus of Shakespeare's play, John Wilkes Booth assumed that his act would be gratefully applauded; and like his role model, he was astonished by the hostility it elicited among a public whose sympathy for the fallen leader he had **grievously** underestimated. Near the end he wrote in his diary, "After being hunted like a dog…, with every man's hand against me, I am here in deep despair. And why? For doing what Brutus was honored for."

John F. Andrews   October 1990

guarded   *GAR did*

cautious; careful; watchful

An article in the section of *The New York Times* devoted to the forward lines of lifestyle makes note of a trend: instead of meeting with others socially at restaurants couples are actually inviting friends over to their homes for dinner. Another article in the same section reports that members of cutting-edge households are putting photographs of family members into frames and then making arrangements of the photographs on a wall. From a different newspaper comes a story about people forsaking conventional psychotherapy and, as psychologists look on with **guarded** hope, seeking emotional well-being by telling humorous stories to friends and then joining in the laughter.

Cullen Murphy   August 1997

> ✳ Since the 1960s, lifestyle has referred to one's outward style of living. When the psychologist Alfred Adler (1870-1937) coined the word in 1929, however, he was describing the way life is lived, choices made and actions taken as determined by one's early childhood experiences.

gulf   *guhlf*

a wide gap or separation

"I try very hard to go out there every show and do at least one thing that the band had no idea I was gonna call for," Haggard told me. "It's an adrenaline kick. It keeps me on my toes. It damn sure keeps them on theirs!" No remark could convey more tellingly the **gulf** between Haggard and the stars of nineties country music, whose concerts — sonically perfect and choreographed down to the hip-wiggle — mime the twinkly perfection of their videos.

Tony Scherman   August 1996

gull *guhl*
to deceive; cheat; dupe; take in

America has always taken pride in its innovativeness. Not all sorts of innovation, however, lead to higher productivity. Sometimes companies can increase their profits more by figuring out how to avoid taxes than by producing better products; sometimes they can maximize their wealth by gulling unwary investors rather than by actually inventing goods that yield high returns.

Joseph Stiglitz   October 2002

gusto *GUHS toh*
vigorous enjoyment; enthusiastic appreciation; zest

Bizet: L'Arlésienne *Suites Nos. 1 and 2; Suite from* Carmen *(Paul Paray conducting Detroit Symphony Orchestra; Mercury MG-50135: 12").* Mr. Paray eschews subtleties in favor of unabashed gusto, as if he were conducting a summer band concert, and the engineers join in the festival mood: every time the cymbals clash, you will think lightning has struck the pergola.

John M. Conly   August 1957

hobnob

Never have I enjoyed youth so thoroughly as in my old age. In writing *Dialogues in Limbo* and *The Last Puritan*, I have drunk the pleasure of life more pure, more joyful, than it ever was when mingled with all the hidden anxieties and little annoyances of actual living. Nothing is inherently and invincibly young except spirit. And spirit can enter a human being perhaps better in the quiet of old age and dwell there more undisturbed than in the turmoil of adventure. But it must be in solitude. I do not need or desire to hobnob artificially with other old men in order to revisit them in their salad days, and to renew my own.

George Santayana   May 1952

see page 209

hagiography   *hay gee AH gruh fee*
a worshipful biography: originally, a biography of a saint: Greek, hagio, *holy +* graphein, *to write*

> Brief memoirs of Austen written by her descendents amount to hagiographies. Her great-nephew edited and bowdlerized the first edition of her letters in 1884, claiming that "no malice lurked beneath" Austen's wit, which is like saying that no alcohol lurks in claret.
>
> Lee Siegel   January 1998

hag-ridden   *HAG ri din*
tormented, obsessed or harrassed by worry or dread

> A man never writes better, or more easily, than when regular work — not too pressing — keeps his hand in play. So Sir Walter Scott, hag-ridden by debt, if he finished a novel in the morning began another in the afternoon, because, as he explained, it was less difficult to keep the machine running than to start it again after a rest.
>
> Bradford Torrey   March 1906

> ✳ Raid and blackmail were among the words Sir Walter Scott drew from obscure Scottish and English books and gave new life to in his novels and poems. He also revived the old Scottish words canny, uncanny, gruesome and glamour, using glamour much as he found it, to mean a magic spell or enchantment. Up until 1808, the adjective bluff, describing a person, meant loudmouthed and rough. Scott gave it a new meaning when he applied it in *Ivanhoe* to the jovial and blunt Friar Tuck. While old Scottish law refers to murderers captured with the red hand, it was Scott, in *Ivanhoe*, who described outlaws being caught redhanded. Since the 14th century, stalwart had

meant strong and sturdy, but Scott revived its neglected 16th-century meaning of courageous. He coined at least one word from scratch: free lance. Today, freelances write and draw; in *Ivanhoe* they were mercenaries, fighting for whoever paid them, and carried spear-like weapons called lances.

haj   *hahj*

a pilgrimage: the haj is the pilgimage to Mecca that every Muslim is expected to make at least once

The restored cottage, which has been open to tourists since 1891 (Woodrow Wilson came here on a cycling tour in 1899), is the Kaabah of a Lake District *haj*, a must-see for all pilgrims. Wordsworth wrote many of his finest poems here, including "Michael," "Ode: Intimations of Immortality," and the first version of his masterpiece, *The Prelude*. Every scribbling somebody dropped by for a visit at one time or another. Coleridge was a constant visitor, as, later, was the poet laureate Robert Southey, better remembered today for being the butt of Byron's derisive wit than for his own verse (though his children's story "The Three Bears" is as certain of immortality as anything ever written). Dorothy Wordsworth kept a trenchant, entertaining journal of her life with the poets in the cottage. And after the Wordsworths moved out, in 1808, to settle in another house nearby, Thomas De Quincey took the place over and wrote *Confessions of an English Opium-Eater*, a vivid, anecdotal account of his life and nightmares in Dove Cottage.

Jamie James   June 2000

❋ Within the courtyard of Mecca's Great Mosque is the Kaabah, a cube-shaped building that is Islam's holiest site, and the focal point of the Muslim's pilgrimage to Mecca, Mohammed's birthplace. All the world's mosques face in the direction of the Kaaba, and wherever a Muslim prays, he or she faces in that direction.

hamper   *HAM puhr*

to keep from moving or acting freely; hold back; hinder

The progress of man has never been impeded by preconceived ideas regarding his abilities, his proper interests, and his appropriate activities. Woman has always been so hampered.

Faith Fairfield   June 1926

hapless   *HAP lis*

tending to encounter misfortune; unlucky; unfortunate

If you listened to the radio at all in the years 1937 to 1950 (and if you were alive to be doing much of anything back then, you probably listened to the radio quite a lot), then you must have heard Ray Erlenborn. Not heard of, mind you — just heard. He wasn't one of those sonorous voices announcing grim news from Europe, or an intergalactic gangster purring threats at Buck Rogers, or a hapless family man yelping above the din of comedic mayhem. He was, instead, the *thrummmmm* of tanks chugging into battle, the *woo-wooooosh* of a spaceship accelerating toward Altair 7, and the *wheeeeeeee-crash!* of a comic hero barreling out the front door, late for work, and running headlong into the mailman. Erlenborn was a master of sound effects in the heyday of radio.

Adam Goodheart   June 2000

harangue *huh RANG*
a long or scolding speech; tirade

Once, during a political campaign, I attended a meeting held by J. Frank Norris, the evangelist who once was tried on a killing charge out in Texas. He was speaking in behalf of one of Georgia's demagogues and, after a harangue in which God and Jesus and hellfire and eternal life were tossed about between deep-pulled breaths, he said: — "All those who think we ought to nail to the fence the hides of the newspaper editors who don't support these things, stand up." They all stood.

Ralph McGill   September 1944

harbor *HAHR ber*
to hold a thought or feeling within oneself

Much as they dislike admitting it, feminists generally harbor or have harbored categorical anger toward men. Some would say that such anger is simply an initial stage in the development of a feminist consciousness, but it is also an organizing tool and a fact of life for many women who believe they live in a sexist world.

Wendy Kaminer   October 1993

hard-boiled *HAHRD boild*
tough; unsentimental; callous

Ross Thomas, who died last winter at the age of sixty-nine, has often been compared to another writer of hard-boiled fiction — Raymond Chandler. Both were spellbinding storytellers; no matter how fast one galloped through their books, one read the last chapter at a crawl, in order to delay its end ("Can't put it down" also means "Try to make it last").

Tony Hiss   November 1996

hardened   *HAHRD uhnd*
toughened; habituated

Philadelphia, on a low-lying spit of land between two rivers, has little to recommend it except its suburbs, which are beautiful, accessible, and salubrious. And with the advent of the motor car everyone lives out of town except a few hardened souls who prefer dirt and noise to quiet and fresh air.

A. Edward Newton   May 1932

hard-nosed   *HAHRD nohzd*
tough; practical; harshly realistic

Tuberculosis is another disease that one might call a biological expression of social inequality, because it primarily affects the poor, the homeless, and the addicted. Yet it was New York City's hard-nosed decision, in the early 1990s, to require that everyone who needed medication take it daily, in front of a health worker, that checked the spread of tuberculosis.

Sally Satel   January 2001

harrowing   *HA roh ing*
extremely disturbing or distressing; frightening

Plane rides can be harrowing in Colombia, where every airport seems to be sitting atop a spiny mountain ridge or facing a cliff. Nevertheless, the country has superb air service, which the well-to-do use frequently and casually, often to visit weekend homes in Miami.

Ben Ryder Howe   May 2000

hauteur   *hoh TER*
a superior manner toward others; formal and cold behavior that suggests one is better than others; snobbery

It is hard to convince a business man that college teaching is work. My business friends, although they may envy me for nothing else, envy me for what they are pleased to call my leisure. One of them, who sat behind a window in a bank and with nicely modulated hauteur, regarded those who approached, never failed to congratulate me on my spare time.

Robert M. Gay   February 1918

headlong   *HED lawng*
heedlessly; recklessly; rashly

The 1960s were full of hope, and in fashion the hope was men. The "peacock revolution" was at hand, led by a vanguard wearing turtleneck sweaters, fitted suits (dignified by historical adjectives — Edwardian, Napoleanic), voluminous cloaks, even jewelry and handbags. Oleg Cassini, Pierre Cardin, Bill Blass, Yves Saint Laurent — the leading designers of women's clothes rushed headlong into menswear, liberating the victims of tradition.

Holly Brubach   April 1983

heady   *HE dee*
intoxicating

I believe in reading, while I'm there, about wherever it is that I've gone. And so I have carried Giuseppe Tomasi di Lampedusa's *The Leopard* with me to Sicily, Jean Rhys's *Wide Sargasso Sea* to Dominica, Carl Hiaasen's novels to Miami. One of the headiest blends of book and place I've ever whipped up for myself was Keri Hulme's multiple-prize-winning *The Bone People* and New Zealand, where the author lives and where the novel is set.

Barbara Wallraff   January 1999

heat   *heet*
intensity of feeling

Dickens, in his preface to *Oliver Twist*, replies with some heat to those "refined and delicate people" who had objected to his introduction of such creatures as Fagin and Sikes and Nancy into the book, as equally offensive to good morals and good taste. After justifying his selection of such persons for romantic treatment, he bluntly tells his censors that he has no respect for their opinion, does not covet their approval, and does not write for their amusement. "I venture," he adds, "to say this without reserve; for I am not aware of any writer in our language, having a respect for himself or held in any respect by his posterity, who has ever descended to the taste of this fastidious class."

Edwin Percy Whipple   October 1876

hegemony   *hi JE muh nee*
leadership or dominance, especially that of one country over another

The political and economic hegemony of Europe is a thing of the past. European civilization will maintain its position only if we activate it so as to meet prevailing conditions and if we are ready to defend it.

Konrad Adenauer   March 1957

hew *hyoo:*
to cut down, make or shape, as with an axe

There was a time when the American who needed a home went into the forest and hewed the logs himself. He needed very little cooperation except for the heavy work of frame raising, when he called the neighbors in and made a party of it.

Arthur C. Holden   June 1938

to conform; follow closely; uphold

The legendary — and legendarily ruthless — Republican political consultant Lee Atwater hewed to the adage that a campaign should frame its opponent before the opponent can frame himself.

Joshua Green   June 2004

heyday *HAY day*
the period of greatest success or prosperity; prime

In the heyday of scientific Marxism people in Russia gave their children names such as Villior (a Russian acronym for "Vladimir Lenin, Initiator of the October Revolution") and Remizan (an acronym for "she participated in world revolution"), names that today must make their bearers feel like dolts.

Cullen Murphy   February 2000

hidebound *HIGHD bownd*
obstinately conservative; inflexible

In Western ballet conventional movements such as an arabesque or entrechat or pirouette are freely used by a choreographer to express certain ideas or types, not to mention the clever and dramatic use of the mime. But does not convention often become an embarrassment, even an impediment? Even in such a poetic ballet as *Les Sylphides* the male dancer looks slightly ridiculous. It is this hidebound convention which has led to new growths in the dance styles of the West — movements led by such dancers as Mary Wigman, Martha Graham, Kurt Jooss, who go completely outside the conventions of classical ballet to revitalize the new dance.

Narayana Menon   October 1953

hierophant *HIGH yuhr oh fant*
an interpreter of sacred mysteries or esoteric principles

To plain people there is an aura of mystery about gold; partly because, as money, they never see it. It sits in subterranean fortresses of incredible complexity, and from their gloomy silence works its queer alchemy upon the fate of nations by processes that only its hierophants can comprehend.

William Orton   February 1932

highbrow   *HIGH brow*
a person having or affecting highly cultivated, intellectual tastes

Eugene O'Neill is the one American dramatist who enjoys a great reputation in England. Not only the critics and the highbrows, but a considerable portion of the theatergoing public, have seen and read his plays and rejoiced in that skill of his in probing what Mr. Ashley Dukes calls "the motive of illusion — the study of that infinite capacity of self-deception which has been the despair of the moralist, the joy of the cynic and the stumbling-block of the reformer."

Neil Forbes Grant   March 1926

highminded   *HIGH MIGHN did*
having high principles, ideals or feelings ("highmindedness" is the noun)

I suspect I am not the only one who since September 11 has found himself reading a paperback edition of the Koran that was bought a few years ago in a fit of highmindedness but was never actually opened.

David Brooks   March 2003

high-water mark   *high WAW tuhr mahrk*
the highest point attained

Movies reflect changing social attitudes toward journalism, and have from time to time critically examined and influenced the profession. The 1976 classic *All the President's Men* was the high-water mark for reportorial heroism on film, showing the Fourth Estate vigilantly protecting the public from the corrupt and the powerful.

Mark Bowden   March 2004

 ❉ The Fourth Estate became a synonym for England's press in the 18th century, a reference to its place alongside England's three traditional estates, or political classes — the clergy (the Lords Spiritual), the nobility (the Lords Temporal) and all other citizens (Commons).

historiography   *his taw ree AH gruh fee*
the writing of history; also, the study of the techniques of historical research and historical writing

The study of slavery is the glory of American historiography. No other aspect of our history has inspired scholarship of such sophistication and subtlety. (In fact, the single greatest work of U.S. history since the Second World War, Eugene Genovese's *Roll, Jordan, Roll,* examines the world of the slaves.)

Benjamin Schwarz   September 2003

histrionic   *his tree AH nik*
relating to acting or the art of acting

Mary Pickford's salary didn't jump from $50 to $10,000 a week before World War I because she was a fine actress (although she was one of the first to demonstrate what film acting was) but because she was America's Sweetheart. This was no mere publicity slogan. She literally was. And women didn't tear the clothes off Valentino because they were so impressed with the histrionic talent he revealed in *The Four Horsemen of the Apocalypse.*

Budd Schulberg   November 1947

❋ Between its first appearance in writing in 1589 and the beginning of the 18th century, the word actress did not refer to a woman performer, but to a woman who did something, as in, "She was the major actress in her family's good fortune." Because women were not permitted to perform on the English stage until after 1660 (boys and young men played women's roles), there was no need for a word to distinguish women from men performers. The word actress is not recorded in print as a term for female actors until 1700.

hitherto   *HI th:uhr too:*
until this time; as yet

British road manners used to be the best of any thickly populated country in Europe. This is no longer the case. Britain's cities have become maelstroms of desperate effort to get in, out, and, above all, on. London taxi drivers, hitherto as faultlessly mannered a breed as the Afghan hound, are today cranky, crotchety, and jealous on the road. To them there are only two important rules: keep moving fast, in order to earn as much as possible; and observe a minimum degree of politeness toward passengers, in order to secure a decent tip largely untaxed, and therefore all the more profitable.

Terence Prittie   May 1964

hoary   *HAW ree*
very old; venerable; time-honored

It is a hoary rule of marketing that a rise in price that puts a commodity out of reach of the many may increase its attractiveness to the few.

Timothy Kalich   October 1987

hobbyhorse   *HAH bee hawrs*
a topic that one frequently brings up or dwells on; a favorite pursuit or pastime

For reasons that I argued at length some years ago in this magazine, a congressionally based party always has trouble when it comes to mounting a campaign for the presidency. Members of Congress come to enjoy frolicking in their pools of personal influence, dabbling with the agencies whose funds or legislation they control, mounting investigations, riding their pet hobbyhorse through a set of hearings or on a foreign tour. Few of them, at heart, pine for the discipline of responsibility that falls on them when their party also controls the executive branch of government and is judged by the voters on how well its policies and programs perform.

David S. Broder   March 1974

hobnob   *HAHB nahb*
to be on familiar terms with someone; rub elbows

Never have I enjoyed youth so thoroughly as in my old age. In writing *Dialogues in Limbo* and *The Last Puritan*, I have drunk the pleasure of life more pure, more joyful, than it ever was when mingled with all the hidden anxieties and little annoyances of actual living. Nothing is inherently and invincibly young except spirit. And spirit can enter a human being perhaps better in the quiet of old age and dwell there more undisturbed than in the turmoil of adventure. But it must be in solitude. I do not need or desire to hobnob artificially with other old men in order to revisit them in their salad days, and to renew my own.

George Santayana   May 1952

homely   *HOHM lee*
simple; plain

Much charity must be extended to a man who thinks he can reach the presidency. As Lincoln said, in homely phrase, "No one knows how that worm gnaws until he has it"; and the worm gnawed at Webster's heart for twenty years. The North alone could have made him president, and he came down from his high place and bowed to the South, who received him only to throw him aside. In wrath of spirit he advised his friends to support the party he had always resisted, the party of slavery and secession. The waters of bitterness went over him, and the sun of his greatness set in clouds.

Henry Cabot Lodge   February 1882

homogeneous   *hoh muh JEE nee uhs*
similar or identical; of the same kind

We are so accustomed to speak of India as if it constituted one country, and were inhabited by a homogeneous people, that it is difficult to understand that not even in Europe are nations to be found more unlike to one another than in British India. In Hindostan and the Deccan there are ten different civilized nations, resembling each other no more than Danes resemble Italians, or Spaniards Poles.

Charles Creighton Hazewell   November 1857

uniform in structure or composition throughout

The merit of Diaghilev was that he was able to breathe new life into the ballet, to change its form, to coordinate the different elements of which it was composed, to make it completely homogeneous, and to raise it to the highest degree of art.

Igor Stravinsky   November 1953

horde   *hawrd*
a large moving group; swarm

The queen honeybee, the queen Army ant, and the kings and queens of termite colonies are alike surrounded by hordes of attendants during every moment of their long lives, and are fed, cleaned, and guarded without cessation.

Caryl P. Haskins   March 1946

hortatory   *HAWR tuh taw ree*
serving to encourage; urging strongly; exhorting

In 1989 the American Bar Association approved "Guidelines for the Appointment and Performance of Counsel in Death Penalty Cases," which set rigorous standards. Invaluable though these guidelines may be in establishing goals for state and local governments, they remain purely hortatory and are rarely put into practice.

Alan Berlow   November 1999

hosannahs   *hoh ZA niz*
prayerful praise

When we arrived in New York, we found a day of extreme brilliance. It would be impossible ever to forget the first sight of groups of slender towers that form the skyline of New York City, chanting hosannahs to an autumn sky.

Sir Osbert Sitwell   February 1962

hotbed   *HAHT bed*
a place that fosters rapid growth or extensive activity, especially in an undesirable way

Most of the houses which the poor occupy are the property of persons who receive from them a rent very large in proportion to their value. No other class of houses gives, on an average, a larger return upon the capital invested in it. The rents which the poor pay, though paid in small sums, are usually enormous in comparison with the accommodation afforded. The houses are crowded from top to bottom. Many of them are built without reference to the comfort or health of their occupants, but with the sole object of getting the largest return for the smallest outlay. They are hotbeds of disease, and exposed to constant peril from fire. Now it seems plain that here is an occasion for the interposition of municipal authority. In spite of the jealousy (proper within certain limits) with which governmental interference with private property is regarded in this country, it is a manifest dereliction of duty on the part of our city authorities not to exercise a strict supervision over these houses. The interests which are chiefly affected by their condition are not private, but public interests.

Charles Eliot Norton   June 1860

howler *HOW ler*
an amusing or ridiculous blunder

I am convinced that I will never see a computer that can take a recording of normal conversation and convert it into text, or one that can translate a document from Japanese to English without numerous howlers.

James Fallows   March 1996

huckster *HUHK ster*
to promote or advertise in an overly aggressive or showy manner

If we permit noise, ballyhoo, and theater to influence us in the selection of the people who are to run the country, why should we object to the same methods in the selection of meritorious achievements in the film business? If we can huckster a President into the White House, why cannot we huckster the agonized Miss Joan Crawford or the hard and beautiful Miss Olivia de Havilland into possession of one of those golden statuettes which express the motion picture industry's frantic desire to kiss itself on the back of its neck?

Raymond Chandler   March 1948

humbug *HUHM buhg*
a person who claims to be other than what he or she is; an impostor; fraud

People, especially members of an orchestra, may gossip about some directors and whisper that they are no more than humbugs; but no such slander is ever breathed against Toscanini. He has a marvelous ability to get the best out of musicians, to inspire them to play above themselves. He is passionately intense in rehearsal, though deceptively stolid at the actual concert. He has no superficial tricks of showmanship and is, if anything, an awkward figure on the stand. He has a certain nobility of expression — high forehead, prominent nose, moustache that might once have been fierce, and receding hair; and these features are transfused with a personality that quickly communicates itself to an audience.

Alexander W. Williams   March 1938

humdrum   *HUHM druhm*
monotonous; dull; boring

Just as Disneyland presents a vision of Main Street, USA, that is very far afield from the real thing, so Stewart presents a vision of domesticity that involves as much make-believe as practicality, that is filled with allure and prettiness rather than the drudgery and exhaustion of which we are all so wary. She lectures not on the humdrum reality of sweeping the kitchen floor every night but on the correct way to store two dozen specialty brooms. Not on washing the dishes meal after relentless meal but on the advisability of transferring dishwashing liquid from its unattractive plastic bottle to a cut-glass cruet with a silver stopper.

Caitlin Flanagan   September 2002

hurly-burly   *HUHR lee BUHR lee*
hubbub; commotion; tumult

Kashgar's main event, the Yekshenbe Bazari, or Sunday Bazaar, dates back 2,000 years. It is a gathering of medieval aspect, a hurly-burly of trade conducted by 100,000 Uighurs from surrounding villages. Well before I reached the bazaar grounds, by way of a bridge across the Tuman River, I could see the dust kicked up by legions of donkeys, rickshaws, and customers. Soon I came upon rows of stands where villagers were buying clothes and selling peppers, doling nuts into sacks, sampling spices. Pyramids of apples stood next to piles of figs. Men haggled over goats, women over cloth. You could find someone to break a horse or geld a stallion in the market; you could buy a sheep whole or assemble a slaughtered one from its component parts; you could have a molar pulled by a toothless dentist with iron tongs and blackened fingernails.

Jeffrey Tayler   September 1999

husband   *HUZ bind*
to use economically or sparingly; conserve

I left New York in an agreeable frame of mind. I had a railroad ticket to San Francisco, a steamship ticket from that port to a group of Pacific islands four thousand miles farther on, and nearly eight hundred dollars in cash. Wheels would be turning and propellers spinning under me for many days; I was going from winter to perpetual summer, and by **husbanding** my resources I could loaf, if I chose, for two or three months after arriving at my destination, one of the authentic ends of the earth. There was reason for contentment, and as I watched the snowy landscape flowing past I considered myself a fortunate man.

James Norman Hall   October 1926

husk   *huhsk*
the useless or worthless outside covering of anything

Jazz aficionados have always enjoyed nothing more than debating the relative merits of different performers. But when conversation turns to Billie Holiday, the only way to start a fight is to state a preference for early, middle, or late — her jaunty recordings of the 1930s, her diva-like ballads of the 1940s, or her work from the 1950s, when she had almost nothing left but compensated for her **husk** of a voice with the intimacy of her phrasing (closer to speech than song).

Francis Davis   November 2000

hybrid   *HIGH brid*
having a mixed origin or composition

Much ado has been made recently about women's boxing, particularly now that Muhammad Ali's daughter, Laila, has entered the ring. Books and movies have suddenly appeared, and **hybrid** offshoots of the sport, such as the "cardio-boxing" being taught at health clubs and featured in various women's magazines, have proliferated. Pre-teen clothing catalogues are now selling T-shirts that say GIRL BOXING. Although much of this is pure marketing hype, there is a growing group of women who take boxing quite seriously.

Daniel Boyne   December 2001

hypothesis   *high PAH thu sis*
a supposition based on observed facts that can be tested by further investigation

The origin of species, like all origination, like the institution of any other natural state or order, is beyond our immediate ken. We see or may learn how things go on; we can only frame **hypotheses** as to how they began.

Asa Gray   October 1860

impious

The opposition to science in the past was by no means surprising. Men of science affirmed things that were contrary to what everybody had believed; they upset preconceived ideas and were thought to be destitute of reverence. Anaxagoras taught that the sun was a red-hot stone and that the moon was made of earth. For this impiety he was banished from Athens, for was it not well known that the sun was a god and the moon a goddess? It was only the power over natural forces conferred by science that led bit by bit to a toleration of scientists, and even this was a very slow process, because their powers were at first attributed to magic.

Bertrand Russell   November 1949

see page 221

I

iconic *igh KAH nik*
representing in a single image an overall picture or truth; symbolic

> One of the iconic sights in airport men's rooms is a line of well-dressed gentlemen standing at urinals, all of them conducting phone conversations, wires dangling from ear to chin.

> Cullen Murphy   October 2003

idiopathic *i dee oh PATH ik*
designating a disease of unknown origin or cause

> Epilepsy can be caused by congenital abnormalities, tumors, viruses, and injuries to the brain, but most cases of epilepsy are idiopathic: their cause is unknown.

> Eve LaPlante   November 1988

ignoble *ig NOH buhl*
of low character

> Most modern tragedies are not true tragedies, for they are not about truly tragic characters. Mr. Dreiser's *American Tragedy*, for example, is not a true tragedy, for the motives of his actors are so trivial, their natures so ignoble, that the emotion stirred in the reader is not tragic awe at man's powers, but pitying disgust at his futility.

> David Cecil   September 1932

ignoramus *ig nuh RAY muhs*
an ignorant and stupid person

> Many words in the form that is now mandatory were originally just mistakes, and many of these mistakes were forced into the language by eager ignoramuses

determined to make it conform to some notion of their own. The *s* was put in *island*, for instance, in sheer pedantic ignorance. The second *r* doesn't belong in *trousers*, nor the *g* in *arraign*, nor the *t* in *deviltry*, nor the *n* in *passenger* and *messenger*. Nor, so far as English is concerned, does that first *c* in *arctic* which so many people twist their mouths so strenuously to pronounce.

Bergen Evans   March 1960

illimitable   *i LI mi tuh buhl*
without bounds; immeasurable

What animated Columbus more than anything else, more than God or glory or gold, must surely have been those primal passions of curiosity and wonder, the response to the challenge of the unknown, the need to go where none had gone before. That everlasting quest for new frontiers continues today as earthlings burst terrestrial bonds and begin the endless voyage beyond planet and galaxy into the illimitable dark.

Arthur M. Schlesinger Jr.   September 1992

imbibe   *im BIGHB*
to drink in; take in; absorb

Do we imbibe our families' psychological issues and concerns along with the mother's milk that we drink?

Maggie Scarf   November 1986

immanent   *I muh nint*
existing within; inherent

Milton believed that God's will is immanent in man and in human society. He saw that, to compass a larger vision of that will, men must be free to think and speak and act.

George A. Gordon   January 1909

immolate   *I muh layt*
to offer in sacrifice

Only rarely, and almost never when still alive, does a poet become the object of a cult. Sylvia Plath, age thirty, died in London in 1963, leaving behind her a sheaf of terrifying poems. Since then, and especially in the past year, poem after poem has been written to her memory by people who never knew her work while she was alive. The fable of "her abrupt, defiant death," as Robert Lowell puts it, sees her as immolated on the altar of a cruel society, her poems the outraged byproduct of her last agony.

Peter Davison   August 1966

immutable   *i MYOO: tuh buhl*
never changing or varying; unalterable

The Darwinian theory is erected on the primary foundation of a natural law acting through all time, — a persistent force which is applied to all creation, immutable, unceasing, eternal; which determined the revolutions of the igneous vapor out of which worlds were first evolved; which determines now the color and shape of a rose-bud, the fall of the summer leaves, the course of a rippling brook, the sparkle of a diamond; which gives light to the sun and beauty to a woman's eye. It rejects utterly the idea of special creation, and maintains that the globe, as it exists to-day with all its myriad inhabitants, is only one phase of that primeval vapor which by the force of that law has reached its present state.

Charles James Sprague   October 1866

impalpable   *im PAL puh buhl*
unable to be felt by touching; intangible

It is the lack of practical advantages and material rewards that makes the business man dubious of teaching as a profession. In any practical sense it certainly is the most futile of professions. Possibly the business man, contemplating himself as one product of teaching, catches a hint of the futility — But that is neither here nor there; commonly enough, at any rate, he cannot see why any human being should pursue a vocation the results of which are so impalpable. A physician cures diseases and makes money; a lawyer wins cases and makes money; even a clergyman, although he makes little money, secures conversions and fills churches; but what, what does the college professor do?

Robert M. Gay   February 1918

impasse   *IM pas*
a situation in which no advancement is possible; a standstill in affairs

Remembering that human nature remains the same, that inventions are always with us, and that men almost invariably learn by experience too late, — "si jeunesse savait, si vieillesse pouvait," — civilization appears to be in an *impasse*. When we are assured by statesmen that the bad old world must and shall pass away, we naturally ask ourselves why — failing any real change of directing mood — it should become anything but worse. Must we, then, throw up our hands and say, "Well, we're only human beings: we do what we can, and after all, in some respects the world is better than it was, even if we *are* heading for a conflagration more hideous than the last"? Or is there any way in which we can try to struggle up out of the *impasse*?

John Galsworthy   February 1920

✳ The French *Si jeunesse savait, si vieillesse pouvait* translates to "If you knew, if old age could." It's another version of "youth is wasted on the young."

impecunious   *im pi KYOO: nee uhs*
having no money; poor; penniless

No stranger should expect an author to send him or her his photograph. These pictures cost money, and it may not be convenient to an **impecunious** celebrity to furnish them to the applicants, who are becoming singularly numerous.

Oliver Wendell Holmes   January 1883

imperative   *im PE ruh tiv*
absolutely necessary; urgently needing action

I cannot think that we shall have what wholly deserves to be called an educated womanhood until we have dissipated the idea, still so prevalent even among women themselves, that a woman needs to have a definite occupation only until she marries, or if she fails to marry. That "a woman must choose between marriage and a career" is the most detestable of all the woman platitudes in the entire collection, because, while most of these platitudes are merely stupid, this one is wholly vicious. It has been so incessantly reiterated, to the accompaniment of much shallow sentimentalizing on the sacredness of home and mother, that the public has never been allowed a quiet moment to reflect on its injustice, and to realize how possible, and therefore **imperative**, is its removal along with other ancient injustices.

Mary Leal Harkness   March 1914

impertinent   *im PER tuh nint*
not showing proper respect or manners; presumptuous; inappropriate

The publication of Mark Twain's new story, *The Prince and the Pauper*, supplies a rather striking instance in point, — or, at least, supplies material for illustration of the tendency of writers whose position is fixed and prosperous to give their faculties a new and unexpected range, and strive for a totally different order of production from any previously accomplished. It would be **impertinent** to pronounce too confidently upon the author's motive, but what he has done is, in one particular, plain to every comprehension. He has written a book which no reader, not even a critical expert, would think of attributing to him, if his name were withheld from the title-page. There is nothing in its purpose, its method, or its style of treatment that corresponds with any of the numerous works by the same hand.

Edward Howard House   December 1881

Charles Dickens, whose chief impression of his first American visit was the thousands of "bores" he met, reported that an impertinent little boy on a stagecoach near Harrisburg dared accost him, "Well, now, stranger, I guess you find this a'most like an English a'ternoon — hey?" "It is unnecessary to add," wrote the irritable creator of Little Nell and Oliver Twist, "that I thirsted for his blood."

Dixon Wechter   December 1938

impious   *IM pee uhs*
lacking reverence for God ("impiety" is the noun)

The opposition to science in the past was by no means surprising. Men of science affirmed things that were contrary to what everybody had believed; they upset preconceived ideas and were thought to be destitute of reverence. Anaxagoras taught that the sun was a red-hot stone and that the moon was made of earth. For this impiety he was banished from Athens, for was it not well known that the sun was a god and the moon a goddess? It was only the power over natural forces conferred by science that led bit by bit to a toleration of scientists, and even this was a very slow process, because their powers were at first attributed to magic.

Bertrand Russell   November 1949

implacable   *im PLA kuh buhl*
incapable of being appeased or pacified; inflexible; relentless

I observed an exaggerated form of the American ambivalence toward China in the late Henry Luce, with whom I traveled around Asia some years ago. Born in China of missionary parents, he was torn between his love for the Chinese and his implacable hatred of Communism, and this schizophrenia prompted him to irrational outbursts. He would explode at the suggestion that the Communist Chinese were successful, with the argument that "Communists can't be successful," and, with equal vehemence, he would explode at the suggestion that the Communist Chinese were failing, with the argument that "Chinese can't fail."

Stanley Karnow   October 1973

implicit   *im PLI sit*
understood though not expressly stated; implied

My first television exposure was local, in Atlanta: the *Woody Willow* show. Woody was a puppet, who was entirely up-front about being made of wood. His friend, oddly enough (perhaps there was some implicit lesson about disparate types getting along), was Tillie the Termite.

Roy Blount Jr.   June 1998

imponderables   *im PAHN duh ruh buhls*
things that connot be conclusively determined or explained

To weigh the minuscule but real risk of a smallpox attack against the minuscule but real risk of complications from a vaccine is to weigh imponderables. No public-health expert is any more qualified to make this call than is the person who will have to live with the consequences.

Jonathan Rauch   December 2001

importunity   *im pawr TOO: nuh tee*
an insistent or pressing demand

The faithful slave husband in Kentucky, who had refused to escape from a master who trusted him, when he was about to be sold "down river," came to her as a pattern of Uncle Tom, and the scenes of the story began to form themselves in her mind. "The first part of the book ever committed to writing [this is the statement of Mrs. Stowe] was the death of Uncle Tom. This scene presented itself almost as a tangible vision to her mind while sitting at the communion-table in the little church in Brunswick. She was perfectly overcome by it, and could scarcely restrain the convulsion of tears and sobbings that shook her frame. She hastened home and wrote it, and, her husband being away, read it to her two sons of ten and twelve years of age. The little fellows broke out into convulsions of weeping, one of them saying through his sobs, 'Oh, mamma, slavery is the most cursed thing in the world!' From that time the story can less be said to have been composed by her than imposed upon her. Scenes, incidents, conversations rushed upon her with a vividness and importunity that would not be denied. The book insisted upon getting itself into being, and would take no denial."

Charles Dudley Warner   September 1896

impoverish   *im PAH vuh rish*
to make poor; reduce to poverty ("impoverished" is the adjective and "impoverishment" the noun)

Take the gods out of the *Iliad*, and you diminish the heroes. The battlefield of Greek and Trojan would, in the absence of the gods, seem as petty as a lamp-lit town over which hung no firmament of stars. We may not be able to explain why this is so, but we know that it is so. We know that in the presence of the stars we feel an exaltation and liberation of the spirit such as we do not feel in the light of the lamps in a street. It is as though the stars enlarged our world and gave us the freedom of the universe. If we could imagine the extinction of the stars we should think of the world as an infinitely impoverished place. Literature, I believe, would suffer an equal impoverishment as a result of the death of the gods.

Robert Lynd   September 1928

impracticable *im PRAK ti kuh buhl*

not capable of being carried out in practice

Any man who studies the social condition of the poor knows that liquor works more ruin than any other one cause. He knows also, however, that it is simply impracticable to extirpate the habit entirely, and that to attempt too much often results merely in accomplishing too little; and he knows, moreover, that for a man alone to drink whiskey in a bar-room is one thing, and for men with their families to drink light wines or beer in respectable restaurants is quite a different thing. The average citizen, who does not think at all, and the average politician of the baser sort, who thinks only about his own personal advantage, find it easiest to disregard these facts, and to pass a liquor law which will please the temperance people, and then trust to the police department to enforce it with such laxity as to please the intemperate.

Theodore Roosevelt September 1897

❋ The words impracticable and impractical are often used interchangeably, but there is a difference in what the two denote. Constructing a tunnel beneath the Pacific Ocean between San Francisco and Hong Kong would be impracticable — that is, unfeasible or perhaps impossible. By contrast, constructing a tunnel under a stream that a person could easily leap over would be impractical — possible but not useful or worth the trouble.

impresario *im pruh SA ree oh*

one who produces or sponsors entertainments, especially the manager of an opera, ballet, concert company or individual artist: a term usually applied to producers made famous by their successes

Grace Bumbry is a 26-year-old Negro girl from St. Louis who, like many other young American singers, went to Europe to learn her trade. Two leading, if rather contrasting, figures in the entertainment world have taken an interest in her — Arthur Godfrey, the broadcaster, who put her on his show when she won a high school singing contest, and Sol Hurok, the impresario, who has helped guide her career and this winter arranged for her formal American debut in two Carnegie Hall concerts.

Herbert Kupferberg March 1963

improvident *im PRAH vuh duhnt*

without regard to the future; not cautious or wise ("improvidently" is the adverb)

The right to strike is of inestimable importance to unions, and it cannot be impaired or weakened without great public danger involving the substitution of the Fascist state for the American system of free government. It is a weapon, however, which should not be used recklessly or **improvidently**, nor as the result of hot blood generated by acrimonious and unsuccessful negotiations.

George W. Alger   June 1940

imputation   *im pyoo: TAY shuhn*
a charge against; accusation

Gandhi's spirituality has been discounted, on the ground that he is a politician. Yet every seer or founder of a creed, or system, has been a politician. Gandhi has his own answer to these **imputations** on his good faith. "Jesus," he said, "in my humble opinion, was a prince among politicians. He did render unto Cæsar the things that were Cæsar's. The politics of his time consisted in securing the welfare of the people by teaching them not to be seduced by the trinkets of the priests and Pharisees."

Edmund Candler   July 1922

inane   *i NAYN*
lacking meaning or substance; foolish; silly ("inanity" is the noun)

Among the more **inane** statements ever to achieve immortality is F. Scott Fitzgerald's famous observation in *The Last Tycoon*, "There are no second acts in American lives." This country is premised on second acts.

Cullen Murphy   January/February 2003

In European countries men are often free thinkers and *esprits forts*, while their women still cling passionately to seemingly outworn creeds. Things are different in America. There may be a certain **inanity** in some of the more popular "uplift" movements, but there is certainly more general practical radicalism among American women than among American men of the same social stratum. And the radicalism women go in for is not mere "lip service," as is often the case with men. They are willing to pay the price of freedom with their bodies and their souls.

Moritz J. Bonn   September 1928

✱ *Esprits forts* (French, strong spirits) are those who profess superiority
to conventional thinking or current prejudices.

incandescent   *in kin DE sint*
brilliantly glowing

On March 31, 1952, something happened for which music lovers around the world had been waiting, none too patiently, for a quarter century. Arturo Toscanini, eighty-five years and six days old, walked into Carnegie Hall to put on RCA Victor records his incandescent interpretation of Beethoven's *Ninth Symphony.* Patently he had rededicated himself all anew to the score, after fifty years' acquaintance with it. Each note sounded as if it might have been written the day before. As he played, there grew in the minds of his listeners the inescapable conviction that they never really had heard the symphony until now. Quite possibly they hadn't; quite possibly nobody had.

John M. Conly October 1952

incidental music *in suh DEN tuhl MYOO: zik*

music composed to accompany a dramatic work or to fill intervals between scenes

As You Like It is probably the most beautiful and the most difficult of all Shakespearean comedies. It is pervaded by an atmosphere of poetry, which renders it alike attractive to young and old playgoers. The dialogue abounds in wit and pleasantry; the characters are all entertaining, and that of Rosalind is one well calculated to excite the ambition of any young and pretty actress. Besides all this there is a good deal of pleasing incidental music. The reason why it always fails is probably because it is impossible, with any ordinary human company, to strike the exact line between the real and the ideal suggested by the text.

Arthur George Sedgwick March 1881

⁜ Probably the most famous piece of incidental music is Felix Mendelssohn's "Wedding March," the music played at weddings after the officiating person says, "I now pronounce you husband and wife." Composed in 1843 along with other music to accompany Shakespeare's *Midsummer Night's Dream*, the custom of playing it at weddings began with its performance at the wedding of Queen Victoria's daughter, Princess Victoria, in 1858. The other traditional wedding music, "The Bridal Chorus" from Richard Wagner's opera *Lohengrin*, is popularly known as "Here Comes the Bride." It has been played at American weddings since the Civil War.

incipient *in SI pee int*

in the first stage of existence; just beginning to exist or appear

I was rather a fat little girl: my moon-round face, which was surrounded by green-gold curls, had, strangely for so small a child — indeed for any child — the eyes of someone who had witnessed and foretold all the tragedy of the world. Perhaps I, at four years old, knew the incipient anguish of the poet I was to become.

Dame Edith Sitwell March 1965

incontestable   *in kuhn TES tuh buhl*
indisputable; unarguable; unquestionable

As recently as 1950 Lionel Trilling could proclaim, as if it were incontestable, that American Conservatives had no ideas, only "irritable mental gestures." Today, though many conservatives remain irritable, ideas they possess in abundance. Conservative thinking has not only claimed the presidency; it has spread throughout our political and intellectual life and stands poised to become the dominant strain in American public policy.

Gregg Easterbrook   January 1986

incorrigible   *in KAW ri juh buhl*
incapable of being corrected or reformed

Those of us who knew the Good Gray Poet in his best days of health, who saw him day and night, before and after his watches with his sick and maimed soldier boys, feel that a great privilege was ours. To live with one who was, and could be, as has been said of another, an "incorrigible optimist" in the midst of slaughter and all the horrors of war, a man who felt that after all, the world was pretty good, and men and women not so bad as they were pictured, was uplifting and helpful in those awful days, and all other days, and the last word that must be said of Walt Whitman, was that he was first and last and forever an Optimist.

Ellen M. Calder   June 1907

incubator   *INK yuh bay tuhr*
an environment that promotes the growth or development of something

The most disquieting aspect of natural selection as observed on Earth is that it channels intellect to predators. Most bright animals are carnivores: stalking requires tactics, pattern recognition, and, for social animals, coordinated action, all incubators of brainpower.

Gregg Easterbrook   August 1988

inculcate   *in KUHL kayt*
to impress something upon the mind of another by frequent instruction or repetition; implant; instill

Unfortunately, the child of insecure parents often becomes an insecure person himself, because insecure parents cannot inculcate security in their children or create an environment in which the children can develop a sense of security on their own.

Bruno Bettelheim   November 1985

incunabula   *in kuh NAH byuh luh*
books printed before 1500, during the first decades after the invention of the printing press; the earliest stages in the development of anything: Latin, in, in + cunabula, *a cradle*

> In the fifty years after 1455, when Gutenberg had perfected the printing press and movable type he had been working on for years, the printing revolution swept Europe and completely changed its economy and its psychology. But the books printed during the first fifty years, the ones called incunabula, contained largely the same texts that monks, in their scriptoria, had for centuries laboriously copied by hand: religious tracts and whatever remained of the writings of antiquity.
>
> Peter F. Drucker   October 1999

indecorous   *in DE kuh ruhs*
lacking good taste in manners and conduct; unseemly

> Though it may seem indecorous to discuss rigor mortis regarding something you're going to eat, the subject is of central concern to anyone interested in fish. If fish is left at ambient temperature for even a few hours — the time it takes to enter rigor mortis — the texture will irremediably suffer. If it is frozen immediately, the thawed fish can be superior.
>
> Corby Kummer   August 1992

indemnify   *in DEM nuh figh*
to repay or compensate for what has been lost or damaged ("indemnification" is the noun)

> Today, nearly half a century after the liberation of the Nazi concentration camps, the Federal Republic of Germany has paid out more than $50 billion in the form of reparations to the State of Israel and indemnification to Holocaust survivors. The German Finance Ministry estimates that it will pay out almost $20 billion more by the year 2030, when according to its current calculations the last survivor will have died.
>
> Michael Z. Wise   October 1993

indictment   *in DIGHT mint*
a strong charge; accusation; serious criticism

> Our notion now of suburbia in the fifties is that it was essentially benign — sometimes gawky, often dull, but on the whole healthy and happy. But in the fifties themselves virtually everything written about the suburbs was negative, even alarmed. The indictment can be summed up in one word: conformity. Working for huge corporations, living in tract homes, surrounded by spookily similar neighbors, the new

middle-class Americans had lost their feelings of pride, meaning, and identity. They wanted only to blend unobtrusively into a group.

Nicholas Lemann   November 1989

✳ Gawky, which usually describes a person of awkward or ungainly gait or posture, derives from the 14th-century English word *gouki*, meaning foolish.

indifferent   *in DI frint*
showing no interest, concern or feeling; unmoved ("indifference" is the noun)

Recently I have given a lot of thought to the underlying causes of crime, and I have about concluded that the greatest cause of crime today is public indifference and public ignorance of the problems of penology. The average citizen is completely sold on the idea of punishment as a crime deterrent. There is sound reasoning to support that position. The average citizen, however, goes further and feels that punishment is a cure for crime. And by no stretch of the imagination can statistical figures furnish that position the slightest support.

Erle Stanley Gardner   March 1958

indignant   *in DIG nint*
feeling anger mingled with scorn or contempt over something regarded as unjust ("indignantly" is the adverb)

For the most part, Argentina's military rulers have reacted indignantly to criticism from abroad on their attitude toward human rights. Some of them suggest that the criticism is the work of an international communist conspiracy, intent on embarrassing them and forcing them to ease up on the guerillas. Others say smugly that in comparison to Uganda, the Soviet Union, or Cambodia, there is no human rights problem in Argentina.

Joseph B. Treaster   November 1977

Most of the students in the composers' department of the Conservatory were musicians of a mature age, and it must have been rather galling for them to have a youngster of thirteen in their midst. I made matters worse by introducing a statistical chart of mistakes made by the class. I don't blame my fellow students for being indignant.

Sergei Prokofiev   July 1947

indisposition   *in dis puh ZI shuhn*
a minor ailment, slight illness or temporary discomfort

It was astonishing to me that anyone could smoke so much and drink so much and keep perfectly well. I actually do not remember that in those days Mr. Churchill ever had an indisposition when he was with us.

Eleanor Roosevelt   March 1965

❋ The passage above appeared in the article "Churchill at the White House" that Eleanor Roosevelt wrote in 1959 at the invitation of Edward Weeks, *The Atlantic's* editor. It was one of several articles he requested from people who knew or studied Churchill so *The Atlantic* could have them ready for a special issue whenever Sir Winston, who was in his eighties, died. Churchill died in January 1965, at 91, and *The Atlantic's* tribute issue appeared in March. Eleanor Roosevelt had died in 1962, at 78.

indolence   *IN duh lins*
idleness; inactivity

The Atlantic bluefin tuna is part of a global family (*Scombridae*) that includes the largest and the fastest of the ocean's finfish. Anglers who have taken the bluefin on rod and reel will tell you it is the bravest and most beautiful of game fish. I have watched 1000-pound bluefins move at 50 mph through the clear waters of the Gulf of Maine, have seen them laze in iridescent indolence just beneath the surface, and have been awed by the grace of their tapering bulk.

John N. Cole   December 1976

induce   *in DOO:S*
to bring about; persuade; prevail upon; influence

Manet once remarked to Monet, "As Renoir's friend you ought to induce him to give up painting. You can see for yourself he's not cut out for it." Sisley protested to Renoir, "You're mad; what an idea to paint trees blue and the earth violet."

Lee Simonson   May 1946

ineffectual   *i ni FEK choo uhl*
not capable of performing the required duties; inadequate

For the oppressive but ineffectual governments that rule much of the Middle East, finding targets to blame serves a useful, indeed an essential, purpose — to explain the poverty that they have failed to alleviate and to justify the tyranny that they have introduced. They seek to deflect the mounting anger of their unhappy subjects toward other, outside targets.

Bernard Lewis   January 2002

ineluctable   *in uh LUK tuh buhl*
unavoidable; certain; inevitable

When you have the historical picture before you, and can see how Indo-European gradually slipped into Germanic, Germanic into Anglo-Saxon, and Anglo-Saxon into the English of Chaucer, then Shakespeare, and then Henry James, the process of linguistic change seems as ineluctable and impersonal as continental drift. From this Olympian point of view, not even the Norman invasion had much of an effect on the structure of the language, and all the tirades of all the grammarians since the Renaissance sound like the prattlings of landscape gardeners who hope by frantic efforts to keep Alaska from bumping into Asia.

Geoffrey Nunberg   December 1983

ineradicable   *in i RA di kuh buhl*
impossible to uproot, eradicate or erase

Perhaps the most ineradicable bad idea of recent decades has been the yellow Smiley face. Released into the ecosystem in 1963, Smiley and mutations like Frowney have by now colonized every inch of the planet. Smiley-face sweatshirts are today worn by peshmerga guerrillas in Kurdistan and child mercenaries in Liberia. Smiley's creator, Harvey R. Ball, died not long ago, at the age of seventy-nine. One can't help wondering, did friends and family wear Smiley at the funeral? Or did they wear Frowney?

Cullen Murphy   September 2003

inertia   *in ER shuh*
resistance to action or change

In the opera house the public is chary of novelty and insists on the repetition of the same operas year after year. The repertoire in symphony concert halls consists largely of performances of hackneyed music, generally bearing the stamp of nineteenth-century Romanticism. The inertia of managers, conductors, and performers is largely responsible for the rut in which the record companies now find themselves.

Moses Smith   August 1945

inexorable   *in EKS uh ruh buhl*
unrelenting; unalterable; unstoppable

Food and clothing are drastically rationed in Israel today; the necessity to import virtually all commodities, and to purchase them in hard currency, has subjected the economy to the inexorable regimentation of controls, priorities, allocations, and red tape. Only time plus peace plus credit can alleviate the situation.

The *Atlantic* Editors   January 1952

inexplicable   *in EKS pli kuh buhl*
incapable of being explained or accounted for

Rarely have I found sitters altogether pleased with their portraits. Understanding is rare, and the sitter usually wants to be flattered. How Goya ever got away with his superb portraits of the Spanish Royal Family is still an inexplicable mystery. I recall the naïve expression of one of my sitters who asked me if his nose was as I depicted it, and, when I assured him that it was so, cajolingly exclaimed, "Can't you cheat nature a little?"

Jacob Epstein   November 1940

infinitesimal   *in fi nuh TE suh muhl*
tiny; infinitely or immeasurably small

If, during the infinitesimal period of time which elapses between the beginning of the upward swing of the club and its impact with the ball, the golfer allows any one single sensation, or idea, to divert his attention — consciously or unconsciously — from the little round image on his retina, he does not properly "perceive" that ball; and of course, by consequence, does not properly hit it.

Arnold Haultain   June 1910

infra dig   *in fruh DIG*
beneath one's dignity: Latin, infra dignitatum

It is no longer considered "sissy" for boys, or queer and *infra dig* for men, to take a serious interest in music, as was true when I was a boy; we can now hear superb performances of the best music by college glee clubs.

Henry S. Drinker Jr.   February 1934

ingenuous   *in JEN yoo: uhs*
innocently frank; open-hearted; lacking in worldy experience

Some twenty years ago, when American sailing ships dotted every sea, a great many of the boys who ran away from their country homes in New England made their way to Boston, filled with the inspiring purpose of going to sea. The sailing vessel has been largely superseded in these latter days by the steamship; and the novelist does not find it possible to fire the imagination of youth by taking a deck hand or a stoker for his hero. The ingenuous country lad who boasts an American parentage is therefore seldom seen nowadays haunting the wharves for a chance to ship before the mast.

James Mokeller Bugby   November 1879

inherent   *in HE rint*
relating to a quality found within that gives something its worth; existing in someone or something as a permanent attribute; innate; intrinsic ("inherently" is the adverb)

> The truth is that even the best wines cost only about $10 a bottle to produce, and they are not inherently rare. If the initial cost is tripled to allow for profits along the path of distribution, one can reasonably conclude that retail prices above $30 are based on speculation, image, and hype.

> William Langewiesche   December 2000

inimical   *i NI mi kuhl*
in opposition; unfavorable; harmful; incompatible

> The idea that formal education was unnecessary or even inimical to economic success was a staple of American popular culture from Franklin's time until the mid-twentieth century. In works as adoring as Horatio Alger's novels and as condemnatory as Theodore Dreiser's *The Financier*, the self-made man always drops out of school and becomes a kind of apprentice to an older businessman as the first step on the road to riches.

> Nicholas Lemann   August 1995

inimitable   *in I mi tuh buhl*
unable to be imitated

> Even though he is the one twentieth-century American composer whose music is played all the time and everywhere, Gershwin is an isolated and inimitable figure — the only popular composer of this century whose works have made a lasting dent in the granitic façade of the classical canon.

> David Schiff   October 1998

injunction   *in JUHNK shuhn*
a command or order from a person of authority

> Some men are born great, some achieve greatness, and some have great catchphrases said to them. James Montgomery Doohan is an honorary member of that last category. He was the guy who spent four decades on the receiving end of the request "Beam me up, Scotty"— if not on TV, where no character on *Star Trek* ever actually uttered those words, at least in real life, where fans would cheerfully bark the injunction across crowded airport concourses in distant lands, and rush-hour drivers would lurch across four lanes of freeway traffic to yell it out the window at him.

> Mark Steyn   October 2005

inner sanctum   *I nuhr SANGK tuhm*
a private or secret place known only to a few people; a place of almost
sacred privacy

When Dr. Henry Kissinger was appointed President Nixon's chief aide on world affairs, he liked to amuse his friends by impersonating Peter Sellers impersonating Dr. Strangelove, who might have been an impersonation of Dr. Kissinger himself. Like Strangelove, Kissinger made his fame as an expert on nuclear war; like him he is a Central European; and like him, his voice is heard in the inner sanctum of government. Unlike Strangelove, Kissinger is a political scientist, and physicists Edward Teller and Wernher von Braun have better claims to being the inspiration for the hero of the famous film. Further, whereas Strangelove was, to say the least, screwed up, Kissinger is cool, humorous, and most of the time, detached.

Nora Beloff   December 1969

inordinate   *in AWR duh nit*
beyond expectation; excessive ("inordinately" is the adverb)

I am not inordinately fond of, or interested in, children; their appeal to me is a physical appeal such as the young of other animals make. I have never felt in the least sentimental about them, or no more sentimental than one becomes for a moment over a puppy or a kitten. In so far as I understand their minds, the understanding is based on the observation, casual enough and mostly unconscious, which I give to people generally; on memories of my own childhood; and on the imagination which every writer must bring to memory and observation.

A. A. Milne   June 1939

inquisitorial   *in kwi zuh TAW ree uhl*
intensively or offensively questioning

The French peasant is essentially an individualist. While he does look to the government for its assistance in raising the prices of farm products and blames it when they fall below his expectations, he also resents any prying into his private affairs. He instinctively resists inquisitorial methods and all regimentation. Hence his reluctance to depositing money in the banks, and the persistent survival of the legendary woolen stocking which has meant so much to the country in times of national emergency.

A. Gaulin   September 1936

✱ Hiding one's money in a woolen stocking is the equivalent of the English-language expression about hiding money under the mattress.

inscrutable   *in SKROO: tuh buhl*
impenetrable; baffling

Shortly before he went into the theater for what would turn out to be his final performance, John Wilkes Booth stopped for a drink in a nearby tavern. According to one account, an acquaintance laughingly remarked that the young Booth "would never be as great as his father." With "an inscrutable smile" Booth assured his critic that "when I leave the stage, I will be the most talked-about man in America."

John F. Andrews   October 1990

insensate   *in SEN sayt*
not capable of feeling

If we could ever get through thinking of the automobile as an exaggerated horse and treat it as a powerful, insensate machine requiring a vastly more careful selection of driver than any span of horses, one more gleam of sanity would be added to the few now pervading the motor mania.

Seth K. Humphrey   December 1931

insidious   *in SI dee is*
watching for an opportunity to ensnare; treacherous

Three insidious temptations assail the biographer: to suppress, to invent, and to sit in judgment, and of these the earliest and most frequent is suppression. In the Middle Ages, indeed, it was rendered inevitable by the purpose which biography was intended to fulfill: to produce a noble example.

Iris Origo   February 1959

inspissate   *in SPI sayt*
to thicken, as by evaporation; condense ("inspissated" is the adjective)

The vital ingredient of bird's nest soup is not feathers, sticks, twigs, or grass, but, as is known to epicures, it is the inspissated saliva of adult swiftlets. This is a secretion from the salivary glands of certain swiftlets, with which they make their nests. The saliva hardens on exposure to the air into something like isinglass, and this is the edible ingredient of birds' nests.

Agnes Newton Keith   August 1951

✳ Isinglass has nothing to do with glass. The name derives from the Dutch word *huizenblas*, sturgeon bladder, a form of gelatin prepared from the swim bladders of sturgeon (*huizen*) and other freshwater fish. It is used to clarify, or remove suspended particles in, wines and beers, as well as to stiffen jellies, and to make glues and cements. Isinglass's resemblance to a type of thinly sliced, transparent mica used in place of window glass led English-speaking people to also apply the word to the mineral it looked like. And not only does isinglass have nothing to do with glass — *isin* has no meaning at all; it just has a more English-friendly sound and look than *huizen*. This kind of false derivation is called a folk etymology, the seemingly logical story behind a word based on its sound, spelling or meaning, but a misunderstanding of the word's true etymology. For other folk etymologies, see the sidelight for the passage for ramble.

insurgency   *in SER jin see*
an organized rebellion aimed at overthrowing a government through the use of subversion and armed conflict

Last year Colombia, the only country in the Americas that is still fighting a major guerrilla insurgency, saw its government's decade-long losing streak continue. Army bases were overrun, villages were leveled, and images of refugees and shell-shocked soldiers filled the nightly news.

Ben Ryder Howe   May 2000

insurmountable   *in ser MOWN tuh buhl*
unable to be overcome

No young nation has approached the task against heavier odds. Israel's problems are ubiquitous — social, economic, political, military, psychological. Viewed objectively, dispassionately, they appear to be insurmountable. Yet the state exists, expands, grows every day in stature as living proof of the founders' unquenchable fire and the relentless determination of its people.

The *Atlantic* Editors   January 1952

intact   *in TAKT*
not broken; left entire; untouched; uninjured; undiminished

The big estate owners were the bitterest opponents of the state park and parkway program on Long Island. They said they would fight to the death to keep their ancestral acres intact and to exclude the riffraff from town, but they sold to developers who in most cases literally hacked the estates to pieces.

Robert Moses   December 1950

❊ America's first parkway was Eastern Parkway in Brooklyn, New York, a tree-lined boulevard more than two miles long that was built between 1870 and 1874. It was designed by Frederick Law

Olmstead and Calvert Vaux, the founders of American landscape architecture, who coined the word parkway in 1866 to describe a road expressly built for "pleasure-riding and driving." Today, a road with parkway in its name often indicates one on which commercial traffic is prohibited.

integrated   *IN tuh gray tid*
having various traits, tendencies, feelings and attitudes in one harmonious personality

I guess that today the psychiatrists would call my father an integrated man. For him life was not a series of insulated cubicles, each hermetically sealed from the others, one for personal emotion, one for business, one for politics, one for family, one for education, and one for social life. For him private feelings, business, politics, family, education, and social life were all parts of a single life process with no clear line that separated one from the other. He used to say, "My best friends are my children, and then my books," but it was perfectly obvious that he was a vital part of everything that touched his life.

Hubert H. Humphrey   November 1966

intercourse   *IN tuhr kawrs*
dealings or communications between persons or groups

The personal history of Jane Austen belongs to the close of the last and the beginning of the present century. Her father through forty years was rector of a parish in the South of England. Mr. Austen was a man of great taste in all literary matters; from him his daughter inherited many of her gifts. He probably guided her early education and influenced the direction of her genius. Her life was passed chiefly in the country. Bath, then a fashionable watering-place, with occasional glimpses of London, must have afforded all the intercourse which she held with what is called "the world."

Anna Morton Waterston   February 1863

✱ Intercourse, a strong, useful word that once strictly meant dealings or communications between people, is rarely used today except with reference to sex. The *Oxford English Dictionary*'s earliest citation for intercourse in its nonsexual sense is from 1494. Its first citation of intercourse in its sexual sense is dated more than 300 years later, 1798. The citation is from the British economist Thomas Malthus's *Essay on the Principle of Population*, in which he wrote of "illicit intercourse between the sexes." From the 15th century through the 19th, one still could say intercourse without its meaning sexual intercourse. Early in the 20th century, however, the single word intercourse became the equivalent of sexual intercourse and fell out of use in its other sense.

interdict   *in tuhr DIKT*
to intercept ("interdiction" is the noun)

> The Reagan Administration, early in the President's first term of office, proclaimed a war on drug trafficking, and from the outset the war has been waged primarily at the nation's borders. It has been a war, in other words, largely of interdiction.

> James Lieber   January 1986

interregnum   *in tuh REG nuhm*
the time between two reigns or governments, or two events

> In 1932-1933 a long interregnum between the election and a March inauguration was still constitutionally mandated. Poor Herbert Hoover had to lead the country as a lame duck for a third of a year.

> Garry Wills   April 1994

intersperse   *in tuhr SPERS*
to scatter among other things; place at intervals

> Nobody has ever surpassed Conrad in ability to spin a sea yarn that holds your attention to the end; to tell a story of seafaring interspersed with the most true and beautiful descriptions of vessels under sail, of the ocean in all its moods, and of the effect of the sea on human character.

> Samuel Eliot Morison   September 1955

intimate   *IN tuh mayt*
to suggest indirectly; hint; imply

> It is not a pretty thing to ponder — that in the spring of 1941 the leaders of American thought, from the President on down, can shake oratorical or editorial fists at the aggressors to their hearts' content, can intimate repeatedly that the defeat of the Axis is essential to American safety, but can never so much as breathe that some American boy might get hurt in the process.

> Stewart Alsop   May 1941

invective   *in VEK tiv*
a violent verbal attack; strong criticism; insult

> Adlai Stevenson was considered an *egghead* in his 1952 race with Dwight Eisenhower — a dubious distinction that didn't help him that November. LBJ's claim that Gerald Ford wasn't smart enough to "*chew gum and walk at the same time*" is now secure in the treasury of political invective. But of course, as David Hess, a

state representative in New Hampshire, observed recently, when it comes to politics "people are suspicious of the four-point-O, straight-A guy."

J. E. Lighter   March 2000

✳ Egghead, a slang term for an intellectual person, derived from the belief that such people had high foreheads. The term first appeared in print in 1907 but was popularized during the 1952 American presidential campaign as a disparaging, anti-intellectual description of the baldish Democratic candidate Adlai Stevenson, who was known for his intellect and wit. Parrying the epithet at the University of Wisconsin during the campaign in 1952, Stevenson told his audience, "Eggheads of the world, unite — you have nothing to lose but your yolks."

inverse   *IN vers*
reversed in order or relation; the direct opposite

I know a shrewd and slightly cynical publisher who insists that the popularity of a piece of literature is always in an inverse ratio to its excellence. This is a pleasing and easily-remembered formula. It collapses, however, when you say "Hamlet."

Bliss Perry   March 1907

inveterate   *in VE tuh rit*
persisting in an ingrained habit; habitual

Charles Ives was an inveterate borrower; in his Fourth Symphony the second movement alone quotes at least two dozen tunes by other composers.

Charles C. Mann   September 1998

of long standing; deep-rooted

An inveterate hatred of war appears throughout the *Iliad*, and Homer smuggles into Book Twenty-three a bitter comment on the monstrous slavery it entails by awarding the winner of the wrestling match a copper cauldron worth twelve oxen and the loser a captive Trojan noblewoman, valued as highly as four because she is skilled at the loom.

Robert Graves   November 1959

invincible   *in VIN suh buhl*
unable to be overcome; unconquerable

During the dreary centuries through which the Sierra lay in darkness, crushed beneath the ice folds of the glacial winter, there was a steady invincible advance toward the warm life and beauty of to-day; and it is just where the glaciers crushed most destructively that the greatest amount of beauty is made manifest. But as these landscapes have succeeded the preglacial landscapes, so they in turn are giving place to others already planned and foreseen. The granite domes and pavements, apparently imperishable, we take as symbols of permanence, while these crumbling peaks, down whose frosty gullies avalanches are ever falling, are symbols of change and decay. Yet all alike, fast or slow, are surely vanishing away.

John Muir   August 1899

inviolable   *in VIGH uh luh buhl*
secure from assault or trespass; sacred

If in an ideal democracy everyone votes, people could simply be required to participate. This is how Australians reasoned when they instituted compulsory voting after their turnout rate fell to 58 percent in 1922. Since then the turnout in Australia has never fallen below 90 percent, even though the maximum fine for not voting is only about $30, and judges readily accept any reasonable excuse. However, American political culture is based on John Locke's views on individual rights, whereas Australian culture was shaped by Jeremy Bentham's concept of the greatest good for the greatest number. Most Americans would probably assert that they have an inviolable right *not* to vote.

Martin P. Wattenberg   October 1998

ipso facto   *IP soh FAK toh*
by that very fact

We sometimes hear parents say, "I don't see why my children have turned out so differently, when I have trained them all exactly alike." That is reason enough. No two are alike, and the training that is right for one is *ipso facto* wrong for another.

James Champlin Fernald   September 1900

irredentist   *i ri DEN tist*
the policy of seeking to recover territory culturally or historically related to one's nation but now subject to a foreign government

Since its creation after the First World War, Iraq has been a fragile entity, with its Sunni Muslim elite dominating restless Shiites and Kurds. In the aftermath of the Gulf War, Syria, Iran, and Turkey — each of which has irredentist claims on Iraq — have encouraged and abetted turmoil there.

Christopher Layne   July 1991

irrefutable   *i ruh FYOO: tuh buhl*
impossible to deny or disprove ("irrefutably" is the adverb)

Most of the stock arguments in favor of suffrage seem to me to be so irrefutably true as to be absolutely bromidic. Women are certainly "people." They are certainly "equal" to men. If they have property, they certainly ought to have a part in the management of public affairs in the locality where it lies. It is eminently "fair," for all these reasons, that women should vote if they wish to, and the majority of them apparently do wish to — the majority, that is, of the whole country, not the majority in certain sections of the country where it is still unpopular. And though they are still untrained in politics, there seems to be no reason why they should not acquire experience, and develop talents along these lines; for so far they have proved that they can do anything that men can do, and do it well. Anyone unconvinced of this before the late war must be certain — even if reluctantly certain — of it now.

Frances Parkinson Keyes   February 1920

In an interesting letter addressed but not sent to the author P. D. Boborykin, Tolstoy defended his avoidance of social problems. "The aims of art," he wrote, "are incommensurable (as they say in mathematics) with social aims. The aim of an artist is not to resolve a question irrefutably, but to compel one to love life in all its manifestations, and these are inexhaustible. If I were told that I could write a novel in which I could indisputably establish as true my point of view on all social questions, I would not dedicate two hours to such a work; but if I were told that what I wrote would be read twenty years from now by those who are children today, and that they would weep and laugh over it and fall in love with the life in it, then I would dedicate all my existence and all my powers to it."

Ernest J. Simmons   April 1946

irresolute   *i RE zuh loo:t*
wavering in decision, purpose or opinion; undecided; uncertain

I have never ordered a dessert for lunch that I have not looked with envy and despair upon the superior one chosen by my companion. The donkey who starved to death irresolute between two bales of hay, not knowing which to attack first, I can understand like a brother.

Roger Lewis   December 1927

irretrievable   *i ruh TREE vuh buhl*
that which cannot be restored or recalled ("irretrievably" is the adverb)

The old-fashioned dignity of Washington Square has been irretrievably compromised by a modern corporation building which adds insult to injury by wearing on its façade the Latin motto *perstando et prestando utilitati*. Furthermore, this insolent structure so dwarfs the Washington Arch as to give it the artificial air of the frosted show-piece of a confectioner's window.

Alvan F. Sanborn   October 1906

✳ Because most 19th- and early 20th-century high school and college graduates were presumed to be familiar with Latin and classical Greek, phrases and passages in those languages were usually not translated or footnoted in magazines and books intended for readers with those levels of education. *Perstando et prestando utilitati* translates as "persevering and excelling in useful activity." Alvan F. Sanborn was probably unaware that the same motto that he found offensive on the façade of a commercial building on Washington Square was on the original seal of New York University, several of whose academic buildings bordered the Square in 1906. N.Y.U. was founded in 1831 as the University of the City of New York. When its name was changed in 1896, a new seal was designed and its motto shortened to *Perstare et Praestare*, "to persevere and excel."

irrevocable   *i RE vuh kuh buhl*
impossible to undo or change; irreversible ("irrevocably" is the adverb)

Few sensations, or rather sentiments, are more inextricably made up of pleasure and sadness than that with which we contemplate (as is not infrequent in some old gallery of Europe) a portrait which deeply interests us, and whose history is irrevocably lost. A better homily on the evanescence of human love and fame can scarcely be imagined: a face alive with moral personality and human charms, such as win and warm our stranger eyes, — yet the name, subject, artist, owner, all lost in oblivion!

Henry Theodore Tuckerman   February 1858

itinerant   *igh TI nuh rint*
traveling from place to place as part of one's work

With a very few exceptions the professional pianist to-day is nothing more than an itinerant advertising medium for the manufacturer whose piano he plays. In fact, if piano houses were not in deadly competition to get rid of their wares, the amount of music made in this country would easily be cut in half, for their largess penetrates into all the cracks and crannies of the business.

William E. Walter   January 1908

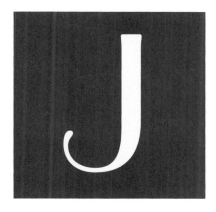

jejune

In Henry Adams, I discovered not only the prototype of the modern thinker but also someone who is more interesting: a viper-toothed, puling, supercilious crank, thwarted in ambition, aging gracelessly, mad at the cosmos, and ashamed of his own jejune ideals. He is nevertheless very dear to me. And he appears in my front-hall mirror.

P. J. O'Rourke   December 2002

see page 246

jar *jahr*

to jolt or shock ("jarring" is the adjective)

> The visual contrasts in Iraq are jarring: on the one hand, traces of Babylon, Assyria, and Sumeria; on the other, the most advanced plutonium breeder reactor.
>
> Claudia Wright   April 1979

jaundiced *JAWN dist*

viewing everything from a negative point of view; cynical

> Even the most jaundiced observer must admit that business is ethically better than it used to be. The milleniuum has not arrived. Human nature has not changed. Men are just as selfish and self-seeking as they ever were. But business has learned the priceless truth, laid down by Benjamin Franklin, and scores of philosophers before him, that honesty is really the best policy. It has learned that the only source of prosperity is the public, which buys and pays, that on its treatment of that public depends, in the long run, its success, and that a permanent customer who comes back is a greater asset than the profit on the first sale.
>
> Earnest Elmo Calkins   February 1928

> ✻ From the belief that to a person with jaundice everything looked yellow, the expression "a jaundiced eye" arose, meaning a prejudiced eye, one that sees only faults.

jaunty *JAWN tee*

lighthearted and self-confident in manner ("jauntily" is the adverb)

> It will be remembered how jauntily Sir Walter Scott, when he wanted a motto for the heading of a chapter in one of his novels, used indifferently some snatch of a Scottish song, or two or three lines of his own, invented on the spur of the moment,

and accredited to some indefinite Old Ballad or Old Play. So it was with Whittier. If he had a story or legend handy when he wished to give expression to some poetic thought or kindly sentiment, well and good, he used it; but if he had not, then he made it; and many of his poems which have all the air of a leaf out of some old book, as "The Gift of Tritemius," for example, are wholly his own.

Horace Elisha Scudder   November 1894

jeer *jeer*
to make fun of in a rude, sarcastic manner; mock; scoff

In 1879 the Impressionists — among them Degas, Monet, Sisley, and Renoir — organized their first exposition. It was apropos of this exhibition that the press coined the word "impressionist" as a term of ridicule. Desperate for funds, the following year they held their first public auction, with police in attendance to prevent a riot, while spectators jeered and howled at every bid. The seventy-three pictures brought 11,496 francs, an average of about 156 fr. ($31) apiece.

Lee Simonson   May 1946

jejune *juh JOO:N*
unsatisfying to the mind or soul; dull; flat; insipid

In Henry Adams, I discovered not only the prototype of the modern thinker but also someone who is more interesting: a viper-toothed, puling, supercilious crank, thwarted in ambition, aging gracelessly, mad at the cosmos, and ashamed of his own jejune ideals. He is nevertheless very dear to me. And he appears in my front-hall mirror.

P. J. O'Rourke   December 2002

je ne sais quoi *zhuhn say KWAH*
something elusive, or hard to describe or express: French, I do not know what

In presenting Sinatra with a Grammy Legend award in 1994, Bono, of the Irish rock group U2, waxed poetic: "Rock-and-roll people love Frank Sinatra because Frank Sinatra has got what we want — swagger and attitude." But Sinatra singing a ballad could be courtly and compassionate, and much of what Bono and Bruce Springsteen, too, applaud as swagger in his up-tempo performances was actually swing — the *je ne sais quoi* of jazz but a commodity foreign to most of today's rock and pop.

Francis Davis   September 1998

jeremiad *je ruh MIGH uhd*
a long lamentation or mournful complaint expressing disapproval or warning of disaster: an allusion to the Lamentations of Jeremiah in the Bible

In his Baccalaureate Address for 1961, President A. Whitney Griswold of Yale said, among other things: "I shall not attempt to recite here all the worst things that are said about us or to refute them by pointing out that just as bad (or worse) things go on in the countries which say them. Neither shall I attempt to itemize the short-comings which we ourselves acknowledge. It is enough to remind ourselves of the nature of the great, national, hundred per cent American jeremiad. It goes like this. We are soft. We are spoiled. We are lazy, flabby, undisciplined, in poor physical con-dition, poorly educated, beguiled with gadgets, bedazzled by sex, uninterested in anything but our own comfort, unprepared for the responsibilities fate has placed upon us, unready for our destiny. In a word, we are decadent."

Robert Moses   January 1962

jingoistic   *JING goh IS tik*
showing extreme chauvinism or nationalism and favoring a belligerent
foreign policy

When he was alive many critics thought Kipling to be a bad writer, and also a bul-lying and jingoistic one, and many readers today agree. Moreover, much of Kipling's work, inarguably, was hasty and poorly written. Dick Heldar, in *The Light That Failed* (1890), says, "Four-fifths of everybody's work must be bad," and one feels Kipling speaking more truly than he knew when his character adds, "But the remnant is worth the trouble for its own sake."

Christopher Hitchens   June 2002

jocose   *joh KOHS*
joking; playful; jesting ("jocosely" is the adverb)

Our new domain comprised several acres of land, and my husband took great plea-sure in laying out an extensive fruit and flower garden and in building a fine hot-house. We removed to this abode on a lovely summer day; and when we entered the grounds I involuntarily exclaimed, "This is green peace!" Somehow, the nickname, jocosely given, remained in use. The estate still stands on legal records as "the Green Peace Estate." Friends would sometimes ask us, "How are you getting on at Green Beans, — is that the name?"

Julia Ward Howe   March 1899

❋ When Julia Ward Howe (1819-1910) died at the age of 91, she had been a renowned magazine editor, an active abolitionist, a founder of the women's suffrage movement, and a fighter for equal opportunity for women. Her lasting fame, though, rests on her having written the words to the "Battle Hymn of the Republic" when she was 42, to the tune of "John Brown's Body," a well-known war song. The "Battle Hymn" retained the "Glory, glory hallelujah" choruses from the older song between each verse. Her inspiration for the song came during a visit to Washington in the fall of 1861, after seeing Union soldiers rush off on horseback to repulse a Confederate attack nearby. In a March 1899 *Atlantic* article of reminiscences, Howe said that after sleeping "quite soundly" that night, "I awoke in the gray of the morning twilight; and as I lay waiting for the dawn, the long lines of the desired poem began to twine themselves in my mind. Having thought out all the stanzas, I said to myself, 'I must get up and write these verses down, lest I fall asleep again and forget them.' So, with a sudden effort, I sprang out of bed, and found in the dimness an old stump of a pen, which I remembered to have used the day before. I scrawled the verses almost without looking at the paper. I had learned to do this when, on previous occasions, attacks of versification had visited me in the night, and I feared to have recourse to a light lest I should wake the baby, who slept near me. I was always obliged to decipher my scrawl before another night intervened, as it was legible only while the matter was fresh in my mind. At this time, having completed my writing, I returned to bed and fell asleep, with the reflection, 'I like this better than most things that I have written.'" An *Atlantic* editor gave the song its title, and Howe's five stanzas were published on the first page of the February 1862 issue.

jostle *JAH suhl*
to bump or push, as in a crowd; to vie with for an advantage or position
("jostling" is the adjective)

Isolation, in this world of jostling nations with a thousand strands of interwoven interests, is an impossible condition. No one nation can hope to flourish in self-contained security at the expense of others or without due regard for their well-being.

E. F. Benson   February 1934

jovial *JOH vee uhl*
joyous; mirthful

Our first notable landscape painter, Thomas Cole, went to England in 1829 with a selection of his paintings to be put on exhibition. The English came, and saw, and were far from conquered. The foliage of this man's trees was all bright red and yellow! As such a thing was never seen in nature as they knew it, they felt that this was a school of art that needed to be nipped in the bud; and so the critics pooh-poohed, and the visitors had many a jovial nudge over the young artist and his new departure in painting.

Charles D. Stewart   November 1934

judicious   *joo: DI shuhs*
showing good judgment; wise

It was at New York that, in the midst of ovations, Dickens, irritated by newspaper comments on his speeches regarding copyright, seems to have begun to dislike his entertainers. His American friends advised him not to introduce the subject of copyright into his speeches. He appears to have attributed to cowardice what was intended by them as judicious advice. They doubtless thought the cause he advocated would be hindered rather than advanced by his appearance before the public, not as a guest of the nation whom all men were eager to honor, but as an English citizen urging a change in the domestic policy of the United States.

Edwin Percy Whipple   April 1887

jurisprudence   *joo ris PROO: duhns*
the application of legal principles and theories to legal problems, especially
classic or recurrent legal questions

Some critics say that voucher use at religious schools violates the Constitution's ban on "establishment of religion," but the better view of the Supreme Court's confusing jurisprudence here suggests that's wrong. After all, no one thinks that federal student loans are unconstitutional when they are used by students to attend Notre Dame.

Matthew Miller   July 1999

keystone

The modern computer is more than a sophisticated indexing or adding machine, or a miniaturized library; it is the keystone for a new communications medium whose capacities and implications we are only beginning to realize.

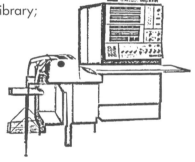

Arthur R. Miller   November 1967

see page 254

kaleidoscopic *kuh ligh duh SKAH pik*
exhibiting many facets or patterns; continually changing

In the kaleidoscopic machinery of opera, the dancers are the most difficult to satis-
fy. Think what an enormous difference a slightly faster speed of the music can make
to a complicated pirouette or to a monstrously high jump into the air! Aware of most
conductors' gross inability to feel with their feet, the Paris Opera has a special ballet conductor who takes the place of the evening's regular maestro as soon as the
danse divertissement is about to start.

Erich Leinsdorf   November 1959

keen *keen*
to utter in a shrill, wailing tone, as for the dead: from the Irish caoin-im, *I wail*

Electronic music-making devices followed remarkably soon after the early radios
and amplifiers, in the 1920's. The best known are the electronic (Hammond) organ
and the eerie theramin, which keened like a musical saw when the performer passed
his hands through the air above it.

Carter Harman   December 1968

✤ The theramin was invented in 1919 by the Russian physicist Lev
Sergievitch Termen (1896-1993), better known by his Anglicized
name, Leon Theramin. Its tremulous, otherworldly sound — something like a ghostly, falsetto human voice — is often heard in science
fiction and horror films, although the theramin's sound can be quite
pleasant, dreamy and lyrical. Its best known movie appearance was in
the 1945 feature *Spellbound*. The theramin is played not by touch, but
by moving one's hands back and forth through the air a foot or two
in front of it, in an electronic field formed by two metal antennas that
project from a metal cabinet, one for pitch and the other for volume.

Hearing about this new use for electricity, Lenin invited Theramin to his Kremlin office, and was so taken by the instrument's sound that he asked the inventor to teach him how to play it. Robert Moog's interest in the theramin led to his inventing the synthesizer that bears his surname.

keystone   *KEE stohn*
the part that supports or holds together all the others; main part: after the central, topmost stone of an arch regarded as holding the others in place

The modern computer is more than a sophisticated indexing or adding machine, or a miniaturized library; it is the keystone for a new communications medium whose capacities and implications we are only beginning to realize.

Arthur R. Miller   November 1967

kinship   *KIN ship*
close connection; relationship by nature or qualities

A tale which may well be truthful recounts that when Shalom Aleichem (a pen name which means "peace be with you," the traditional Hebraic greeting) came to America from Russia, Mark Twain went to call on him, and said, "I wanted to meet you because I understand I am known as the American Shalom Aleichem." It was a graceful way of acknowledging that the Yiddish writer had long been spoken of as the Jewish Mark Twain, and of expressing the literary kinship of two writers who were shrewd and affectonate observers of humanity.

Herbert Kupferberg January 1965

kitsch   *kitch*
artistically shallow or cute art, art objects or writing, calculated for popular taste: German, gaudy trash

What most Americans know about Hawaii is kitsch — grass skirts and ukuleles, pupu platters and Don Ho — culminating in James Michener's fitfully factual pot-boiler and finally degenerating into some tacky prime-time cop shows. The islands never had a native bard to explain them to the rest of the world, as the American frontier had Mark Twain and the South had William Faulkner.

Jamie James   February 1999

kleptocracy   *klep TAH kruh see*
a government whose leaders steal from it

The corruption in Zaire is legendary. The "kleptocracy" has its roots in the nineteenth-century Congo Free State: Belgium's King Leopold II used profits from the export of the country's extensive natural resources to build a personal fortune — profits extracted under conditions of forced labor that included killing workers and chopping off hands if quotas were not met.

Bill Berkeley   August 1993

kvell   *kvel*
to burst with pride: Yiddish

Good families have a chief, or a heroine, or a founder — someone around whom others cluster, whose achievements, as the Yiddish word has it, let them *kvell*, and whose example spurs them on to like feats.

Jane Howard   May 1978

L

leitmotif

People have pointed out the influence of Wagner's music on my work.
Certainly I do not disclaim this influence. In particular, I followed Wagner
in the use of the leitmotif, which I carried over into the work of language.
Not as Tolstoy and Zola use it, or as I used it myself in *Buddenbrooks*,
naturalistically and as a meaning of characterization — so to speak,
mechanically. I sought to employ it in its musical sense. My first attempts
were in *Tonio Kroger*. But the technique I there
employed is in *The Magic Mountain* greatly
expanded; it is used in a very much more
complicated and all-pervasive way. That is why I
make my presumptuous plea to my readers to read the
book twice. Only so can one really penetrate and enjoy its musical
association of ideas. The first time, the reader learns the thematic
material; he is then in a position to read the symbolic and allusive
formulas both forwards and backwards.

Thomas Mann   January 1953

see page 264

labyrinth *LA buh rinth*
an intricate network of winding passages where it is easy to lose one's way

The Roman catacombs consist for the most part of a subterranean labyrinth of passages, cut through the soft volcanic rock of the Campagna, so narrow as rarely to admit of two persons walking abreast easily, but here and there on either side opening into chambers of varying size and form.

Charles Eliot Norton   March 1858

✳ In Greek mythology, the labyrinth was an underground maze of great complexity that the architect Daedalus built for King Minos of Crete. In it, Minos confined the Minotaur, a monster with the body of a man and the head of a bull, which every year devoured seven youths and seven maidens whom Minos placed in the labyrinth. The Minotaur was finally slain by Theseus, who unwound a ball of string as he wandered through the maze and wound it up again to find his way out.

lachrymose *LA kruh mos*
calculated to provoke tears; mawkish: Latin, lacrima, *tears*

In 1907 the author of *Sister Carrie*, widely considered the most degenerate novel of the decade, was employed by the Butterick Publishing Company, of New York, in the improbable role of editor of their trio of genteel women's magazines. From a desk the size of a billiard table in an office of comparable scale, Dreiser acquired the lachrymose poetry and lackluster fiction that filled the pages of the Delineator.

Nancy Caldwell Sorel   November 1989

lackey   *LA kee*
a follower who carries out another's orders like a servant; toady

Since Marxism is a creed of class conflict, it is not strange that its disciples should be vials of wrath. Neither is it astonishing that Mensheviks, Bolsheviks, and Trotskyites should hate one another more fantastically than they hate the "lackeys of the bourgeoisie," for in all religious feuds heretics are more detestable than infidels.

Frederick L. Schuman   June 1946

laconic   *luh KAH nik*
using few words; brief and to the point; terse; concise

The most elaborate car I ever sold was a 40 h.p. Mercedes fitted with a body made by one of the famous London coachbuilders to the order of a well-known New York lawyer, who told me he wanted the most expensive car I could produce. I enlisted the services of cabinetmakers, plumbers, and others, to install a basin, drawers and closet for clothes, and goodness knows what besides. The buyer was delighted and, after signing his check, instructed my secretary to send cables to ten acquaintances bearing the laconic message: "I have just purchased a $40,000 automobile"!

John E. Hutton   December 1948

lacuna   *luh KYOO: nuh*
an empty space; missing part; gap

My wife and I have been away from the United States for nine years, and our children are eleven and nine, so American history is mostly something they have learned — or haven't learned — from their parents. July 4 is one of the times when the American in me feels a twinge of unease about the great lacunae in our children's understanding of who they are and is prompted to try to fill the gaps.

Charles Trueheart   July/August 2001

laissez-faire   *le say FAIR*
the principle that the economy works best if private industry is not regulated and markets are free: French, allow to do

Although I have made a fortune in the financial markets, I now fear that the untrammeled intensification of laissez-faire capitalism and the spread of market values into all areas of life is endangering our open and democratic society. The main enemy of the open society, I believe, is no longer the communist but the capitalist threat.

George Soros   February 1997

non-interference in the affairs of others

The only printed warnings I can remember from childhood are BEWARE OF DOG and the cloth tag on mattresses that was never to be removed, under penalty of law. Today warnings are virtually a design feature of any product. To be sure, many cautionary announcements are essential. Hong Kong's televised "Falling Objects Kill" campaign, which portrays what can happen when a refrigerator tossed from an apartment window lands on a schoolgirl riding a bike, is an urgent necessity in a city of high-rise congestion and laissez-faire sensibilities. At the other end of the spectrum is the warning label on those accordionlike cardboard sun-blockers that stretch above the dashboard: "Do not drive with sunshield in place."

Cullen Murphy   September 1999

laity *LAY uh tee*
those persons who are not members of a particular profession, as distinguished
from those who are

The public should be taught that all normal eyes require glasses for near vision about the age of forty or forty-five; that postponing their use later than this age causes an effort of the accommodation which does harm. The prejudice to the use of glasses seems to be dying out, and the laity are realizing more and more the necessity of paying attention to the eyes.

A. B. Norton   November 1902

lambaste *lam BAYST*
to verbally thrash; scold sharply

In 1915, when *The Genius*, just published, was being lambasted by critics, Theodore Dreiser got a fervent letter of support from a young poet in Washington, D.C. Touched, Dreiser wrote back his thanks and added "a kindly bit of advice" in closing: "Never bother to know me, personally. Remain illusioned, if you can."

Michael Lydon   August 1993

lambent *LAM buhnt*
shining with a soft, clear light; playing lightly and brilliantly on or over a
surface, said of wit or style

We believe that Shakespeare, like all other great poets, instinctively used the dialect which he found current, and that his words are not more wrested from their ordinary meaning than followed necessarily from the unwonted weight of thought or stress of passion they were called on to support. He needed not to mask familiar thoughts in the weeds of unfamiliar phraseology; for the life that was in his mind could transfuse the language of every day with an intelligent vivacity that makes it seem lambent with fiery purpose and at each new reading a new creation.

James Russell Lowell   January 1859

lament   *luh MENT*
an expression of regret or disappointment

The common lament on our campuses is the dearth of "major poets," and the critics are scuttling to find one. If they cannot find him, surely they can invent him: study someone until he turns out to be major by simply dominating the course catalogues. The distinction between major and minor in poetry has not often been useful except when discriminating between a Homer, a Dante, a Shakespeare, a Goethe—and the others. Yet today critics pick over the contemporary and near-contemporary crops of poetry with all the concentration of cannery workers sorting and grading fruit.

Peter Davison   October 1967

languid   *LANG gwid*
without vigor or vitality, as though by choice ("languidly" is the adverb)

A great dancer seems to move more slowly through any given exercise because there is no waste motion whatsoever, and therefore in fact there is more time for movement. Margot Fonteyn is notable for this quality. She is like the stillness in the heart of the hurricane and appears to be moving languidly, until one shuts one's eyes and listens to the music, which may be pumping out a presto.

Agnes De Mille   December 1960

lark   *lahrk*
a merry, carefree episode or adventure embarked on with little forethought

Few things could be more shocking to the sensibilities of a fashionable New York family than to inquire whether they intended going to Coney Island for the season. Occasionally, indeed, a "heavy swell" of the fashionable avenue will take a turn down there with his team, "by way of a lark," but he does this in the confidence that he is not likely to be brought face to face with any of his set, and his account of things when he returns to the city includes nothing of Coney Island with its vulgar associations and motley crowd.

Charles Dawson Shanley   September 1874

latterday   *LA tuhr day*
belonging to present times or those recent by comparison; modern

Some of our latterday historians, in their desire for dispassionateness, have unfortunately not realized that history, even at lowest ebb, is drama. By treating the facts in such a fashion as to disguise the personalities, the clash of will, the inner tumult, these historians have not achieved historical objectivity but departed from it. It is Trotsky's sense of the inherent drama of society, seasoned by his close respect for facts, that gives him the attributes of a great historian.

Lewis Mumford   December 1932

✳ The Church of Jesus Christ of Latter-day Saints (its adherents are commonly known as Mormons) was founded in 1830 by Joseph Smith, who gave the religion that name in 1838. The revelations he received that led to its founding, he said, declared that it was the first true church since the one Jesus founded, and as Jesus's followers were called saints, his followers were to be called saints as well. They were to be "Latter-day" saints to indicate that they would witness Jesus's reappearance on earth — the Second Coming — and prepare the world for its last days.

lavish   *LA vish*
to give or bestow in abundance or excess

Since the surface writing, the direction, the photography, the editing, the visual tricks, and all the other phases of this complex art have been steadily improving while content has lagged, it seems that more and more technique is lavished on less and less, until today the average Hollywood film comes off the assembly line like a well-made can: canned love, canned adventure, canned psychiatry, canned history, canned spiritual values, hermetically sealed, untouched by human hand or human heart.

Budd Schulberg   November 1947

leach   *leech*
to filter into and gradually permeate; drain into

The Protocols of Zion, with its clumsy passages about a Jewish drive for world domination, was a concoction of the secret police in czarist Russia — a fact not conceded by the Russian government until 1993, a century after the toxins had leached into the anti-Semitic world.

Cullen Murphy   December 2004

legacy   *LE guh see*
anything handed down from a predecessor or from the past

I was at my father's elbow constantly, watching him, listening to him, debating with him. It was the luckiest legacy he could have left me. My life since he died has been fortunate, personally and politically. My happinesses have been more than any man should expect. I have sat in the councils of the great and been a part of the drama of our age. But all these things have had meaning and purpose because I had the priceless good fortune of spending almost every day of my childhood, and many nights, working at the side of a wise and sensitive man for whom idealism was not a cold creed but a way of life.

Hubert H. Humphrey   November 1966

legerdemain   *le jer duh MAYN*
trickery; deception; any artful trick

Perhaps nothing has done more to vulgarize the fairy than its introduction upon the stage; the charm of the fairy tale is in its divorce from human experience; the charm of the stage is in its realization, in miniature, of human life. If the frog is heard to speak, if the dog is turned before one's eyes into a prince, by having cold water dashed over it, the charm of the fairy tale has fled, and in its place we have only the perplexing pleasure of legerdemain. The effect of producing these scenes upon the stage is to bring them one step nearer to sensuous reality, and one step further from imaginative reality; and since the real life of fairy is in the imagination, a cruel wrong is done when it is dragged from its shadowy hiding-place and made to turn into ashes under the calcium light of the understanding.

Horace Elisha Scudder   November 1875

leitmotif   *LIGHT moh teef*
a dominant or recurring theme: German, leading motive

People have pointed out the influence of Wagner's music on my work. Certainly I do not disclaim this influence. In particular, I followed Wagner in the use of the leitmotif, which I carried over into the work of language. Not as Tolstoy and Zola use it, or as I used it myself in *Buddenbrooks*, naturalistically and as a meaning of characterization — so to speak, mechanically. I sought to employ it in its musical sense. My first attempts were in *Tonio Kröger*. But the technique I there employed is in *The Magic Mountain* greatly expanded; it is used in a very much more complicated and all-pervasive way. That is why I make my presumptuous plea to my readers to read the book twice. Only so can one really penetrate and enjoy its musical association of ideas. The first time, the reader learns the thematic material; he is then in a position to read the symbolic and allusive formulas both forwards and backwards.

Thomas Mann   January 1953

✳ In music, a leitmotif is a phrase or theme associated throughout the work with a particular character, place, emotion or idea. Many leitmotifs may be heard in a single opera, both vocally and instrumentally.

While each leitmotif has one basic melody, it may occur each time with different harmony, tempo or instrumentation. In Sergei Prokofief's orchestral work *Peter and the Wolf*, each character not only has a leitmotif but is represented by a different instrument of the orchestra. Most movies have leitmotifs in their background music, such as the menacing shark leitmotif in *Jaws* and the murderous violin screech in *Psycho*.

leonine   *LEE uh nighn*
like a lion

Toscanini is barely over five feet tall, though his head is large and leonine; and he looks even smaller in his working clothes, which consist of a black alpaca jacket, buttoned to the neck, gray striped trousers, and black, elastic-sided Italian shoes.

John M. Conly   October 1952

❧ Leonine is one of several words that describe an animal-like resemblance or characteristic. Ursine means bearlike; vulpine, foxlike; bovine, cowlike; lupine, wolflike; and porcine, piglike. An aquiline nose is one that is hooked or curved like an eagle's beak.

leverage   *LE vuh rij*
to apply a strategic advantage

In its most ambitious form the conditional bequest leverages great wealth in an attack on time itself, attempting to ensure that at least some small thing in the universe will never change. Isabella Stewart Gardner gave her Boston mansion and her vast art collection to the public, but decreed that if any of the art or furnishings were moved from their locations the entire bequest was to be auctioned off in Paris, the proceeds going to Harvard University.

Cullen Murphy   April 1994

limn   *lighm*
to draw or paint a picture of; portray graphically in words

When, at some future day, the psychology of music is elaborated, it may be possible to discern a composer's character in his work, to draw his musical portrait as firmly as Holbein limned the courtiers of Henry the Eighth. For, if we put something of ourselves into what are commonly regarded as indifferent acts, how intimately must we express ourselves in anything which moves us so profoundly as music does!

Redfern Mason   February 1909

lion's share   *LIGH uhnz shair*
the largest portion

At the end of the day the problem with health-care spending is not that it's ineffi-
cient but that it's redistributive. Each year the small fraction of people who are very
sick account for the lion's share of health-care spending. They are different people,
of course, from year to year, and the odds are that all of us, once or twice in our
lives, will take our turns as mega-medical consumers. Since none but the very
wealthiest families can sustain the cost of big-ticket medical episodes, the risk has
to be partially socialized, either privately through insurance or publicly through the
tax system. I may not want to help pay for your heart attack, but I'll need you to
kick in, one way or another, for the cost of my cancer.

Charles R. Morris   December 1999

lip service   *LIP ser vis*
verbal support or agreement that is not backed up by deed

In the old world that is crumbling to pieces as I write, nations strove with each other
to win supremacy in the means of destruction. The defunct League of Nations, whatever its shortcomings, had in its conception of world peace an area of thought which
we should do well to cultivate. While lip-service to international equality and justice
was not found wanting, signatories of the League Covenant did not have the courage
actively to implement the principles enunciated so piously by their representatives
round the conference table. China, Abyssinia, Spain, Poland, and other militarily
weak nations became the victims of aggression, and the democracies, which should
have seen the writing on the wall, did little more than make futile protests.

Madame Chiang Kai-Shek   May 1942

litmus test   *LIT muhs test*
a test that uses a single indicator to determine the finding: from a test in which
litmus paper turns blue when dipped in an alkali and red when dipped in an acid

It's hard, honestly, to imagine any politician's incurring serious political damage
because of a decision to send his or her children to private school — or, for that matter, because of a weak commitment to public education. Fealty to the ideal of public
school is no longer a litmus test, even for most Democrats. Half a century from now
the Clinton years may be remembered as the years when public education lost its hold
on American hearts and minds — a transformation as profound as it was unintended.

Margaret Talbot   February 2001

littoral   *LI tuh ruhl*
a shore or coastal region, including the land and water that touch each other

The historian Erich S. Gruen has observed that Rome's expansion throughout the Mediterranean littoral may well have been motivated not by an appetite for conquest per se but because it was thought necessary for the security of the core homeland.

Robert D. Kaplan   July/August 2003

loath *lohth*
unwilling; reluctant

Shakespeare is a biographer's nightmare. Not because the information about him is so overwhelming or incriminating but because it is so slight and so stubbornly innocuous. We forgive our great poets almost anything — suicide (Sylvia Plath), homicide (Ben Jonson), incest (William Wordsworth), hubris (Oscar Wilde), drunkenness (Edgar Allan Poe), insanity (Friedrich Nietzsche), sexual excess of every description (Byron, Shelley, Houellebecq — who not?). What we are loath to forgive is quiet respectability.

Cristina Nehring   December 2004

loathe *lohth*
to feel intense dislike or disgust; abhor

I have loathed fairies ever since the days of Tinker Bell and the mean slyness of the Alcott fairy who gave the bracelet that pricked. Loathed them at first furtively and guiltily, knowing them to be somehow the literary disguise of adult authority, the power and the sermon sneaking in on silly rainbow wings with thin legs and gauzy dresses, all-wise, all-powerful under its fragility, always beautiful (for the fat and forty love the image of themselves in golden hair, barefooted on the flowers), insistent as mosquitoes, preaching at the helpless human child.

Josephine Johnson   September 1953

locus classicus *LOH kuhs KLA si kuhs*
a passage often cited as authoritative to explain a subject or word; a standard passage (especially one by an ancient author) that is viewed as the principal authority on a subject

The first volume (A-G) of the new Supplement of the *Oxford English Dictionary* identifies me as providing the *locus classicus* for the term "the Establishment" when I first used it in its contemporary meaning in 1955. I have to confess that I feel as if I have been knighted, and a friend has suggested that I should henceforth insist that envelopes be addressed to me as "Henry Fairlie, *l.c.*" Certainly, when I first gazed at the entry, I wondered if there was anyplace left to go but down.

Henry Fairlie   January 1975

✳ Since its publication in 1928, any serious discussion about a word's meaning or origin has been virtually impossible without considering what the *Oxford English Dictionary* says about it. The *OED* not only defines the various senses of every word in the English language but, citing dates and authors, provides a history of their use through examples from books, periodicals and other sources. Oxford University scholars began work on the *OED* in 1879, planning to publish a 7,000-page, four-volume dictionary in ten years at a cost of £9,000. Forty-nine years later, in 1928, the 16,000 page, 20-volume dictionary was completed. It cost £300,000. The *OED* gathered its entries from hundreds of volunteers worldwide who pored through books and periodicals, writing words and passages, titles and dates on slips of paper and mailing them to the editors, who selected the examples, defined the words and researched the etymologies. Supplements composed of new words and new senses of old words have appeared since 1928, but with the complete *OED* now available online as well as in print, new material appears on its Web site almost daily. From the beginning, what distinguished the *OED* from even the monumental dictionaries of Samuel Johnson (1755) and Noah Webster (1828) was its goal to include every word in the English language, every sense and every meaning, not just those selected by the author as worthy of inclusion in the language. The lexicographer should be "a historian, not a gatekeeper of language," said Richard Trench, one of the *OED*'s founders.

locution   *loh KYOO: shuhn*

a word, phrase or expression

In the Chicago ghetto poor blacks use the verb stay instead of live, as in "I stay at Robert Taylor Homes." Besides implying an inconstant life, this comes from a perfectly sensible sharecroppers' locution: "I stay at the Smiths' place." Another northern ghetto term that comes from southern town life is "getting over," which is less translatable but means, roughly, doing what is necessary to survive and, if possible, succeed. While it does not cover violence, it would apply to hustling as well as to more legitimate pursuits. It comes from the idea of crossing the Jordan River to get to the Promised Land.

Nicholas Lemann   June 1986

lodestone   *LOHD stohn*

a magnet: from geology, a stone containing magnetic oxide of iron

Adlai Stevenson and I both arrived in Washington at the outset of the New Deal, he a refugee from a Chicago law firm, and I fresh out of law school. Roosevelt's inauguration made Washington an irresistible lodestone for young lawyers with a mission.

George W. Ball   May 1966

lofty   *LAWF tee*
having high purpose; elevated ("loftiness" is the noun)

The loftiness of the *Times* is an asset when it comes to standing up to popular opinion or the bullying of government. But when you set out to assemble and connect with the most demanding readers in the world, it is not acceptable to serve them eat-your-peas journalism and insist that they swallow it as a duty of citizenship. If you want to reach members of this quality audience who are between the ages of twenty and forty, you have to penetrate the worlds of style and popular culture. If the *Times's* journalism continues to show contempt for the vernacular of those worlds, the paper will continue to lose subscribers. To explore every aspect of American and global experience does not mean pandering. It does mean that the serial ups and downs of a Britney Spears are a sociological and economic phenomenon that is, as a reflection of contemporary American culture, worthy of serious reporting.

Howell Raines   May 2004

loom   *loo:m*
to come into view, or appear to the mind, in a magnified and threatening form

When, some years ago, I set out to write about Sir Francis Bacon, the undertaking loomed frighteningly large. Not only had Bacon been written about copiously for more than three hundred years, but I had chosen as subject a man who was a world in himself; a Renaissance man, as many-sided as Da Vinci; at once a scientific thinker, an observer of human nature, and a writer of cool, quick, mellifluous prose, which at its best is unmatched in our language.

Catherine Drinker Bowen   January 1966

loquacious   *loh KWAY shuhs*
very talkative

Indians are a loquacious people. They gather in knots on street corners and talk — about politics, about economics, about American-Soviet affairs, about Indira Gandhi, about themselves, about anything.

Pranay Gupte   August 1977

louche   *loo:sh*
questionable; shady; dubious

We walked and walked. At last we came to a wide stone square, serene and gorgeous in the long, slanting light. People stood or lounged on a set of steps, awaiting the nightly opening of the Odéon, the architectural focus of the square. Across the way was a glass-fronted restaurant, La Méditerranée. We liked the setting, we liked the restaurant's looks, we liked the posted menu: not too haughty, not too louche, but juuuust right.

Barbara Wallraff   October 1999

lout   *lowt*
one who behaves in a rude, offensive and sometimes aggressive way

The public always knew the basic contradictions: Sinatra was vicious and sweet-hearted; he hated racial and religious bigotry and consorted with killers; he was a man of easy elegance and he was a lout. But while those paradoxes contributed to his mystique, they never defined it.

Benjamin Schwarz   July/August 2005

lubricable   *LOO: bruh kuh buhl*
capable of being stimulated or encouraged by drink

A distinguished British newspaper proprietor had died, and his paper was under the competitive necessity of making as much of his death as a very liberal hyperbole would allow. So the editor summoned the paper's best writer and drummed into him the herculean expectations the paper had for the obituary he was to write. The writer, who was known to possess a lubricable genius, was taken to a hotel room, furnished with a typewriter and paper, and locked in for the night. Early the next morning the editor opened the door to find the writer slumped over his typewriter, asleep, an empty whiskey bottle at his feet. The room was littered with crumpled sheets of paper, and on the sheet in the typewriter were these words: "Not since the death of Jesus Christ ...."

Jack Beatty   April 1990

lubricate   *LOO: bruh kayt*
to serve to smooth the progress or reduce the friction of a situation

"A good dinner lubricates business," said Dr. Johnson, and laughter, however caused, lubricates a dinner almost as much as wine, which in these degenerate days is hard to come upon — with safety.

A. Edward Newton   May 1932

lubricious   *loo: BRI shuhs*
characterized by lust; wanton

In 1975, when the movie *The Stepford Wives* first came out, it was widely regarded as a chilling parable about men's fears of feminism, a tale of horror that also worked as a social satire on sexism. Sure, it struck some women's liberationists as a ham-fisted attempt to cash in on the movement. But Ira Levin, who wrote the novel on which the movie was based, seems to have been in earnest — or as earnest as he could be with a brisk little potboiler in which suburban husbands band together to replace their wives with lubricious and empty-headed robots.

Margaret Talbot   December 2003

   ❋ Within minutes after the Czech playwright Karel Čapek (1890-1938) was inspired to write a play about mechanical people that take over the world, he asked his brother Josef what he should call them. "Robots," his brother said, *robota* being the Czech word for labor. The play, *R.U.R.* (Rossum's Universal Robots is the factory where they are made), was first performed in 1921. Prior to *R.U.R.* a robot-like device was called an automaton.

ludicrous   *LOO: duh kris*
so absurd, ridiculous or exaggerated as to be laughable

Lincoln's humor often served a useful purpose. Abstruse points became clear to the slowest minds on a jury when Lincoln explained them with a story; and his quick perception of the ludicrous and the ridiculous enabled him to unmask pretense and vanity and hold things in true perspective.

Benjamin B. Thomas   February 1954

   ❋ When Senator Stephen A. Douglas called him a "two-faced man," Lincoln said: "I leave it to my audience. If I had another face, do you think I would wear this one?"

lugubrious   *loo GOO: bree uhs*
exaggeratedly mournful, dismal or gloomy, especially in a way that seems ludicrous ("lugubriously" is the adverb)

Kissinger could barely conceal his contempt for those European diplomats who had to consult their cabinets or their divided parliaments before committing themselves. Besides, he felt, allies are a hindrance to superpower diplomacy, and he kept them out of his act. He now finds his own congressional support eroded, and lugubriously laments, as if it were a fatal flaw in democracy, that Congress should have such power to check him.

Thomas Griffith   July 1976

lurid   *LOO rid*
vivid in a harsh or shocking way; gruesome; sensational

One hundred years ago the first Sherlock Holmes story, "A Study in Scarlet," was published in *Beeton's Christmas Annual*, a lurid journal of cheap fiction. No one noticed. Only one major reviewer bothered to read it, and he thought it was unoriginal and sensational.

Cait Murphy   March 1987

lustrous   *LUS truhs*
having a sheen or gloss

Kalamata are the best-known Greek olives, and are unmistakable for their elegant almond shape that comes to a sharp point, like a comma, and their lustrous eggplant color.

Corby Kummer   June 1993

mote

In some schoolroom long ago,
with chalk motes drifting in the
sunbeams, I had been instructed
that the line "the moan of doves

in immemorial elms" was a near perfect onomatopoeia.

Christopher Hitchens   October 2003

see page 288

Machiavellian *ma kee a VEL ee uhn*
characterized by the political principles and methods of expediency, craftiness and dishonesty set forth in Machiavelli's book The Prince

Englishmen and Americans are alike in thinking their own nations virtuous and innocent, while other governments are suspected of acting on Machiavellian principles.

W. R. Inge   March 1922

maelstrom *MAYL struhm*
a swirling mass; a state of turbulence or confusion; a whirlpool: after one off the west coast of Norway, which reputedly sucked in and destroyed ships

To pass from Williamsburg to New York is to pass from a costumed colonialism to a motorized maelstrom. The congestion in the pre-Christmas season was the worst I have ever experienced. Indeed, the traffic was so snail-like and frustrating that people took to walking for sheer relief.

Edward Weeks   January 1961

magisterial *ma ji STIR ee uhl*
showing the skill or knowledge of a master; authoritative

THE FIRST WORLD WAR, VOLUME I: TO ARMS, *by Hew Strachan. Oxford, 1180 pages, $45.00.* "Definitive" is a much overused word, but this work merits the term. The first of a three-volume history that explores nearly every aspect of the war, from finance to ideology to diplomacy to armaments, it combines depth with staggering breadth, acute analysis with magisterial narrative.

Benjamin Schwarz   December 2001

magnanimous   *mag NA nuh muhs*
noble and generous in spirit and conduct; above petty resentment or jealousy;
forgiving ("magnanimously" is the adverb)

A better definition of education than Milton's has never been given: "I call a complete and generous education that which fits a man to perform justly, skillfully, and magnanimously, all the offices, both private and public, of peace and war."

George A. Gordon   January 1909

mainstay   *MAYN stay*
a chief support; something on which one relies

The New England groundfishery is collapsing. For hundreds of years Georges Bank, one of the world's most prolific fishing grounds, has produced seemingly inexhaustible supplies of cod, haddock, and yellowtail flounder — three species of bottom-dwellers known as groundfish. Today the bank's rich waters are nearly empty of those fish, which were once a mainstay of the New England fishing industry.

Deborah Cramer   June 1995

makeweight   *MAYK wayt*
a quantity added to make up a certain weight; a counterbalance or counterweight

Kissinger's greatest triumph was the opening to China, the most dramatic shift in the balance of power since the Cold War began. The decision to elevate outcast, isolated China to the position of a makeweight against Russia was Nixon's (perhaps suggested to him by De Gaulle). Kissinger brilliantly brought it off and has not since cheaply exploited it, has not sought to exacerbate the quarrel between the two communist countries or taken sides. That is statesmanship.

Thomas Griffith   July 1976

malady   *MA luh dee*
a disease; illness

The debasement of language is a major malady, one of the most serious problems of our time.

Robert Manning   April 1971

malaise   *muh LAYZ*
uneasiness of mind or spirit

I've been known of an afternoon to set off on a walk — to clear my head, take a break from my desk — and eventually find myself at Filene's Basement. The Basement,

Boston's famous discount store, the first of its kind in the world, accommodates a peculiar mood of mine: a jumble of dreaminess, despair, and distraction. At the office such a cluttered malaise is unbearable. But at the Basement my mood seems to find its reflection in the store's carnival of disorder, and something like calm takes over.

Kate Bolick   January 2001

malign   *muh LIGHN*
to speak harmful untruths about; speak about with strong ill-will; slander; defame ("maligned" is the adjective)

Skunks are a horribly maligned animal. Everyone shuns them. Everyone accuses them, and without ascertaining the facts, of various crimes, such as hen killing and egg sucking. Actually, they don't do so much damage; on the contrary, they are the natural enemies of vermin of all sorts and are among man's best friends in the country.

Louise Dickinson Rich   July 1942

manumission   *man yoo: MI shuhn*
a freeing or being freed from slavery; liberation; emancipation

Between the Revolution and the War of 1812 Virginians freed more slaves than they did at any other period before the Civil War. Although this might seem to point to the power of revolutionary ideology, historians in fact attribute these manumissions largely to the influence of evangelicalism, which characterized slavery not just as an abridgment of natural rights but also as a "horrid evil." Virginia's white evangelicals became convinced of the sinfulness of slavery because of the shared spiritual life of whites and blacks. Even if Jefferson, who represented the acme of political and cultural sophistication, believed that blacks and whites could never join together in society, Baptists and Methodists — black slaves and lower-class whites — were in fact trying to create an interracial society.

Benjamin Schwarz   March 1997

marginalize   *MAHR jin uh lighz*
to remove from the center or mainstream; to relegate to the periphery of a concern, issue or event ("marginalization" is the noun)

The marginalization of sub-Saharan Africa in the 1980s has been relentless. Its share of world trade is half what it was thirty years ago. Private investment is virtually nonexistent. Aid money from the United States is dropping, and total global aid to Africa has stagnated. With the Cold War winding down, superpower competition in sub-Saharan Africa is on the wane — a welcome development in certain ways, no doubt, but one guaranteed to make Africa seem all the more irrelevant.

David Ewing Duncan   July 1990

marry *MA ree*
to join closely; unite

Pork is my default meat — the one I use when I can't think of anything else to buy, the one that can marry with any number of sauces, and the one that can be cooked in the time it takes to wash the utensils used to prepare the rest of the meal.

Corby Kummer   December 1988

maverick *MA vuh rik*
a person who takes an independent stand, as in politics, refusing to conform to the group

Through the whole of his public life, the President has been jeered at or sneered at by the Republican branch of his family, the branch that has glorified the career and the personality of Theodore Roosevelt. Not only have these kinsmen opposed him politically, which is their undeniable privilege, but Cousin Franklin has even been stigmatized as the "maverick" of the clan, an imputation that could not fail to rankle.

J. Frederick Essary   December 1937

✳ Samuel A. Maverick (1803-1870) was a Texas lawyer who accepted 400 head of cattle in lieu of a $1,200 debt. Having little interest in cattle ownership, he left the cattle unbranded, and little by little most of them found their way into other people's herds and received their brands. The term Maverick caught on as a name for any stray, unbranded cattle.

mawkish *MAW kish*
sickeningly sentimental; insincerely emotional

This year of Howells's eightieth birthday is also the centenary of Jane Austen's death — fitly, because he has honored himself in honoring her, and because she too loved reality and made successful war, from her provincial citadel, on superstition, on mawkish sensibility, and on the tinsel romanticism of the fashion then current. The years in which she was quietly fulfilling her allotted task were, like this year, made terrible by war and the pouring out of blood; yet she pursued her way and kept her faith, in a quietude untroubled by the great stirrings of empire abroad.

Helen Thomas Follett and Wilson Follett   March 1917

maxim *MAK suhm*
a concisely expressed principle or rule of conduct; a statement of a general truth

In one of his letters, Thomas Jefferson remarked that in matters of religion "the maxim of civil government" should be reversed and we should rather say, "Divided we stand, united, we fall." In this remark Jefferson was setting forth with classic terseness an idea that has come to be regarded as essentially American: the separation of Church and State.

Bernard Lewis   September 1990

One of my favorite psychological maxims, which I attribute to the psychoanalyst Myron Gunther, is "Every adolescent needs an adult to help him grow up, and it can't be a parent."

Scott Turow   December 2005

mealy-mouthed   *MEE lee mowth:d*
hesitant to state facts or opinions simply and directly; afraid to speak one's mind

A 1996 poll asked scientists whether they believed in God, and the pollsters set the bar high — no mealy-mouthed evasions such as "I believe in the totality of all that exists" or "in what is beautiful and unknown"; rather, they insisted on a real biblical God, one believers could pray to and actually get an answer from. About 40 percent of scientists said yes to a belief in this kind of God — about the same percentage found in a similar poll in 1916. Only when we look at the most elite scientists — members of the National Academy of Sciences — do we find a strong majority of atheists and agnostics.

Paul Bloom   December 2005

measure   *ME zhuhr*
extent; capacity

It is a misfortune for Mr. Whistler that he once gave the measure of his talent, and a very high measure it was. The portrait of his mother, painted some years ago, and exhibited this year in New York, is so noble and admirable a picture, such a masterpiece of tone, of feeling, of the power to render life, that the fruits of his brush offered to the public more lately have seemed in comparison very crude.

Henry James Jr.   August 1882

✳ Henry James Jr. was not a lone critic of James McNeill Whistler's work. For most of his life, Whistler, who left America in his twenties to live in France and England, saw some of his most ambitious works rejected by exhibitions in those countries. Today he is considered among the most important 19th-century influences on American and European art.

medley   *MED lee*
a mixture of things; assortment

> The news of the day as it reaches the newspaper office is an incredible medley of fact, propaganda, rumor, suspicion, clues, hopes, and fears, and the task of selecting and ordering that news is one of the truly sacred and priestly offices in a democracy. For the newspaper is in all literalness the bible of democracy, the book out of which a people determines its conduct. It is the only book they read every day.

> Walter Lippmann   November 1919

mellifluous   *muh LI floo: uhs*
sweet-sounding or smooth flowing: Latin, mel, *honey* + fluere, *to flow*

> In Paris, where the sense of style is everywhere, so that one looks around for the one mind that planned it all, Hemingway achieved such an instinct for how words should sound and how a sentence should hang, that very often the "true sentence" pleased him because it was the mellifluous sentence, the artly balanced sentence. In time Hemingway became as fond of his sentences as a matador of his veronicas, and the "true sentences" were too often a run of sentences chic and marvelously phrased, displays of his technique.

> Alfred Kazin   June 1964

melodrama   *ME luh drah muh*
a play or film that exaggerates emotion and emphasizes plot or action at the expense of characterization

> It seems obvious that if the Victorian theater had been as receptive to the literary imagination as the Elizabethan was, Dickens would have been a playwright, like Shakespeare, rather than a novelist; but the Victorian theater was in fact trivial and philistine, reducing tragedy to melodrama and comedy to farce.

> David Lodge   May 2002

mephitic   *muh FI tik*
foul-smelling

> For centuries Bilbao was an industrial dynamo, an international center for shipbuilding, shipping, mining, and metallurgy, and also banking, and it produced many noble stone buildings and many wealthy Bilbainos. But all that industry turned the air a sooty yellow and the River Nervion, which runs through Bilbao, a mephitic white. In the late 1980s the region's political leaders decided to move industry out of the city, in order to attract more service and high-tech companies. Today the air is clean, and the water is verging on it.

> Marisa Bartolucci   October 2000

mercenary   *MER suh ne ree*
motivated solely by a desire for monetary or material gain; greedy

I have observed that most people have less difficulty in selecting the good from the bad than they do in getting the right things together. To help our patrons at this point, we assemble the costume with all its accessories in one of our private selling rooms. Our sales staff is trained to suggest tactfully a change in color or detail, and recommend conscientiously the correct thing without regard to any mercenary interest of a larger sale. Mrs. Nieman, my brothers, or I may be called in to pass final judgment. We have no hesitancy in "killing" a sale if we feel that the customer is buying the wrong dress or fur or hat.

Stanley Marcus   December 1948

meritocracy   *me ruh TAH kruh see*
a group of people whose progress is based on ability and talent rather than on class privilege or wealth; leadership by able and talented people ("meritocratic" is the adjective)

Elites and upper classes have always been controversial for Americans, and since the Revolution we have viewed them with particular suspicion. Yet a century of sociology has concluded that an elite is a practical necessity for any society. The real question is, what kind of elite will you have — an open, meritocratic elite that is continually refreshed from other strata of society, or a closed and exclusive elite that withdraws into castelike isolation and merely seeks to perpetuate its privileges?

Adam Bellow   July/August 2003

messianic   *me see A nik*
having the characteristics of a liberator or savior

Deep within us lies a certain strain of longing for genius, a genius worship, that might be described as messianic: the hope that a genius will come along to save us from our technological, philosophical, spiritual, or aesthetic impasse. Is there anything wrong with cherishing this ideal?

Marjorie Garber   December 2002

métier   *may TYAY*
the work that one is particularly suited for; one's area of expertise or strength

It was not until I wrote *Ethan Frome* that I suddenly felt in full control of my *métier*, as an artisan should be of his tools. I mention this because, when *Ethan Frome* first appeared, I was severely criticized by the reviewers for what was considered the clumsy structure of the tale. I had pondered long on this structure, had felt its peculiar difficulties, and possible awkwardness, but could think of no alternative which would serve as well in the given case; and though I am far from thinking *Ethan Frome* my best novel, and am bored and even exasperated when I am told that it is, I am still sure that its structure is not its weak point.

Edith Wharton   April 1933

✽ Ellery Sedgwick, *The Atlantic's* editor from 1909 to 1938, dealt with Edith Wharton differently from most writers whose work appeared in the magazine. As he explained in a November 1947 *Atlantic* article: "As a contributor grows in importance and success, the editor's touch must be lighter and more delicate. Discipline is relaxed and whims are indulged. But standards are standards, and I do not believe an editor should come to heel at any author's whistle. I recall small but characteristic altercations with Mrs. Wharton. She lived in Paris and wrote by Jamesian standards. Her spelling and punctuation followed the English tradition. The *Atlantic* usage was its own but it followed the main currents of American practice. So it was that when the 'u's' were taken out of Mrs. Wharton's 'parlours' and 'colours' and semicolons were substituted for her dashes, she altered to the original form every correction made in her galley proofs. It was very obvious that the *Atlantic* reader, noticing variant spelling and punctuation in the magazine, would ascribe the deviations simply to careless proofreading; and careless proofreading the editor abhorred. The issue was joined. *Atlantic* habits must be respected, but Mrs. Wharton was an artist and the work of artists must not be retouched. I pondered the question, printed the article precisely as the author demanded, and simply subjoined this footnote: — In this story certain divergencies in spelling and punctuation from the established practice of *The Atlantic* are made at the request of the author. Mrs. Wharton was irritated, but after all, she had had her woman's way and the editor his professional satisfaction."

miffed   *mift*
annoyed; in a huff

Gephardt is similar to Bill Clinton in one way and different in most others. The similarity is in the way he listens. Many politicians are visibly miffed when they have to sit still while someone else is the center of attention. At best they remain engaged only long enough to figure out which of the many prepared-answer tapes their brains should start playing as soon as the other person has finished speaking. Gephardt, like Clinton, uses eye contact and a range of facial expressions to suggest that he really is listening — that his attention and time, a politician's scarcest commodities, are completely yours while you speak.

James Fallows   November 1997

militate   *MI luh tayt*
to operate or work against; be directed against

Predominance of intellect does not necessarily imply true wisdom; for in reality an impulsive, restless activity of mind seems often to militate against calm reflection.

Paul Elmer More   December 1898

minion   *MIN yin*
a servile follower

In 1957 a former *Collier's* magazine writer named Vance Packard published an investigative report about the American advertising industry's efforts to maneuver consumers into buying goods they neither needed nor wanted. These machinations did not rely on slick imagery, exaggerated claims, or outright deception — tools whose use had subjected marketers and their minions on Madison Avenue to ridicule or censure since the days of P. T. Barnum. Packard's charge was more specific and startling. Advertisers, he claimed, were using hidden symbols to goad the unconscious mind and the body under its control into the act of acquisition.

Randall Rothenberg   June 1997

minister   *MI nis tuhr*
to attend to the comfort or needs of another; care for someone who is ill

One only watched her breathing through the night, — he who for fifteen years had ministered to her with all the tenderness of a woman. It was a night devoid of suffering *to her*. As morning approached, and for two hours previous to the dread moment, she seemed to be in a partial ecstasy; and though not apparently conscious of the coming on of death, she gave her husband all those holy words of love, all the consolation of an oft-repeated blessing, whose value death has made priceless. Such moments are too sacred for the common pen, which pauses as the woman-poet raises herself up to die in the arms of her poet-husband. He knew not that death had robbed him of his treasure, until the drooping form grew chill and froze his heart's blood. At half past four, on the morning of the 29th of June, Elizabeth Barrett Browning died of congestion of the lungs. Her last words were, "It is beautiful."

Kate Field   September 1861

mint   *mint*
new or in its original condition

The selling of souls has now made its way onto eBay, the online auction house, providing a literal answer to the rhetorical question from the Gospel of Mark: "For what shall it profit a man, if he shall gain the whole world and lose his own soul?" The online traffic in souls became public two years ago when a man named Adam Burtle, of Woodinville, Washington, put up an eBay listing that read "20 yr-old Seattle boy's SOUL, hardly used." Burtle went on, "Please realize, I make no warranties as to the condition of the soul. As of now, it is near mint condition, with only minor scratches." By the time eBay officials stepped in (eBay insists that auctioned items consist of merchandise that can physically change hands), the price had reached $400, and Burtle's soul had been bought by a woman in the Midwest.

Cullen Murphy   April 2003

minuscule *MI ni skyoo:l*
exceedingly small

Princeton is an automatic underdog when it plays any major basketball school, because its stringent recruiting rules limit it to players of high academic achievement. Academic excellence doesn't preclude basketball excellence, of course, but the pool of players who can maintain both is minuscule.

Sam Toperoff   November 1989

Parents who decide that the time has come to teach their children about money usually begin by opening savings accounts. The kids are intrigued at first by the notion that a bank will pay them for doing nothing, but their enthusiasm disappears when they realize that the interest rate is minuscule and, furthermore, their parents don't intend to give them access to their principal. To a kid, a savings account is just a black hole that swallows birthday checks.

David Owen   April 1998

mired *MIGH uhrd*
stuck in a situation difficult to emerge from; bogged down

Centuries ago, when Europe was mired in its feudal Dark Ages, the sages of a flourishing Islamic civilization opened an era of great scientific and philosophical discovery. The ideas of the ancient Greeks and Romans might never have been introduced to Europe were it not for the Islamic historians and philosophers who rediscovered and revived them.

Toby Lester   January 1999

misnomer *mis NOH muhr*
a misapplied name, especially one that conveys a misleading impression

It is a well-known fact that no nation in the world has such a variety and abundance of the best food that Nature gives as we ourselves. She teems with such bounty to her adopted children that it has often seemed to me a misnomer to call our country "Father-land," —*Mother*-land she is for the whole earth, with her broad lap of plenty sloping from the Rocky Mountains down to the very Atlantic shore, as if inviting the hungry nations to come over to it and be fed.

Zina Fay Peirce   December 1868

mitigate   *MI tuh gayt*
to make less severe; lessen the trouble caused by; alleviate

Congress last year spent ten million dollars in the corn-borer campaign, and the total effect was to mitigate very slightly the ravages of this insect pest. Scientists on the job report that the slow westward march of the corn borer will not stop with Ohio and Michigan, but will inevitably continue until the whole corn belt is covered.

James E. Boyle   October 1929

✳ Residents of the Wolverine State refer to themselves as Michiganians, Michiganites or Michiganders. Each demonym (a word that describes the people of a place: *demos*, people + *nym*, name) is proudly worn, but the last originated as an insult. In a July 1848 speech before the U. S. House of Representatives, Michigander is what Abraham Lincoln called Lewis Cass, a presidential candidate from Michigan who favored extending slavery to the territories newly won in the Mexican War. Michigander blended the state's name with gander, the male goose, and a synonym for fool. Cass's opponents thought he looked like a goose, as well.

modus operandi   *MOH dus ah puh RAN dee*
a way of doing something; mode of operation

From my late adolescence through my early twenties my weekend *modus operandi* was to come in at around five in the morning and sleep heavily till three or so in the afternoon.

Joseph Epstein   February 2002

modus vivendi   *MOH duhs vi VEN dee*
a way of living that enables two parties or groups to coexist peacefully

The most comprehensive explanation of the causes of immigration a century ago is to be found in the disruptions visited on European society by population growth and the Industrial Revolution. The United States was, to use the language of the law, the incidental beneficiary of that upheaval. The swelling immigrant neighborhoods in turn-of-the-century American cities were, in effect, by-products of the urbanization of Europe. And once landed in America, immigrants accommodated themselves to the larger society — not always easily assimilating, but at least working out a modus vivendi — without the kinds of conflicts that have afflicted other multinational societies.

David M. Kennedy   November 1996

molt   *mohlt*
to shed all or part of an outer covering, such as feathers or skin, in the process of acquiring new growth

Early in life lobsters molt frequently — up to twenty-five times in their first five years. After that they molt about once a year for a while, and when they're bigger, the rate drops again.

Trevor Corson   April 2002

momentum   *moh MEN tuhm*
the force or speed of an object in motion

Hurrying with the never ebbing crowd along her streets, living the eager life with the others, amazed daily at the momentum of the place, seeing there is scarcely any people of the globe for which the town is not an asylum, one feels it a duty, almost a command, to put the thing down in words, and give the world an idea of the city's energy and achievement. It is this which has given some of the best known writers of the West the "sacramental view of literature," as one of them ironically expressed it. For Chicago has a passionate zest for life; it is arrogant, swaggering, half drunken with pride, puffed up at its benevolence, its large-mindedness, and its ingenuity; and it conceals, as a blustering young man will conceal a virtue or a tenderness, the nostalgia for beauty which yearns in its heart.

Elia W. Peattie   December 1899

monkey   *MUHN kee*
to meddle, tamper or interfere with

Good fresh chèvre should be pure white and spreadable, without the chalky, dry, crumble-to-bits texture of many logs. You can seldom find it so pure, because fresh goat-cheese logs are so often flavored with things like jalapeño or cracked peppercorns. As with many mild foods people monkey with, if the flavor is subtle, varied, and good on its own, there's not much point to piling on extra ingredients.

Corby Kummer   December 2005

monochromatic   *mah nuh KRUH ma tik*
having one color

Winter lacks the pyrotechnics of spring, the brute, strapping joy of summer, the old sugary nostalgia of autumn. It's just cold and elegant, monochromatic, somnolent.

Rick Bass   January 2000

morass   *muh RAS*
a complicated, confused or entangling situation that is difficult to escape from:
in its literal sense, a swamp or bog

I hope a great many other young wives write in as I have — I'd hate to think of all American womanhood weltering in the morass of self-pity described by Mrs. Cyrus. Mrs. Cyrus just can't make me sorry for myself.

Rhona Ryan Wilber   June 1947

> ✻ Rhona Ryan Wilber is responding here to the author of an *Atlantic* article critical of mothers who say their children are "all that really matters" in their lives. A passage from that article appears in this book under self-abnegation.

moratorium   *maw ruh TAW ree uhm*
a temporary, official suspension of an activity

The annual meeting of the International Whaling Commission this month in Monaco promises to be a contentious affair, as Japan and Norway renew their efforts to modify the eleven-year-old international moratorium on commercial whaling so that they can hunt minke whales without censure.

Mark Derr   October 1997

mores   *MAW rayz*
the shared habits, manners and customs of a community or social group

American popular culture and mores have penetrated far more deeply and widely in Middle Eastern society than was ever possible for the elitist cultures of Britain and France.

Bernard Lewis   February 1993

morphology   *mawr FAH luh jee*
the form and structure of an animal or plant

The oldest archaeological evidence of dogs with a morphology distinct from that of wolves is from about 12,000 years ago in the Middle East, suggesting an evolution coinciding with the rise of the first agricultural settlements and permanent villages, and pre-dating the domestication of other animals, including sheep and goats, by a few thousand years.

Stephen Budiansky   July 1991

mote *moht*
a speck of dust or other tiny particle

In some schoolroom long ago, with chalk motes drifting in the sunbeams, I had been instructed that the line "the moan of doves in immemorial elms" was a near perfect onomatopoeia.

Christopher Hitchens   October 2003

> ✳ Onomatopoeia, Latin for the making of words, is commonly known to mean the formation and use of words to imitate sounds — ding dong, toot, meow, purr, burp. Another class of onomatopoeic word, however, imitates not the sound of a thing but the sense of a thing — breeze, loathe, picky, oops, wow, stuck, tickle, dazzle, twirp, rinky-dink.

mulct *mulkt*
to get payment from unwillingly, as by coercion or deceit

In any understanding of the problem of industrial racketeering it is important to grasp this essential. The racketeer pays for his right to mulct others, not only of their money and possessions, but also of their legal rights. He is a protected person. He is always protected in his privilege to violate the law and the rights of others. It must be assumed, even where it cannot be proved, that he pays for such protection. Whether he splits with politicians or works under some other arrangement, the racketeer is responsible to the politician. The man higher up in every racket is a politician.

George E. Sokolsky   September 1938

multifarious *muhl tuh FAI ree uhs*
having great variety or diversity; made up of many parts or kinds

Where did you hear, before jazz was invented, such multifarious stirring, heaving, wrestling of independent voices as there are in a jazz orchestra? The saxophone bleats a turgid song; the clarinets turn capers of their own; the violins come forward with an obbligato; a saucy flute darts up and down the scale, never missing the right note on the right choral; the trombone lumberingly slides off on a tangent; the drum and xylophone put rhythmic highlights into these kaleidoscopic shiftings; the cornet is suddenly heard above the turmoil, with good-natured brazenness. Chaos in order, — orchestral technic of master craftsmen, – music that is recklessly fantastic, joyously grotesque, — such is good jazz. A superb, incomparable creation, inescapable yet elusive; something it is almost impossible to put in score upon a page of paper.

Carl Engel   August 1922

✳ When Adolphe Sax (1814 -1894), a Belgian instrument maker, brought his newly invented bass horn to Paris in 1842 and played it for Hector Berlioz, the composer fell in love with it. "It cries, it sighs and dreams," Berlioz wrote in a Parisian journal, describing the beauty of its tones, including "the most beautiful low voice known to this day." He called it *le saxophon*. It was intended for military bands, where it would provide the middle voice between the brass and the woodwinds, and Sax convinced the French war minister to include it in all of France's regimental bands. He received a patent in 1846, but other manufacturers were so infuriated with having many of their band instruments supplanted by the saxophone that they formed the Association of United Instrument Makers and brought a series of baseless lawsuits against him. Sax did not lose the lawsuits, but the cost of fighting them and dealing with jealous competitors drove him to bankruptcy three times.

multiplicity   *muhl tuh PLI suh tee*
a large number

President Kennedy paid a famous tribute to the multiplicity of Jefferson's talents, but they have always been regarded as astonishing. James Parton, one of Jefferson's nineteenth-century biographers, gave his dazzling range of abilities a dramatic accent when he characterized his subject as a man who "could calculate an eclipse, survey an estate, tie an artery, plan an edifice, try a cause, break a horse, dance a minuet, and play the violin." And Parton was describing a young Jefferson who had not yet written the Declaration.

Douglas L. Wilson   November 1992

✳ The tribute President Kennedy paid to Jefferson occurred at a White House dinner honoring Nobel Prize winners, on April 29, 1962. "I think this is the most extraordinary collection of talent, of human knowledge, that has ever been gathered together at the White House," the president said, "with the possible exception of when Thomas Jefferson dined alone."

mum   *muhm*
silent; not speaking

Depreciate your wares. Learn from the Tennessee innkeeper who described his establishment as "not the largest hotel in the burg; not newly furnished throughout; no free 'bus to trains; not the best grub the market affords; but simply clean beds and good food. 25 cents a sleep, 25 cents an eat. Toothpicks and ice water thrown in. Try us! Pay up! And if not satisfied keep mum."

Rollin Lynde Hart   May 1904

munificent *myoo: NI fuh sint*
showing great generosity; bountiful

If it be true, as has been said, of Dr. Johnson that his sturdy self-respect led him to invent the modern publisher as a substitute for the old-fashioned patron, a fresh item is added to the debt of gratitude which the world owes to the stout old lexicographer. Of the miseries of doing literary work at the dictation or under the auspices of a munificent patron, few recent writers can have any idea, now that literature has come to be an acknowledged article of merchandise, as much as hops or calico. Yet these miseries were very substantial, and were no doubt injurious to the growth of good literature. The frequent liability to gross insult, hardly relieved by yet grosser flattery; the fulsome dedications, composed in return for scanty stipends grudgingly doled out; the subjection of high scholarship and talent to the ignorant whim of some patronizing duke or princess, — such are the unwholesome conditions under which great writers have too often worked. Among the beneficial changes that have been wrought in the world since the beginning of the last century we should not forget the slow revolution which has substituted the agency of the publisher for that of the Mæcenas, in the creation and diffusion of literature.

John Fiske January 1882

❊ Gaius Maecenas (c. 70-8 B.C.) was a Roman statesman who helped support writers in the reign of his friend Augustus (27 B.C. – A.D. 14), among them Virgil and Horace. Since the mid-16th century, wealthy patrons of artists, writers and composers have been known as Maecenas. Samuel Johnson completed his great *Dictionary* without the help of a Maecenas, receiving financial support only from a few booksellers who stood to profit from the book. Hoping for support from the Earl of Chesterfield, he dedicated the book's proposal to him, was given £10 initially, then ignored. Johnson's definition of patron in the *Dictionary* was a swipe at Chesterfield: "One who countenances, supports or protects. Commonly a wretch who supports with insolence, and is paid with flattery."

mutatis mutandis *moo: TAH tis moo: TAN dis*
with all due adjustments or modifications having been made (used when comparing two or more cases or situations): Latin, things being changed that have to be changed

Thatcher quite often spoke of her reverence for Sir Winston Churchill, whom she did not in fact much resemble, except in this regard: *mutatis mutandis*, he, too, was an outsider.

Geoffrey Wheatcroft December 1991

myopia   *migh OH pee uh*
lack of understanding or foresight; narrow-mindedness; short-sightedness:
Greek, myops, *shortsighted*

East Asia has never been a terribly successful field for American diplomacy. There are undoubtedly many reasons for this, and surely that shortcoming for which the United States is continually indicted — cultural and historical myopia — has contributed enormously to its failures in the region. Americans have always seen East Asia not for what it is but for what it can do to them or for them: the region is either danger or opportunity — either a new "ground war in Asia" or a new China market.

Benjamin Schwarz   June 1996

nest egg

There are four odd facts about Mr. Nixon that tell a good deal about the man. First, he is the kind of man who, before putting his legs up on a silk-covered stool or ottoman, goes into the bathroom and gets a towel to put under his legs. Second, as a Navy lieutenant in World War II, this young and presumably unworldly Quaker played such brilliant poker that he came home with a nest egg of around $10,000. Third, although most people think of him as the archetypal Wasp, he is very much an Irishman and, on his father's side, that special breed, a Black Irishman. Fourth, on his mother's side, he is a descendant of a line of successful itinerant lady preachers.

Stewart Alsop   February 1972

see page 299

naif *nah EEF*
a naïve person

Raintree County was borne on a river of hype. A thousand-page first novel by a crinkly-eyed Indiana naif who (the legend already went) had brought his bulky manuscript to Houghton Mifflin in a battered suitcase, *Raintree County* was a corn-fed, swaggering, patriotic, highfalutin, and occasionally naughty yarn. "It attempts no less," declared its astonishingly heedless publisher, "than a complete embodiment of the American Myth."

Charles Trueheart   September 1994

namby-pamby *NAM bee PAM bee*
weakly sentimental; insipid; wishy-washy

Elementary school pupils are fascinated with nature, computers, space exploration, the power of the atom, cartoon characters, far more than they are with abstract numbers and the namby-pamby adventures of the children in traditional readers. The smart teacher takes advantage of these preoccupations to motivate reading, writing, math, and social studies.

Benjamin Spock, M.D.   April 1984

✳ Namby-pamby originated as the nickname that the poet Henry Carey (1687-1743) gave to Ambrose Philips (1675-1749), whose poetry about children he criticized as being cloyingly sentimental. Carey wrote a parody of Philips's verse titled "Namby Pamby," imitating the way a child might say "Ambrose Philips." Namby-pamby is a word form called reduplication, the repetition of a word, or the changing of a part of a word, to create the second half of a word pair. First-order reduplications are plain repetitions: choo-choo, goody-goody. In second-order reduplications, the first letter of the second word is changed: fuddy-duddy, itsy-bitsy, okey-dokey, roly-poly. Third-order duplications change the interior of the first word: dilly-dally, fiddle-faddle, wishy-washy, zig-zag.

nebulous *NEB yuh lis*
unclear; vague; indefinite; ill-defined; hazy

Spenser is a great name; but he is the only undramatic poet of his time who could be placed above, or on a level with, Wordsworth, Byron, Shelley, Coleridge, or Tennyson. There is a list, somewhere, of two hundred names of poets who belonged to the Elizabethan age, — mostly mere nebulous appearances, which require a telescope of the greatest power to separate into individual stars. Few of them can be made to shine with as steady a lustre as the ordinary versemen who contribute to our magazines.

Edwin Percy Whipple April 1868

necropolis *nuh KRAH puh lis*
a cemetery, especially one belonging to an ancient city

A small passageway in the south exterior wall of St. Peter's Basilica leads into an eerily intact Roman necropolis that underlies the entire center aisle. The passage becomes the main street of a miniature city of the dead, fronted by ornate two-story mausoleums on which Christ and the Apostles stand alongside Apollo, Isis, Bacchus, and rampaging satyrs. This necropolis first came to light in the Renaissance, when the basilica was rebuilt: pontiffs and architects watched in horror as an endless stream of pagan relics issued from the floor of Catholicism's most sacred church.

Tom Mueller   April 1997

nefarious *ni FAI ree uhs*
wicked; villainous: with implications of group activity that is secret and crafty

Macau, forty-five minutes away by boat, has a bad reputation among Hong Kongers as a tacky place for gambling and various nefarious pursuits, but in my two days there I didn't once set foot in a den of iniquity, and I left wishing that I had allotted it at least twice as much time.

Jamie James   May 2001

Ever since Elisabeth Föörster-Nietzsche edited her brother's final manuscripts (and in some cases actually forged whole passages) to reflect her own anti-Semitic and fascist views, it has become almost a tradition in the philosophical community to suspect the editors, colleagues, or relatives of philosophers of nefarious behavior with their literary remains. Thus rumors abound concerning the manuscripts of Charles Sanders Peirce, George Santayana, and Martin Heidegger, to name just a few.

Evelyn Toynton   June 1997

nemesis   *NE muh sis*
something that is the inevitable cause of someone's downfall or defeat

If George W. Bush knows what's good for him, he won't run for a second term — the nemesis of presidential reputation. If Bill Clinton had retired after one term, both he and the public would have been spared his impeachment over the Lewinsky matter. A single-term Ronald Reagan would not have somnambulated into the impeachment-worthy Iran-contra affair. If Richard Nixon hadn't run again, "Watergate" would refer merely to the complex at the corner of Virginia Avenue and Rock Creek Parkway, in the District of Columbia. If FDR had not won a third term, in 1940, he would have been remembered as much for his dictatorial attempt to pack the Supreme Court, among other hubristic second-term blunders, as for the New Deal.

Jack Beatty   September 2003

✱ Nemesis, the Greek goddess of retribution, punishes hubris, the exaggerated pride and self-confidence that lead someone to believe that he or she is above the gods. The prime example of hubris and its nemesis in classical literature is Oedipus, who ignores a prophesy that he will kill his father and marry his mother.

neologism   *nee AH luh ji zuhm*
a new word, or a new meaning for an established word

To persons of a certain temperament any word seems bad when it is new, because it is new. But every old word was new once; all have had to run the same gauntlet. Neologisms that, because they answer to some continuing need, are destined to last are, *ipso facto*, good. They may not seem so to us now, but we are bound to come to it.

Wilson Follett   March 1938

✱ Here are former neologisms that ran the gauntlet and survived, along with the dates of their first documented appearance in print and the people who coined them:

agnostic	1870	Thomas Huxley
antediluvian	1646	Sir Thomas Browne
centrifugal	1687	Sir Isaac Newton
debunk	1923	William Woodward

ecology	1873	Ernst Haeckel
folklore	1846	William John Thoms
genocide	1943	Raphael Lemkin
international	1780	Jeremy Bentham
kindergarten	1852	Friedrich Froebel
mascot	1880	Edmond Audran
nihilism	1817	Ivan Turgenev
nostalgia	1688	Johannes Hofer
schizophrenia	1910	Eugene Bleuler
self-help	1831	Thomas Carlyle
witticism	1677	John Dryden
workaholic	1968	Wayne Oates

ne plus ultra   *nee pluhs UHL truh*
the highest point capable of being reached; the acme; the ultimate: Latin, not more beyond

There are now hundreds of thousands of bloggers, individuals who publish news, commentary, and other content on their own idiosyncratic Web sites. Some boast readerships exceeding those of prestigious print magazines, but most number their faithful in the double and triple digits. Find the one who shares your tastes and leanings, and you'll have attained the ne plus ultra of bespoke media: the ghostly double of yourself.

William Powers   January/February 2005

nepotism   *NE puh ti zuhm*
favoritism or unfair preference in hiring or promoting a relative or friend

Helen Thomas, the former UPI Washington correspondent, declared in a column that the Bush Administration had become "a family affair, reeking of nepotism." (Nepotism is often said to reek, as though it were a pile of dirty laundry.) "You'd think an administration headed by the son of a former president might be a teensy bit leery of appearing to foster a culture of nepotism," Andrew Sullivan wrote in *The New Republic*. Sullivan produced a long list of people who had gotten jobs in Washington through such connections, and concluded, "All this nepotism is a worrisome sign that America's political class is becoming increasingly insular."

Adam Bellow   July/August 2003

✳ Nepotism, from the Latin *nepos,* nephew or grandchild, was applied originally to the favoritism shown to popes' nephews at the Papal Court in Rome during the Middle Ages.

nest egg   *NEST eg*

money set aside as a reserve; money serving as a nucleus for the acquisition of more

There are four odd facts about Mr. Nixon that tell a good deal about the man. First, he is the kind of man who, before putting his legs up on a silk-covered stool or ottoman, goes into the bathroom and gets a towel to put under his legs. Second, as a Navy lieutenant in World War II, this young and presumably unworldly Quaker played such brilliant poker that he came home with a nest egg of around $10,000. Third, although most people think of him as the archetypal Wasp, he is very much an Irishman and, on his father's side, that special breed, a Black Irishman. Fourth, on his mother's side, he is a descendant of a line of successful itinerant lady preachers.

Stewart Alsop   February 1972

✳ Because most Irish people are fair-skinned, fair-haired and blue- or green-eyed, those who are dark-featured are sometimes referred to as "Black Irish," a term originally used by the Irish in America but not in Ireland. The genetic history for this divergence is unknown, although migrations and invasions more than two millennia ago from the Iberian peninsula may account for it. The explanation that the ancestors of today's Black Irish sailed with the ill-fated Spanish Armada, were shipwrecked off the coast of Ireland in 1588 and had children with Irish women, is generally thought a myth, as very few Spanish sailors survived. Another unproven explanation is that "Black Irish" was originally applied to those who immigrated to America from Ireland to escape the potato famine of 1847, known as the Black Blight.

nexus   *NEK sis*

a central point or point of convergence; a focus; meeting-place

Near the archaeological museum, on the edge of Spaccanapoli, is the refreshingly green and relaxed Piazza Bellini, a nexus of antiques dealers and the city's flourishing booksellers — Naples is one of Italy's great bibliophile centers. Bookstalls like the ones along Paris's Left Bank, selling both new and used books, line the streets on and leading from the square.

Corby Kummer   August 1997

The Rise of Silas Lapham, our first and best analysis of the self-made man and of the social implications of his money, is a tragedy whose significance reaches nearly the whole of self-made America. Written at the nexus of so many tendencies and interests, the novel remains today as poignantly contemporary as ever, a drama of transitions not yet more than half-accomplished. We clamor still for "the great American novel"? Why, we have been reading it these thirty years and more.

Helen Thomas Follett and Wilson Follett   March 1917

nil *nil*
nothing; zero

> Do You Remember? Radio's Greatest Themes. *Eddie Layton at the Hammond organ; Epic BN-26146 (stereo) and LN-24146.* Musically, the value of this record is slight, not to say nil, but nostalgically, ah, that's another question.

> Herbert Kupferberg   September 1965

NIMBY *NIM bee*
an acronym for Not In My Back Yard, denoting an attitude ascribed to persons who object to the placing of something they regard as detrimental or hazardous in their own neighborhood, while not raising objections to similar developments elsewhere

> In the United States noise awareness centers on airports, specifically in the unending NIMBY controversies over where new airports should be built.

> John Sedgwick   November 1991

> ✳ The first documented use of NIMBY was by Emilie Travel Livezey in the November 6, 1980 issue of *The Christian Science Monitor*: "People are now thoroughly alert to the dangers of hazardous chemical wastes. The very thought of having even a secure landfill anywhere near them is anathema to most Americans today. It's an attitude referred to in the trade as NIMBY — 'not in my backyard.'"

noisome *NOI suhm*
having a bad smell; foul-smelling ("noisomeness" is the noun)

> The first flower to bloom in this latitude, when the winter frost loosens its grip upon the sod, is not the fragrant arbutus, nor the delicate hepatica, nor the waxen bloodroot, as the poets would have us think, but the gross, uncouth, and noisome skunk cabbage; and this same skunk cabbage is, for all its grossness and noisomeness and uncouthness, at once a product and a prophecy of the oncoming spring. If a great moral transformation is really going on in New York, it is only natural that it should be attended, as great moral transformations nearly always have been, with unlovely excesses.

> Alvan F. Sanborn   October 1906

nominal   NAH muh nuhl
in name only; not actually; so-called

I am amazed, in retrospect, to recall how well Paris was eating up to the very eve of the German occupation. There was talk of ration cards, but they had not been actually introduced except in the case of sugar. Such nominal restrictions as existed on the consumption of meat and pastries and alcohol were of a very mild character and were easily evaded.

William Henry Chamberlin   September 1940

nonce   nahns
the present; the time being

It is an axiom that nations learn more readily from defeat than from victory, and though for the nonce Germany is prohibited from building tanks, her post-war military reviews and textbooks bear ample witness to the study that is being devoted to them and their tactics.

Captain B. H. Liddell Hart   September 1925

✱ Nonce words are those invented by a writer for the nonce, intended for one-time use to serve a need at hand. Many of today's common words began as nonce words. James Murray, the first editor of the *Oxford English Dictionary*, coined the term. He applied it when he needed to describe a word being considered for inclusion in the *OED* when only one example of it could be found in print. The single example of gossipaceous, meaning full of gossip, which Charles Darwin invented in an 1849 letter to a colleague, did not make it into the *OED*, while linguipotence, coined by Samuel Taylor Coleridge in 1820, and meaning mastery of languages, did.

noncommittal   nahn kuh MI tuhl
not committing oneself to a particular view or course of action; not revealing what one feels or thinks

Once, when I had spent several minutes explaining to a boy the technical construction of Shelley's "Ode to the West Wind," I spoke to him rather caustically about his failure to apprehend what I had been trying to say. He looked a trifle discomfited, but made no reply. A few days later, I was attempting desperately on a very cold morning to start my car, and the same lad, passing the garage door and observing my futile movements, came in. "Can I help you, sir?" he inquired courteously. Embarrassed, I grunted a noncommittal response; whereupon he lifted the radiator hood, peered into the bowels of the engine, took from his pocket a small screw driver, made one or two motions, and said, "I think it'll go now, sir." Sure enough, it did. Then he expounded to me, with the forbearance of a father instructing his child, some mystery of the carburetor which I could not apprehend. Observing my perplexity, he directed my attention to the mechanism itself and, without the slightest trace of annoyance, showed me what had been wrong. He was a better teacher than I had been. To this day, when a boy wrinkles his forehead over the difference between a metaphor and a synecdoche, I remember the carburetor, moderate my wrath, and start again.

Claude M. Fuess   October 1932

nonentity   *nahn EN tuh tee*
a person regarded as being unimportant or insignificant

Professional musicians sometimes like to give the impression that theirs is the best job of all in that they're being paid to do what they would be doing just for fun. Stardom is frequently a variation on that theme. But to Presley's way of thinking, becoming a star was the only alternative to the role of total nonentity to which his family's low social standing and his own shyness might otherwise have doomed him.

Francis Davis   October 1994

nostrum   *NAH struhm*
a pet scheme or favorite remedy for bringing about some social or political reform or improvement: Latin, our own, from nostrum's original and literal meaning of a quack medicine (although in its figurative sense, the word is not necessarily derogatory)

U.S. schools today are the product of three different educational eras: the agricultural (which produced the nine-month school year), the industrial (which emphasized rote learning and regimentation to fit the rhythms of mass production), and what might be called the experimental (which promoted a range of nostrums, from sex education to Whole Language, often at the expense of basic skills). Each of these has left its own layer of sediment to muck things up in the present.

James P. Pinkerton   January/February 2003

notwithstanding   *naht with STAN ding*
although; despite; nevertheless

The Hickory throws out its branches at first very obliquely from the shaft; afterwards the lower ones bend down as the tree increases in size, and acquire an irregular and contorted shape; for, notwithstanding their toughness, they bend easily to the weight of their fruit and foliage. This tree is celebrated in the United States for the toughness of its wood; and the term Hickory is used as emblematical of a sturdy and vigorous character.

Wilson Flagg   September 1860

nouveau riche   *noo: voh REESH*

a person who has recently become rich: usually used disparagingly to imply a flashy display of wealth intended to impress, and a lack of taste and culture ("nouveaux riches" is the plural)

Angelenos have perhaps an even greater cultural inferiority complex than did, say, the late nineteenth-century New York robber barons or the Chicago meat-packers. They know that the East Coast elite often regard them as sun-baked nouveaux riches or flakes, or both; they have heard Johnny Carson's joke that the only live culture in Los Angeles is in its yogurt.

Charles Lockwood and Christopher B. Leinberger   January 1988

noxious   *NAHK shuhs*

injurious; harmful; unwholesome

True it is that the dance to which jazz music has been coupled is not precisely setting an example of modesty and grace. True, also, that certain modern dance-perversions have called up music that is as noxious as the breath of Belial. Only by a bold stretch of fancy can this delirious caterwauling be brought under the head of music proper — or improper; as noise, its significance at times becomes eloquent to the point of leaving little or nothing to the imagination.

Carl Engel   August 1922

nuanced   *NOO: ahnst*

exhibiting small, delicate or subtle variations

The explanation usually given for Sinatra's spotty track record on screen is that he didn't take acting as seriously as he did singing. The way I see it, anyone capable of giving performances as nuanced and watchable as Sinatra's in *From Here to Eternity*, *The Man With the Golden Arm*, *Some Came Running*, and *The Manchurian Candidate* has nothing to apologize for.

Francis Davis   September 1998

nubile   *NOO: bighl*

fully developed sexually; marriageable: applied almost exclusively to women

In innumerable parts of the world the season of love is a time which the nubile of each sex devote to dancing in each other's presence, — sometimes one sex, sometimes the other, sometimes both, in the frantic effort to display all the force and energy, the skill and endurance, the beauty and grace, which at this moment are yearning within them to be poured into the vital stream of the race's life.

Havelock Ellis   February 1914

nugatory *NOO: guh taw ree*
trifling; worthless

Why do I continually misspell certain words, so that I have an actual vocabulary of spelling errors? Why do I make the same grammatical mistake in Latin again and again? Why can't I see at once what it means to organize a piece of writing? Why did Newton have to wait for inspiration till he saw the apple fall? The answer is our inveterate tendency to get into ruts. So far removed is the essence of learning from becoming routinized that, when this happens to us, learning stops. To continue we have to jolt ourselves out of the rut, to try out alternatives, to overcome a limited and specific stupidity which, like a paralysis, can frustrate and render nugatory the will to learn. To put it otherwise, we are all strongly subject to mental cramp. When the great genius breaks with the past, and achieves a profoundly original and significant regrouping of experience, we exclaim: 'Inspiration!' We should do better to call it learning.

James L. Mursell   June 1935

nurture *NER cher*
to nourish, support, foster or maintain; further the development of ("nurturing" is the noun)

If the Basques have succeeded in preserving themselves as a people, it has been through the proud nurturing of their rural traditions. With a population that numbers not much more than two million, in a territory about the size of Connecticut, the Basques remain a people apart. Genetically distinct from every other group in Europe, the Basques are thought to be the direct descendants of Cro-Magnon man, having survived the Indo-Aryan invasion with their culture intact.

Marisa Bartolucci   October 2000

orthography

Noah Webster, poor, sturdy, independent, with a rude but surprising knowledge of philology, revolted in every nerve and fibre of his being against the enervating influence of the colonial past. The spirit of nationality had entered into his soul. He felt that the nation which he saw growing up about him was too great to take its orthography or its pronunciation blindly and obediently from the mother land. It was a new country and a new nation, and Webster determined that so far as in him lay it should have linguistic independence.

Henry Cabot Lodge   May 1883

see page 312

obdurate   *AHB duh rit*
stubbornly resistant; unyielding; obstinate

Political principles have not been able to make black and white Americans truly one people; they cannot wash away the color line, which remains the fundamental and most obdurate problem of American life.

Benjamin Schwarz   March 1997

obeisance   *oh BAY suhns*
a gesture of respect or reverence

Beginning in 1932, Hemingway lived in Cuba off and on for nearly three decades and through three wives, and devout tourists, mostly European and Canadian, trek like pilgrims along the Stations of the Papa, making obeisance where the great man lived, worked, and, mostly, drank.

Wayne Curtis   October 2005

obloquy   *AH bluh kwee*
censure, blame or abusive language aimed at a person or thing by the general public

In 1859 appeared Darwin's work, *On the Origin of Species, by Means of Natural Selection, or the Preservation of Favored Races in the Struggle for Life.* Like its predecessors, it was a firebrand thrown into the scientific camp. Like his predecessors, the author drew down obloquy and anathemas from the clergy, sarcasm and vituperation from the laity, and a host of replies from writers of all grades. Like his predecessor, the author of the "Vestiges," he might have said, in the words of Agassiz: "The history of the sciences is present to tell us that there are few of the great truths now recognized which have not been treated as chimerical and blasphemous before they were demonstrated."

Charles James Sprague   October 1866

✳ *Vestiges of the Natural History of Creation,* published anonymously in England in 1844, proposed a theory of evolution that preceded *The Origin of Species* by 14 years and not only influenced Darwin's ideas, but helped prepare society for their impact. *Vestiges* described an infinite universe, an earth that changed geologically through time, and the development of life on earth from its earliest forms. In highly religious 19th-century England, much controversy greeted the book. In 1884, long after his death, the author of the *Vestiges* was revealed to be Robert Chambers (1802-1871), an eminent Scottish publisher and writer.

obscurantist *uhb SKYOO ruhn tist*
opposed to human progress, enlightenment or the spread of knowledge
("obscurantism" is the noun)

The excessive Biblicism of orthodox Protestantism is — contrary to popular impression — considerably more obscurantist, culturally, than Catholicism. For Catholicism incorporates the best in the humanistic tradition of Western culture, while Protestant obscurantism turns its back on every insight not directly derived from scripture. In this strategy it manages to give many a scriptural truth an invalid, literalistic meaning.

Reinhold Niebuhr   February 1948

obsequies *AHB suh kweez*
funeral rites

The funeral procession of the late President of the United States has passed through the land from Washington to his final resting place in the heart of the prairies. Along the line of more than fifteen hundred miles his remains were borne, as it were, through continued lines of the people; and the number of mourners and the sincerity and unanimity of grief were such as never before attended the obsequies of a human being; so that the terrible catastrophe of his end hardly struck more awe than the majestic sorrow of the people.

George Bancroft   June 1865

obsequious *uhb SEE kwee uhs*
showing too great a willingness to serve and obey; overly submissive; fawning

One of the best known Whistler stories is that of the answer to a lady who declared that there was no one but but Whistler and Velasquez: "Madam, why drag in Velasquez?" An obsequious follower actually inquired of the Master whether he really meant this.

Gamaliel Bradford   April 1921

obtain   *ahb TAYN*
to be prevalent, customary or established

The American miracle may be represented in a number of ways, political and economic as well as cultural. But it can be argued that the supreme triumph of the American people is to have produced the largest homogeneous cultural unit on earth. Neither China or Russia, comparable though each is in extent and population, can claim that the official language of the state is understood from border to border or that the values that obtain among the governing and intellectual class of the capital are the raw material of public life in the remotest province.

John Keegan   April 1984

obtuse   *ahb TOO:S*
slow to understand; unfeeling; callous; thick-headed ("obtuseness" is the noun)

Twenty thousand British and Canadian soldiers were routinely killed on single mornings just by being sent out of their trenches at the Somme River. At Verdun on the first day of their attack the Germans fired one million shells on the French lines. Not until the war was almost over did the hopelessness, the criminal uselessness, of all this penetrate the populations at large. Then, finally, the truth began entering the despised civilians' minds that so many had been killed and gassed and maimed only through the self-satisfied obtuseness of their officers, and "pacifism" ceased to be a dirty word.

Hans Koning   September 1997

obviate   *AHB vee ayt*
to make unnecessary; prevent or avoid by anticipatory measures

> Curlylocks, Curlylocks, wilt though be mine?
> Thou shalt not wash dishes, nor yet feed the swine,
> But sit on a cushion and sew a fine seam,
> And feed upon strawberries, sugar and cream.

What a complete illustration of the unenlightened attitude toward women! The wooer, after tickling the young lady's vanity by an allusion to her coiffure, attempts to induce her to become his chattel by assuring her that, denied any share in their common labor and reduced to enervating indolence, she shall waste her time and ruin her eyesight on worthless needlework while she is pampered with a dangerous diet of fruit, sugar, and fat which will serve only to obviate in time the need for the cushion.

Bergen Evans   December 1934

   ✱ See also avarice, delectation, engender and sullen for other passages in which Bergen Evans provides his tongue-in-cheek analyses of nursery rhymes.

odoriferous   *oh duh RI fuh ris*
giving off a strong, usually offensive odor

Paul Revere rode out beyond Cambridge to Lexington once, and on toward Concord. That highway is now a through-traffic artery which eventually becomes the famous Mohawk Trail. Most of its length it is a swiftly moving steel and rubber river between banks of "hot-dog" kennels, fried-clam stands, filling stations, and other odoriferous and ugly reminders of this progressive age. On past Hawthorne's "Wayside" and Emerson's white dwelling it sweeps, and you wonder what would have happened to Hawthorne's delicate nerves or Emerson's serenity had those artists been forced to work beside this roaring torrent.

Walter Prichard Eaton   May 1930

oenologist   *ee NAH luh jist*
an expert in or connoisseur of wines and wine-making

In the discovery and providing of favorable conditions for the nurturing of the great European grape varieties, I believe that the more enlightened California vintners, with the guidance of such conscientious and painstaking oenologists as make up the staff of the University of California, are well on the road to distinguished achievement in fine wine making.

Charles R. Codman   June 1941

oeuvre   *ERV ruh*
the works of an artist, composer or writer, regarded collectively

At the highest level of competitive chess, players are so familiar with one another's games that they can practically read their opponents' minds. The memorization of opening theory and the intensive study of an opponent's oeuvre so dominate the modern game that when two grand masters square off, the first twenty moves unfold like a stale sitcom plot.

Rene Chun   December 2002

omniscient   *ahm NI shuhnt*
having infinite knowledge; all-knowing ("omniscience" is the noun)

It is related by Ovid that Lykaon, king of Arkadia, once invited Zeus to dinner, and served up for him a dish of human flesh, in order to test the god's omniscience. But the trick miserably failed, and the impious monarch received the punishment which his crime had merited. He was transformed into a wolf, that he might henceforth feed upon the viands with which he had dared to pollute the table of the king of Olympos.

John Fiske   August 1871

onerous   *AH nuh ruhs*
burdensome; oppressive

If there is any issue on which this year's presidential contenders seem stereotyped, it is the environment. George W. Bush is seen as a pro-business oilman who would let polluters run amok, Al Gore as a fanatical tree-hugger who would terrorize industry with onerous ecological restrictions.

Gregg Easterbrook   September 2000

opportunist   *ah puhr TOO: nist*
a person who exploits circumstances or opportunities as they occur to gain
immediate advantage, without regard to principles

The growing "free" market in China is mostly about well-connected entrepreneurs speculating with public funds, pocketing the profits, and assigning the losses to the state. When Chinese workers pen Marxist manifestos and take to the streets against their new capitalist oppressors, it is these government opportunists about whom they are up in arms.

Trevor Corson   February 2000

opprobrium   *uh PROH bree uhm*
disgrace arising from a person's shameful or dishonorable conduct

The World Court adjudicates civil disputes among nations — quarrels over borders, or fishing rights, or the meaning of treaties, or the right to deem another country an aggressor. It has no power of enforcement or credible threat of punishment for noncompliance. Its only leverage is moral gravitas. The court weighs in, and lets opprobrium or vindication fall where it may. Many states ignore it when they wish. The United States sharply restricted its conditions for accepting the court's jurisdiction after Reagan-era decisions against it in a dispute with Nicaragua.

Charles Trueheart   April 2000

orbit   *AWR bit*
the ordinary range of activity or experience

Traditionally, universities regarded patents as being outside their orbit, generally believing that proprietary claims were fundamentally at odds with their obligation to disseminate knowledge as broadly as possible. Today nearly every research university in the country has a technology-licensing office, and some have gone further. Johns Hopkins Medical School, for example, has established an internal venture-capital fund to bankroll commercially promising lines of research.

Eyal Press and Jennifer Washburn   March 2000

organic   *awr GA nik*
developing gradually and naturally; not forced or contrived

Liberty is not something that can be created by a document; neither is it something which, when created, can be laid away in a document, a completed work. It is an organic principle, a principle of life, renewing and being renewed. Democratic institutions are never done; they are like living tissue, always a-making. It is a strenuous thing, this of living the life of a free people; and our success in it depends upon training, not upon clever invention.

Woodrow Wilson   November 1889

orthography   *awr THAH gruh fee*
a system of spelling

Noah Webster, poor, sturdy, independent, with a rude but surprising knowledge of philology, revolted in every nerve and fibre of his being against the enervating influence of the colonial past. The spirit of nationality had entered into his soul. He felt that the nation which he saw growing up about him was too great to take its orthography or its pronunciation blindly and obediently from the mother land. It was a new country and a new nation, and Webster determined that so far as in him lay it should have linguistic independence.

Henry Cabot Lodge   May 1883

✳ When Noah Webster published *A Grammatical Institute of the English Language* in 1783 (renamed *The American Spelling Book* in 1787), his purpose was not just educational, it was patriotic. He considered the British primers used in American schools as ineffectual, and their use a sign of American dependence on England. Seeing how greatly spelling and pronunciation varied from state to state, region to region and even house to house, and the difficulties members of different immigrant groups had understanding one another's speech, he feared what that would mean for the nation's future. And so he set out as a 24-year-old schoolmaster in Goshen, New York, to develop a system of education that would standardize American spelling and pronunciation and unify the nation's language. His spelling book introduced new ways to teach and learn spelling and pronunciation, making it easy for all American children to pronounce words the same way. One method was the rhymed spelling list, one of which was cap, gap, lap, map, rap and tap. In his first speller, Webster changed publick to public and made zee the American way to say the letter z, instead of the British zed. In later spellers and dictionaries he removed the u from colour, honour and humour, and ended defence, offence and pretence with se. From the middle of the 19th century until the early part of the 20th century, Webster's spelling books sold a million or more copies a year, and his *American Spelling Book* received the first U. S. copyright. He was unsuccessful, however, in getting Americans to adopt a complete overhaul of their spelling, in which words would be spelled the way they sounded — cloke, spunge, fether, medicin, leef, ruf and blud.

oscillate   *AH suh layt*
to swing back and forth ("oscillation" is the noun)

To be a young man with literary aspirations is not to be particularly happy. At first, the desire to write is more strong than is a clear perception of what one wants to write and how one will write it. There are surprising oscillations of mood. One moment the young writer is energetic and hopeful. The next he is catapulted into a fit of despair with his faith in himself infirm, his self-confidence shattered and broken, his view of the future one in which he sees futile self-sacrifices ending only in dismal failure.

James T. Farrell   September 1938

outlandish   *owt LAN dish*
exceedingly odd, strange or peculiar; highly unconventional; outrageous; bizarre

Constitutional protection for animals is not an outlandish proposition. The late U.S. Supreme Court Justice William O. Douglas wrote once, in a dissenting opinion, that the day should come when "all of the forms of life . . . will stand before the court — the pileated woodpecker as well as the coyote and bear, the lemmings as well as the trout in the streams."

Steven Zak   March 1989

outstrip   *owt STRIP*
to get ahead of; leave behind; excel; surpass

As a saving in the time given up to writing, the phonograph promises to far outstrip the typewriter. The business man can dictate to the phonograph as fast as he can talk, and the wax cylinder, inclosed in a suitable box, can be sent off by mail to read out its message perhaps thousands of miles away. Or else, as is now done in Mr. Edison's laboratory in Orange, N. J., the typewriter girl can print out upon paper what her employer has dictated to the phonograph. For the reporter, the editor, and the author who can dictate, a device has been adapted to the phonograph which causes it to stop its message at every tenth word, and to continue only when a spring is touched. Thus, the editor can dictate his article to the phonograph as he does now to his stenographer, and when the printer at the case gets the resulting phonogram the instrument will dictate to him in short sentences. If he cannot set up the sentence at one hearing, it will repeat its ten words. If he is satisfied, it reads out ten words more. I really see no reason why the newspaper of the future should not come to the subscriber in the shape of a phonogram.

Philip G. Hubert Jr.   February 1889

overarching   *oh vuhr AR ching*
encompassing all that is within its scope; all-embracing

On the eve of the takeover of the U.S. embassy in Iran, in 1979, American officials desperately fed secret documents into the embassy's paper shredders. Over the next several years, while waiting for satellite dishes and *Baywatch* to arrive, the Iranians painstakingly stitched the documents back together. They ultimately published the reconstituted intelligence files in some sixty volumes, under the overarching title *Documents From the U.S. Espionage Den.*

Cullen Murphy   May 2002

oxymoron   *ahks uh MAW ron*
a figure of speech in which opposite terms are combined to create a seemingly contradictory idea: Greek, oxy, *sharp +* moros, *foolish*

Let us be clear: "humane killing" is an oxymoron. The best we can hope for in killing animals is that death be as quick and as nearly painless as possible. Experience has shown that in the whaling industry this is largely achieved — just as it is in the food industries that kill millions of cattle, sheep, pigs, and chickens every day.

William Aron, William T. Burke and Milton Freeman   May 1999

P

polity

In France everything speaks of long familiar intercourse between the earth and its inhabitants; every field has a name, a history, a distinct place of its own in the village polity; every blade of grass is there by an old feudal right which has long since dispossessed the worthless aboriginal weed.

Edith Wharton   December 1906

see page 338

315

pacific *puh SI fik*
of a peaceful nature; calm; tranquil

> Though sometimes the pigheadedness of mankind puts me in a huff, my nature is essentially pacific.

> Glanville Smith   April 1940

paean *PEE uhn*
a song or hymn of joy, triumph or praise: originally, in ancient Greece, a hymn of thanksgiving to Apollo or another god for victory or survival in battle

> *Walden* is probably our only, as it is certainly our first, nature classic. It lives because it has the real breath of life; it embodies a fresh and unique personality, and portrays an experiment in the art of living close to nature, in a racy and invigorating style. It is a pæan in praise of that kind of noble poverty which takes the shine out of wealth completely. All the same, most of its readers would doubtless prefer the lot of the young men, his townsmen, to whom Thoreau refers, "whose misfortune it is to have inherited farms, houses, barns, cattle, and farming tools" — things, he added, that "are more easily acquired than got rid of."

> John Burroughs   April 1919

painstaking *PAYNZ tay king*
expending great care, effort and attention ("painstakingly" is the adverb)

> In the former Soviet Union there was a literary genre called *samizdat* (the word means "self-published" in Russian) that consisted of subversive political manifestos and unsanctioned — that is, good — poetry and fiction, circulated only in type-scripts, painstakingly reproduced by volunteer typists who smashed their keys through four or five sheets of carbon paper at a time. Famous typescripts never

published in the USSR included Boris Pasternak's *Doctor Zhivago* and Aleksandr Solzhenitsyn's *The Gulag Archipelago.*

Alex Beam   November 2005

palimpsest *PA limp sest*
a parchment or other writing surface that has been written on more than once, with the earlier writing incompletely erased and often still legible: thus, an object or a place whose older layers or aspects are apparent beneath its surface

All great books are symbolical myths, overlaid like palimpsests with the meanings that men at various times assign to them.

Clifton Fadiman   October 1943

palisade *pa luh SAYD*
a row of tall pointed stakes set in the ground as an enclosure or fence to keep out the enemy; a line of anything resembling such a fence, as cliffs or buildings

Incredible as it seems, people get used to New York, and the perpetual drama of the city does not strike them in the face. In my mind that drama is always present, but never did it strike me so forcibly as on the first morning I went to work in the big town. In the business world of the city I had not one friend, and when I tumbled out of my Pullman berth and found myself standing on Forty-second Street at seven o'clock in the morning, I knew I was in for the fight of my life. The palisade of buildings scowled across the way as if each one were an active belligerent. It was the metropolis against me, and the odds were on the metropolis. I laugh now as I see myself clenching my fist and shaking it at the big bank opposite, muttering to myself: "Damn you, New York. I will wring a living out of you yet."

Ellery Sedgwick   September 1946

pall *pawl*
a covering, such as cloud or smoke, that darkens or obscures an area

In 1950 a gigantic fire burned over an area of 10,000 square kilometers of forest in Alberta, Canada. The trees, mostly conifers, were rich in tars and resins, which make oily black smoke. The pall covered about half the land area of the United States, spread across the Atlantic, was detected over Great Britain by aircraft as high as 35,000 feet, and actually reduced the amount of visible light reaching the ground in Western Europe.

Thomas Powers   November 1984

to become boring, stale or wearisome

One of the many wonderful things about a home is that it can be as lively as you please without ever becoming public. The big Cambridge house was in this respect, as in all other respects, a true home. Although I could be entirely alone when I wished, a varied social life awaited me whenever aloneness palled. A father and mother — later, a sister — two successive grandmothers and an aunt (all three of whom sang, or played the piano, or did both, extremely well) and one uncle, plus three or four hearty and jovial servants, were at my almost unlimited disposal.

E.E. Cummings   April 1953

❋ While it is commonly believed that the poet and artist Edward Estlin Cummings (1894-1962), better known as E. E. Cummings, preferred his name in all lowercase letters, it was his publishers who liked it that way, taking their cue from his unorthodox use of lowercase letters in his poetry. Cummings himself intended his name to be written in the traditional manner.

palliate   *PA lee ayt*
to lessen or alleviate an illness or problem without effecting a cure or solution ("palliation" is the noun)

For the third time within the memory of men who still feel themselves young, the President of the United States has been struck down by an assassin. Each of these crimes was as wanton as it was remediless. No shadow of excuse or palliation — except upon the charitable presumption of insanity — can be found for the vainglorious actor, the disappointed office seeker, and the self-confessed anarchist, who treacherously took the lives of Lincoln, Garfield, and McKinley.

Bliss Perry   October 1901

panacea   *pa nuh SEE uh*
a supposed remedy or solution for all illnesses or problems; a cure-all

Many popular articles on the control of the Mississippi give expression to favorite panaceas. The general public, the sentimental conservationists, and the Bureau of Forestry, all give great weight to reforestation. The responsible civil engineers of the country generally dismiss it as having no practical relation to flood control.

Arthur E. Morgan   November 1927

pandemic   *pan DE mik*
a disease affecting a country, continent or global area and claiming a large proportion of its population

"Pandemic" is not another word for "epidemic," any more than "hurricane" is another word for "breeze." Influenza becomes epidemic every year in some part of the world. It creeps into a city, — sometimes in winter, sometimes in summer, — attacks the children and young adults, and burns itself out a month later. Once in three, in eleven, twenty, or even thirty years, one of these epidemics explodes into a pandemic and sweeps around the world. No medical man knows yet what it is that keeps it local, or sends it rampaging across continents, any more than meteorologists can put their fingers on the precise combination of low and high pressure areas that will turn an ordinary Caribbean gale into another 1938 New England hurricane.

Mona Gardner   February 1941

pander *PAN duhr*
to cater to or profit from the weaknesses or vices of others

I believe that this generation is capable of doing the right thing, and that politicians might well discover that it is better to appeal to their nobler instincts than to pander to their baser ones.

Peter G. Peterson   May 1996

panegyric *pa nuh JI rik*
a public speech or piece of writing praising a person, event or achievement

Perennial panegyrics are written, and rightly, on the unerring instinct and undying spirit of the noble salmon, battling their way up raging torrents to consummate racial reproduction at the cost of their own lives. But there are many instances of salmon giving up on a river and quitting it forever when they find man-made changes there intolerable.

John Stuart Martin   June 1965

paradigm *PA ruh dighm*
a pattern, example or model

As the Strip in all its impermanence has. flourished, Las Vegas's old downtown has languished — it's the paradigm, after all, for what has happened in a city near you.

Richard Todd   February 2001

a set of assumptions, concepts, values and practices of a particular discipline at a given time

Slowly but surely, higher education is evolving a new paradigm for undergraduate study that erodes the long-standing divide between liberal and professional education. Many liberal arts colleges now offer courses and majors in professional fields; professional disciplines, meanwhile, have become more serious about the arts and sciences. Moreover, universities are encouraging students to include both liberal arts and professional coursework in their programs of study, while internships and other kinds of off-campus experience have gained widespread acceptance in both liberal and professional disciplines.

Richard M. Freeland   October 2004

parameters   *puh RA muh terz*
boundaries or limits

I turned forty recently, so it's time I started planning my midlife crisis. I'm not going to have it right away, but something this humiliating requires preparation. First I've got to set some general parameters. For example, I envision something more dramatic than a red convertible but less drastic than a sex-change operation. I'm not inclined toward the Brian Wilson-style spend-three-years-in-bed crisis; on the other hand, I wouldn't want to go off soul-searching amid Tibetan Sherpas at a Himalayan base camp, which involves more physical exertion than I'm up for. I want to achieve the traditional goals of the midlife crisis — several acts of epic selfishness, maximum possible embarrassment to my children, maybe a hair weave — but I don't want to do anything that might cause my wife to cast meaningful glances at the butcher knives.

David Brooks   March 2002

paramount   *PA ruh mownt*
ranking higher than any other; supreme

America seeks a world in which American interests are paramount, but it does not covet anyone else's land, nor does it wish to subjugate any other peoples. The United States is deeply interested in extracting wealth from other lands and peoples, but in our enlightened time it is understood that the efficient way to do this is through commerce, not through the old, costly, dangerous, and tedious business of conquest, colonization, plunder, and taxation. AOL-Time-Warner-Disney-God will eventually get everybody's money, and no one will have to get shot.

Michael Kelly   October 2001

parlous   *PAHR luhs*
precarious; perilous

Ernest Hemingway's house just outside Havana is called Finca Vigía. You aren't allowed inside. It's in parlous condition, and it's filled with small, pilferable items, such as unopened letters and a rubber stamp that reads "I never answer letters, Ernest Hemingway." You are, however, permitted to stroll around the outside and crane your neck through open windows and doors, from which you can see the interior much as the author left it in 1960.

Wayne Curtis   October 2005

parody *PA ruh dee*
a humorous or satirical imitation of the content or style of another work
(a "parodist" is one who practices this art)

The doctrine of "fair use" permits brief passages from a book to be quoted in a book review or a critical essay; and the parodist of a copyrighted work is permitted to copy as much of that work as is necessary to enable readers to recognize the new work as a parody.

Richard A. Posner   April 2002

parrot *PA ruht*
to repeat or imitate mechanically or mindlessly

The celebrated panoramas and points of view are not the favorite haunts of great painters. They do not need to travel far for their subjects. Mr. Ruskin tells us that Turner did not paint the high Alps, nor the *cumulus,* the grandest form of cloud. Calame gives us the nooks and lanes, the rocks and hills, of Switzerland, rather than the high peaks; Lambinet, an apple-orchard, a row of pollard-elms, or a weedy pond, — not cataracts or forests. This is not affectation or timidity, but an instinct that the famous scenes are no breaks in the order of Nature, — that what is seen in them is visible elsewhere as well, only not so obvious, and that the office of Art is not to parrot what is already distinct, but to reveal it where it is obscure.

James Eliot Cabot   February 1864

parsimonious *pahr suh MOH nee uhs*
overly careful in spending; stingy; tight-fisted ("parsimony" is the noun)

Style varies with every temperament. Sometimes it is torrential, sometimes combative. Occasionally it is achieved through a certain parsimony in words. In a satirical passage understatement always tells. I chance on an excellent example in the opening sentence of a story by that intermittent and malformed genius, Ambrose Bierce. "Early one June morning in 1872, I murdered my father — an act which made a deep impression on me at the time."

Ellery Sedgwick   November 1947

passé *pa SAY*
out of date; behind the times

The Czech Republic might be considered passé. It has been half a dozen years since young Americans flocked to Prague for its cheap, dreamy bohemian life. Prague remains the capital of the real Bohemia — Bohemia and Moravia being the two provinces that make up the Czech Republic. But Prague was discovered by the tour buses and became clichéd, and the young dreamers moved on to Bratislava or Minsk.

James Fallows   June 1998

✻ The popular image of the bohemian lifestyle — painters and writers living in garrets, spending afternoons and evenings in cafés talking art and philosophy, scraping out a living — existed long before 1849. But that was the year that Henry Murger, a 27-year-old Parisian journalist, gave the lifestyle its name. He published a novel depicting the life he and his friends led in 1840s Paris, calling it *Scenes de la Vie de Boheme*. Since these artists and writers seemed to have no permanent home, "bohemian" accrued to them from the similarity of their lifestyle to the gypsies of Bohemia. From Murger's book, Giacomo Puccini created the opera *La Boheme* in 1896.

pastoral *pas TAW ruhl*

rural

Last summer I visited England with intent to explore its highways and byways in search of cathedrals, almshouses, inns, and cottages, but chiefly of that pastoral charm which pervades the pages of such old books as *Our Village* and *Selborne*. It was a delightful outing, for England is still England, war or no war, and in the country one is less conscious of change, the change the economist commends, in the course of which a people sloughs off the habit and habits that have no right to exist, except that they are old and picturesque and human and lovable.

Earnest Elmo Calkins September 1925

patrician *puh TRI shuhn*

noble; aristocratic

The leading investment personality of the 1970s, Louis Rukeyser, for more than thirty years the host of TV's *Wall Street Week*, had the patrician profile of a Founding Father, the flowing hair of a concert pianist, and the clubby nasal voice of a Harvard English professor. He was a true blue blood or a smooth fraud or some of both.

Walter Kirn November 2004

patronize *PAY truh nighz*

to behave in an offensively condescending manner toward; to be helpful in a haughty way, as if dealing with an inferior ("patronizingly" is the adverb)

Nothing gives me the feeling of having been born several decades too late quite like the modern "literary" best seller. Give me a time-tested masterpiece or what critics patronizingly call a fun read — *Sister Carrie* or just plain *Carrie*. Give me anything, in fact, as long as it doesn't have a recent prize jury's seal of approval on the front and a clutch of precious raves on the back. In the bookstore I'll sometimes sample what all the fuss is about, but one glance at the affected prose — "furious dabs of tulips stuttering," say, or "in the dark before the day yet was" — and I'm hightailing it to the friendly black spines of the Penguin Classics.

B. R. Myers   July/August 2001

peccadillo   *pe kuh DI lo*
a small or petty fault or offense

Perhaps your husband smokes? If so, at what period of the twenty-four hours have you invariably found Mr. — most lenient to your little pecuniary peccadilloes? Is he not always most good-natured when his cigar is about one-third consumed, the ash evenly burnt and adherent, and not fallen into his shirt-bosom? Depend upon it, tobacco is a great soother of domestic differences.

David William Cheever   August 1860

pecuniary   *pi KYOO: nee ai ree*
pertaining to money

The conversion of women into a crypto-servant class was an economic accomplishment of the first importance. Menial employed servants were available only to a minority of the pre-industrial population; the servant-wife is available, democratically, to almost the entire present male population. Were the workers so employed subject to pecuniary compensation, they would be by far the largest single category in the labor force.

John Kenneth Galbraith   August 1973

pellucid   *puh LOO: sid*
transparent or translucent; clear

I am reminded of the river of my youth, as it was fifty years ago and has now become in my old age. Fifty years ago the Russian River was a scene of constant rustic beauty. There were deep pools, with sparkling riffles pellucid and gin-clear in the summertime, where the minnows sported in the shallows. Game fish boiled in the deep runs, where a sack of crawfish could be captured by the judicious use of a small net and a piece of fresh liver any evening, and where smallmouth bass could be lured from the deeper water with a popper or a fly.

Clark C. Van Fleet   July 1964

penumbra   *puh NUHM bruh*
a partial shade or shadow bordering upon a fuller or darker one

Whether as a result of our effort to build a unified nation out of diverse racial material, or as an accompaniment of an intellectual simplicity unaware of the penumbra of ideas beyond its own mental margins, or as the product of innate conservatism, we have throughout our country, North, South, East, and West, stressed conformity and looked askance upon difference. To our Puritan tradition irregularity in party or creed, divergence in social theory or in literary form, have all smacked of immorality.

Cornelia James Cannon   September 1925

penuriousness   *puh NYOO ree uhs nis*
stinginess; frugality

Emily Dickinson is one of our most original writers, a force destined to endure in American letters. There is no doubt that critics are justified in complaining that her work is often cryptic in thought and unmelodious in expression. Almost all of her poems are written in short measures, in which the effect of curt brevity is increased by her verbal **penuriousness**. Compression and epigrammatical ambush are her aids; she proceeds, without preparation or apology, by sudden, sharp zigzags. What intelligence a reader has must be exercised in the poetic game of hare-and-hounds, where ellipses, inversions, and unexpected climaxes mislead those who pursue sweet reasonableness.

Martha Hale Shackford   January 1913

✳ In the children's game hare and hounds (also called paper chase) the hares, with a head start, run off to a designated place, leaving a trail of paper scraps for the hounds to follow. By leaving false trails of paper, the hares can throw the hounds off the scent. If a hare reaches the finish without being caught, it becomes a hound in a new round.

perdurable   *per DOO ruh buhl*
lasting; enduring

The lingering stigma associated in the new Russia with towns more than 101 kilometers (sixty-three miles) outside Moscow or other big cities reflects a **perdurable** Soviet legacy: the division of the land into favored urban areas and a neglected, poverty-stricken hinterland.

Jeffrey Tayler   February 1999

peremptory   *puh REMP tuh ree*
without further debate or question ("peremptorily" is the adverb)

There had formerly been much complaint of the brutal treatment by police of innocent citizens. This was stopped **peremptorily** by the obvious expedient of dismissing from the force the first two or three men who were found guilty of brutality. On the other hand, we made the force understand that in the event of any emergency requiring them to use their weapons against either a mob or an individual criminal, the police board backed them up without reservation. Our sympathy was for the friends, and not the foes, of order.

Theodore Roosevelt   September 1897

perforce   *puhr FAWRS*
by necessity

Of such planets as doubtless circle round other suns we as yet know nothing. Our search is **perforce** confined at present to the members of our own solar family.

Percival Lowell   May 1895

permeate   *PER mee ayt*
to pass into and affect every part of; penetrate and spread throughout; pervade

A none-of-my-business attitude **permeates** the firearms distribution chain from production to final sale, allowing gunmakers and gun marketers to promote the killing power of their weapons while disavowing any responsibility for their use in crime.

Erik Larson   January 1993

permutation   *per myuh TAY shuhn*
variation; change; alteration; transformation

Steinbeck has been interested in writing for as long as he can remember. When he was four, he discovered, to his flabbergasted delight, that "high" rhymed with "fly," and from that day to this the **permutations** and combinations of words have charmed and fascinated him.

Lewis Gannett   December 1945

peroration   *pe ruh RAY shuhn*
a long speech containing lofty and often pompous language

Macmillan is not always happy when addressing a mass audience; sometimes he is too witty, and sometimes he goes off into a Churchillian **peroration** that sounds phony and second-rate. Where he excels is in private conversation. Completely relaxed, filling his pipe, sipping a whisky and soda, he gives an impression of friendly naturalness.

Hugh Massingham   November 1958

perpetuate   *per PE choo: ayt*
to cause to continue; make endless

The legend of the South Seas, whether the time be 1762 or 1962, resurrects a vague but distant place of scented breezes and ivory beaches, tiny scrubbed islands ringed with pink coral and peopled with slim, carefree natives who swim and dance and make love, a myopic vision relentlessly perpetuated by film directors and travel editors.

Christopher Lucas   November 1967

✳ Beach originally meant the wave-worn pebbles that make up what we now call the beach. Today, we go to the beach. Originally, though, one walked upon the beach, meaning upon the pebbles. Gradually, the term became transferred to the pebbled area itself. The origin of the word beach is unknown; etymologists assume it had to have an earlier form in a different language, but have been unable to trace it back earlier than 16th-century English.

perquisite   *PER kwuh zit*
a benefit, privilege or advantage over and above regular salary

Kissinger is a man fascinated by power, a student of it, a ruthless seeker of it, a respecter of others who have it, a skilled wielder of it, and sometimes, alas, a man intoxicated by it. His love of the perquisites of power, the television camera's attention, the long black limos, the special plane, is so evident to everyone that in self-defense Kissinger can only wittily confess his weakness.

Thomas Griffith   July 1976

per se   *puhr SAY*
in or by itself

I am not persuaded by anything I have read or know that the presence of a few Communists among the teaching profession in this country constitutes an emergency; I cannot agree that the refusal to incriminate one's self before an investigating committee is *per se* proper ground for wrecking the professional life of a teacher, however foolish I may think he is; and I only regret that I cannot put my faith into more impressive words. Unless some unforeseen turn of events should alter the present posture of affairs, I believe that long-run wisdom in the United States is to leave reason free to combat error.

Howard Mumford Jones   June 1953

persiflage   *PER suh flazh*
light, frivolous or flippant writing or speaking

Without getting all bollixed up in Platonist categories, it's not too farfetched to suggest that what used to make American films recognizably American was not how they looked but how their screenwriters made them sound. Through the work of journalists like Herman Mankiewicz and Ben Hecht and playwrights like Robert Sherwood, the American talkie came to value word over image, persiflage over mise-en-scène, verbal swagger over visual sweep.

David Kipen   June 2004

> ✳ *Mise-en-scène* (French, what's put into the scene) is the combined elements of a play or movie's appearance — the scenery, props, lighting and performance.

perspicacity   *per spuh KA suh tee*
keenness of insight, perception or understanding

When an author writes "Chapter I" at the top of a blank page, he is starting out on a strange and often dangerous adventure. Without knowing it always, he is going to tell us all about himself, but he feels perfectly safe because he masquerades as a dozen different people and never credits the reader with enough perspicacity to find him out.

Julian Green   December 1941

persuasion   *per SWAY zhuhn*
a deep conviction or belief

The image of our sixteenth President, at once brooding and benign, casts its spell over all who visit the Lincoln Memorial in Washington. Political leaders and reformers of many persuasions have invoked this icon of American civil religion. At a low point of the Vietnam War, President Richard Nixon engaged anti-war protesters in a dramatic midnight dialogue at the Lincoln Memorial. During the civil-rights march on Washington in 1963 Martin Luther King Jr. stood in front of the memorial and began his "I Have a Dream" speech with the words "Fivescore years ago, a great American, in whose symbolic shadow we stand today, signed the Emancipation Proclamation."

James M. McPherson   November 1995

pertinacity   *per tun NA suh tee*
resolute or stubborn adherence to a purpose or opinion; persistent determination

Horace Greely was a queer compound of bone, brain, and self-will. The current impression that he lacked pluck and pertinacity is entirely without foundation. He had indomitable self-assertion, and was game to the last. He cared not a cent about fashion in speech, manners, or dress. While I worked under him, although I saw him every day and heard his voice through the open doors, I never once heard him say "Good morning" or "Good evening," "How d' ye do" or "Good-bye," or inquire about anybody's health. But he scrupulously answered every letter that came to him, and generally tilted his chair forward on its legs and answered it on the spot, so that the writer could get a reply in the next mail. His conscience was abnormally developed on that one subject, and he probably wrote many thousand letters which did not need writing, and thus shortened his life.

William A. Croffut   February 1930

pertinent   *PER tuh nint*
relevant; to the point

I was looking for an old quotation, something to the effect of "Political office should be held only by men who don't want it." I thought this was from *The Education of Henry Adams,* which I remembered as being a trenchant criticism of politics, as pertinent today as when it was written, in 1905. I got out my copy, unopened since college — and maybe unopened then, if Monarch Notes were available. ("Trenchant criticism ... as pertinent today ..." certainly sounds like Monarch Notes.) I began to skim, became fascinated, and actually read the thing.

P. J. O'Rourke   December 2002

perturb   *per TERB*
to disturb the regular order or course; to cause disorder or irregularity in; to unsettle ("perturbation" is the noun)

Recently I took a six-week journey across China. It was my first trip back since I came to the United States to study, in 1985. In the course of my visit I saw — I felt — the perturbations of profound and chaotic social change. China's stunning hurtle from a centrally planned economy to a free market has set off an economic explosion and generated tremendous prosperity.

Xiao-huang Yin   April 1994

perversity   *per VER suh tee*
the disposition or tendency to act in a manner contrary to what is right or reasonable; contrariness

We should all be grateful for a certain perversity in human nature. In my own case, what doubles the pleasure of reading is the subconscious feeling that I ought, most of the time, to be doing something else.

Carl S. Patton   February 1922

pettifoggery   *PE tee fah guh ree*
trivial objections; pettiness: originally applied to lawyers who habitually argue over petty details

> What was done for Shakespeare and his readers by scholarship, by painful investigation, by comparison of texts, by research into the social fashions and intellectual habits of the past, although it often degenerated into literary pettifoggery, was on the whole of real worth and no small service. For most of these critics sought only to discover what it was that Shakespeare had actually written, and what there was in the history and the literature of his time that would make his meaning clear; and although they had their little pride in their little excavations, they were truly modest, and sought to illustrate their subject rather than themselves. They seemed to work in a moleish fashion; but after all, moles have a way of getting at the roots of things. We can forgive much pedantry for the sake of what some pedants have done for us.
>
> Richard Grant White   May 1884

petulant   *PE chuh luhnt*
impatient or irritable over petty things

> Herbert Spencer was not merely petulant when he said that to play billiards perfectly argued a misspent life. He stated a profound truth.
>
> Simeon Strunsky   August 1914

philanderer   *fuh LAN der er*
a married man who has numerous love affairs ("philander" is the verb)

> Dreiser was a hypochondriac, drank too much, and had a nervous habit of folding and refolding his handkerchief. He philandered, and philandered on his philanderings; despite buckteeth, a cast in one eye, and a shambling gait, he attracted women with what one called his animal magnetism. He quarreled with publishers over royalty statements and movie studios over script control, and even quarreled with H. L. Mencken, who had fought at his side in early battles against the censors.
>
> Michael Lydon   August 1993

philippic   *fi LI pik*
a bitter verbal attack

> MAD IN AMERICA *by Robert Whitaker. Perseus, 330 pages, $27.00.* People who concern themselves with the treatment of the mentally ill can generally be put into one of two categories: those who push drugs, and those who push therapy. In this historical philippic the medical reporter Robert Whitaker firmly sides with the latter. He marshals all the attributes of investigative journalism — the liberal use of quotation marks, the tireless attention to malfeasance, the deep-rooted mistrust of authority —

to argue that what he stubbornly calls "mad medicine" is and always has been misguided in its emphasis on physical therapies.

Daniel Smith   March 2002

phlegmatic *fleg MA tik*
having a calm, sluggish temperament; unemotional; unexcitable

The love-madness of a young mother for her tiny infant, poetical and picturesque as it is, is harmful in many ways. It is to a great extent a sensuous obsession to which in this country the husband and father is, all too often, ruthlessly sacrificed. If this sacrifice were in the least justified by the needs of the infant, there would be little to criticize; but it is distinctly not so justified in the average middle-class household. A phlegmatic nurse whose ministrations are rooted in duty alone, is not only equally as good for the baby, but is very much better.

Anna A. Rogers   March 1908

physiognomy *fi zee AHG nuh mee*
the general appearance or external features of a thing

Sequoias are trees that the familiar pines and firs seem to know nothing about, lonely, silent, serene, with a physiognomy almost godlike, and so old that thousands of them still living had already counted their years by tens of centuries when Columbus set sail from Spain, and were in the vigor of youth or middle age when the star led the Chaldean sages to the infant Saviour's cradle. As far as man is concerned, they are the same yesterday, today, and forever, emblems of permanence.

John Muir   March 1901

picaresque *pi kuh RESK*
dealing with humorous, earthy, colorful and often bizarre adventures

As a story writer, I have always been intrigued by that kind of story in which the hero chases through exciting, picaresque dangers in order to acquire a small box or a sealed bottle or a talismanic ring, or a sword or grail containing *the* answer.

Wolf Mankowitz   March 1962

piecemeal *PEES meel*
in small amounts; gradually; separately

The exigencies of magazine life call for serial novels, yet it is not impossible that as the publication of novels in separate monthly parts has ceased, so the fashion of printing works of fiction in successive numbers of a monthly or weekly magazine may pass away, for it is only a fashion. Now and then a novel, like *The Pickwick Papers* or *Vanity Fair,* is all the more enjoyable for being read at intervals, and the reader is helped by having his fiction doled out to him instead of putting himself under bonds to read his novel by piecemeal. We suspect even that this serial mode has some influence upon a writer, and that he looks after the articulation of his work more carefully than he would if it were to appear in the first instance as a book. Yet it is manifest that a work of art in literature ought to be quite independent of its mere mode of publication, and the final issue in book form certainly gives the reader a better opportunity for regarding it as a whole than when it was constantly interrupting itself.

Horace Elisha Scudder   July 1889

pied-à-terre   *pee ay de TAIR*
a second residence used only occasionally: French, foot on the ground

New York is a lodestone to the literary talent of the entire United States. As a centre for the printing and distribution of books and magazines it has no New World and few Old World rivals. Where publishers are gathered together, there authors likewise must reside, or at least possess what the French call a *pied-à-terre.*

Alvan F. Sanborn   October 1906

piffle   *PI fuhl*
nonsense; twaddle

It is customary to suppose that every unmarried woman bears the secret scar of an unfinished romance or disappointment, but that is all piffle. It sounds like the talk in a girls' school when the favorite teachers are discussed. There are disappointments and there are tragedies. But nearly all women who constitutionally want to be married are married — if not to one man, to another. I know very many spinsters, and wistfulness is not their quality.

Margaret Lynn   May 1934

pigeon   *PI jin*
a person easily deceived or gulled; dupe

No doubt the avaricious poker players in the Pacific rear areas where Lieutenant Nixon served out his war thought that this young Quaker would be a nice fat pigeon. Instead, he soon turned out to be one of the most aggressively successful poker players in the Navy. Today, his lack of any overburdening ideology makes it possible for him to use the talents which made him a brilliant poker player to their fullest, unencumbered by ideological convictions. It makes it possible for him to "finesse" (this Nixonian verb, rather surprisingly, is borrowed from bridge, not poker) his natural enemies, the liberal Democrats.

Stewart Alsop   February 1972

pigeonhole   *PI jin hohl*
to place in a category; classify; label ("pigeonholing" is the noun)

Neither a strict classicist like George Szell nor a mystic romantic like Klaus Tennstedt — though he could be elegantly classical or prophetically mystical or sensual or jazzy — Bernstein the conductor resists critical pigeonholing.

David Schiff   June 1993

✳ When in August of 1876 Mark Twain wrote to William Dean Howells, *The Atlantic's* editor, about the novel he had been working on, he used pigeonhole in another sense, meaning to set aside with little intent of finishing. "I have written 400 pages on it therefore it is very nearly half done," he wrote. "It is Huck Finn's Autobiography. I like it only tolerably well, as far as I have got, & may possibly pigeonhole or burn the MS when it is done." He pigeonholed it until 1884.

pillory   *PI luh ree*
to publicly ridicule or abuse: the pillory, an instrument of shame in Europe since at least the Middle Ages, and later in the United States, was a device consisting of a board with holes for the head and hands, in which offenders were locked and exposed to public scorn ("pilloried" is the adjective)

Fifteen years ago, when Ionesco's first play, *La Cantatrice Chauve (The Bald Soprano)*, was put on at the Left Bank theater of Les Nictambules, few in the audience were aware that they were witnessing a radically new kind of theater. There were catcalls and boos. What did the author mean by writing a play in which no bald-headed singer appears, into which a fireman strays when there isn't the whiff of a fire, and in which the dialogue, from the first line to the last, seems bent on defying every canon of rational speech? The reception was so hostile that Ionesco had to be restrained by his friends from climbing onto the stage to defend his pilloried work.

Curtis Cate   April 1966

pious hope   *PIGH uhs HOHP*
an unrealistic hope expressed in order to preserve an appearance of optimism

Red China did not enter the war with the object of throwing over her own prestige and sacrificing her power position at the last moment. To expect such stupid generosity of her is almost criminal folly. The Chinese aim is to defeat the United States and UN coalition, and possibly, beyond that, to expand her territory. So when our statesmen express the pious hope that in a "reconciliation period" which follows a truce, Red China can be persuaded to withdraw, they are blind to fundamental political realities. Red China can't withdraw; nor can water flow uphill.

Brigadier General S. L. A. Marshall   September 1953

piquant *PEE kuhnt*
exciting interest or curiosity; stimulating; provocative ("piquancy" is the noun)

In the summer of 1953 we got jobs together as counselors at a Jewish camp in the Poconos, where I had worked the year before, and there at night we took off for the woods. What with the obstacles to passion having to be surmounted again and again, our erotic life, along with the sheer thrill of its newness, had the underground piquancy of adultery. Even more than lovers, we became, through this drama of concealment and secrecy, the closest of companions and the most devoted of friends.

Philip Roth   December 1987

pitfall *PIT fawl*
an unsuspected danger or error into which a person is liable to fall; trap

Analogical argument — the inferring of a further degree of resemblance from an observed degree — is one of the greatest pitfalls of popular thinking. In medicine it formerly led to what was known as the doctrine of signatures, by which walnuts were prescribed for brain troubles because walnut meats look something like minia-ture brains, foxes' lungs were prescribed for asthma because foxes were thought to have unusual respiratory powers, and bear grease was rubbed on the head for bald-ness because bears have hairy coats. Hundreds of futile remedies were based on such false analogies and they have not all been cleared off druggists' shelves yet, though the survivors are, no doubt, "scientifically" prepared and packaged.

Bergen Evans   April 1946

pithy *PI th:ee*
saying much in a few words ("pithiness" is the noun)

With his melodic fertility and swift working habits, he might have turned out a suc-cession of Broadway musicals. Or, with his musical cleverness and pithiness, he could have been a master of the television singing commercial, which actually is as sharp, concise, and effective a musical form as any our society has evolved. So per-haps it's just as well to leave Mozart in his own century.

Herbert Kupferberg   December 1965

plaint *playnt*
an audible expression of sorrow or grief; lamentation; grieving

Sound has no power to express a profounder emotion of utter loneliness than the loon's cry. Standing in piny darkness on the lake's bank, or floating in dimness of mist or glimmer of twilight on its surface, you hear this wailing note, and all possibility of human tenancy by the shore or human voyaging is annihilated. You can fancy no response to this signal of solitude disturbed, and again it comes sadly over the water, the despairing plaint of some companionless and incomplete existence, exiled from happiness it has never known, and conscious only of blank and utter want.

Theodore Winthrop   September 1862

platitude   *PLA tuh too:d*
a commonplace or trite remark, especially one uttered as if it were fresh or original

For those who have learned the pleasures of political clichés, the best and the most come in the presidential year and in much of the year before it. Post-presidential years bring the books that reporters write to make their platitudes endure.

Martin Plissner   January 1980

plaudits   *PLAW dits*
enthusiastic praise or approval; applause

Mayor Rudolph Giuliani, later to be described as an American Churchill, laid the groundwork for his own plaudits by announcing, just after the aggression of September 11 against his city, that he was reading a book about Churchill's wartime premiership "and nothing is more inspirational than the speeches and reflections of Winston Churchill about how to deal with that." Ronald Reagan hung a portrait of Churchill in the Situation Room of the White House soon after taking power; the first President Bush allowed Jack Kemp to compare him to Churchill during the Gulf War; the second President Bush asked the British embassy in Washington to help furnish him with a bronze bust of Churchill, which now holds pride of place in the Oval Office.

Christopher Hitchens   April 2002

plum   *pluhm*
something choice or desirable

Mark Twain went into publishing on his own with my father as his partner and titular head of Charles L. Webster & Company. Both partners were on the lookout for new books and it was Mark Twain who came up with the prize plum, the *Personal Memoirs of U.S. Grant.* This work, which broke all records in American biography, was to be printed in two volumes, and Volume One came off the press late in 1885. But Grant himself did not live to see his autobiography published; he died on July 23, less than one week after his final correcting of the manuscript. Actually, his last bit of writing was the revision of the prospectus advertising the book: he made the changes, as he explained on the margin, because he was afraid feelings might be hurt by something he had said.

Samuel Charles Webster   November 1944

✳ In the early 18th century, plum was a slang word for the sum of £100,000, as in "He's worth a plum." By the early 19th century, anything choice could be a plum.

plume *ploo:m*
to indulge in self-congratulation; to feel vainly self-satisfied

Would men ever get anywhere, do you think, if they fussed around with as many disconnected things as most women do? And the worst of our case is that we are rather inclined to point with pride to what is really one of the most vicious habits of our sex. We have all seen the swelling satisfaction with which the comely young school-ma'am, complimented upon a pretty gown, announces, "made it myself." And we have all heard the chorus of admiring approbation following the announcement — joined in it, perhaps, and asked to borrow the pattern. But really, viewed in the light of reason, what is there about the feat upon which she should so plume herself? Suppose that a man should point proudly to his nether garments and say, "Lo! I made these trousers." I have not a mental picture of even the most economical of his fellow clerks, or mail-carriers, or clergymen, or school-teachers, crowding around to admire and cry, "What a splendid way to spend your time out of business hours! And it looks just like a tailor-made."

Mary Leal Harkness   March 1914

plump *pluhmp*
to be wholeheartedly in favor of; give an unqualified vote for

Near the wooden arch that announces the Serengeti National park, giraffes are daintily occupied in nibbling the tops of acacia trees. Let those who will, rear lion cubs; I'd plump for a baby giraffe, not more than seven feet tall. Inquisitive and nervy, the giraffes pose with their leaning-tower necks at unlikely angles and scrutinize you through tremendous eyelashes, don't like what they see, and amble or bound away in motion like no other creature. They never seem real; unicorns would be as probable.

Martha Gellhorn   January 1966

plunder *PLUHN duhr*
to take with illegal force or appropriate wrongfully

For the sake of the American author who is now robbed, for the sake of the foreign author who is now plundered, for the sake of that vast body of people who read books in the United States, and upon whom we now force all the worst and cheapest stuff that the presses of the world pour forth, a bill for international copyright ought to be passed. Most of all, it ought to be passed for the sake of the country's honor and good name. It does not become the United States, holding high place in the forefront of the nations, to stand like a highway robber beside the pathway of civilization, and rob the foreign author of his property with one hand, while it deprives the American author of his rights with the other.

Henry Cabot Lodge   August 1890

to devastate for financial gain

So far our government has done nothing effective with its forests, though the best in the world, but is like a rich and foolish spendthrift who has inherited a magnificent estate in perfect order, and then has left his rich fields and meadows, forests and parks, to be sold and plundered and wasted at will, depending on their inexhaustible abundance.

John Muir   August 1897

plutocracy   *ploo: TAHK ruh see*
government by the wealthy or by a group of wealthy people who control
the government

The United States began with a mixture of democracy and plutocracy, and it is with us still. On the date our Constitution was adopted, in most states a man had to own a certain amount of property in order to vote and a greater amount of property in order to hold office. Other states had a substantial poll tax. In only one — Vermont — were all adult males entitled to vote. Not until well into the nineteenth century did "manhood suffrage" become the basic rule rather than the exception. It took constitutional amendments to extend suffrage to black men and, considerably later, to women, black or white.

Charles Rembar   March 1981

poetaster   *POH uh tas ter*
a writer of poor or trashy verse; a rhymester: the suffix aster, *meaning inferior*
or not genuine, has also ended words applied to politicians (politicaster) and
grammarians (grammaticaster)

The poetaster who has tasted type is done for. He is like the man who has once been a candidate for the Presidency. He feeds on the madder of his delusion all his days, and his very bones grow red with the glow of his foolish fancy.

Oliver Wendell Holmes   October 1858

✳ Madder is a plant, the root of which produces strong dyes of red, pink, rust, brown, purple, orange and red. When animals feed on madder their bones turn red, but no other tissues are affected, a condition that allowed 19th-century physiologists to study bone development. Madder has been used as a textile dye since the time of ancient Egypt, and is still used today for handmade dyes.

pointed *POYN tid*
hitting the mark; penetrating; incisive

HAIR *(Original Broadway Cast; RCA Victor LSO-1150)*. It still rocks, but *Hair* was a more pungent and pointed show before it moved uptown from off-Broadway, and that original-cast album (LSO-1143) had more zip and zest than this Broadway version.

Herbert Kupferberg   September 1968

✳ When Bertram G. Work, B. F. Goodrich's president in 1923, renamed the company's galoshes the Zipper, it wasn't because of the sliding fastener that closed them but because he wanted a zippier name than Mystic Boot, the original name for his company's rubber and fabric boots. Zipper did not yet exist, but zip did, and it meant to move briskly or with speed. Within two years zipper had become the common name for the device, wherever it was used.

polarized *POH luh righzd*
intensely divided on opposite sides of an issue

As party lines have hardened and drawn apart, acrimony has grown between Democratic and Republican politicians, further separating the parties in what has become a vicious cycle. The political scientist Gary C. Jacobson, of the University of California at San Diego, finds that Democrats and Republicans not only enter Congress further apart ideologically, but also become more polarized the longer they stay in Congress's fiercely partisan environment.

Jonathan Rauch   January/February 2005

polemical *puh LE muh kuhl*
argumentative

An essay is a thing of the imagination. If there is information in an essay, it is by-the-by, and if there is an opinion, one need not trust it for the long run. A genuine essay rarely has an educational, polemical, or sociopolitical use; it is the movement of a free mind at play. Though it is written in prose, it is closer in kind to poetry than to any other form. Like a poem, a genuine essay is made of language and character and mood and temperament and pluck and chance.

Cynthia Ozick   September 1998

polity *PAH luh tee*
an organized society or community of people; a state

In France everything speaks of long familiar intercourse between the earth and its inhabitants; every field has a name, a history, a distinct place of its own in the village polity; every blade of grass is there by an old feudal right which has long since dispossessed the worthless aboriginal weed.

Edith Wharton   December 1906

poltroon   *pahl TROO:N*
an utter, miserable, worthless coward ("poltroonishly" is the adverb)

When John Murray and Thomas Moore poltroonishly burnt Byron's memoirs, the crime affected quite a number of people. The thought of all those indiscreet confessions, outrageous jokes, amorous scandals, and diatribes against Robert Southey dispersing into common London soot has maddened generations of the scholarly, the poetical, and the prurient.

Phoebe-Lou Adams   February 1968

postprandial   *pohst PRAN dee uhl*
after a meal, especially after dinner

Jules Huret, a French journalist who was in Argentina around 1910, visited one of the aristocratic residences on the pampas where he attended, wide-eyed, postprandial discussions of Mallarmé's poems and Debussy's preludes which were worthy of the salons of the Paris elite.

Tomás Eloy Martinez   December 1990

postulate   *PAHS chuh layt*
to assume without proof to be true, real or necessary, especially as a basis
for argument

The supremacist ideology of the Bush Administration stands in opposition to the principles of an open society, which recognize that people have different views and that nobody is in possession of the ultimate truth. The supremacist ideology postulates that just because we are stronger than others, we know better and have right on our side.

George Soros   December 2003

posture   *PAHS chuhr*
an official stand or position

Woodrow Wilson instinctively reacted to the onset of the Great War by issuing a proclamation of neutrality. But as the conflict grew in scale and duration, wreaking devastation previously unimaginable, he became increasingly convinced that isolation was no longer a viable posture for the United States.

David M. Kennedy   March 2005

pragmatic   *prag MA tik*
concerned with actual practice, not theory; practical

The complaint will be heard that a school cannot be all things to all people — cannot be place of education, health-care clinic, settlement house, and neighborhood recreation center rolled into one. The pragmatic response is that a school must in fact be all these things.

Michael J. Barrett   November 1990

prattle   *PRA tuhl*
to be talkative about trifles; chatter idly

"Montaigne and Howell's Letters," says Thackeray, "are my bedside books. If I wake at night, I have one or other of them to prattle me to sleep again. They talk about themselves forever, and don't weary me. I like to hear them tell their old stories over and over again. *I read them in the dozy hours, and only half remember them.*" In the frank veracity of this last confession there lies a pleasant truth which it is wholesome to hear from such excellent and undisputed authority. Many people have told us about the advantage of remembering what we read, and have imparted severe counsels as to ways and means. Thackeray and Charles Lamb alone have ventured to hint at the equal delight of forgetting, and of returning to some well-loved volume with recollections softened into an agreeable haze.

Agnes Repplier   July 1894

precarious   *pri KAI ree uhs*
dangerously uncertain ("precariously" is the adverb)

For the last four centuries the combative nationalism of Western civilization has been leading the world deeper and deeper into a sea of troubles, where the great ships of state now manoeuvre precariously, amid cross-currents, hidden shoals, sudden tempests, and impenetrable fogs. To extricate the fortunes of mankind from conditions so unstable will prove no easy task, for they are interwoven with the structure of the modern world — part, almost, of its substance.

L. P. Jacks   February 1923

preeminent   *pree E muh nint*
excelling or distinguished beyond others, especially in a particular quality
("preeminence" is the noun)

In our opinion, *Great Expectations* is a work which proves that we may expect from Dickens a series of romances far exceeding in power and artistic skill the productions which have already given him such a preëminence among the novelists of the age.

Edwin Percy Whipple   September 1861

preface   *PRE fis*
to make introductory remarks

The centennial birthday of George Washington was duly honored in the city which he had founded and which bore his name. Divine services were performed at the Capitol, and later in the day there was a dinner at Brown's Hotel, at which Daniel Webster prefaced the first toast in honor of the Father of his Country by an eloquent speech of an hour in length.

Ben Perley Poore   June 1880

prefigure   *pree FI gyuhr*
to come before in a similar form; suggest beforehand

The thrust of the Enlightenment, like the Greek humanism that prefigured it, was Promethean: the knowledge it generated was to liberate mankind by lifting it above the savage world.

Edward O. Wilson   March 1998

prelapsarian   *pree lap SE ree uhn*
of the time before the fall of man; a time of human innocence

Revisionists tend to portray pre-Columbian America as an Arcadia. The most read-able statement of the case is by Kirkpatrick Sale, in his graceful and passionate book *The Conquest of Paradise* (1990). Sale envisages a continent where people lived in "balanced and fruitful harmony" with nature and with one another, "an untouched world, a prelapsarian Eden of astonishing plenitude ... functioning to all intents and purposes in its original primal state," green and pure, until European violence smashed the human and ecological utopia.

Arthur M. Schelsinger Jr.   September 1992

prelude   *PRAY loo:d*
an introduction to a larger work, as in music, drama or literature; preface

Few events in American literary history have been more curious than the sudden rise of Emily Dickinson into a posthumous fame only more accentuated by the utter-ly recluse character of her life and by her aversion to even a literary publicity. The lines which form a prelude to the published volume of her poems are the only ones that have come to light indicating even a temporary desire to come in contact with the great world of readers; she seems to have had no reference, in all the rest, to any-thing but her own thought and a few friends.

Thomas Wentworth Higginson   October 1891

✳ In 1862, Thomas Wentworth Higginson published an article in *The Atlantic* seeking new voices. Saying that "every editor is always hungering and thirsting after novelties," he invited young poets and writers to submit their work. Emily Dickinson responded with a letter and four poems. "Are you too deeply occupied to say if my verse is alive?" she asked. So began a 25-year correspondence, until Dickinson's death in 1886. And although Higginson found in those first poems "a wholly new and original poetic genius," as he wrote in *The Atlantic* after her death, he didn't quite know what to make of their unconventional form and ideas. Despite seeing her uniqueness, he never encouraged her to publish her work. And except for a few of her 1,800 poems, she never did. Although Higginson helped to publish a book of her poems after she died, it was not without changing many words and much punctuation, to make the poems conform to what he considered the public's concept of poetry. Others who published her poems posthumously did the same until a three-volume set that Thomas H. Johnson published in 1955 presented them in much the same unconventional way she had written them.

preoccupy   *pree AH kyuh pigh*
to be constantly on the mind ("preoccupation" is the noun)

Consciously or not, we take it so much for granted that high school is a social education, with the formal kind eating dust, that we have no idea how exotic a spectacle it presents to the rest of the planet. "I always thought all of the notions about cliques and crowds, and the preoccupation with fashions that I had seen in American movies was the invention of Hollywood," says a Turkish grad student quoted in Murray Milner Jr.'s *Freaks, Geeks,* and *Cool Kids.* "Then when I came to the U.S. for the first time as an exchange student my junior year in secondary school, I was stunned to see that many of the images actually existed."

Tom Carson   July/August 2004

preponderance   *pruh PAHN duh ruhns*
superiority in number, influence or importance

Even supposing the war should end to-morrow, and the army melt into the mass of the population within the year, what an incalculable preponderance will there be of military titles and pretensions for at least half a century to come! Every country-neighborhood will have its general or two, its three or four colonels, half a dozen majors, and captains without end, — besides non-commissioned officers and privates, more than the recruiting offices ever knew of, — all with their campaign stories, which will become the staple of fireside-talk forevermore.

Nathaniel Hawthorne   July 1862

prerogative   *prugh RAH guh tiv*
an exclusive right or privilege

> The Second Amendment presumes (as did the framers) that private citizens will possess private arms; Madison referred offhandedly to "the advantage of being armed, which the Americans possess." But Madison also implied that the right to bear arms is based in the obligation of citizens to band together as a militia to defend the common good, as opposed to the prerogative of citizens to take up arms individually in pursuit of self-interest and happiness.
>
> Wendy Kaminer   March 1996

presage   *PRE sij*
to signify beforehand; portend; foreshadow

> Fifty years ago the meteoric shower of 1833 showed that the less cultivated class, even in America, still looked upon the accidents of the skies as signs of heavenly wrath and portents of coming ills. Now even the least educated no longer ask, What does this presage? but What is its cause? Naturalism has advanced fast and far in the last century.
>
> N. S. Shaler   April 1884

> Mark Twain believed that his birth in a Halley's Comet year presaged his death the next time Halley's Comet came around, seventy-five years later. The only reason anyone remembers this fact is that we now know Twain was right.
>
> Cullen Murphy   November 1993

prescient   *PRE shuhnt*
knowing things before they happen or come into being; having a foreknowledge

> Neville Shute, formerly of the British Navy, is one of the most prescient of novelists; his novels, warmblooded and appealing in their depiction of human nature, have a way of looking ahead and of warning and foretelling. In *Ordeal,* which was published nearly twenty years ago, he foreshadowed the Blitz and what it would do to England, Southampton in particular. In *On the Beach* (Morrow, $3.95), his latest, which the Book-of-the-Month Club, prompted by the disarmament discussions, has moved up for midsummer publication, he makes the appalling revelation of how lethal radiation had become in 1963 in the aftermath of the third world war.
>
> Edward Weeks   August 1957

presentiment   *pri ZEN tuh muhnt*
a sense that something is about to occur; a premonition; foreboding

All through the winter the horses hauled twenty-foot logs out of the woods and piled them in great heaps on the ice of the lakes and rivers, and when the riverbed was full, on the banks. In March came the first warm winds; dirt began to show in the road ruts, the six-foot icicles on the camp eaves began to drip and finally came a night when the lumberjack smelled that the ice would go out before morning. From beneath his bunk, or his fir-bough pillow, he fished a pair of old cork boots, filed their inch-long spikes to gleaming points, and then, as he was lovingly greasing them, there would come an earthshaking tremor and a tremendous roar of cracking ice and leaping water from the river, to confirm his presentiment.

Robert E. Pike   July 1963

presentism   *PRE zint iz uhm*
the application of contemporary standards to the past

I asked seven anthropologists, archaeologists, and historians if they would rather have been a typical Indian or a typical European in 1491. None was delighted by the question, because it required judging the past by the standards of today — a fallacy disparaged as "presentism" by social scientists. But every one chose to be an Indian. Some early colonists gave the same answer.

Charles C. Mann   March 2002

presumptuous   *pruh ZUHMP choo: uhs*
overstepping one's appropriate place; unduly confident or bold

You have been told, of course, that I am to speak about *Joseph and His Brothers,* a tetralogy of novels or epic in prose, of which the final volume, *Joseph the Provider,* is just about to be completed. Let me say first that I was quite startled and disconcerted when Archibald MacLeish suggested this book to me as my topic for tonight — I was much more inclined to refuse than to accept. Would it not seem terribly presumptuous, vain, and egocentric if I talked today, and here, about my own affairs, my own work — in other words, about highly personal and private matters instead of general and important ones, of the great cares and hopes of our time, of the war and its objectives?

Thomas Mann   February 1943

pretentious   *pri TEN shuhs*
making an exaggerated outward show; affectedly grand; showy; ostentatious

Istanbul's food, much of it blessedly based on long-cooked vegetables, is often wonderful and, except at a few pretentious restaurants, is served in simple surroundings that provide few clues to its quality.

Corby Kummer   January 1995

claiming an undeserved distinction ("pretention" is the noun)

The technique of gearing appeals to the social class most likely to enjoy your product would seem to be a step toward rationality in marketing. One of the notable cases of ill-considered selling occurred in Chicago when one of the leading brewers developed social pretensions for its brew, which had long been popular with the tavern-type clientele. The brewer's advertising men, in an effort to give the brew more class, began showing it being sipped by fox hunters, concert pianists, and drawing-room socialites. Sales did pick up slightly in the better residential areas but began falling disastrously with old customers. The boys in the tavern found the brew didn't taste right any more, though the formula was unchanged.

Vance Packard   August 1957

preternatural   *pree tuhr NA chuh ruhl*
beyond what is natural; surpassing the normal("preternaturally" is the adverb)

The shrewdest judges of polio's impact on Roosevelt are two authors who themselves suffered from polio — Geoffrey Ward and Hugh Gregory Gallagher. There is no sentimentality in these men's views of Roosevelt. They both see that what polio did was to make him preternaturally aware of others' perceptions of him. This increased his determination to control those perceptions. People were made uncomfortable by his discomfort. He needed to distract them, to direct their attention to subjects he preferred, to keep them amused, impressed, entertained. That meant he had to perfect a deceptive ease, a casual aplomb, in the midst of acute distress. He became a consummate actor.

Garry Wills   April 1994

pretext   *PREE tekst*
a false reason or motive put forth to hide the real one; excuse

In 1930 I visited Cambridge University. The anti-Kipling rage, even among young conservatives there, was in full course. It was denied that Kipling had any feeling for color or rhythm, or even the capacity for describing the most elementary sensations. But these were only pretexts. He was despised because he represented an England content with itself, imperialistic, scorning inferior races; because his world was that of the "old school," prejudiced and solid.

Jean Prévost   May 1938

prig *prig*

a person who takes pride in behaving correctly and properly, and in feeling morally superior to others

The question still awaits us, however, What is the public school system achieving for public morals? Just at present there is a movement in various quarters to introduce instruction in the theory of morals into even the lower grades of the schools; but no one seems to be sure that this will not produce self-conscious prigs, or encourage morbid introspection rather than sturdy morality.

William Frederic Slocum Jr.   May 1894

✳ "Mr. Augustus Minns was a bachelor, of about forty as he said — of about eight-and-forty as his friends said. He was always exceedingly clean, precise, and tidy; perhaps somewhat priggish, and the most retiring man in the world." These are the first sentences of Charles Dickens's first published work of fiction, a 4,000-word sketch of London life titled *A Dinner at Poplar Walk*. It appeared under the pseudonym Boz in *Monthly Magazine* in December 1833 and later in the story collection *Sketches* by Boz.

prima facie *prigh muh FAY shee*

self-evident: in law, a prima facie case is one based on evidence sufficient to enable a decision or verdict to be made unless the facts are disproved: Latin, at first sight

The steady accumulation of wrongful convictions and death sentences in the United States constitutes a prima facie case that we are dealing with widespread, systemic flaws in the administration of justice. Until those flaws are corrected, we should declare a moratorium on executions.

Alan Berlow   November 1999

prismatic *priz MA tik*

many-colored; brilliant; dazzling

Merle Haggard is a man of prismatic creativity, a singer, songwriter, bandleader, guitarist, and fiddler — (everything but, as a recent brush with bankruptcy attests, a good businessman). He has written or co-written 346 songs, forty-five more than the legendarily prolific Willie Nelson. As a singer he has sent thirty-eight tunes to No. 1 on Billboard's country chart — more than Nelson and Hank Williams Sr. combined. He has released sixty-eight albums, not counting the bootleg cassettes and CDs one finds on drugstore racks.

Tony Scherman   August 1996

privation   *prigh VAY shuhn*
want of necessities; deprivation; misery

Whatever the future may witness of tragical and pathetic on the stage of public events, it can see nothing so impressively memorable as that which this generation has known in the assassination of Lincoln and Garfield. The men were alike in their typically American origin and character, — from the people, of the people, for the people; acquainted with hardships and privation and toil, and supremely triumphant in their aims. They were both cast in the same noble mould, and were largely gentle, patient, and good; true heroes and exemplars of a democracy whose ideal is the realization in its chiefs of the same virtues which sweeten and enlighten the lowliest life in the commonwealth. History will make certain distinctions between them, but without disturbing the conception of their essential equality, and without affecting the parity of their humane ambition, or separating them in the perpetual remembrance of their common fate.

William Dean Howells   November 1881

problematic   *prah bluh MA tik*
hard to solve or deal with; uncertain; questionable

Rama and Sita, hero and heroine of the epic *Ramayana,* are the ideal couple of the Hindu tradition. My peers and I grew up on tales of his courage and caring, her beauty and strength of character, their appreciative and untroublesome in-laws, their mutual devotion in a time of polygamy. But for young men and women coming of age today, in the aftermath of independence and the women's-liberation movement, the old myth is problematic. How can they ignore the way the epic ends, with Rama banishing an innocent Sita from his kingdom because her virtue has been questioned by some of his subjects?

Chitra Divakaruni   March 2000

Procrustean   *pro KRUH stee uhn*
forcing into conformity at any cost: in Greek mythology, Procrustes is a giant who waylays travelers, ties them to an iron bedstead, and either stretches them or cuts off their legs to make them fit

Philip Young's *Ernest Hemingway,* published in 1953, had attributed much of Hemingway's inspiration or "invention" to his violent experiences as a boy and in World War I. "If you haven't read it, don't bother," Hemingway volunteered. "How would you like it if someone said that everything you've done in your life was done because of some trauma. Young had a theory that was like — you know, the Procrustean bed, and he had to cut me to fit into it."

Robert Manning   August 1965

prodigal *PRAH di guhl*
extravagant; lavish

Critics are prodigal with notions as to what motivated certain compositions of the masters. Brahms's biographers have said that he wrote such and such music because he was "grieving over Clara Schumann," Robert Schumann's wife, with whom Brahms was in love for years. Maybe the critics were right. But what Brahms himself said at the time was, "Some of my best ideas come to me while I am brushing my shoes before dawn."

Catherine Drinker Bowen   November 1961

proffer *PRAH fer*
to put before a person for acceptance; to offer; present

In the spring of the year 1853, I observed, as conductor of the weekly journal, "Household Words," a short poem among the proffered contributions, very different, as I thought, from the shoal of verses perpetually setting through the office of such a periodical, and possessing much more merit. Its authoress was quite unknown to me. She was one Miss Mary Berwick, whom I had never heard of; and she was to be addressed by letter, if addressed at all, at a circulating-library in the western district of London. Through this channel, Miss Berwick was informed that her poem was accepted, and was invited to send another. She complied, and became a regular and frequent contributor. Many letters passed between the journal and Miss Berwick, but Miss Berwick herself was never seen.

Charles Dickens   December 1865

❋ In December 1854 Dickens learned the true identity of Mary Berwick, following a dinner at the home of his old friend Bryan Waller Procter, a playwright, poet and songwriter. Dickens had brought with him a proof of that month's forthcoming issue of his magazine *Household Words* and mentioned to Mrs. Procter that it contained "a very pretty poem, written by a certain Miss Berwick." The next day he learned that Mary Berwick had been at the dinner table: she was the Procters' 29-year-old daughter, Adelaide, whom Dickens had known since she was a child. She had sent in her work under another name because she did not want special consideration, even though she was a well-known writer under her real name. After Adelaide died at the age of 38, in 1864, her parents asked Dickens to write the *Atlantic* article as a memorial to her.

pro forma *pro FAWR muh*
as a matter of form: Latin, for form

Every year, in forbidding executive session, the House Committee on Appropriations clips the long lists of messengers, doorkeepers, and guards from the previous year's departmental authorizations and solemnly pastes them in the new bills. Passed by a *pro forma* vote in the House and Senate, the new law of the land is ready for the signature of the President of the United States. Under a series of Supreme Court decisions, the President is obliged to accept or reject the bill *in toto.*

Lawrence Sullivan   March 1931

prognosticate   *prahg NAH stuh kayt*
to predict or foretell events

Among the signs which are believed by the superstitious to prognosticate future events, those connected with the habits and character of birds have always been regarded as important. So much attention was paid by the ancients to these indications that the word bird was even in Homer's time synonymous with omen. Most birds were considered ominous of good or evil according to the place and manner of their appearance, so that they might be said to flutter with uncertain wings on the confines of disaster and success. Others, however, from their own nature were believed to portend calamity, and although they might occasionally afford a presage of good luck, yet their general reputation was decidedly bad. There is nothing so hard to get rid of as a bad name, and as this is true alike of bipeds with or without feathers, it is not surprising that some of the former have always been regarded as birds of ill omen.

Alexander Young   September 1874

proletarian   *proh luh TAI ree uhn*
of the working class

Although the country was deep in the Depression, there was a heady excitement in the air, a spirit of literary crusading, the sense of a movement. Marxism was in the air, turnover was in the air, and whatever else you could say of them, the writers I knew had the look of being part of a common atmosphere of ideas. It was the age of militancy. So many of the writers who seemed to me, when I was twenty, really to *be* writers wore proletarian scowls on their faces as constant as the cigarette butts pasted in their mouths. There was a proud and conscious carrying on of the literary groups and cenacles of the nineteen twenties, an atmosphere of dash, a writer's sense of a common destiny, that I saw reflected in the faces of James T. Farrell and Robert Cantwell, of Clifford Odets and Elia Kazan.

Alfred Kazin   May 1962

> ❋ A cenacle is a group of writers who gather to discuss their work or interests, as Victor Hugo and other young writers did in the cenacle at his house in Paris in the late 1820s. The French word *cénacle* is derived from the Latin *cenaculum,* dining room. In the Bible (Acts I,

13-14), the cenaculum was the room where Jesus and his disciples ate the Last Supper and where the apostles met after the Ascension.

Promethean   *pruh MEE thee in*
boldly and hugely new; life-bringing

John Kennedy's inaugural address gave stirring expression to a generation's conviction that it possessed powers of Promethean proportions. "The world is very different now," Kennedy proclaimed. "For man holds in his mortal hands the power to abolish all forms of human poverty and all forms of human life."

John Kenneth Galbraith   August 1973

promiscuous   *pruh MI skyoo: uhs*
without plan or purpose; random; casual ("promiscuously" is the adverb)

In 1792 the British navigator George Vancouver led the first European expedition to survey Puget Sound. He found a vast charnel house: human remains "promiscuously scattered about the beach, in great numbers." Smallpox, Vancouver's crew discovered, had preceded them.

Charles C. Mann   March 2002

promontory   *PRAH min taw ree*
a point of high land that juts out into a body of water

One of the earliest recorded sculpture parks is the elaborate garden that the Roman Emporor Tiberius created on the isle of Capri, on the Bay of Naples. When Tiberius retired there, in A.D. 27, he built a large palace on the highest promontory, decorated with marble and bronze statuary.

André Emmerich   August 1996

promulgate   *PRUH muhl gayt*
to make publicly known; proclaim formally; disseminate ("promulgation" is the noun)

Great interest has been awakened, of late, by the promulgation of a new "Theory of Creation"; and non-scientific readers have met with numerous controversial articles in the journals, magazines, and newspapers of the day. The name of Darwin, after having been honorably known for a quarter of a century to the scientists of the world, has become familiar to us all as that of the author of this new theory. A word has been added to our vocabulary. "Darwinian" is now a distinctive epithet wherewith to individualize the new school of thought, and an appellation to designate its votaries.

Charles James Sprague   October 1866

propagate   *PRAH puh gayt*
to cause a plant or animal to multiply or breed by natural reproduction from
the parent stock

Who knows but this chance wild fruit, planted by a cow or a bird on some remote and rocky hill-side, where it is as yet unobserved by man, may be the choicest of all its kind, and foreign potentates shall hear of it, and royal societies seek to propagate it, though the virtues of the perhaps truly crabbed owner of the soil may never be heard of, — at least, beyond the limits of his village? It was thus the Porter and the Baldwin grew.

Henry David Thoreau   November 1862

✳ The "crabbed owner of the soil" whom Thoreau refers to was probably the owner of the land whose wild apples he relished. By crabbed, Thoreau most likely meant physically crooked or gnarled.

propensity   *pruh PEN suh tee*
inclination; tendency

In all parts of the country that abound in woods of any description, we are sure to be greeted by the loud voice of the Blue Jay, one of the most conspicuous tenants of the forest. He has a beautiful outward appearance, under which he conceals an unamiable temper and a propensity to mischief.

Wilson Flagg   March 1859

propitious   *pruh PI shuhs*
presenting favorable circumstances

On the piercingly cold afternoon of January 8, 1927, Picasso was wandering near the Galeries Lafayette in the aimless state of mind advocated by the Surrealists as most propitious for unexpected discoveries and new beginnings, for the intervention of chance and the marvelous. Among the crowd coming out of the Metro was a blonde and beautiful young woman whose face, with its classic Greek nose and blue-gray eyes, he had seen before — in his mind's eye and on his canvases. "He simply grabbed me by the arm," Marie-Thérèse Walter recalled, looking back on the moment that transformed her life, "and said, 'I'm Picasso! You and I are going to do great things together.'" For him it was a moment of recognition and of surrender to a sexual passion unfettered by the conventions of age, matrimony, time, and responsibility.

Arianna Stassinopoulos Huffington   June 1988

prosaic   *proh ZAY ik*
ordinary; commonplace; matter-of-fact; the opposite of poetic

The man of prosaic mind thinks that composition is a matter of so arranging words that they shall convey a meaning that is the sum of their separate meanings. But the poet knows better. He knows that it is a matter of so ordering them that they shall suggest verbally inexpressible meanings between the lines; that they shall, quite literally, set spirits to dancing from sentence to sentence, flashes of intellectual electricity to leaping from page to page, faces to peeping forth at the reader from behind the letters like children from behind tree-trunks.

Harold Goddard   July 1918

prosody   *PRAH suh dee*
the study of the structure of verse

I'm a believer in specialized knowledge for the poet — that is, knowledge in a chosen area which is apart from prosody or the whole question of literature. My own favorite reading is in horticulture and zoology, I would say, and I much prefer reading books in those categories than most poems.

Stanley Kunitz   August 1966

prosthesis   *prahs THEE sis*
an artificial replacement for a part of the body

During Grover Cleveland's second term, in the 1890s, the White House deceived the public by dismissing allegations that surgeons had removed a cancerous growth from the President's mouth; a vulcanized-rubber prosthesis disguised the absence of much of Cleveland's upper left jaw and part of his palate. The public knew nothing about the implant until one of the President's physicians revealed it in 1917, nine years after Cleveland's death.

Robert Dallek   December 2002

prostrate   *PRAH strayt*
helpless; overcome; powerless: literally, to lie with the body extended flat in a horizontal position

That China, which in 1948 was economically prostrate under runaway inflation, maladministered by a weak and corrupt government totally dependent on American aid, incapable of producing motorcycles, much less automobiles, can now fight the United Nations to a draw in Korea, maintain the world's fourth largest air force, produce trucks, jet planes, even establish a nuclear reactor, is an intoxicating spectacle to the Chinese.

Harriet C. Mills   December 1959

protagonist   *proh TA guh nist*
the main character in a story

It is commonly true of Hawthorne's romances that the interest centres in one strongly defined protagonist, to whom the other characters are accessory and subordinate, — perhaps we should rather say a ruling Idea, of which all the characters are fragmentary embodiments. They remind us of a symphony of Beethoven's, in which, though there be variety of parts, yet all are infused with the dominant motive, and heighten its impression by hints and far-away suggestions at the most unexpected moment.

James Russell Lowell   April 1860

protégé   *PROH tuh zhay*
one guided and helped in furthering his or her career by a more influential person

The most frequent complaint against Sondheim is that audiences don't leave the theater humming his melodies, the way they did Gershwin's and Kern's. Sondheim — who was Oscar Hammerstein II's protégé but who also studied with the "serious" composer Milton Babbitt, the author of a 1958 article variously published as "The Composer as Specialist" and "Who Cares If You Listen?" — has often gone to extremes to ensure that audiences won't hum the show on the way to the exits.

Francis Davis   March 1995

prototype   *PROH tuh tighp*
the original or model on which something is based; standard

Monorails have more history than you might think. A patent for the first prototype was registered in 1821, and the first one-track passenger train appeared in 1825, drawn by a single horse. The Philadelphia Centennial Exposition, in 1876, featured a Victorian-looking double-decker steam monorail, and in 1911 the first of the modern monorail cars — those that resemble huge suppositories — made an appearance in Seattle, running on a wooden track.

Wayne Curtis   December 2005

protracted   *proh TRAK tid*
prolonged; extended; drawn out

The U.S. government considered the possibility of a nuclear war with the Soviet Union more seriously during the early Reagan years than at any other time since the Cuban Missile Crisis of 1962. Reagan had spoken in his 1980 campaign about the need for civil-defense programs to help the United States survive a nuclear exchange, and once in office he not only moved to boost civil defense but also approved a new defense-policy document that included plans for waging a protracted nuclear war against the Soviet Union.

James Mann   March 2004

protrude   *proh TROO:D*
to thrust outward

Let us take a simple problem: we wish to point out something. The "natural" way — the "only" way, we might say, is to lift the hand and stretch out the index finger. But the Zuñi, for example, solve the problem otherwise; for them, pointing with the finger is in the grossest taste, as too ostentatious. They protrude the lips, barely turning the head; a swift, fleeting gesture, but enough.

Contributors' Club: Leslie Spier   January 1931

protuberant   *proh TOO: buh ruhnt*
bulging; swelling out; protruding

The mantis is a truly terrifying creature, apparently always willing to engage in a battle even with man. If one alights on the table before you it will stand up on four legs, turn its beastly head on its narrow neck, and stare you straight in the face with its evil protuberant eyes, at the same time presenting its two forearms crooked like a pugilist's and bristling with rows of slender toothlike spines, with which it not only seizes its prey but also its mate, from both of which it sucks the lifeblood.

Ivan Sanderson   August 1937

> ✳ Mantis derives from the Greek *mantis,* prophet or diviner, an allusion to the insect's prayerful posture and to the belief that it could foretell natural events such as famine or the coming of spring.

provenance   *PRAH vuh nins*
origin; derivation; source

No doubt the bell's provenance contributed to its mythic quality: the original bell had been cast in England but had cracked shortly after arriving in Philadelphia, in 1753; it was melted down and recast by two local artisans. Thus the great symbol of American independence really was Made in the USA — or at least in what would soon become the USA.

Witold Rybczynski   June 1998

prudery   *PROO: duh ree*
excessive or affected modesty in behavior, dress or speech, and criticism of a lack of it in others

All generalizations are to be mistrusted; but I think it will scarcely be denied that the art of fiction in the English tongue has been limited by prudery. Of course, limitation in one direction may mean enfranchisement in another; it is possible that

English fiction has extended itself into new interests under compulsion of the very fact that it was debarred from regarding sexual misconduct as the all-embracing and all-sufficing topic.

Gerald Gould   July 1928

prurient *PROO ree uhnt*
characterized by an inordinate interest in sex

Prurient curiosity has no limits; but the press cannot justify the invasion of private life by the claim that its readers like it. The competition between newspapers tends steadily to lower the bars that protect the private citizen against impertinent curiosity; and it is the duty of every editor who recognizes his responsibility as a leader to resist this tendency.

Moorfield Storey   January 1922

puerile *PYOO righl*
immature; juvenile

Sometimes nurturing students means challenging their complaints instead of satisfying their demands for sympathy. I've heard female students declare that any male classmate who makes derogatory remarks about women online or over the telephone is guilty of sexual harassment and should be punished. What are we teaching them if we agree? That they aren't strong enough to withstand a few puerile sexist jokes that may not even be directed at them? That their male classmates don't have the right to make statements that some women deem offensive? There would be no feminist movement if women never dared to give offense.

Wendy Kaminer   September 1997

puissant *PWI suhnt*
powerful; mighty; potent

Years ago someone called steam "that great civilizer." Never has it been more alive, more usefully in the service of man, more puissant, than in this fourth decade of the twentieth century.

George W. Gray   January 1937

punctilio *punk TI lee oh*
a fine point of conduct or etiquette

It is the fashion in the modern world to rate a civilization by its sense of values. In Spain the highest value is human dignity. Read again the conversations between Sancho and his master, and note how mutual is the punctilio between them.

Everywhere in Spain you see instances in high relief of the universal recognition of the respect one man owes to another.

Ellery Sedgwick   September 1931

purblind   *PER blignd*
slow in perceiving or understanding; lacking or incapable of clear mental, moral or spiritual vision

It is hard to understand the mental processes of men like Hitler and Napoleon, who are at times so incomparably shrewder and more perceptive than their fellow men and at times so incomparably purblind.

Clifton Fadiman   May 1942

pussyfoot   *POO see foot*
to shy away from definite commitment or from taking a firm stand

In 1949 everything changed for America when the Soviet Union tested its first atomic bomb. By that time U.S. political leaders had already developed concepts to govern a very long struggle against Soviet communism. Harry Truman, George Kennan, George Marshall, and their colleagues are heroes now because what they explained to the public through the late 1940s and early 1950s proved to be so wise. Could today's leaders look like heroes in fifty years? Yes — if they similarly laid the groundwork for a long, principled, and sustainable struggle. A Truman would tell us that loose nuclear weapons are the real emergency of this moment, and that instead of pussyfooting around we should control them right away. A Kennan would explain the sources of Muslim extremist behavior and how our actions could encourage or retard it. A Marshall would point out how gravely we left ourselves exposed through our reliance on oil from the Persian Gulf.

James Fallows   January/February 2005

pyrotechnics   *pigh ruh TEK niks*
a brilliant or dazzling display ("pyrotechnic" is the adjective)

Is it "the Bilbao effect"? After Frank Gehry's visually pyrotechnic Guggenheim Museum Bilbao opened its doors, in the fall of 1997, and saw more than 1.3 million visitors stream through them within a year, that museum was widely credited with having sparked an economic boom in northern Spain. Now its success seems to be a prime factor in igniting a building boom among art museums all across the United States. In the past four years at least forty American art institutions have announced, begun, or finished additions or new buildings, and a goodly proportion of these involve architecture as spectacle.

Ann Wilson Lloyd   June 2001

querulous

Charles de Gaulle, living in a democratic society that had one (state-controlled) television network, spoke for all chief executives: he used to say that all print reporters were against him, but television belonged to him. It was the classic statement of a politician about journalism: print can be too querulous, can do too much analyzing of motives, can spread too much doubt. But broadcasting is different; it accepts by and large what has been said and passes it on, often uncritically.

David Halberstam   February 1976

see page 359

quagmire *KWAG mighr*
boggy or mushy ground

One comes away from an interview with presidential press secretary Ronald Ziegler with the feeling of having sunk slowly, hopelessly, into a quagmire of marshmallows. But unless a newsman is out of favor, Ziegler is at least accessible to the press. To an unprecedented degree in the modern presidency, President Nixon is not.

David Wise   April 1973

quell *kwel*
to suppress; put an end to; quiet

For the first several decades of the twentieth century the most important tool in scaring and starving remained the warship, able to destroy coastal cities, deliver armies, and blockade nations. A powerful navy was vastly more powerful than a powerful army, and ultimately the only effective defense against a powerful navy was another powerful navy. When Theodore Roosevelt wished to announce that America had come of imperial age, he sent neither ambassadors nor armies around the world but the Great White Fleet. In dealing with the smaller and weaker nations, the visit of a single warship might quell trouble.

Michael Kelly   April 2002

querulous *KWE ruh luhs*
given to complaining and finding fault; peevish; grumbling

Charles de Gaulle, living in a democratic society that had one (state-controlled) television network, spoke for all chief executives: he used to say that all print reporters were against him, but television belonged to him. It was the classic statement of a politician about journalism: print can be too querulous, can do too much analyzing of motives, can spread too much doubt. But broadcasting is different; it accepts by and large what has been said and passes it on, often uncritically.

David Halberstam   February 1976

quibble   *KWI buhl*
to argue, criticize or object in a petty fashion

Southern writers may quibble as they please about slavery not being the cause of the war. Nobody denies that there were other causes, many of them, lying deep in difference of climate, difference of breeding, difference of local temperament. But no one can seriously maintain that any of those other causes, or all of them together, could have led to any sectional quarrel that might not have been easily settled, if it had not been for the dark phantom, the terrible midnight incubus of slavery.

Gamaliel Bradford   December 1910

> ✳ In medieval times, an incubus was believed to be an evil spirit that descended upon sleeping women and had sexual intercourse with them as they slept (Latin, *incubare*, to lie down upon). The incubus's female equivalent was the succubus (*succubare,* to lie under). Metaphorically, an incubus represents a frightful burden.

quick study   *KWIK STUH dee*
a person who learns something new remarkably quickly

Even though the era of the tyrant conductor is long gone, musicians do not choose the music they play, and have little input into musical interpretation. Rehearsals are timed to the second, starting at the stroke of ten in the morning and ending precisely at twelve-thirty, with a fifteen-minute break. In three or four rehearsals musicians must put together a concert program that may contain a work they have never played before. They are all quick studies, but the rigid constraints on rehearsal time create an emergency-room tension and a frustrating sense of artistic compromise.

David Schiff   August 1997

quietus   *kwigh EE tuhs*
anything that serves to suppress, curb or eliminate

I like to think that I am responsible in some measure for Trollope's present vogue, both with readers and with collectors. I have always delighted in him because of his humor, and his marvelous pictures of nineteenth-century English life. After his death a quietus was put to his fame by the publication of his *Autobiography.* In it he described the perfunctory way in which he wrote his novels, and, his own generation of readers dying with him, the next would have nothing to do with him. "How can novels so produced be anything but stupid?" it was said.

A. Edward Newton   December 1926

✳ Anthony Trollope says in his autobiography that his writing day began each morning at 5:30, when his servant awoke him and gave him coffee, and ended three hours later. During that time, he said, he wrote a thousand words an hour, 250 words every 15 minutes. R. H. Super, a scholar who examined some of Trollope's 300,000-word manuscripts, doubted that Trollope counted every word, day after day. "Trollope had a far easier way of keeping track of the length of his novels," Super wrote. "He invariably wrote on paper of the same size, eight inches by ten inches, and since the margins were fairly regular and his handwriting was consistent, each page had approximately the same number of words." Trollope wrote 47 novels, more than 40 short stories, three biographies and five travel books.

quip *kwip*
a witty remark or reply; jest; gibe

Late in his life, within the memory of people in middle age today, Frost became more and less than a famous poet: he became a sort of national totem. His humor had a great deal to do with it. Like Mark Twain, Frost attracted a huge public with the charm and informality of his talk; and as with Mark Twain, a darkness lay beneath the humor. (Thus the quip he voiced toward the end of his life: "Forgive, 0 Lord, my little jokes on Thee / And I'll forgive Thy great big one on me.") Frost attained a larger audience during his lifetime than did any serious American poet who had preceded him.

Peter Davison   December 2000

quirk *kwerk*
a deviation from a regular course or pattern; peculiarity

To Saddam, the present global domination by the West, particularly the United States, is just a phase. America is infidel and inferior. It lacks the rich ancient heritage of Iraq and other Arab states. Its place at the summit of the world powers is just a historical quirk, an aberration, a consequence of its having acquired technological advantages. It cannot endure.

Mark Bowden   May 2002

quotidian *kwoh TI dee uhn*
undertaken or experienced daily; everyday

As our Supreme Court justices have become remote from the real world, they've also become more reluctant to do real work — especially the sort of quotidian chores done by prior justices to ensure the smooth functioning of the judicial system. The

Court's overall productivity — as measured by the number of full, signed decisions — has fallen by almost half since 1985. Clerks draft almost all the opinions and perform almost all the screening that leads to the dismissal without comment of 99 percent of all petitions for review. Many of the cases dismissed are the sort that could be used to wring clear perversities and inefficiencies out of our litigation system — especially out of commercial and personal-injury litigation.

Stuart Taylor Jr.   September 2005

quotient   *KWOH shuhnt*
the number of times a thing occurs within something else; quota; rate

I spent the last days of the first Gulf War's phony peace in Baghdad, and I am spending the last days of this one's in Kuwait, soon to take part in the experiment of "embedding," as the jargon has it, some 500 journalists with the U.S. military for the duration of what is generally expected to be a short, exceedingly one-sided conflict. On the whole, I'd say, the phoniness quotient is down this time. We are spared, at least, much of the death-and-destruction-and-quagmire talk that preceded the last conflict here.

Michael Kelly   May 2003

Revisionism

How things have changed in a century! Political, religious, and social differences, far from vanishing, place Columbus today in the center of a worldwide cultural civil war. The great hero of the nineteenth century seems well on the way to becoming the great villain of the twenty-first. Columbus, it is now charged, far from being the pioneer of progress and enlightenment, was in fact the pioneer of oppression, racism, slavery, rape, theft, vandalism, extermination, and ecological desolation. The revisionist reaction, it must be said, has been under way for a while. As far back as the quadricentennial, Justin Winsor, a historian and bibliographer of early America, published a soberly critical biography, arguing that Columbus had left the New World "a legacy of devastation and crime."

Arthur M. Schlesinger Jr.   September 1992

see page 384

rabid *RA bid*
irrationally extreme in opinion or practice

> On a pleasant evening in the spring of 1934, after one of the President's Fireside Chats, I met a friend in front of my house as I was about to take a walk in the park before retiring. I asked him if he had heard the talk. "No," he said. "I was at Tom's house. And he's such a rabid Roosevelt hater he won't listen to him. He only reads enough of what he says to be able to take issue with him."

> George V. Denny Jr.   September 1942

racy *RAY see*
slightly improper or indelicate; risqué

> *In Dubious Battle* was the first of three very different Steinbeck books dealing with migratory farm laborers on the California fruit farms, and it was the bitterest of the three. "I guess it is a brutal book," he wrote when he was still at work on it, in February, 1935, "more brutal because there is no author's moral point of view. The speech of workingmen may seem a little bit racy to the ladies' clubs, but since ladies' clubs won't believe that such things go on anyway, it doesn't matter. I know this speech and I'm sick of workingmen being gelded of their natural expression until they talk with a fine Oxonian flavor....A workingman bereft of his profanity is a silent man."

> Lewis Gannett   December 1945

rail *rail*
to use bitter, harsh or abusive language, usually in print or public speech; complain violently

> In 1557 Queen Mary I gave control of all printing and book sales to a single guild,

the Stationers' Company. Guild members bought manuscripts outright from writers and then had the exclusive right to print and sell them forever. The Crown even granted exclusive rights to print the works of long-dead writers like Plato and Virgil. In return the guild helped the Crown to censor "seditious and heretical books." Protected by its statutory monopoly, the guild charged such high prices that John Locke railed against "the company of ignorant and lazy stationers." Radically, Locke proposed that the guild should voluntarily allow anyone to publish writers who had been dead for more than a millennium. The guild ignored him.

Charles C. Mann   September 1998

No American poet has proclaimed his contempt for this country more noisily than Allen Ginsberg. Ever since he first recited "Howl" in a San Francisco coffeehouse, in 1956, Ginsberg has been railing against the horrors of urban life, the stupidity of our government, and the crimes of what used to be called the military-industrial complex.

James Atlas   December 1984

raiment   *RAY muhnt*
decorative, ceremonial or fine clothing

As we wander on through the wood, all the labyrinths of summer are buried beneath one white inviting pathway, and the pledge of perfect loneliness is given by the unbroken surface of the all-revealing snow. There appears nothing living except a downy woodpecker, whirling round and round upon a young beech-stem, and a few sparrows, plump with grass-seed and hurrying with jerking flight down the sunny glade. But the trees furnish society enough. What a congress of ermined kings is this circle of hemlocks, which stand, white in their soft raiment, around the dais of this woodland pond! Are they held here, like the sovereigns in the palace of the Sleeping Beauty, till some mortal breaks their spell?

Thomas Wentworth Higginson   February 1862

raison d'être   *RAY zawn DET ruh*
reason for being; ground for existence: French

A most convincing proof of the joy-giving qualities of chamber-music is the attitude of the professional musician toward it. One rarely hears of the reporter haunting the police court during off hours, or of the mail-carrier indulging in a holiday walking-tour. But many a jaded teacher and slave of the orchestra finds his real *raison d'être* in playing chamber-music "for fun."

Robert Haven Schauffler   April 1911

rake   *rayk*
a fashionable man of immoral character

Auden met the stunningly handsome eighteen-year-old Kallman in 1939 and decided immediately that he had found the man of his dreams. But Kallman really was a **rake**, sexually incompatible with Auden and endlessly promiscuous. There ensued a lifelong folie à deux in which Auden played the role of perfect wife to Kallman's philandering husband. The situation made Auden feel both absurd and virtuous.

David Schiff   November 1997

❋ A folie à deux is a relationship in which two people share, support or reinforce the other's delusional beliefs or ideas. (French: *folie,* madness + *à,* between + *deux,* two)

ramble   *RAM buhl*
a walk for pleasure or recreation without a fixed route in mind

Shelley often called me for a long **ramble** on the heath, or into regions which I then thought far distant; and I went with him rather than with my father, because he walked faster, and talked with me while he walked, instead of being lost in his own thoughts and conversing only at intervals. A love of wandering seemed to possess him in the most literal sense; his rambles appeared to be without design, or any limit but my fatigue; and when I was "done up," he carried me home in his arms, on his shoulder, or pickback.

Thornton Hunt   February 1863

❋ Long before there was piggyback (1843 is the first citation in the *Oxford English Dictionary*), there were pick pack (1564), pick a pack (1722) and hyphened variations. Although its origin is uncertain, pick pack may have derived from the German *huckepack,* meaning "on the back and shoulders of another person or animal," or *huckeback,* "to carry a load on one's back." Piggyback arose through folk etymology, the process by which an unfamiliar-sounding word takes on a more familiar or English sound and spelling. As with all folk etymology, the word's meaning has nothing to do with the word whose sound it has adapted — in this case, pig. In a similar manner, belfry, from the Middle English *berfrey,* or tower, has nothing to do with bell. Carryall, from the French *cariole,* a small, one-horse carriage that can hold several people, has nothing to do with carry or all. Crayfish, from the French *écrevisse,* is not a fish. Forlorn hope, a desperate undertaking, is from *verloren hoop,* Dutch for "lost troop," a group of soldiers assigned to make an attack. Humble pie is a pie made of *umbles,* the innards of deer, and was formerly fed to servants. And Jerusalem artichokes are so called from the Italian *girasole,* sunflower, and have no connection to Jerusalem.

rancor   *RANG ker*
bitter, longlasting ill feeling; deep-seated ill will

A punch in the nose might seem to be an intensely personal thing — much more so, for example, than pushing the queen's rook's pawn on a board of checkered squares. Yet I have been astonished to hear of enmities and feuds in the game of chess, that epitome of abstract combat. The queen's rook's pawn sems to have occasioned a surprising lot of rancor and fury. I find it difficult to understand, but then I have been merely a boxer, a devotee of one of the most noted of all physical-contest sports.

Gene Tunney   June 1939

rank   *rangk*
growing vigorously and coarsely; overly luxuriant

Going up the side of a cliff about the first of November, I saw a vigorous young apple-tree, which, planted by birds or cows, had shot up amid the rocks and open woods there, and had now much fruit on it, uninjured by the frosts, when all cultivated apples were gathered. It was a rank wild growth, with many green leaves on it still, and made an impression of thorniness. The fruit was hard and green, but looked as if it would be palatable in the winter.

Henry David Thoreau   November 1862

rankle   *RANG kuhl*
to cause persistent irritation or resentment

De Musset, the melancholy poet of the disenchantments of life, and Heine, the sad mocker of the changefulness of life, are very light offenders against the serene or stagnant world of well-regulated people, compared with the positive, the unmitigated, the caustic poet Baudelaire. If you confront him, you will never forget him; he will not let you forget him. He plants his thought in your mind and it rankles there, the painful proof of a real and contemporary experience, that never has had so intense and bold a representative as the wretched author of *Les Fleurs du Mal*.

Eugene Benson   February 1869

rapacious   *ruh PA shuhs*
taking by force; plundering ("rapacity" is the noun)

A lot of nonsense has been written by literary critics, and others, about "the human spirit," tempting one to point out that the human spirit has always been remarkable more for greed and rapacity than for the exalted qualities the term usually celebrates. Yet occasionally a book rekindles our affection for the human race, and *A Fine Balance* is one. Although the suffering within it should be unbearable to observe, the reading experience is in fact strangely joyful.

Brooke Allen   September 2002

rara avis   *RAY ruh AY vis*
a person of a type seldom encountered; someone unique or exceptional: Latin, rare bird

A generation ago the native-born, homebred American Zionist was a *rara avis* indeed. Some few of the species were about, men of insight and courage — Louis D. Brandeis, for example.

Rabbi Milton Steinberg   February 1945

rarefied   *RAIR uh fighd*
in a realm with few others; singular

William Butler Yeats first appears, in the memories of his contemporaries, as a rarefied human being: a tall, dark-visaged young man who walked the streets of Dublin and London in a poetic hat, cloak, and flowing tie, intoning verses. The young man's more solid qualities were not then apparent to the casual observer. But it was during these early years that Yeats was building himself, step by step, into a person who could not only cope with reality but bend it to his will. He tells, in one of his autobiographies, of his determination to overcome his young diffidence. Realizing that he was "only self-possessed with people he knew intimately," he would go to a strange house "for a wretched hour for schooling's sake." And because he wished "to be able to play with hostile minds" he trained out of himself, in the midst of harsh discussion, the sensitive tendency "to become silent at rudeness."

Louise Bogan   May 1938

rash   *rash*
a large number of instances within a brief period

The recent art-market collapse hit New York hard, causing a wave of closures and bankruptcies, and the gallery world that has since emerged has dismayed many by teetering between two extremes: a few glossy mega-dealers who have the muscle to move the market their way, and a rash of smaller, scruffier galleries that often struggle to stay afloat. Yet even through the darkest days new dealers and spaces have continued to appear.

Carol Kino   July 1996

hasty; reckless ("rashly" is the adverb)

President Kennedy entered the White House in the conviction that Presidents should stay at home. In 1960, when Candidate Nixon rashly promised to go to Eastern Europe if elected, Candidate Kennedy replied, "If I am elected, I will go to Washington."

Carroll Kilpatrick   May 1965

ratiocination   *ra shee ah si NAY shuhn*
the process of logical reasoning

We cannot explain an inspiration. Our chief feeling about it is that it is not the result of our own ratiocinations, but that it came to us from elsewhere. And if we happen to have a precognitive dream, how can we possibly ascribe it to our own powers? Often we do not even know until afterward that the dream represented foreknowledge, or knowledge of something that happened at a distance.

Carl Jung   January 1963

> ✳ Edgar Allen Poe described his detective stories as "tales of ratiocination" in which a "web" of mystery surrounding a crime is logically unwound. Poe's "The Murders in the Rue Morgue (1841)," "The Mystery of Marie Rogêt" (1842) and "The Purloined Letter" (1845) established the modern detective story, the main element of which is the brilliant but eccentric private detective who by deductive reasoning solves cases that baffle the police.

ravage   *RA vij*
to devastate; bring heavy destruction on; lay waste

Only thirty years ago, the great Central Valley of California, five hundred miles long and fifty miles wide, was one bed of golden and purple flowers. Now it is ploughed and pastured out of existence, gone forever, — scarce a memory of it left in fence corners and along the bluffs of the streams. The gardens of the Sierra also, and the noble forests in both the reserved and the unreserved portions, are sadly hacked and trampled, notwithstanding the ruggedness of the topography, — all excepting those of the parks guarded by a few soldiers. In the noblest forests of the world, the ground, once divinely beautiful, is desolate and repulsive, like a face ravaged by disease. This is true also of many other Pacific Coast and Rocky Mountain valleys and forests. The same fate, sooner or later, is awaiting them all, unless awakening public opinion comes forward to stop it.

John Muir   January 1898

rebuff   *ri BUHF*
a blunt refusal of a request or offer

Could anyone outside the Vatican have foreseen that Karol Wojtyla would be elected

Pope? Could anyone even inside the Vatican have foreseen the direction his pontificate would take — the 100-plus foreign trips; the plethora of canonizations; the opening to Judaism and the rebuff to Anglicanism; the challenge to communism in Poland and then throughout the Eastern bloc; the apology to Galileo; the photo op with Castro; the abrupt declarations that matters of ordination and sexuality, which had only just begun to receive informed attention from the world's Catholics, were closed to further discussion? The answer, of course, is no. Even so, the spectacular misreading of John Paul shows the perils of interpreting any Pope in terms of his curriculum vitae.

Christopher Hitchens   September 2004

rebuke   *ruh BYOO:K*
to criticize; reprimand; chide

The closing scene of the *Phaedo* is as simple as it is moving. It does nothing but recount the facts: the bringing of the poison; Socrates brushing aside delay; the uncontrollable tears of the beloved disciples — tears which Socrates gently rebukes; the calm of Socrates himself in the very face of death. Stretched out on his bed, while the poison begins to paralyze his body, Socrates' last words are a brief request: to pay a cock to Aesculapius, patron of medicine. For Socrates has been healed — of life. He has chosen immortality, not the endlessness of time, but the timelessness of reason and justice.

Irwin Edman   February 1953

recast   *ree KAST*
to refashion or rework

Renditions of the Kerouac myth rarely mention that although he did write the original version of *On the Road* in one burst on his legendary teletype paper rolls, he rewrote and recast it many times in the seven or eight years before it was published.

Ralph Lombreglia   August 1996

recede   *ree SEED*
to become less; diminish; become more distant

Fear that the memory of the Holocaust may recede with time has in recent years prompted an international outpouring of books and films, and a proliferation of monuments to the Holocaust's victims.

Michael Z. Wise   October 1993

recherché   *ruh SHAIR shay*
carefully sought out; rare; exotic

Reader, have you ever eaten snails or horsemeat.? I have eaten both and I prefer snails; snails are, indeed, a great delicacy, and at the sign of L'Escargot d'Or, or the Golden Snail, a very old establishment near the Halles, they are always included in any very recherché meal; indeed, in the neighborhood of the Halles there are a dozen places which announce the interesting fact that snails are there served, by large effigies of the animal or reptile — or whatever it is — in gold, swinging from brackets over their doors.

A. Edward Newton   June 1928

recoil   *ri KOIL*
to draw back suddenly as in fear, surprise or disgust

I believe that if chance had produced the helicopter for general use before the automobile was invented, people would recoil in dismay at the hazards of a Sunday drive on a modern highway in what would be, to them, a newfangled dangerous contraption.

Igor Sikorsky   September 1942

reconcile   *RE kuhn sighl*
to make one thing consistent with another, in fact or in one's mind; to bring into agreement

When I entered Harvard in the fall of 1924, I was not only a Christian, I was also an avowed candidate for the ministry. Then for four years I underwent a process of mental readjustment which shook my little world to its foundations. Through it all only one thing was clear to me: if I could reconcile religion with intelligence, I knew that I could go on into my chosen career fortified by the experience; if I could not, every consideration of honor would compel me to make other plans. In the end I gave up the ministry.

Philip E. Wentworth   June 1932

recondite   *RE kuhn dight*
beyond ordinary knowledge or understanding; dealing with complex or difficult subjects

Frustration confronts the general reader shopping for an annotated edition of the King James Version of the Bible. It's the single greatest work of English literature (even the most ungodly H. L. Mencken pronounced it "probably the most beautiful piece of writing in all the literature of the world"), and no one who hasn't read it thoroughly should be considered well educated. But, of course, the Bible generally is a recondite book, full of obscure religious, historical, ethnographic, calendrical, even agricultural references.

Benjamin Schwarz   November 2003

recrudescence   *ree kroo: DE suhns*
a breaking out again or coming into renewed activity after a period of inactivity

The spread of private and sectarian schools in this country in the last twenty years has gone along with a very great increase in the proportion of citizens of alien traditions and customs in our midst. The withdrawal from the public schools of more and more of the children of those already Americanized greatly enhances the difficulty of making a unit of this inchoate mass of human beings that we call America. What does such a shift of large numbers of children signify? One can think of it only as the recrudescence in this country of the aristocratic, sectarian, exclusive traditions of the older European civilizations — attitudes incompatible with belief in democracy, with groupings determined by individual ability and capacity independent of inherited class or religious associations.

Cornelia James Cannon   November 1923

recur   *ri KER*
to return to the mind

The sensitiveness to varying phases of nature which appears in Longfellow's poems recurs to one as he reads the frequent notes, in diary and letters, of the welcome which the poet gave the spring, the spirit with which he encountered the winter. It was his custom to walk before sunrise. "Resumed my morning walks," he says one 9th of January, "after the long snow blockade. Was out by half past six, the moon shining; in the east just an explosion of light through broken clouds." And again: "A vigorous, cold day. Ah, how cold it is! My walk before sunrise I keep up very conscientiously, and because I really enjoy the fresh air. But to-day the wind scourged my ears sharply. These extremes of climate make me feel melancholy. Even when not cold myself, I cannot help thinking how many others are so."

Horace Elisha Scudder   May 1886

redoubtable   *ree DOW tuh buhl*
commanding respect or reverence

Will someone with time on his hands unearth for me a certain compound fracture of the infinitive that must have set an all-time world's record for the language? That redoubtable infinitive-dynamiter, Thomas Hardy, achieved in an early edition of one of his novels — *Far from the Madding Crowd,* unless my memory is shamefully at fault — *a split infinitive within a split infinitive:* that is, an infinitive broken off after *to* in favor of an adverbial parenthesis so highly developed as to contain within itself a casual split infinitive of the common to-sincerely-admire pattern. When I tried to refer to this feat of virtuosity, years after my first awed discovery, I failed to run it down in the edition at hand. Did someone induce Hardy to destroy it, perhaps by asking his publishers for a plate correction?

Wilson Follett   November 1938

redound   ri DOWND
to return as a reward or consequence for having done something; rebound

Mr. Polk meant to vindicate his Mexican policy by the private papers which he preserved so carefully; but this vindication was evidently staked upon the expectation that public gratitude would redound because of the splendid expansion that he gave to our national boundaries. He toiled and he despoiled for the glory of the American Union; but he could see nothing wrong in his despicable treatment of Mexico, in the crime he perpetrated against liberty and the sacred rights of property. He was not the kind of patriot to place himself at another's point of view, and could feel no tender compunctions for an adversary, and least of all for a weak one.

James Schouler   September 1895

reductio ad absurdum   ri DUHK tee oh ad ab SER duhm
the application of a rule or principle so strictly or literally that the result is ridiculous

Most of us have completely forgotten that *mob* was once *mobile vulgus*, and that Jonathan Swift inveighed against its slang abbreviation. Surely the rage for shortening reached a *reductio ad absurdum* when circa was made circ., an abbreviation which, with its period, is exactly as long as the original!

Contributors' Club: Harry T. Baker   June 1921

❋ When James Murray, the editor of the *Oxford English Dictionary,* was asked by a correspondent whether "whisky" or "whiskey" was the correct spelling, he replied: "Both forms are current and equally correct or incorrect. When in a hurry you may save a fraction of time by writing *whisky,* and when lingering over it you may prolong it to *whiskey.*"

reductive   ruh DUHK tuhv
oversimplifying complex things and ignoring their subtleties or important details

The great men of the past whose names have given an adjective to the language are by that very fact most vulnerable to the reductive treatment. Everybody knows what "Machiavellian" means, and "Rabelaisian"; everybody uses the terms "Platonic" and "Byronic" and relies on them to express certain commonplace notions in frequent use. Unfortunately, this common application of proper names yields but a detached fragment of the truth, and sometimes less than a fragment — a mere shadow of it. With regard to "Byronic," the reduction is truly *ad absurdum,* for the adjective refers to the man exclusively and to a single mood only — one of the poet's fictional types has engrossed his name.

Jacques Barzun   August 1953

reel   *reel*
to stagger, as if thrown off balance

Look at us. While the world — ours as well as the other fellow's, if you grant the brotherhood of man — is consumed by such obscene cruelties that the imagination mercifully reels, we blow thin drafts of words down the necks of one another. Mr. Henry Ford bids us supply Nazis and English with weapons so that they may both be destroyed — "then the United States can play the rôle for which it has the strength and the ability." The rôle, that is, of cosmic undertaker and ghoul prowling amid the ruins of Europe. This is the terrible idea of our greatest industrialist.

David L. Cohn   April 1941

reflexive   *ri FLEKS iv*
automatic; habitual; unthinking ("reflexively" is the adverb)

Sesame Street is reflexively admired by almost everyone, but I suspect that adults would praise it less if they watched it more. *Sesame Street* may not be schlock, but kids often watch it the way they watch schlock: like zombies. Four hours of television a day is much too much, even if it's Bert and Ernie.

David Owen   October 1986

refractory   *ri FRAK tuh ree*
resistant to authority or control; stubborn; obstinate; rebellious

Our father confessed that as a boy he had been very lazy — not thoroughly lazy, of course, for he had been an avid reader, had played the violin and written poetry, but lazy as a pupil. He received poor marks and was refractory toward his teachers.

Erika and Klaus Mann   April 1939

unyielding to treatment

Physicians are referring their patients to acupuncturists for chronic pain, anxiety, a variety of musculoskeletal problems, and neurological conditions that have proved refractory to conventional treatments.

James S. Gordon   October 1992

register *RE jis ter*
the total range of an instrument or voice

Despite a popular misconception, the hardest notes to play musically on the trumpet aren't the high, loud ones. Low — down around middle C and lower — is the most difficult part of the register. It's not easy to get a tone down there that someone will want to listen to, especially playing soft. As you lessen the flow of air through the horn in an effort to play soft, the sound will sometimes just disappear, right in the middle of a note.

Carl Vigeland   November 1999

rejoinder *ri JOIN der*
a quick reply to a question or remark, especially a witty or critical one

Admiral Takijiro Onishi was one of the few voices warning that an attack on Pearl Harbor might make the Americans "so insanely mad" that all hope for compromise would go up in flames. Everyone knew that if the Americans should choose to fight a war to the finish, Japan was almost certainly doomed. The Emperor, a diminutive figure revered by his people as the son of God, a taciturn man who usually sat impassive during these ritualized conferences, appreciated the perils ahead. He sharply reminded his military leaders that China's extensive hinterland had cheated Japan of victory on the Asian mainland, and that the Pacific was "boundless." To that cryptic utterance there was no effective rejoinder. The plan was approved.

David M. Kennedy   March 1999

relish *RE lish*
enjoyment of the taste or flavor of something

My personal acquaintance with Douglas Jerrold began in the spring of 1851. I had always had a keen relish for his wit and fancy; I felt a peculiar interest in a man who, like myself, had started in life in the Navy; and one of the things poor Douglas prided himself on was his readiness to know and recognize young fellows fighting in his own profession.

James Hannay   November 1857

✳ The passage above is the first paragraph of the first article in the first issue of *The Atlantic Monthly,* November 1857. Inasmuch as a major goal of *The Atlantic's* founders was to make the magazine a platform for American writing at a time when it was held in low esteem compared with British literature, it is noteworthy that this first article was written by a Scotsman about an Englishman. Douglas Jerrold (1803-1857) is today largely forgotten, but in his time he was a celebrated editor, publisher, playwright and wit. His continuous contributions to *Punch* magazine, from its founding in 1841 until shortly before his death, brought him fame as the comic and satiric equal of Charles Dickens and Henry Makepeace Thackeray (both of whom were pallbearers at his funeral). He went to sea in 1813 as an apprentice and was transferred to active duty in April 1815, on a ship carrying troops to fight Napoleon in Belgium. In July, his ship brought back wounded from the battle of Waterloo, and in October he quit the navy, having seen enough of war. He was 13.

remonstrate   *re MAHN strayt*
to say or plead in protest, objection or disapproval ("remonstrance" is the noun)

As our Spanish War was about to break out, it was said that one of our diplomats in Europe was approached by a high official of a foreign government who told him that the European nations were proposing to send a remonstrance to this country. Our diplomat, we were told, advised against it on the ground that we should pay no attention to it. What, pay no attention to the general opinion of Europe! No, none whatever. Instead of being chagrined, even those of us who disapproved of the war thought this answer worthy of our nation. Our people were not to be deterred from what most of them thought the noble cause of intervening in behalf of the maltreated Cubans because Europe did not see it as we did.

A. Lawrence Lowell   July 1934

remote   *ri MOHT*
set apart or distant from others in manner; withdrawn; reserved; aloof

In ordinary social intercourse, Wilson was shy, remote, and difficult. He himself admits it and others agree. On the other hand, when the ice was once broken and the barriers down, the President's charm was unusual and almost unfailing. The ungraciousness of the harsh features and stiff manner was forgotten in the winning, sympathetic smile and especially in the vivid ease and insinuating charm of the varied and piquant speech.

Gamaliel Bradford   February 1931

remove   *ri MOO:V*
the distance between one thing and another

In the eyes of children, anything can happen, for so little has happened before; for us, at a remove, we know what is likely and what is impossible, and so our propensity to astonishment is much less.

Alastair Reid   April 1963

remuneration   *ri myoo: nuh RAY shuhn*
payment for work or services performed; reward; compensation

If the quality of the men and women taking up the profession of teaching to-day is inferior to what it was a generation ago, the blame must rest on our shoulders. We have failed to show the members of the teaching profession the high honor which is their due, and to give them the adequate remuneration which is their right. We owe them sympathy and understanding in the gigantic task which is laid upon them.

Cornelia James Cannon   November 1923

renounce   *ri NOWNS*
to give up in a complete and formal manner

Icelandic surnames are unstable from one generation to the next. Sverrir Hermannsson's surname is Hermannsson because he is the son of a man whose first name was Hermann; if Sverrir had a daughter named Asta, she would become Asta Sverrirsdottir. The name laws stipulate, among other things, that a newborn child must be christened with a traditional Icelandic name before its birth can be registered. The adoption of a family name — a once-popular "Danish" fashion — is proscribed, although those that were in existence before the law's promulgation are permitted. In addition, foreigners granted Icelandic citizenship must renounce their original names and take new, Icelandic ones.

Brad Leithauser   September 1987

rent   *rent*
torn through

Again the Guinea jungle comes wonderfully to the eye and mysteriously to the mind; again my khakis and sneakers are skin-comfortable; again I am squatted on a pleasant mat of leaves in a miniature gorge, miles back of my Kartabo bungalow. Life elsewhere has already become unthinkable. I recall a place boiling with worried people, rent with unpleasing sounds, and beset with unsatisfactory pleasures. It is, I believe, called New York.

William Beebe   March 1921

repartee   *re pahr TAY*
conversation marked by quick and witty replies

Austen's style is one of English literature's marvels. Her repartee is sometimes as dazzling as anything in Sheridan, and is one reason that her perpetual hope of seeing exciting theater was disappointed wherever she went.

Lee Siegel   January 1998

replicate   RE pli kayt
to make a copy or reproduction from a model or original

The nation-states of Europe and Europe's offshoots, and their industrial economies, are the results of centuries of slow and painstaking growth. In retrospect, it was absurd to suppose that at the click of fingers they could be replicated throughout Africa after the brief sojourn there of the European imperialists. Africa would surely be better off today if the colonial powers either had remained for another generation or had never gone there in the first place.

Geoffrey Wheatcroft   November 1990

repose   ri POHZ
quiet or peaceful inaction; calmness; tranquillity

To rush through the world in automobiles means to accustom the eye to the rapid flight of impressions, and spoils the inner eye for the fancies of repose.

Hugo Münsterberg   March 1909

repository   ruh PAH zuh taw ree
something serving as a center of accumulation or storage

The National Archives in Washington now has about five billion documents in storage. Nationwide, federal repositories have another 19 million cubic feet of them, which in boxes set end to end would stretch from coast to coast.

Cullen Murphy   May 1996

reprehensible   re pri HEN suh buhl
deserving severe blame or censure; shameful

It is held rather reprehensible to say it, but I do not see why every girl has not as good a right as every boy to dream of fame, and to be put in the way of reaching fame. If ninety-nine per cent of the girls fail of even the smallest title to fame, just as ninety-nine per cent of the boys do, yet the level of their lives must inevitably be raised by the education and the educational ideals which we should provide for them all for the sake of the hundredth girl. The supreme ideal which I hope that our schools may some day inspire is that every girl should discover something, whether of fame-bringing probabilities or not, which will seem to her worthy of being a life-work.

Mary Leal Harkness   March 1914

reproach   *ri PROHCH*
to criticize someone for not being successful or not doing what is expected

The worker has been made a mere cog in a big machine, and yet he is constantly reproached for being without initiative. The careful specialization of labor has cut the majority of wage-earners off from any chance of having their ambitions realized. Industry has been deliberately graded in a great hierarchy, and then the lowest level, upon which the whole superstructure rests, is reproached by well-meaning people for not raising itself by its boot-straps.

Randolph S. Bourne   March 1914

strong disapproval or blame

It is a common saying in England that America is governed by newspapers, — and this by way of sneer, according to the charming fashion of Englishmen. But long ago Jefferson anticipated and met this reproach, when he said, "I would rather live in a country with newspapers and without a government, than in a country with a government but without newspapers." The alternative is seldom presented nowadays; indeed, it has been found easier to overthrow a government at Paris, Madrid, Mexico, or Rome, than to stop a well-managed newspaper.

Franklin Benjamin Sanborn   July 1874

✻ The more complete rendering of what Thomas Jefferson actually wrote to Colonel Edward Carrington on January 16, 1787 is: "The basis of our government being the opinion of the people, the very first object should be to keep that right; and were it left to me to decide whether we should have a government without newspapers, or newspapers without a government, I should not hesitate for a moment to prefer the latter. But I should mean that every man should receive those papers and be capable of reading them."

reproof   *ri PROO:F*
disapproval of something said or done; reprimand

Our childhood grows in value as we grow in years. It is to that time that every one refers the influence which reaches to his present and somehow moulds it. It may have been an insignificant circumstance, — a word, — a book,— praise or reproof; but from it has flowed all that he is.

Ralph Waldo Emerson   September 1858

republican   *ri PUB li kuhn*
relating to a form of government in which the supreme power rests in the body of citizens entitled to vote for leaders responsible to them

In Brandeis's view, big business threatened self-government in two ways — directly, by overwhelming democratic institutions and defying their control, and indirectly, by eroding the moral and civic capacities that equip workers to think and act as citizens. Brandeis brought long-standing republican themes into the twentieth-century debate: like Jefferson, he viewed concentrated power, whether economic or political, as inimical to liberty.

Michael J. Sandel   March 1996

repugnant   *ri PUHG nuhnt*
repulsive; distasteful; offensive

Cocoa powder is seldom seen in Italian bars, and cinnamon is an unknown embell-ishment. On a cappuccino there's just beautifully creamy foam. But could someone please tell me where the custom of serving espresso with a sliver of lemon peel came from? Not from the Italians, who regard this practice as a repugnant American aber-ration. Coffee aficionados despise it, because the acidity in the peel's oil ruins the balance of the acidity in the coffee.

Corby Kummer   November 1990

resilience   *ri ZIL yins*
the ability to bounce back or recover quickly from a setback or loss

Runaways did not bring down slavery, though the issues they raised and the prob-lems they created helped to bring on the war that would destroy slavery. By their very presence and persistence they testified to the resilience of the human spirit in a nation whose Constitution and laws sanctioned slave catchers. As much as any of the Revolutionary patriots and Founding Fathers, we need to recall these plantation rebels and outlaws — mostly unsung in their own time — who individually or col-lectively tried, in the face of overwhelming odds, to give meaning to abstract notions of independence and freedom.

Leon F. Litwack   November 1999

resolution   *re zuh LOO: shuhn*
in music, a note or chord to which the harmony moves when progressing from dissonance to consonance

Mendelssohn went to call on a friend, the story runs, and learned that he was still abed. Going to the piano, he played one loud chord of the seventh and sat down to await events. In a moment a commotion was heard above, boots were thrown on the floor, and soon the sluggard rushed down the stairs to the piano and played the resolution of the chord.

Lucy Elliot Keeler   January 1914

resonate   *RE zuh nayt*
to strike a sympathetic chord; be responsive to

One reason Confucius has resonated with twentieth-century intellectuals is that his religiosity — or lack thereof — is remarkably congruent with our time. He appeared to encourage obedience to the will of "heaven" and reverent observance of religious rites — the ancient Chinese practice of offering sacrifices to the spirits of one's ancestors, for example — while remaining agnostic on the question of whether a supernatural world actually exists.

Charlotte Allen   April 1999

resoundingly   *ri ZOWN ding lee*
emphatically; quite noticeably

John Milton once said that a poet's life should itself be "a true poem." He himself failed resoundingly in this ideal, not just because his life was tragic but because it was sprawling, petty, punctuated by long stretches of nothingness, thick on work but thin on grace.

Cristina Nehring   April 2004

respite   *RE spit*
an interval of relief or rest

The habit of fighting is deeply ingrained in human nature, though one cannot accept the contention of certain European thinkers that war is the normal condition of things and peace a mere necessary respite.

Sisley Huddleston   February 1925

resurgence   *ri SER jins*
a rising again

The 1990s saw a resurgence of poetry in American culture, especially poetry read aloud. Today poets fill auditoriums, lecture halls, and urban performance spaces in a way not seen, perhaps, since the 1950s, when Dylan Thomas popularized public poetry readings as he toured the United States, and the work of Allen Ginsberg and his fellow Beats thrived as much in performance as on the printed page. Poetry slams and the rise of "spoken word" or "performance poetry" — influenced by rap and hip-hop musical styles — are now a pop-culture phenomenon.

Wen Stephenson   April 2000

resuscitate   *ri SUH suh tayt*
to bring back to life; revive

A recent historian of dancing, in a book published so lately as 1906, declared that "the ballet is now a thing of the past, and, with the modern change of ideas, a thing that is never likely to be resuscitated." That historian never mentioned Russian ballet, yet his book was scarcely published before the Russian ballet arrived, to scatter ridicule over his rash prophecy by raising the ballet to a pitch of perfection it can rarely have surpassed, as an expressive, emotional, even passionate form of living art.

Havelock Ellis   February 1914

retiring   *ri TIGH ring*
reserved; shy

It was at Villino Trollope that we first saw the wonderfully clever author, George Eliot. She is a woman of forty, perhaps, of large frame and fair Saxon coloring. In heaviness of jaw and height of cheek-bone she greatly resembles a German; nor are her features unlike those of Wordsworth, judging from his pictures. The expression of her face is gentle and amiable, while her manner is particularly timid and retiring. In conversation Mrs. Lewes is most entertaining, and her interest in young writers is a trait which immediately takes captive all persons of this class. We shall not forget with what kindness and earnestness she addressed a young girl who had just begun to handle a pen, how frankly she related her own literary experience, and how gently she suggested advice. True genius is always allied to humility, and in seeing Mrs. Lewes do the work of a good Samaritan so unobtrusively, we learned to respect the woman as much as we had ever admired the writer.

Kate Field   December 1864

retrofit   *RE troh fit*
to modify with new parts

The *Esprit,* like most of the dozens of hotel barges plying their trade in various regions of France, has been retrofitted with heating and air-conditioning, guest cabins (the *Esprit's* are very clean and comfortable, though far from sybaritic), a dining room, a bar and lounge, and, out on deck, patio chairs, pots of geraniums, and a rack of bicycles.

Barbara Wallraff   February 1996

revel   *RE vuhl*
to enjoy oneself greatly; take intense pleasure

Mrs. Coolidge likes, revels in, the social world, which her husband detests and avoids. He hates to talk — she loves it; and when she utters the superfluous she gives it a grace and charm which makes it seem more indispensable than the necessary, as indeed no doubt it is.

Gamaliel Bradford   January 1930

revenant   *RE vuh nuhnt*
returning to a place after a long absence

Perón, like Franco and Salazar, survived the supposed defeat of fascism in the Second World War, and he kept on torturing Argentina with his revenant third and fourth acts, ultimately dying and then ruling by posthumous proxy through the cult of his dead wife and the actual agency of his second one, the charmless Isabel.

Christopher Hitchens   September 2004

revere   *ruh VEER*
to regard with deep and awed respect

Swift frankly hated Ireland, but once there, he became a fiercely eloquent advocate of fair and decent treatment of the island and is revered as the father of Irish independence.

Phoebe-Lou Adams   June 1999

revile   *ruh VIGHL*
to use abusive or contemptuous language in speaking to or about

Fruit and vegetable growers in the state now rely on a thriving black market in labor — and without it more farms would disappear. Illegal immigrants, widely reviled and depicted as welfare cheats, are in effect subsidizing the most important sector of the California economy.

Eric Schlosser   November 1995

revisionism   *ruh VI zhuh ni zuhm*
the revising or reinterpretation of a traditionally accepted historical event or movement; an attempt to re-evaluate and restate the past based on newly acquired standards ("revisionist" is the adjective)

How things have changed in a century! Political, religious, and social differences, far from vanishing, place Columbus today in the center of a worldwide cultural civil war. The great hero of the nineteenth century seems well on the way to becoming the great villain of the twenty-first. Columbus, it is now charged, far from being the pioneer of progress and enlightenment, was in fact the pioneer of oppression, racism, slavery, rape, theft, vandalism, extermination, and ecological desolation. The revisionist reaction, it must be said, has been under way for a while. As far back as the quadricentennial, Justin Winsor, a historian and bibliographer of early America, published a soberly critical biography, arguing that Columbus had left the New World "a legacy of devastation and crime."

Arthur M. Schlesinger Jr.   September 1992

ridicule   *RI di kyoo:l*
words intended to mock, belittle or make fun of a person or idea

Edison has devoted nearly two years to the task of making the phonograph of commercial use. He believes that he has succeeded. Whether or not the instrument shall enter into every-day life, as the telephone has done, is a question for the future. Certainly it is now a far greater wonder than it was in 1875, and it has reached a point where it cannot again be dropped by the scientific world. Whether Mr. Edison, or Mr. Bell, or some one else puts the final touches which will take the apparatus out of the laboratory and make it practical for common use does not much matter. Some one will certainly do it. Those persons who smile incredulously when it is said that the perfected phonograph will do away with letter-writing, will read to us, will sing and play for us, will give us books, music, plays, speeches, at almost no cost, and become a constant source of instruction and amusement, must have forgotten the ridicule they heaped upon the rumor that an American inventor proposed to talk from New York to Chicago. The achievements of the phonograph will at best be less wonderful than those of the telephone.

Philip G. Hubert Jr.   February 1889

rift   *rift*
an open break in a previously friendly relationship

The core problem within the ghetto is the vicious circle created by the lack of decent housing, decent jobs and adequate education. The failure of these three fundamental institutions has led to alienation of the ghetto from the rest of the urban area as well as to deep political rifts between the two communities.

Stokely Carmichael and Charles V. Hamilton   October 1967

riposte   *ri POHST*
a sharp, swift response or retort; counterstroke: from the fencing term meaning a quick thrust after parrying a lunge

In October of 1992 President George Bush readied an arsenal of one-liners for use in his first televised debate with Bill Clinton — lines that in the end he could not work in. If Clinton had stumbled in the area of foreign affairs, Bush was prepared with ripostes. "Now I know what to get you for Christmas — a world globe," was one possibility. Had a Clinton gaffe involved the name of some world leader, Bush was ready with this: "If you ever go on Jeopardy, don't choose the category Foreign Heads of State."

Cullen Murphy   July 2000

risqué   *ris KAY*
very close to being sexually improper or indecent; off-color; suggestive

It used to be that the curious reader in quest of the risqué had to go to the scrofulous French novel, but how pallid it was and is, compared with the modern native product. If, a century from now, the social historian should read many best sellers of our time, he would be forced to conclude that male and female Americans of this period were wholly engaged in amorous and extramarital affairs, with incidental excursions into business, politics, war, and so forth. For nowadays affairs are as automatic in a novel as corpses in a detective story; the only question is how many are required.

Douglas Bush   January 1959

riven   *RI vuhn*
torn apart or split

Iraq has a one-man thugocracy, so the removal of Saddam would threaten to disintegrate the entire ethnically riven country if we weren't to act fast and pragmatically install people who could actually govern. Therefore we should forswear any evangelical lust to implement democracy overnight in a country with no tradition of it.

Robert D. Kaplan   November 2002

riverine   *RI ver een*
on or near the banks of a river

Riverine data in some form have been collected by all civilizations, so essential are rivers to commerce and agriculture. Records of the annual high-water level of the Nile, for example, are complete all the way back to A.D. 622, save for one large gap in the early modern period.

Cullen Murphy   January 1995

robber baron   *RAH buhr BA ruhn*
a U.S. financier or industrialist of the late 19th century who became wealthy by unethical means, such as exploiting labor and natural resources and corrupting legislators: the original robber baron was a noble who robbed people passing through his domain

Old houses bursting with antiques have shaped the prevailing notion of what a bed-and-breakfast should be. In a beautiful section of Louisville, I was given a suite at the top of a grand staircase in a Victorian mansion worthy of a robber baron. At breakfast, laid out next to a tall bay window, the host supplied my table with an elaborate silver service that accentuated the architectural splendor.

Philip Langdon   September 1993

roistering   *ROI stuh ring*
lively and noisy; revelling; boisterous

Who in my generation was not moved by Hemingway the writer and fascinated by Hemingway the maker of his own legend? "Veteran out of the wars before he was twenty," as Archibald MacLeish described him. "Famous at twenty-five; thirty a master." Wine-stained moods in the sidewalk cafés and roistering nights in Left Bank *boîtes*. Walking home alone in the rain. Talk of death, and scenes of it, in the Spanish sun. Treks and trophies in Tanganyika's green hills. Duck-shooting in the Venetian marshes. Fighting in, and writing about, two world wars. Loving and drinking and fishing out of Key West and Havana. Swaggering into Toots Shor's or posturing in *Life* magazine or talking a verbless sort of Choctaw for the notebooks of Lillian Ross and the pages of the *New Yorker.*

Robert Manning   August 1965

romanticize   *roh MAN tuh sighz*
to describe, think of or interpret something in an idealized way; glamorize
("romanticization" is the noun)

A newcomer certain to create a stir has just appeared on the scene. Norman Mailer's first novel, *The Naked and the Dead* (Rinehart, $4.00), strikes me as being by far the most impressive piece of fiction to date about Americans in the Second World War. The author, a veteran of the Pacific, is twenty-five years old. Mailer's concern is with the individual and the way of life that formed him. He uses the shocks and tensions of war as a corrosive agent which bites through to the hard core of truth about men. *The Naked and the Dead* is vastly more mature, intellectually, than the war novels of the twenties, with their romanticization of chronic mutiny. Artistically, it rates comparison with the best of them.

Charles J. Rolo   June 1948

rout   *rowt*
a disorderly flight

However glorious the history of art may be, the history of artists is quite another matter. And in any well-ordered household the very thought that one of the young may turn out to be an artist can be a cause for general alarm. It may be a point of great pride to have a Van Gogh on the living-room wall, but the prospect of having Van Gogh himself in the living room would put a good many devoted art lovers to rout.

Ben Shahn   August 1957

rue   *roo:*

regret

I first read Marquand's novels twenty-odd years ago. Back then they swept me up in nostalgia for a time I'd never actually known — my parents' youth, hinted at in anecdotes and glimpsed in old photographs. The outdated, elusive glamour of movies from the 1930s and 1940s surrounded his characters, who religiously dress for dinner, keep eccentric retainers, and wait a prescribed amount of time before using one another's first names. Re-reading these books today, I find that the nostalgia and the glamour are undiminished — and that the dialogue occasionally has a cinematic brittleness. But more striking to me now (perhaps for obvious reasons) is the way in which he regularly tapped into the rue and longing of middle age.

Martha Spaulding   May 2004

S

sedentary

To appreciate the wild and sharp flavors of these October fruits, it is necessary that you be breathing the sharp October or November air. The out-door air and exercise which the walker gets give a different tone to his palate, and he craves a fruit which the sedentary would call harsh and crabbed. They must be eaten in the fields, when your system is all aglow with exercise, when the frosty weather nips your fingers, the wind rattles the bare boughs or rustles the few remaining leaves, and the jay is heard screaming around. What is sour in the house a bracing walk makes sweet. Some of these apples might be labelled, "To be eaten in the wind."

Henry David Thoreau   November 1862

see page 399

S

sacred cow *SAY krid KOW*
anything treated as immune from criticism or change: an allusion to the fact
that Hindus hold the cow sacred

> No newspaper is freer from outside control. Mr. Ochs is inordinately proud, as he has
> every right to be, that the *Times* has no Ivory Towers, no Sacred Cows. The high-
> placed in any field are to him not Sacred Cows but high-bred Holsteins, provided
> they live up to their breeding. Hence his resentment flares up the more sternly when
> they indicate a meretricious desire for preferential grazing ground in his columns.
>
> Benjamin Stolberg   December 1926

> So organized and so vociferous are dog lovers that dogs have become, so to speak,
> sacred cows. They stand on an equal basis with Mother and the Flag, just a little
> higher than clergymen and doctors. A man who would gladly put his mother on a
> leash or tie her to a tree will burst into weeping oratorical defense of his dog if he is
> asked to restrain it.
>
> Robert Fontaine   December 1963

sagacity *suh GA suh tee*
the quality of being discerning, sound in judgment and farsighted;
wisdom; shrewdness

> There are few birds that equal the Crow in sagacity. He observes many things that
> would seem to require the faculties of a rational being. He judges with accuracy,
> from the deportment of the person approaching him, if he is prepared to do him an
> injury; and seems to pay no regard to one who is strolling the fields in search of
> flowers or for recreation. On such occasions, one may get so near him as to observe
> his manners, and even to note the varying shades of his plumage. But in vain does

the sportsman endeavor to approach him. So sure is he to fly at the right moment for his safety, that one might suppose he could measure the distance of gunshot.

Wilson Flagg   March 1859

sage *sayj*
a person of profound wisdom

In 1857 Henry Wadsworth Longfellow, along with Harriet Beecher Stowe, Ralph Waldo Emerson, Oliver Wendell Holmes, John Greenleaf Whittier, James Russell Lowell, and other three-handled New England sages, founded *The Atlantic Monthly*. Our original mission was to free the slaves and bridge the chasm between the old culture of Europe and the new culture of America: to import the old and export the new.

Peter Davison   February 2001

salient *SAYL yint*
standing out from the rest; prominent; conspicuous; noticeable

The determination of the average man, of the small bourgeois, the peasant, and the farmer, to maintain a life as intact as possible from the problems and pressures of the age is a salient feature of contemporary Europe. Everywhere it contrasts sharply with the immense confusions of politics and economics.

Sir Arthur Willert   September 1937

sallow *SA loh*
weak and sickly; pale; lackluster

As we seek perfection in our officials through an increasingly intense legal scrutiny, and reap an increasingly sallow form of mediocrity instead, there will come times — perhaps dangerous and violent times — when we will be more forgiving toward those who were supremely imperfect in their character yet unafraid to challenge the public mood.

Robert D. Kaplan   June 1999

sally *SA lee*
a quick witticism; quip

The challenge of facing a large audience, expectant but unaroused; the laughter that greets a sally at the outset, then the stillness as the power of imagery and ideas takes hold; the response that flows, audibly or inaudibly, from the audience to the speaker; the fresh extemporizing without which a lecture is dead; the tension and timing as the talk nears the hour; and the unexpected conclusion — this is what every professional speaker comes to know.

Edward Weeks   December 1960

salubrious   *suh LOO: bree uhs*
physically or mentally healthful

Travelers planning a trip to Australia this fall for the Olympic Games might consider getting away from the crowds for a week in scenic, salubrious Tasmania. North American fall is the Antipodean spring, a good time to visit.

Jamie James   March 2000

salutary   *SA lyuh te ree*
calculated to bring about a better condition or to remedy some evil; beneficial

Perhaps a troglodyte, by concealing his comings and goings, might achieve a state of perfect privacy. But most of us are subject to the close scrutiny of friends and neighbors, which we reciprocate with lively interest. Our peccadilloes are fair game for local gossip; and as long as such gossip remains a purely amateur sport it is relatively harmless and may even have a salutary social effect.

Mitchell Dawson   October 1932

sanctum sanctorum   *SANGK tuhm sangk TOH ruhm*
the holiest of holy places

Across the emerald pool fell a shimmering image of lotus-shaped cupolas and copper-gilt walls. Dhoti-clad men lowered themselves on chains into the water to perform ablutions; women in saris murmured prayers in Punjabi. Such a domain of peace and piety — the Golden Temple, the sanctum sanctorum of Sikhism — had been impossible to imagine while navigating the clamorous lanes of Amritsar outside. The temple was orderly, efficient, with gurus on duty in shrines around its sides, and with Sikh bookstores and a museum of Sikh history at its entrance. Sikh guards, dressed in robes of alabaster white and turbans of royal blue, patrolled the chalk-soft marble walkways with spears, enforcing a discipline and solemnity foreign to places of worship elsewhere in India.

Jeffrey Tayler   November 1999

sangfroid   *sahn FWAH*
cool self-possession or composure in trying circumstances: French, cold blood

Ulysses S. Grant "was not excited by [danger], but was simply indifferent to it, was calm when others were aroused," according to his military secretary. "I have often seen him sit erect in his saddle when everyone else instinctively shrank as a shell burst in the neighborhood." A Union soldier put it thus: "Ulysses don't scare worth a damn." The uninhibited can manifest this same sangfroid in situations, from boardroom conferences to political debates, that entail social rather than physical risk.

Garry Wills   April 1994

sanguinary *SANG gwi nai ree*
accompanied by bloodshed; characterized by slaughter

Our original Thirteen Colonies were badly disunited at the beginning of our War of Independence. If Great Britain had turned us loose in disgust at the very beginning, there would have been sanguinary fighting between our Tories and our extreme revolutionaries. It was the common war against the British and their alien mercenaries that forced us to settle all internal issues as quickly and constructively as possible — with the result that, by the time we had our freedom, civil war was impossible. In spite of the deep-going differences between the slaveholding South and the free North, it took us two generations to work up a civil war.

Owen Lattimore   July 1938

sap *sap*
to deplete or weaken gradually; undermine; exhaust; drain

War is associated with bursting shells, ruined cities, devastated fields, maimed men, military cemeteries. Yet there have been few wars in which economic pressure has not been a vital or even deciding factor. It was Lincoln's blockade which sapped the strength of the Confederacy; Great Britain's grip on the sea was all-important in bringing Germany to her knees in 1918.

T. J. Wertenbaker   January 1936

sardonic *sahr DAH nik*
showing an amused attitude toward someone or something that suggests a criticism but does not express it; bitterly or ironically humorous

"The Great War," used interchangeably with "the First World War" (so named in 1918 by a sardonic English journalist, who knew it would not be the last such conflict), engendered in Britain a sense of loss that endures to this day; it remains the great divide in Britons' sense of their history.

Benjamin Schwarz   May 1999

sashay *sa SHAY*
to move or walk in a casual, gliding fashion

In 1976, when Jimmy Carter moved his family from Plains, Georgia, to Washington, D.C., it went without saying that his nine-year-old daughter, Amy, would attend a public school. Early in his campaign Carter had more or less promised that no child of his would be found sashaying through the halls of an elite prep school. After all, he was running as a homespun outsider; and as a matter of practical politics, the teachers' unions would certainly have regarded a decision to send Amy to private school as a betrayal, and would have punished Carter for it.

Margaret Talbot   February 2001

satiated *SAY shee ay tid*
supplied to excess; satisfied to the point of boredom; glutted

The verdict which public opinion has pronounced, or, rather, is from time to time pronouncing, on the writings of George Eliot is certainly a very complicated one. That she is an acute delineator of character, a subtle humorist, a master of English, a universal observer and a comprehensive student, a profound moralist, — all this is part of her established reputation. That she is, besides this, a poet of great force and originality would, if we took as the test the most widely published criticism, be also established. That she has also succeeded, — in an age in which the public has been satiated with novels, and critics have begun even to doubt whether novel-writing were not a thing of the past, — if not in founding a new school of novel-writing, at least in proving that this literary form could be adapted, in skilful hands, to purposes which her predecessors had never dreamed of.

Arthur George Sedgwick   April 1873

satrap *SA trap*
a despotic, subordinate official; petty tyrant

Within thirteen years after Lenin's death, Stalin, emerging swiftly from obscurity, had got rid of all the senior revolutionaries, and a great part of the communist rank and file, either by shooting or imprisonment. He had also broken the Red Army as a potentially independent force by shooting practically the whole of the high command and a large proportion of the officers' corps. He ruled despotically, surrounded by a group of personally appointed satraps. By means of the secret police he exercised a ruthless and appallingly wasteful terror throughout the land.

Edward Crankshaw   July 1959

  ✳ Satraps were provincial governors in ancient Persia. The Old Persian word *shathrapavan* means protector of the country.

saunter *SAWN ter*
to walk in a relaxed, leisurely way; stroll

I have met with but one or two persons in the course of my life who understood the art of Walking, that is, of taking walks, — who had a genius, so to speak, for *sauntering*: which word is beautifully derived "from idle people who roved about the country, in the Middle Ages, and asked charity, under pretense of going *à la Sainte Terre*," to the Holy Land, till the children exclaimed, "There goes a *Sainte-Terrer*," a Saunterer, a Holy-Lander. They who never go to the Holy Land in their walks, as they pretend, are indeed mere idlers and vagabonds; but they who do go there are saunterers in the good sense, such as I mean.

Henry David Thoreau   June 1862

✳ Thoreau's derivation of saunter is charming but not borne out by modern etymological research. While its origin is obscure, it may have come from the Middle English *santren,* to muse, be in a reverie.

savant   *suh VAHNT*
a person of deep learning; eminent scholar

Returning to my American home, I read, after a few days, in the local newspaper (the *Newport Mercury*), that I was reported to have enjoyed myself greatly in England, and to have been kindly received, "especially among servants and rascals." An investigation by the indignant editor revealed the fact that the scrap had been copied from another newspaper; and that a felicitous misprint had substituted the offending words for the original designation of my English friends as savants and radicals.

Thomas Wentworth Higginson   December 1897

savory   *SAY vuh ree*
having an agreeable pungent or salty taste

Pancetta is ubiquitous in Italian cooking, serving with onion, carrot, celery, and parsley as a base for nearly every savory sauce and stew.

Corby Kummer   February 1990

scabrous   *SKA bruhs*
scandalous; indecent; shocking

A Madman's Manifesto, *by August Strindberg (1895).* Strindberg intended this scabrous roman à clef about his tormented marriage to the actress and feminist Siri von Essen to serve as a suicide note. He got cold feet about killing himself but decided to humiliate her anyway by publishing this devil's banquet of unseemly allegations. (He accused Von Essen of promiscuity, drunkenness, and lesbianism.) A more loathsome yet absorbing example of misogynistic dementia would be hard to find.

Terry Castle   September 2004

scathing   *SKAY th:ing*
bitterly severe; searing; withering

Bleak House, the 1853 classic by Charles Dickens, is a scathing indictment of a legal system that served no one but lawyers. The novel is based on a nineteenth-century British inheritance dispute that raged for generations until nothing was left to fight over, because the entire value of the estate had been consumed by legal fees and court costs.

Edwin Chen   July 1984

schadenfreude   *SHAH duhn froy duh*
pleasure at another's misfortune: German, schaden, *harm +* freude, *joy*

In the underselling, overanalyzed world of literary fiction, the disappointing second novel is as familiar as baseball's fizzled phenom or the stock market's burst bubble. Reviews announcing the failure of last year's prodigy to "fulfill the early promise" of what so proudly was hailed are written and read with a sort of exhilarated letdown. Knowingness and schadenfreude abound.

Thomas Mallon   October 2002

schmaltz   *shmahltz*
exaggerated sentimentality in music, drama or other art form; mawkishness:
Yiddish, melted chicken fat

Philip Furia, my favorite scholar of Broadway lyrics, says that Porter's wit turned into schmaltz whenever he wrote a romantic ballad. Call me a sap, but I find songs like "Ev'ry Time We Say Goodbye" and "I Concentrate on You" — or even that parody of itself, "I Love You" — as psychologically compelling as the snappier "Just One of Those Things" or "It's All Right With Me."

David Schiff   July/August 2004

screed   *skreed*
a long, tiresome speech or piece of writing; diatribe; harangue

In the old-style newspaper, in spite of the fact that the editorial articles were usually anonymous, the editor's name appeared among the standing notices somewhere in every issue, or was so well known to the public that we talked about "what Greeley thought," of this or that, or wondered "whether Bryant was going to support a certain ticket," or shook our heads over the latest sensational screed in Bennett's paper.

Francis E. Leupp   February 1910

scrofulous   *SKRAH fyuh luhs*
morally corrupt; degenerate

In its craze for listeners, radio has become the most incestuous of all arts. There is hardly a successful radio program which has not provoked a dozen scrofulous little imitations, designed to look as nearly like the original as the laws of plagiarism will allow. The parentage of virtually every program can be directly traced to the few original minds who entered broadcasting in its formative years.

John Crosby   January 1948

scrupulous   *SKROO: pyuh luhs*
extremely careful to do the precisely correct thing

It was thirty-seven years ago that Dr. Holmes published in the first number of this magazine the opening paper of a series which gave distinction at once to *The Atlantic Monthly*. Since that day scarcely a volume has appeared without a word from him, and many of the volumes contain a poem, paper, or chapter of a novel in every number. So identified had he become with the fortunes of the magazine that, the day after his death, I received a communication addressed to him as editor. It was very fortunate for all of us that he never was its editor, for he would have been so scrupulous that he would have expended his energies on other people's work, and we should have missed some of his own.

Horace Elisha Scudder   December 1894

scurrilous   *SKUH ruh luhs*
indecent or abusive; foulmouthed; coarse

Charles Comiskey, a legendary baseball figure, first called clubhouse visitors "fanatics," and Ty Cobb called fans "bugs," a scurrilous slang synonym for "zealot" or "enthusiast." Cobb occasionally rushed into the grandstands to stamp his opinion on the face of the customer who criticized his play.

Jim Brosnan   April 1964

scurvy   *SKER vee*
low; vile; contemptible; worthless

When we meet a man who is well-dressed, and whose external demeanor is that of a gentleman, we are prone to infer that he is also a man of upright principles and honorable feelings. But we are very often mistaken in this inference; the nice garment proves to be little better than a nice disguise; and the robe of respectability may cover the heart of a very scurvy fellow.

Park Godwin   January 1858

scuttle   *SKUH tuhl*
to run with quick, hasty steps, especially away from danger; scurry

All ballplayers like Connie Mack. Some managers enjoy slapping a fine on a recalcitrant star; Connie has other and possibly subtler methods. A player jumps from a taxi before the hotel, nods good-night to Mack, who is standing at the entrance, and goes up in the elevator. But Connie knows youth like the master of a boarding school. He merely walks round to the back entrance in time to catch the player scuttling out like a bad boy. Lots of managers would seize the moment to burst into a lecture, winding up with a fine. Connie doesn't need to. The man sees him, turns round, and goes back to his room and bed.

John R. Tunis   August 1940

searing   *SEER ing*
burning; scorching

Foreigners often find Americans as a group more than a little hard to take, in their overt nationalism, deep religiosity, proud vulgarity, unashamed sentimentality, battered but defiant idealism, and propensity for searing public debate. These are precisely the qualities that are disappearing in Europe. Traumatized by world war and absolutist political ideologies, Western Europe's political elites have been working for decades to neutralize passion altogether.

Robert D. Kaplan   July/August 2004

secular   *SE kyuh ler*
pertaining to the worldly as opposed to the religious

Although the Catholic Church suppressed a recent attempt to conduct the Sacrament of Penance by e-mail, there is a secular Apology Room on the Web that encourages visitors to "anonymously share with others" their shortcomings, and to beg forgiveness.

Cullen Murphy   April 2003

To judge by rates of churchgoing, Iceland is the most secular country on earth, with a pathetic two percent weekly attendance. But four out of five Icelanders say that they pray, and the same proportion believe in life after death.

Paul Bloom   December 2005

sedentary   *SE den TE ree*
marked by much sitting and little moving about; accustomed to sitting still

To appreciate the wild and sharp flavors of these October fruits, it is necessary that you be breathing the sharp October or November air. The out-door air and exercise which the walker gets give a different tone to his palate, and he craves a fruit which the sedentary would call harsh and crabbed. They must be eaten in the fields, when your system is all aglow with exercise, when the frosty weather nips your fingers, the wind rattles the bare boughs or rustles the few remaining leaves, and the jay is heard screaming around. What is sour in the house a bracing walk makes sweet. Some of these apples might be labelled, "To be eaten in the wind."

Henry David Thoreau   November 1862

sedition   *suh DI shuhn*
the stirring up of discontent, resistance or rebellion against the government ("seditious" is the adjective)

> The grand jury's function of screening the prosecution's cases has been solidly established in this country from earliest times. In 1734, William Cosby, a particularly incompetent royal governor of New York, was stung by the attacks upon him carried in the New York *Weekly Journal.* Cosby had his handpicked chief justice indicate to the grand jury that John Pete Zenger, the paper's printer, had committed the crime of seditious libel. The grand jury refused to indict, and repeated its refusal when Cosby tried again several months later. The fact that Zenger was later charged in an information and that he won his acquittal through the heroic efforts of his lawyer, Andrew Hamilton, does not change the fact that for the best part of a year the grand jury stood between a thoroughly ruthless executive and an unjustly accused citizen.

Judge Irving R. Kaufman   April 1962

> ✳ An information is the formal charging document that sets forth an accusation or criminal charge brought by the public prosecutor.

sedulous   *SE juh luhs*
working hard and steadily; diligent; constant; persistent

> The moral traits of U. S. Grant are tolerably well understood by the country, and a belief in them undoubtedly did very much towards elevating him to power; but there still exists in some quarters a mistrust of his intellectual ability, an uncertainty as to whether he possesses the faculties necessary in a statesman, especially at so delicate and dangerous a crisis as that through which this nation is passing. The characteristic reserve of the man, his persistent shrinking from self-assertion, his sedulous avoidance of display of any sort, have contributed to this anxiety. For Americans, of all people, are least used to this reserve.

Adam Badeau   May 1869

seedy   *SEE dee*
shabby and unkempt; worn

> Mr. Le Carré's characters, deprived of the traditional heroics of espionage, are mostly seedy and querulous civil servants, burdened by nagging wives and able to keep themselves going only by the illusory image of themselves as still carrying on their brave work of World War II.

William Barrett   August 1965

seer   *SEE uhr*
a person said to be able to foretell events

> Through most of his time in public life Kennan has been known as farsighted —
> almost as a seer. During the early forties, when many Americans, including our
> President, had warm feelings toward the Soviets, Kennan repeatedly warned his supe-
> riors in the government that this outlook was based on wishful thinking and on a
> total misunderstanding of Russian politics, Russian intentions, and Russian history.

> William Whitworth   April 1989

self-abnegation   *self ab nuh GAY shuhn*
setting aside one's self interest for the sake of others

> One sometimes hears the "well-adjusted" mother express her self-abnegation in
> heroic terms. "After all," she says, "the children come first. They're all that really
> matters." If the purpose of an adult human being is to rear a child or two so that
> those children can in turn rear children, ad infinitum, then life is unquestionably the
> absurd treadmill it sometimes seems and there is nothing to do but relax. How can
> the mother who believes she herself doesn't matter rear her children *for* anything?
> The only bearable theory is that we bring our children up to adulthood because we
> believe in adulthood — in its satisfactions and in the possibilities it offers for infi-
> nite growth and development.

> Della D. Cyrus   March 1947

self-deprecation   *self de pruh KAY shuhn*
the belittling, undervaluing or disparaging of the value of one's own talent,
ability or accomplishments

> I am not a boastful person. In fact, self-deprecation is generally judged to be one of
> my most winning attributes. I am always ready to discuss my personal defects —
> irritability, untidiness, permanent panel of blubber between bust and waist which
> can't be exercised away.

> Mary Killen   May 2001

sententious   *sen TEN shuhs*
full of maxims or proverbs in a way that is trite and moralizing
("sententiousness" is the noun)

> Don Quixote, famously, is the first major work of Western literature to take ordi-
> nary human life for its subject — specifically, a life that is replete with accidents,
> fiascoes, and indignities — and make it over into something luminous with mean-
> ing. It does so without pomp or sententiousness — it's the friendliest and least

formal of all the Great Books — yet will overwhelm you, in the end, with its moral and imaginative splendor.

Terry Castle   January/February 2004

sentinel   SEN tuh nuhl
a person or thing that guards or stands watch; sentry

There is probably no record in history of a change in the international reputation of a country as profound and as rapid as that which Turkey has undergone since 1918. Twenty years ago it was the "Sick Man of Europe"; Carlyle's phrase, "the unspeakable Turk," was actually used on the floor of the United States Senate in the early twenties. Today Turkey is the bastion against Naziism, the Eastern sentinel of democracy and freedom, and one of the most popular and most respected small nations in the world.

Peter F. Drucker   April 1941

sepulchral   suh PUHL kruhl
as though from the grave; gloomy; mournful

Sometimes, when I see my little boy hugging himself with delight at the near prospect of the kindergarten, I go back in memory forty years and more to the day when I was dragged, a howling captive, to school, as a punishment for being bad at home. I remember, as though it were yesterday, my progress up the street in the vengeful grasp of an exasperated servant, and my reception by the aged monster — most fitly named Madame Bruin — who kept the school. She asked no questions, but led me straightway to the cellar, where she plunged me into an empty barrel and put the lid on over me. Applying her horn goggles to the bunghole, to my abject terror, she informed me, in a sepulchral voice, that that was the way bad boys were dealt with in school. When I ceased howling from sheer fright, she took me out and conducted me to the yard, where a big hog had a corner to itself. She bade me observe that one of its ears had been slit half its length. It was because the hog was lazy, and little boys who were that way minded were in danger of similar treatment; in token whereof she clipped a pair of tailor's shears suggestively close to my ear. It was my first lesson in school. I hated it from that hour.

Jacob Riis   November 1899

servile   SER vuhl
like slaves or servants; submissive; cringing; fawning ("servility" is the noun)

Material possessions not only focus people toward private and away from communal life but also encourage docility. The more possessions one has, the more compromises one will make to protect them. The ancient Greeks said that the slave is someone who is intent on filling his belly, which can also mean someone who is intent on safeguarding his possessions. Aristophanes and Euripides, the late-eighteenth-century Scottish philosopher Adam Ferguson, and Tocqueville in the nineteenth century all warned that material prosperity would breed servility and withdrawal, turning people into, in Tocqueville's words, "industrious sheep."

Robert D. Kaplan   December 1997

sesquipedalian   *ses kwi puh DAYL yin*
containing many syllables: Latin, sesquipedalis, *a foot and a half long*

Outside the town, where the cool, pure ponds gaze skyward and the white crooked brooks run whispering their sesquipedalian Indian names, the Maple leaves slant drifting down to the water; there they will sink like galleons with painted sails, or spin away on voyages of chance that end on some little reef of feldspar and horneblende and winking mica schist.

Donald Culross Peattie   March 1949

sham   *sham*
a trick or fraud; something claimed to be genuine but really meant to deceive

Dickens painted the walls of his library at Gads Hill to represent bookshelves in tiers around the entire room. The titles on the sham tomes were likewise of his own invention: *A History of the Middling Ages,* in many volumes; *Has A Cat Nine Lives? Was Shakespeare's Mother's Hair Red?*

Lucy Eliot Keeler   January 1914

shibboleth   *SHI buh lith*
a catchword or formula adopted by a party or sect, by which their adherents or followers may be discerned, or those not their followers may be excluded

The problem of the twentieth century is the problem of the color line; the relation of the darker to the lighter races of men in Asia and Africa, in America and the islands of the sea. It was a phase of this problem that caused the Civil War; and however much they who marched south and north in 1861 may have fixed on the technical points of union and local autonomy as a shibboleth, all nevertheless knew, as we know, that the question of Negro slavery was the deeper cause of the conflict.

W. E. B. Du Bois   March 1901

shoddy   *SHAH dee*
rundown; shabby

The Floridita was once one of those comfortably shoddy Havana saloons where the food was cheap and good and the drinking serious. By then, enjoying a prosperity that was due in no small part to its reputation as the place you could see and maybe even drink with Papa Hemingway, it had taken on a red-plush grandeur and even had a velvet cord to block off the dining room entrance. "It looks crummy now," Hemingway said, "but the drinking's as good as ever."

Robert Manning   August 1965

shrink   *shrink*
to draw back; hesitate

It required no great perspicacity to perceive that the South ruled the democratic party, and that whoever would rise in that party was obliged to serve the South. From this Mr. Buchanan did not shrink. He was the faithful servant of the South for years. He supported all the Southern measures. He was in favor of the annexation of Texas, and he helped on the infamy of the Mexican war, covering the progress of the slavery movement with all sorts of smooth and specious pretexts and excuses, while he kept strictly for home consumption a very mild disapproval of the system of slavery as an abstract theory.

Henry Cabot Lodge   November 1883

shrinking violet   *SHRINGK ing VIGH uh lit*
a very shy or unassuming person

For a time Bacharach was as famous as any of the singers who put his songs on the charts. When *Promises, Promises* opened on Broadway, he eclipsed not only his nearly invisible lyricist but also the show's producer, David Merrick, and the author of its book, Neil Simon, neither of whom was ever accused of being a shrinking violet. People who would have been unable to say for sure who wrote "Raindrops Keep Fallin' on My Head" or "What the World Needs Now Is Love" knew Burt Bacharach by name, just as they might have known the name of Irving Berlin without being able to identify him as the composer of "White Christmas" and "Easter Parade."

Francis Davis   June 1997

shunt   *shuhnt*
to turn aside or out of the way

Sixty years ago few companies thought twice about firing a female employee who became pregnant; now the discrimination against women who have children is more subtle but nevertheless tangible, as they are shunted off into corporate backwaters or kept out of consideration for partnerships or passed over for pay raises.

Gina Maranto   June 1995

signal   *SIG nuhl*
striking; remarkable; notable; significant

The signal error of the American elite after the end of the Cold War was its trust in rationalism, which, it was assumed, would eventually propel the world's societies toward systems based on individual rights and united by American-style capitalism and technology.

Robert D. Kaplan   May 2003

signature   *SIG nuh cher*
typical of or identified with a person, place or time

Trieste's moody winters fill the city with its signature wind, which whips down from the mountains in the northeast to the Adriatic at up to sixty miles an hour. Like the Provencal mistral and the New England nor'easter, this wind bears its own name and legend: la bora is said to periodically cleanse the city of its sins with three-day episodes. The wind seems overly expressive to the understated Triestini, who deem a man who's unnecessarily blustery, all full of himself, l'uomo borioso.

John Donatich   June 2002

simile   *SI muh lee*
a figure of speech in which two essentially unlike things are compared to each other through the use of "like," "as" or another word expressing similarity

Last summer an Englishman created a sensation at the Harvard International Seminar by getting up and saying, "The American girl is like a Jaguar: she's very fast at first, but then she suddenly breaks down and won't move another inch." We can be grateful to our transatlantic cousin for speaking his mind with such John Bullish bluntness. But at the risk of striking a nationalistic note, I must say that he got his similes confused. The American woman isn't like a Jaguar at all; she's like a Thunderbird — sleek, streamlined, difficult to maneuver, and with comfortable room for only one passenger next to the driver.

Don Cortes   August 1957

✳ John Bull is the traditional personification of England and the English character, similar in purpose to America's Uncle Sam. He first appeared in 1712 in a collection of pamphlets satirizing English politics and has been depicted since in stories, plays and, most commonly, caricatures and political cartoons. His creator, John Arbuthnot (1667-1735), a Scottish physician, described him as an "honest, plain-dealing fellow, choleric, bold, and of a very inconstant temper." In drawings made popular in the British humor magazine *Punch* during the 19th century he is stout and hearty, wearing breeches, top hat and a waistcoat with the Union Jack on it. He is often accompanied by a bulldog.

simplistic   *sim PLI stik*
unrealistically or misleadingly simple

Somewhere in every serious political speech are the markers by which a party defines its course. Their colors run back to Jefferson and Hamilton, to Rousseau and Hobbes and the old debates over man's capacity for sensible judgment. They are cast in either/or terms: crime results either from murderous living conditions or from the society's unwillingness to impose firm sanctions on antisocial behavior; poverty is either a social crime of the rich or a psychological failure of the poor; prosperity should trickle down or bubble up. Inevitably the distinctions that bring the loudest cheers at political dinners seem the most inadequate and simplistic the next morning. Sober, thinking people do not see the world in either/or terms.

Harry McPherson   April 1972

simulacrum   *sim yuh LAY kruhm*
something having merely the form or appearance of a certain thing, without possessing its substance or proper qualities; an unreal or superficial likeness ("simulacra" is the plural)

The characters in a good novel are three-dimensional: they have not only height and breadth, but depth. Too often the personages in the traditional biography are two-dimensional. They are flat simulacra. The new biography, adopting the form of the novel, is stereoscopic. Its portraits have depth as well as height. They are painted from life and executed in color.

George Alexander Johnston   March 1929

simulate   *SIM yuh layt*
to give the appearance or effect of

Some critic wrote of Whistler's portrait of Carlyle that it was not life-size. "No," was his reply, "few men are." He cannily made the portrait of Sarasate smaller than life-size, to simulate the effect of seeing the violinist far off on the concert stage.

Lucy Elliot Keeler   January 1914

sinecure   *SIGH ni kyoor*
an office or position that provides an income but requires little or no work

I am very frequently asked what in the world a librarian can find to do with his time, or am perhaps congratulated on my connection with Harvard College Library, on the ground that "being virtually a sinecure office (!) it must leave so much leisure for private study and work of a literary sort." Those who put such questions, or offer such congratulations, are naturally astonished when told that the library affords enough work to employ all my own time, as well as that of twenty assistants; and astonishment is apt to rise to bewilderment when it is added that seventeen of these assistants are occupied chiefly with "cataloguing"; for generally, I find, a library catalogue is assumed to be a thing that is somehow "made" at a single stroke, as Aladdin's palace was built, at intervals of ten or a dozen years, or whenever a "new catalogue "is thought to be needed.

John Fiske   October 1876

sinewy   SI nyuh wee
vigorous; powerful; robust

The English tongue is full of strong words native or adopted to express the blood-born passion of the race for rudeness and resistance, as against polish and all acts to give in: Robust, brawny, athletic, muscular, acrid, harsh, rugged, severe, pluck, grit, effrontery, stern, resistance, bracing, rude, rugged, rough, shaggy, bearded, arrogant, haughty. These words are alive and sinewy, — they walk, look, step, with an air of command. They will often lead the rest, — they will not follow. How can they follow? They will appear strange in company unlike themselves.

Walt Whitman   April 1904

singular   SING yuh ler
one of a kind; unique; remarkable ("singularly" is the adverb)

Mencken's gifts were singularly varied. He was surely one of the great newspapermen of his generation, and of his books probably those dealing with the American language will be longest remembered. He took on the professional philologists and beat them at their own game. He knew more about medicine and the law than any other layman who has passed my way.

Alfred A. Knopf   May 1959

Sisyphean   sis uh FEE uhn
endlessly and uselessly toilsome, as a never-finished task: from the myth of Sisyphus, a cruel king of Corinth, whose punishment in Hades was to push a huge stone up a hill only to have it roll back again before it reached the top

In Webster's Third New International Dictionary, "politics" is defined as, among other things, "the art of adjusting and ordering relationships between individuals and groups in a political community." Even someone in a very small political community (my house) who holds an office that is largely ceremonial (dad) knows what a Sisyphean task it is to be adjusting and ordering relationships between individuals (the kids and the dog) and groups (the whole family packed in the car) for nothing more than a day at the beach.

P. J. O'Rourke   November 2002

skew   *skyoo:*
to slant; distort; warp

Wiffle ball's great advantage over baseball has always been that it requires so few players. Its great disadvantage — from a spectator's standpoint, anyway — is that the ball itself skews the enterprise decidedly in favor of the pitcher. Those who have learned how to fully exploit the ball's aerodynamic idiosyncrasies can throw pitches that dart about like hummingbirds.

Lee Green   June 2002

skinflint   *SKIN flint*
a person who is unwilling to give or spend; a miser

In 1921 France was very much surprised not to be generally supported when she demanded the payment of reparations by the Germans. We were reputed to be misers, exacting and heartless skinflints who insisted on the letter of the law and who did not mind letting our next-door neighbor perish as long as he paid his debt.

Jean Prévost   May 1938

skirt   *skert*
to form the border or edge of; to lie alongside of

There are some trees which are peculiarly American, being confined to the western continent, and unknown in other parts of the world. Among these is the Hickory, a well-known and very common tree, celebrated rather for its usefulness than its beauty. The different trees of this family make an important feature in our landscape: they are not abundant in the forest, but they are conspicuous objects in the open plain, hill, and pasture. Great numbers of them have become standards; we see them following the lines of old stone walls that skirt the bounds and avenues of the farm, in company with the Ash and the Maple.

Wilson Flagg   September 1860

skulduggery   *skuhl DUH guh ree*
unscrupulous behavior; machinations; trickery

Judging from his new book, *A World of Profit,* I should say that Louis Auchincloss is a better novelist for being a good lawyer. New York City will always be his favorite bailiwick, the community where he likes to place his short stories and novels, and in much of the skulduggery in Manhattan, the proxy fights, the amassing of real estate, corporate setups, and divorce suits, lawyers are involved.

Edward Weeks   December 1968

slacker   SLA ker
a person who evades military service in wartime

Many intelligent persons, as well as the great mass of the unthinking, would, now that war is on, have us surrender some of the normal constitutional safeguards of free speech; they would have the plain-clothes men and police officials, our district attorneys, juries, and judges, exercise new vigilance in their control of meetings and public speeches. The excuses for this are the activities of German agents and sympathizers, the encouragement which slackers may receive, and the depressing effect upon our troops of tolerated pacifists and conscientious objectors.

James Harvey Robinson   December 1917

slapdash   SLAP dash
hasty and careless

The very words *Madame* and *Monsieur* seem the essence of civility to me, recently returned to the United States, where a typical salutation is "Hi," and the answer to "How are you?" is likely to be "I'm good." (You are? I'm rather naughty myself.) To the French our hasty, slapdash way of addressing people seems rude. One aspect of French civility is a measured approach to all transactions, whether with a waiter, a taxi driver, or a shop clerk. There's a fraction of a second of eye contact, a "*Bonjour, Madame* [or *Monsieur*]," and often a barely perceptible bow before proceeding to business.

Alice Furlaud   October 2001

sleight of hand   slight uhv HAND
a cleverly executed trick or deception

Thirty-four and a half years ago I was sitting in a nearly empty high school classroom in Philadelphia under the spell of my English teacher and drama coach, D. G. Rosenbaum. I idolized Mr. Rosenbaum (or "Rosey," as we Drama Society brats called him). He had a dark, resonant voice. He had a widow's peak and a moustache and goatee that made him look like Mephistopheles; he hinted that his ancestors were Scottish warlocks. He wore trim black suits, blood-red vests, and pince-nez. He smoked black cigarettes with gold tips, and made them vanish by sleight of hand when the principal was nearby.

Teller (of Penn & Teller)   November 1997

slipshod   *SLIP shahd*
careless in appearance or workmanship; sloppy

I know men, distinguished in the walks of literature, famed for a beautiful style of composition, who do not write a tolerable letter nor answer a note of invitation with propriety. Their sentences are slipshod, their punctuation and spelling beyond criticism, and their manuscript repulsive.

Adams Sherman Hill   June 1858

sloth   *slahth*
a dislike of any kind of physical exertion; laziness; idleness

Some persons object to having a dog on the bed at night; and it must be admitted that he lies a little heavily upon one's limbs; but why be so base as to prefer comfort to companionship! To wake up in the dark night, and put your hand on that warm soft body, to feel the beating of that faithful heart, — is not this better than undisturbed sloth? The best night's rest I ever had was once when a cocker spaniel puppy, who had just recovered from stomach-ache (dose one to two soda-mints), and was a little frightened by the strange experience, curled up on my shoulder like a fur tippet, gently pushed his cold, soft nose into my neck, and there slept sweetly and soundly until morning.

Henry Childs Merwin   January 1910

   ✻ A tippet is a covering for the shoulders, often of fur, with long ends that hang down in front.

slovenly   *SLAH vin lee*
careless and sloppy; negligent

Oliver Twist was the first of Dickens's romances which was subjected to the revision of his dear friend and biographer, John Forster, an accomplished man of letters, recently deceased. Forster read and suggested corrections to everything which Dickens afterwards wrote, and the text of *Oliver Twist* may be supposed to have specially engaged his critical sagacity, as it was the first story on which it was exercised. Yet the text of *Oliver Twist* is left in a slovenly condition, discreditable to both author and reviser. The reader needs to go no further than the opening paragraph to understand what we mean. The frequent use of the colon for the comma in the punctuation of the narrative is particularly exasperating.

Edwin Percy Whipple   October 1876

sluggard   *SLUH gerd*
a habitually lazy, slow or idle person

Democritus, in the 154th Fragment of his *Golden Sayings,* says, "In matters of great weight, go to school with the animals. Learn spinning and weaving from the spider, architecture from the swallow, singing from the swan and the nightingale." This is the sort of advice our forefathers were always wont to give. When they saw a sluggard, they sent him to the ant; when they saw a popinjay, they sent him to the worm; when they saw a buffoon, they sent him to the cow; when they saw a fool, they sent him to the owl. All animate nature took on special characters; peacocks were vain, foxes were cunning, bears were ugly, dogs were lazy, sheep were stupid, oxen were patient, cats were sly, serpents were wise. We began to live in an endless La Fontaine fable.

Contributors' Club: George Boas   November 1920

smug   *smuhg*
narrowly contented with one's own accomplishments and qualities; self-satisfied

Temperamentally opposed as I am to the injection of any kind of "pep" into religious services, whether the merrymakings take the form of revivals, camp meetings, or what not, I looked with aversion at a large poster outside a theater in which religious services were being held on a Sunday evening by a smug evangelist depicted as standing with outstretched hand alongside the legend, "He greets sinners with a smile." So does a bootlegger.

A. Edward Newton   September 1932

sojourn   *SOH jern*
a brief or temporary stay at a place

Travel and sojourn in strange lands teach us more about ourselves than about those lands and the people living in them. They give us a view of ourselves from a new angle, and standards of measurement which bring out our traits in curious and previously unperceived proportions.

Leland Hall   October 1929

solace   *SAH lis*
comfort and consolation

The manner in which movers and shakers wind down their careers frequently has a medieval flavor. Aristocrats of yore often forsook their earthly obligations in late career, entering the cloister and devoting the rest of their lives to study and prayer. In much the same way, modern grandees seek monastic solace in the nonprofit world. Isn't this what the former senator Bob Kerrey has done, taking over the presidency of New School University? And Walter Isaacson, leaving the chairmanship of CNN News Group to become the president of the Aspen Institute?

Cullen Murphy   October 2003

to comfort; console

The Bach family form a whole Milky Way, covering a space of many degrees on the celestial globe of music. From old Veit Bach, the baker and miller of Presburg, in Hungary, who was driven forth by the religious troubles in the sixteenth century to find shelter in Thuringia, and who solaced himself with his lute amid the clatter of his mill, transmitting the same taste to his two sons, and they to their descendants, there were six generations of them who devoted themselves to music, and in each generation two or three stars, at least, of magnitude. At one time every post of cantor, organist, or town musician, in all Thuringia, was occupied by some scion of that stock.

John Sullivan Dwight   May 1885

solicitous   *suh LI suh tis*
showing attention, care or concern for someone's well-being

As the following incident shows, Lee was extremely solicitous about the unnecessary exposure of his men. Once when he was watching the effect of the fire of an advanced battery, a staff officer rode up to him by the approach which was least protected. The general reprimanded him for his carelessness, and when the young man urged that he could not seek cover himself while his chief was in the open, Lee answered sharply, "It is my duty to be here. Go back the way I told you, sir."

Gamaliel Bradford   August 1911

soliloquy   *suh LI luh kwee*
lines spoken aloud by an actor not to the other players but directly to the audience, revealing private thoughts, feelings or intentions

No other piece of English writing has taken such a hold on the English thinking race as Hamlet's soliloquy on suicide. Its matter is the veriest commonplace, — the theme of the college sophomore for generations; parodied, hackneyed, declaimed, misquoted, it still stands the most magnificent piece of writing in English. Why? Because this common thought of this common man is clothed in common words; because the words come straight from his own experience, without garnish or ornament other than that the thought itself wore; because they go straight to the core of the commonest experience of humanity, without other help or assistance than that the understanding alone can furnish. Hamlet, and indeed all of Shakespeare, is an appeal to the general reader. In fact, not much of Shakespeare would have come down to us, had we had to depend on a purely literary public for its transmission to posterity.

Mark H. Liddell   October 1898

soothsayer   *SOO:TH: say er*
a person who professes to foretell the future; seer

The radio commentator in the United States has by now become a national habit. We have venerated most of the merchants of supposed "inside stuff," even hailing some of them as soothsayers.

Robert J. Landry   April 1942

sophistry   *SAH fi stree*
argument based on reasoning that seems plausible but is actually misleading, false and deceptive

That a man named for one of the highest offices in the American system of government could sit silent in the Senate while his colleagues gave his nomination an approval which they must have withheld had he admitted facts which they were entitled to know, was behavior no subsequent conduct can condone. But the apologists for Mr. Justice Black ask us to believe that because he has shown evidence of possessing a social conscience we can afford to overlook this passing dereliction from traditional ethical standards. If ever there was sophistry, if ever there was evasion of the line between right and wrong, it lies in such a contention. The simple fact remains that an office of the highest trust was obtained under false pretenses.

J. Donald Adams   January 1938

✳ On September 13, 1937, one month after Hugo Black's confirmation as U.S. Supreme Court justice, the *Pittsburgh Post-Gazette* charged that he had been, and still was, a member of the Ku Klux Klan. Shortly after that he admitted to an estimated 50 million radio listeners that he had joined the Klan in 1923, as a young trial lawyer in Alabama, but had resigned two years later. He joined it, he said, only because he wanted an "even chance with the juries," as every other corporation lawyer in the area was a member, and so were many judges and jurors. Black went on to become one of the strongest advocates of civil liberties in the history of the Supreme Court.

soporific   *sah puh RI fik*
sleep-inducing; monotonous

In contrast to an alarmingly large body of contemporary music, jazz expects to be listened to. It does not pretend to be soporific even when accused of being an aphrodisiac.

Arnold Sundgaard   July 1955

sotto voce   *SAH toh VOH chee*
in a soft voice, so as not to be overheard: Italian, under the voice

It is true of naughty stories, just as it is of swear-words, that they flourish most lushly

413

where there are most taboos. Robert Graves, the British essayist, catalogues these taboos under three headings — Sex, Religious, and Lavatory; the violation of one or another of these accounts for ninety-nine out of one hundred stories passed along *sotto voce* over the forty-eight states and over the generations.

Burges Johnson   July 1952

spangle   *SPAN guhl*
to cover or decorate with small, bright, glittering objects

Amid the seemingly countless stars that on a clear night spangle the vast dome overhead, there appeared last autumn to be a new-comer, a very large and ruddy one, that rose at sunset through the haze about the horizon. That star was the planet Mars, so conspicuous when in such position as often to be taken for a portent.

Percival Lowell   May 1895

Above all other intellectual qualities, Sir Francis Bacon valued clarity, or said he did. Yet Bacon indulged at times in the most bizarre collection of words, all but incomprehensible and never, so far as I can learn, used before or since — words like *spinosity, assentatorily, illaqueation.* Bacon spoke of the *ways and ambages of God.* (We do find *ambage* in the King James Bible.) "The more subtle forms of sophistry," Bacon writes, "with their illaqueations and redargutions." *Redargution* is a word from old logic, "now rare," the dictionary says. In 1584, a young lawyer wrote that he had been to court to hear Bacon argue his first case, and that Bacon had "spangled his speech with unusual words, somewhat obscure, and as it were, presuming on the judges' capacities."

Catherine Drinker Bowen   January 1966

spare   *spair*
lacking any extras; meager; scanty

Putin's office, in the northwest corner of the second floor, affords a view of Red Square. The office is spare and impersonal, with a somewhat antiquated feel. It has a clunky television and a bank of several dozen phones with heavy handsets — direct lines to the offices of Putin's Kremlin aides and other senior officials.

Paul Starobin   March 2005

spate
a sudden rush, flood or outpouring

Never mind how exquisitely discerning we think we are. In twenty-first-century America our stories have become one and the same: we work to consume, we live to consume, we are what we consume. And not just that; according to a recent spate of appalling — yet intriguing — new books in what one reviewer has called "the growing field of luxe lit," it seems we're all starting to consume the same things. The melting pot is becoming a fondue, as increasing numbers of Americans hurl their hard-earned dollars at such unnecessaries as lattes, gourmet chocolate, Napa wine, massage, lingerie, designer wear, and Mercedes coupes.

Sandra Tsing Loh   December 2003

spawn   *spawn*
to bring forth in great numbers

On a soccer-mad planet — riots occur, work stops, prisoners escape, politicians rise or fall, religious schisms open or close, wars start, all because of soccer matches — the United States has long stood as an oasis of indifference to the world's game. Yes, in recent years the sport has exploded in the United States at the suburban grass roots, and has even **spawned** a cultural archetype: the soccer mom. But soccer at the elite level of play has generally attracted somewhat less interest than, say, ice hockey (though somewhat more than cricket — a foreign curiosity we can't quite get the hang of), and certainly much less than the major American sports. Indeed, with a few significant exceptions, the history of U.S. men's soccer is a long tale of futility.

Scott Stossel   June 2001

> ✳ The *Oxford English Dictionary* cites the date of *soccer mom*'s first appearance in print as October 14, 1982, in the Springfield, Mass., *Morning Union.*

spearhead   *SPEER hed*
a force that precedes others in a thrust or attack; the leading person, element or group in an attack

The free world, with its tremendous moral and material resources, must not remain on the defensive in the face of the Soviet challenge. The economic and psychological **spearheads** of the Soviet drive can be countered and rolled back by creative thinking and imaginative effort on our part. This thinking and effort must be world-wide in scope and commensurate with what is at stake — our very survival in freedom.

Averell Harriman   April 1956

specious   *SPEE shuhs*
seeming to be true but actually a deception; plausible, but in reality fallacious

One does not need to embrace Communism in order to fall prey to its **specious** moral doctrine. The doctrine has seeped through as a result of the effort to view sympathetically an experiment in which, as never before in the world's history, the subordination of means to ends has been glorified. If one may with clear conscience sacrifice an entire generation of men for the purely problematical good of those to come, one may as readily dose one's child with an unproved and potentially fatal antitoxin.

J. Donald Adams   January 1938

splice   *splighs*
to join the ends of two pieces of film or magnetic tape with adhesive

An unsuccessful playwright so ashamed of the profession into which exigency had forced him that for years he hid behind a pseudonym, D. W. Griffith staged a one-man revolution in cinematic technique. The close-up, intercutting for dramatic suspense, dramatic lighting, the moving (or trucking) shot, the flash-back, and the breakdown of a scene into brief individual but component shots spliced together to a dramatically rhythmic plan — these are only a few of Griffith's innovations which accelerated the development not only of American films, but of French, German, Russian, and Italian as well. To this day the French call a close shot *plan américain,* and the Italians, *piano americano.*

Budd Schulberg   November 1947

spoliation   *spoh lee AY shuhn*
the act of injuring, especially beyond reclaim; stripping and taking by force

The spoliation of the Cherokees was a national act, and as such the whole nation assumed its consequences. True, hundreds of thousands of our people protested against the outrage, just as hundreds of thousands protested against slavery; but the judgment that comes upon nations knows nothing of individuals.

George Anson Jackson   March 1890

spur   *sper*
anything that urges, goads, impels or incites; a stimulus to action

Canada is a nation. It is true that a few of her public men feel impelled to deny this from time to time; but these denials are intended only as spurs to urge Canada to more emphatic nationhood. Canada has long ago made up her mind that she is a nation. Now the only workable definition of a nation is that it is any body of people who have made up their minds to be a nation. They do not need to be of the same race, as witness the United States or Great Britain; they do not need to speak the same language, as witness Switzerland; they do not even need to live in the same country, as witness the Jews. They only need to have made up their minds about it. Canada has made up her mind and, despite legal hairsplitting as to whether she is a 'sovereign nation,' or what not, Canada is a nation.

Ramsay Traquair   June 1923

to stimulate

On the outside a timber-framed house looks much the same as a conventional stud-frame house. But on the inside the entire framework of posts and beams is exposed, making a dramatic, rugged outline against walls and ceilings. The rustic beauty of the framework, and its exceptional strength, have spurred a revival of the method since the early 1970's, bringing a seemingly obsolete craft back friom the edge of extinction.

Philip Langdon   December 1988

squalor   *SKWAH luhr*
wretchedness and filth

It is almost impossible now to imagine the claustrophobia which people of imagination and sensibility felt in mid-Victorian England. Its social injustices, the brutal squalor of its submerged population, are still apparent through the rosy hue which our nostalgia has given to an age which offered so much greater security and certainty than our own apocalyptic times. Nevertheless, for almost every major writer or artist of high Victorian times their age seemed a prison house of dreariness and falsity.

Angus Wilson   November 1957

staccato   *stuh KAH toh*
made up of brief, distinct elements or sounds; clipped

I read Montaigne for his rhythm as much as for anything he tells me — the staccato sentences, the cascading examples, the hard little nuggets of epigrammatic insight. "Wherever peccadillos are treated as crimes, crimes are treated as peccadillos."

Phyllis Rose   August 1992

stagy   *STAY jee*
theatrical; artificial

With its neat trolley lanes, geometric parks, rustic flowerpots beside polymer-and-glass buildings, crowded sidewalk benches, and cafés with modish awnings that hang from sandblasted stone and marble façades, Portland exudes a stagy perfection. "View corridors" regulated by municipal ordinances keep new construction from blocking the vistas from downtown of the Cascades and, in particular, Mount Hood.

Robert D. Kaplan   August 1998

stalemate *STAYL mayt*
a situation in which neither side can prevail in a conflict; deadlock; draw

The Soviets can, with their economic warfare, denude Afghanistan of its people, but they can't stop most of the able-bodied male refugees from returning as *mujahideen* for a time and making the occupation a misery with more and more foreign-supplied weapons. Nor can they expect the Afghan fighters to abandon the war as a lost cause — not with their history of ferocious resistance to invaders and not when recovery of their country has become their whole *raison d'etre*. In order to end this limited war the Soviets must widen it — but to widen it would be to heap folly upon recklessness. So the best the Soviets can hope to achieve is a bloody stalemate.

John Keegan   November 1985

stance *stans*
the attitude or view adopted in dealing with a particular situation

Given its economic dynamism, China probably will — in twenty-five years or longer — become a powerful and militarily sophisticated geopolitical actor in East Asia and the eastern Pacific. And so America's overwhelming military and political influence in the region will decline. But the United States has plenty of time to consider the implications of China's rise before it is complete. We must examine our own stance toward the world, and the way we define threats to our national security. In other words, to understand the consequences of China's (slowly) growing ambitions, we have to understand our own.

Benjamin Schwarz   June 2005

stanch *stawnch*
to put a stop to

It proved impossible to stanch the flow of men and supplies from North Vietnam to the South on the Ho Chi Minh Trail. China and the Soviet Union kept the Communists supplied with food and materiel. And the price was staggering. Again, bombing turned out to be perilous for the bombers as well as for the bombed. The North Vietnamese air defenses, augmented by Russian and Chinese support, turned out to be unexpectedly robust, and by the time Johnson ordered an end to the bombing, the United States had lost 818 airmen and 918 aircraft.

Michael Kelly   May 2002

staunch *stawnch*
steadfast; dependable; loyal

Liberia is the oldest republic in Africa, the only country on the continent never to have been a colony or part of an empire, a staunch American friend with the strongest possible cultural and financial ties to the United States. This is what makes Liberia's coup special. Few outsiders — especially those in the U.S. — thought it was possible for this sophisticated African political dynasty, so schooled in the ways of the West, to be overthrown.

Sanford J. Ungar   June 1981

steeped   *steept*
saturated; thoroughly soaked; imbued with

There are some men so blinded by partisan passion that they would rather see the nation remain in peril than see it delivered by a member of the other political party. But they are partisans, not Americans. There are some so steeped in class and caste prejudice that they would prefer to see Hitler lord of America than see American workmen gain another inch. But they are Tories, not Americans. There are some so eaten by avarice that they fear a dictator less than they fear the doctrine that property is not as sacred as the duty of the government to see that famine shall not slaughter the poor. But they are not even civilized men, much less Americans.

Gerald W. Johnson   October 1941

stellar   *STE luhr*
brightly shining; brilliant

John Coltrane died twenty years ago, on July 17, 1967, at the age of forty. In the years since, his influence has only grown, and the stellar avant-garde saxophonist has become a jazz legend of a stature shared only by Louis Armstrong and Charlie Parker.

Edward Strickland   December 1987

stickler   *STIK luhr*
a person who insists on something unyieldingly

Notwithstanding Whitman's fondness for coining words, and using many in uncommon fashions, he was, in a way, a great stickler for the correct use of certain words,— one of which was "paraphernalia," which he insisted could be correctly used only in reference to a bride's belongings or trousseau. We had many amusing discussions about words, and the best dictionary for final settlement of any vexed question, whether it should be Webster or Worcester. He used generally to say, "We will see what Booby says,"—his pet name for either dictionary; but he did not readily allow either one to settle any point.

Ellen M. Calder   June 1907

✳ Although Noah Webster's two-volume *American Dictionary of the English Language* (1825) sold out its first edition of 2,500 sets at $20 each, it was not profitable, and in 1829 he hired Joseph E. Worcester

(1784-1865) to create a one-volume abridgment. After the abridgment was published and selling well, Worcester brought out his own *Comprehensive Pronouncing and Explanatory Dictionary of the English Language* (1830). Webster accused him of plagiarism, Worcester refuted the charge, and the Dictionary War was on, the bitter feelings lasting until the lexicographers' deaths. For years, competition between the dictionaries was active, but after Webster's heirs sold the rights to his dictionary to G. & C. Merriam publishers, Worcester's sales diminished because of Merriam's vigorous marketing and promotion. When the copyright on Webster's 1806 dictionary expired in 1834, the "Webster's" name became public domain, and other publishers used it on their own dictionaries. In 1890 G. & C. Merriam itself added "Webster's" to its dictionary's title for the first time.

stricture *STRIK chuhr*
a limiting or restricting condition; a restraint

Whereas a wedding once provided young people with a moment of transformation so powerful that even a modestly funded event was a momentous one, nowadays — with marriage an iffy bet and with most betrothed couples having already helped themselves to all the liberties of adulthood — the only way to underline the moment is to put on an elaborate and costly show. Further, there were once measures of propriety that held wedding spending in check: no large weddings for second-timers, or older brides, or couples of differing religions, or the visibly pregnant, or cohabitating partners, or couples who would have to assume large debts to throw a lavish reception, or women whose sexual history was extensive and well known. But these strictures have all eroded. With clergymen and parents no longer the guardians of wedding rituals, that role has passed to retailers and party planners, who would happily marry a pair of baboons if someone was willing to foot the bill (indeed, the summer issue of *Martha Stewart Weddings* included "Tips for Making Your Favorite Furry or Feathered Friend a Part of the Festivities").

Caitlin Flanagan   November 2003

strident *STRIGH duhnt*
loud and harsh

By last fall Howard Dean had achieved the unlikely status of front-runner in the crowded race for the Democratic nomination. Yet for all his popularity, the public knew little about him. He built a following almost overnight, mainly because of his strident opposition to the Iraq War and a visceral anger toward the Bush Administration that other candidates were thought to lack.

Joshua Green   June 2004

studied   *STUH deed*
showing a conscious effort to appear natural; not spontaneous; affected; contrived

What I liked most about Camp David was its utter lack of formality. There was no protocol about dress, nor in the table-seating in the dining room, nor, indeed, in the manner of speech. We each received a blue windbreaker marked "Camp David" in letters of gold, and were told that we could dress as we pleased. President Carter wore a pair of faded blue jeans, Vance had on an oversized sweater, and the other Americans were equally casual. The Egyptians were more formal. Sadat may not have worn a tie but the rest of his attire was impeccable, and others in his delegation wore clothes of studied elegance.

Moshe Dayan   June 1981

stultifying   *STUHL tuh figh ing*
dulling to the mind or senses by being repetitive, tedious and boring

The glorious Greeks of antiquity simply refused to do disgusting and menial labor, and the work went undone. But we have become so devitalized that it seems there is no labor so deadly and stultifying but some one can be found to do it. The Greeks doubtless would have howled with mirth at the spectacle of a man spending all his daylight hours bobbing up and down in a little dark cage from the basement to the top-story of a building. And if it were not such a tragedy we might well stop occasionally and jeer at the elevator-boy ourselves. If it were not that this dreary labor is performed for the benefit of our comfortable classes by a member of what we call, with such unconscious self-satirization, the working-class, our sense of humor would not desert us so completely when we contemplate his activity.

Randolph S. Bourne   March 1914

suasion   *SWAY zhuhn*
the act of advising, urging or attempting to convince or persuade toward a desired end; persuasion intended to induce belief or action

Our empire spreads over Western civilization and establishes its dominion over politically self-respecting nations for whom foreign soldiers would represent insufferable badges of foreign rule, but who are able after a fashion to submit to imperial suasion as long as it is hid behind traditional banking ritual and commercial custom. We are the first empire of the world to establish our sway without legions. Our legions are dollars.

Reinhold Niebuhr   May 1930

sui generis   *SOO: ee JE nuh ris*
one of a kind; unique

Jerrold's first papers of mark in *Punch* were those signed "Q." His style was now formed, as his mind was, and these papers bear the stamp of his peculiar way of thinking and writing. Assuredly, his is a peculiar style in the strict sense; and as marked as that of Carlyle or Dickens. You see the self-made man in it, — a something sui generis, — not formed on the "classical models," but which has grown up with a kind of twist in it, like a tree that has had to force its way up surrounded by awkward environments.

James Hannay   November 1857

sullen   *SUH lin*
showing ill humor by morose, unsociable withdrawal; resentfully silent; brooding

> Little Jack Horner sat in a corner
> Eating his Christmas pie.
> He put in his thumb and pulled out a plum,
> And said, "What a good boy am I!"

Obviously a picture of a **sullen** and inhibited child, who, conscious of his own greediness and execrable table manners, soothes himself with dangerous self-laudation. Students of the subject are undecided, but it is not unlikely that there is a sinister political suggestion in the approval expressed at the obtaining of the plum in a manner which openly defies convention.

Bergen Evans   December 1934

✽ See also avarice, delectation, engender and obviate for other
   passages in which Bergen Evans provides his tongue-in-cheek
   analyses of nursery rhymes.

sumptuous   *SUHMP choo: uhs*
magnificent; splendid; lavish; suggesting great expense

In a bid to get New York City to allow its streets to be torn up for the laying of electrical cables, Edison invited the entire city council out to Menlo Park at dusk. He directed the aldermen up a narrow staircase in the dark, and as they grumbled and fumbled their way, he clapped his hands. On came a flood of lights, illuminating a lavishly set dining hall complete with a **sumptuous** feast catered by Delmonico's, then New York's premier restaurant.

Kathleen McAuliffe   December 1995

✴ Delmonico's, opened first as a candy shop and bakery in 1827, became America's first true restaurant in 1830, a public dining room where patrons ordered from a menu. (It closed in 1923, but other restaurants use the name.) In 1876 Ben Wenberg, a sea captain who dined often at Delmonico's, brought chef Charles Ranhofer a recipe for a dish he had enjoyed in South America. The immediately popular dish was named Lobster à la Wenberg, but after Wenberg quarreled with Ranhofer a few months later, the dish appeared on the menu with a mutated version of Wenberg's name. Lobster Newburg had arrived.

supercilious   *soo: per SI lee uhs*
feeling or showing haughty disdain or contemptuous superiority toward someone ("superciliousness" is the noun)

Many otherwise brilliant teachers fail because they lack patience. They expect all their pupils to seize the point after the first explanation; they even somewhat resent having to repeat what seems to them a very simple postulate. It is so easy, from a position of superior knowledge or appreciation, to develop unconsciously an attitude verging on superciliousness.

Claude M. Fuess   October 1932

superfluous   *suh PER floo: uhs*
not needed; unnecessary; irrelevant

Having little use for kings, our Founding Fathers nonetheless knew that monarchy's main virtue is assured continuity. The Roman republic, which was the best model they had in 1787, was at last brought down by civil struggles over succession. So the Founding Fathers invented and gave a Latin title to the office of Vice President. But Ben Franklin suggested he might better be addressed as "Your Superfluous Excellency."

Gerald Ford   July 1974

superlative   *suh PER luh tiv*
a word denoting the highest degree of some quality or attribute

Iceland is a place that seems to generate both superlatives and a people with an appetite for documenting them. Everywhere a visitor goes, he meets statistical boasts and curiosities. Reykjavik is the world's northernmost capital. Its average winter temperature is higher than New York City's. Iceland contains Europe's largest glacier, Vatnajokull, which is as big as Rhode Island and Delaware combined. Iceland was the last country in Europe to be settled.

Brad Leithauser   September 1987

supplant   *suh PLANT*
to forcefully put in place of something else

What, then, is the work before Congress? It is to save the people of the South from themselves, and the nation from detriment on their account. Congress must supplant the evident sectional tendencies of the South by national dispositions and tendencies. It must cause national ideas and objects to take the lead and control the politics of those States. It must cease to recognize the old slave-masters as the only competent persons to rule the South. In a word, it must enfranchise the negro, and by means of the loyal negroes and the loyal white men of the South build up a national party there, and in time bridge the chasm between North and South, so that our country may have a common liberty and a common civilization.

Frederick Douglass   January 1867

supplicant   *SUHP luh kint*
a petitioner

Lobbyists should be denied access to the Capitol. Of course lobbyists are not all sinister; most are simply doing their job. But the number of supplicants gathered round to demand handouts makes it difficult for congressmen to think clearly. Imagine lobbyists for parties in a lawsuit allowed in to see the judge — how credible would his decision be? And having lobbyists crowd outside the chambers of the House and Senate, flashing thumb signs to congressmen like coaches issuing orders to Little Leaguers, is a national disgrace.

Gregg Easterbrook   December 1984

surmise   *ser MIGHZ*
to think or infer without strong evidence; form a notion of on slight proof;
conjecture; guess

There is nothing more bewitching than to have an agreeable woman discover that you are a genius — especially when you have already surmised it yourself.

Gamaliel Bradford   February 1931

sustain   *suh STAYN*
to maintain or prolong; keep up

We cannot sustain the unsustainable. Nor can we finance the unfinanceable. By 2013, when Baby Boomers will be retiring en masse, the annual surplus of Social Security tax revenues over outlays will turn negative. By 2030, when all the Boomers will have reached sixty-five, Social Security alone will be running an annual cash deficit of $766 billion. If Medicare Hospital Insurance is included, and if both programs continue according to current law, the combined cash deficit that year will be $1.7 trillion.

Peter G. Peterson   May 1996

svelte *svelt*
slender and graceful; slim

While we work furiously to pare our waistlines, what are our Russian counterparts doing? One need look no further than the photographs in the daily newspaper. While our svelte first family cavorts energetically about the White House lawns, in what shape do we find the wily Russian Premier and his wife? The answer to this question, however simple, is revealing: round!

John Crawford   October 1962

swath *swahth*
a long strip

Unlike heroin or cocaine, which must be imported, anywhere from a quarter to half of the marijuana used in this country is grown here as well. Although popular stereotypes depict marijuana growers as aging hippies in northern California or Hawaii, the majority of the marijuana now cultivated in the United States is being grown in the nation's midsection — a swath running roughly from the Appalachians west to the Great Plains.

Eric Schlosser   August 1994

sway *sway*
influence or control

The custom of sending young women of the middle class to reside for a time in the houses of the nobility was an ancient one, and seems to have obtained both in France and England. Perhaps the position of maid of honor may be considered a remnant of this curious habit. Still, the idea was no stranger than the modern plan of sending girls to herd together in boarding-schools, under the imperfect sway of a directress who has neither time nor ability to study the individual characters of her charges.

L. D. Morgan   October 1889

sycophant *SIK uh fant*
a person who seeks favor by flattering people of wealth or influence; toady

Pakistan has never been well governed. After the military fought its catastrophic war with India in 1971, hopes were placed on the new democratic leader, Zulfikar Ali

Bhutto, a wealthy landlord from Sind. But Bhutto turned out to be a divisive populist who sowed fear with his security service and surrounded himself with sycophants.

Robert D. Kaplan   September 2000

synopsis *suh NAHP sis*
a condensed version; summary

Almost every New Zealander lives within sight of the mountains or the ocean, or both. The landscapes show long ranges and solitary giants, tipped with alpine glow; there are waterfalls everywhere, some of them among the finest in the world, luxuriant countryside, golden farms, lakes, geysers, volcanoes, forests with miles of pink, white, and red flowering trees in spring; and there are fiords of the sea threading their way around the feet of mountains crowned with glaciers and perpetual snow. The scenery is a synopsis of the best of Norway, Switzerland, Italy, and England, with occasional patches of the Desert of Sahara in the pumice country around the hot lakes.

Henry Demarest Lloyd   December 1899

syzygy *SI zuh jee*
in astronomy, the alignment of three bodies of the solar system along a straight or nearly straight line; here used figuratively to mean a rare conjunction of two stellar figures: Greek, syzygos, *yoked together*

1811-1812. A rich autumn of grape harvesting, of golden forests and red sunset skies. The last but two symphonies and the last violin sonata. Lovely declining days and latter-day loves. And the encounter of two suns, Beethoven and Goethe. It was a brief meeting. For centuries the Fates had been preparing the syzygy of these two stars in the firmament of poetry and music. The hour arrives, and the hour passes; their paths have crossed, and each has gone his way. We must wait another thousand years before such an event can occur again. How I envy those who saw them. I even borrow the eyes off such people, and imagine that I too can see the slumbering images of these men reflected as in a pool.

Romain Rolland   February 1929

T

trope

The United States will never have a true national curriculum (besides *Jeopardy!*), and there will never again be a generation capable of replying "Polk," "Lillie Langtry," "2,005," "Rutherford B. Hayes's," and "Marseilles" to those questions from Go to the Head of the Class. But it probably makes sense to designate a dozen or so things that every American should know. I'm hardly an expert, but my short list would include: the difference between Theodore and Franklin, and between Joe and Eugene; the significance of Booth, Guiteau, Czolgosz, and Oswald; the meaning of the term "tax event"; the price of gasoline in other industrialized countries; the infield-fly rule; how to tell time on a nondigital watch; the custom that people be allowed off an elevator before others get on; the convention that when walking you keep to the right; the fact that a dozen specimens of a single species don't count as one item for Express Lane purposes; and the fact that the now universal linguistic trope "No problem" is not synonymous with "You're welcome."

Cullen Murphy   February 2001

see page 437

tandem *TAN duhm*
one along with the other; together

Respect for the government and respect for the news media have declined in tandem. More and more the two appear to the public to be an undifferentiated establishment — a new Leviathan — composed of rich, famous, powerful people who are divorced from the lives of ordinary people and indifferent to their concerns.

Jonathan Schell   August 1996

✽ In speaking of a "new Leviathan," Jonathan Schell is alluding to the *Leviathan* of Thomas Hobbes (1588-1679), a treatise published in 1651 that asserted that to keep men from anarchy, or from constantly warring against one another, they must agree to be ruled by an absolute monarch or body who will keep the peace and rule them fairly. Hobbes called that overarching state leviathan, alluding to a huge sea creature in the Bible (Isaiah 27:1; Job 41:1; Psalms 104.26). The word is from the Hebrew and means, literally, "that which gathers itself together in folds." Today, by extension, leviathan can mean anything huge and formidable, in comparison with others of its kind.

tatterdemalion *TA ter di MAYL yuhn*
torn and ragged: originally, a person in tattered clothing; ragamuffin

Transylvania presents visitors with none of the logistical hurdles encountered in the hardscrabble lands to its east. Trains go almost everywhere, and tickets cost roughly two dollars an hour for first-class travel (first-class Romanian-style, that is, with tatterdemalion but comfortably upholstered compartments and equally tatterdemalion but solicitous attendants).

Jeffrey Tayler   June 1997

taut   *tawt*
tightly controlled; crisply executed; firm

> Beethoven: Nine Symphonies, Four Overtures (Toscanini, NBC Symphony: RCA Victrola VIC-8000). Lots of the young bloods tend to pooh-pooh Toscanini's taut, no-nonsense approach, but anyone knowing of a more intense and exciting Beethoven package than this is welcome to it.
>
> Herbert Kupferberg   June 1968

tawdry   *TAW dree*
cheap and showy; gaudy; sleazy

> I hold no brief for Hollywood. I have worked there a little over two years, which is far from enough to make me an authority, but more than enough to make me feel pretty thoroughly bored. That should not be so. The making of a picture ought surely to be a rather fascinating adventure. It is not; it is an endless contention of tawdry egos, some of them powerful, almost all of them vociferous, and almost none of them capable of anything much more creative than credit-stealing and self-promotion.
>
> Raymond Chandler   November 1945

taxonomy   *tak SAH nuh mee*
classification

> "What Every American Needs to Know" was the subtitle of *Cultural Literacy* (1987), a work that has now been through several best-selling versions. Here, in a few hundred pages, E. D. Hirsch Jr. and his disciples sought to establish an entire taxonomy of core knowledge — the thousands of dates, names, facts, ideas, and expressions that an educated person can't be seen without: 1066, 1914, Tolstoy, Ellison, Giotto, Jack Sprat, "In the beginning," flapper, uncertainty principle, zeitgeist.
>
> Cullen Murphy   March 2003

teleology   *tee lee AH luh jee*
the study of signs of evidences of design or purpose in the universe

> Although man would fain project a humanity and a teleology upon Nature and thus make her intelligible, would make her yield some support for his emotions, his morality, and his spiritual life, in reality there are no correspondences of this kind in Nature herself.
>
> Paul F. Laubenstein   February 1928

template   *TEM playt*
a pattern to follow

More than any other poet, Longfellow furnished Americans with a template for what poetry was supposed to be: uplifting, patriotic, exotic, dramatic.

Peter Davison   February 2001

✱ A Longfellow poem that many people know by heart is one that few know he wrote:

> There was a little girl, who had a little curl,
> Right in the middle of her forehead.
> When she was good, she was very good indeed,
> But when she was bad she was horrid.

Longfellow's second son, Ernest, explained that "it was while walking up and down with his second daughter, then a baby in his arms, that my father composed and sang to her the well-known lines. Many people think this a Mother-Goose rhyme, but this is the true version and history."

temporize   *TEM puh righz*
to agree or comply temporarily, or evade immediate decision, in order to gain time or avoid argument

India's fear of provoking China is apparent in the way it treats Tibetan refugees. While refusing aid from the United Nations High Commission for Refugees and assuming full responsibility, it has temporized and muddled along with makeshift programs which are no solution to what is obviously a long-term problem. For, unless some other government invites them, the Tibetans are in India to stay.

Bradford Smith   June 1961

tender   *TEN duhr*
to present for acceptance; offer

A few weeks ago emissaries from the game show *Jeopardy!* swept through a quadrant of rural Connecticut, chumming for contestants, and one of my sisters signed up for a quiz. She did pretty well, though she wasn't tendered an invitation. Afterward, at a family gathering, we fielded some of the questions. Hamlet's mother and father? City in South Africa reminiscent of flowers? French word for a newborn's wardrobe? Battle where Cervantes lost the use of his hand? I would like to report that we shouted as one, "Gertrude and Hamlet!" "Bloemfontein!" "Layette!" and "Lepanto!" In truth, we presented a pathetic spectacle of mumbled feints and embarrassed glances.

Cullen Murphy   February 2001

tentative   *TEN tuh tiv*
uncertain; hesitant

I spent my island time idly, listening to the huge eleven-foot-high tides bubble and trickle away across mud flats and observing a tentative raccoon tiptoe out to teach her kits how to dig clams and sea worms while the cove was empty.

Peter Davison   May 1997

terra firma   *TE ruh FER muh*
solid ground

Civilization has been called a dance, but the feet of the dancers do not rest upon terra firma. It is danced upon a tight rope that sways in the breeze. The nerves and muscles of the performers are tense. They wave reckless defiance to the force of gravity, but they are in truth ill equipped for the airy stunt.

Joseph Wood Krutch   December 1927

testament   *TES tuh mint*
tangible proof or evidence

Toward the end of his life the novelist A. B. Guthrie Jr. would peer at the Rocky Mountains through the double picture window of his secluded Montana cabin and fume over the costs of progress. Behind him, on a wall of his second-floor loft study, hung testaments to the celebrated western writer: the Cowboy Hall of Fame certificate recognizing Guthrie as a charter member, the 1950 Pulitzer Prize for *The Way West*, the Academy Award screenwriting nomination for *Shane*. In front of him, though, Bud Guthrie saw a chronicle of decline. Ear Mountain still towered in the distance, but the fields and streams surrounding his boyhood home of Choteau, Montana, had changed, and the land that Guthrie had memorably dubbed "Big Sky" country seemed smaller.

David Whitman   September 2000

throttle   *THRAH tuhl*
to halt the action or utterance of; censor or suppress: literally, choke or strangle

It has yet to be shown that appropriate qualities in consumers' goods prevail in any system where consumer choice is not entirely free, or in other words where producers and distributors are not compelled to compete for consumer patronage by some degree of appeal to quality. Any kind of monopoly which tends to throttle consumer choice or limits it to a single product of a given line of goods is destructive of the necessary motive for production of high and continuously improving quality.

J. B. Matthews   December 1936

timorous *TIM uh ris*
fearful; timid; hesitant

> Mere obedience to law does not measure the greatness of a nation. It can easily be obtained by a strong executive, and most easily of all from a timorous people. Nor is the license of behavior which so often accompanies the absence of law, and which is miscalled liberty, a proof of greatness. The true test is the extent to which the individuals can be trusted to obey self-imposed law.

> John Fletcher Moulton   July 1924

tintinnabulation *tin ti na byoo LAY shuhn*
the ringing sound of bells

> *Strauss: "Also Sprach Zarathustra." Herbert von Karajan conducting Vienna Philharmonic Orchestra; Willi Boskovsky, solo violin; London CS-6129 (stereo).* I do not care as much as I once did for Strauss's immensely scored Zoroaster-Nietzsche oratory, but no one can deny that it makes a wonderful exercise in high fidelity, from the organ snore at the start to the great gonging at the end. I attended the sessions when this version was made by John Culshaw's demonic London engineers. They rented a 2500-pound church bell from a Vienna foundry for the penultimate passage. They also had to hire five men to play it: one to hit it with a sledge, four (in white coats, like hospital orderlies) to leap in and hug it, so it would stop vibrating. The orchestra could not help laughing whenever this happened, but they were able to muffle their mirth with handkerchiefs, so naught went amiss. Karajan, a sound enthusiast himself, got more and more exultant as the taping progressed, and you will see why when, and if, you hear the record. This is about the most tintinnabulation that modern science can give to the listener for five dollars.

> John M. Conly   December 1959

tonic *TAH nik*
an invigorating, refreshing or stimulating influence

> I know of no tonic more useful for a young writer than to read carefully, in the English reviews of sixty or seventy years ago, the crushing criticisms on nearly every author of that epoch who has achieved lasting fame.

> Thomas Wentworth Higginson   December 1867

torpedo *tawr PEE doh*
to destroy; wreck

> Many academics now admit that they engaged in tactical understatement about human-rights abuses in China, because they knew from the example of those

unlucky few who had had their careers torpedoed that China would shut them out, and possibly harrass, imprison, torture, or even execute their Chinese friends.

Lynn Chu   October 1990

totem   *TOH tuhm*
something regarded as a symbol and treated with the kind of respect normally reserved for religious icons

From behind every counter and every desk in every store and office the dour image of "His Excellency Daniel T. arap Moi, C.G.H., M.P., President of the Republic of Kenya and Commander-in-Chief of the Armed Forces," stares impassively into the middle distance. The portrait is a mandatory totem of loyalty. President Moi, who succeeded Kenya's first President, Jomo Kenyatta, in 1978, personifies the rottenness of the Kenyan state. Surrounded by parasites and sycophants, Moi long ago proved himself a shrewd master of Big Man politics: tough enough to crack heads when necessary, he more often adroitly manipulates the flow of cash as the conduit of power.

Bill Berkeley   February 1996

touchstone   *TUHCH stohn*
a basis for comparison; a reference point against which other things can be evaluated: from a type of hard, smooth, black stone formerly used to test the purity of gold or silver by the streak left on it when it was rubbed with the metal

When power leads man towards arrogance, poetry reminds him of his limitations. When power narrows the areas of man's concern, poetry reminds him of the richness and diversity of his existence. When power corrupts, poetry cleanses, for art establishes the basic human truths which must serve as the touchstones of our judgment.

John Fitzgerald Kennedy   February 1964

The first American draft took from a little village in Vermont seventeen of her sons. Before they went away to the wars, thirteen of those boys had never slept a night away from home in all their lives. It is not within the bounds of possibility that the intervening years should leave those boys unchanged. Life in the Vermont village must forever afterward be judged from a different angle. It must be tested on the touchstone of Château-Thierry and the Argonne Forest, which is of sterner stuff than the innocuous domesticities of the daily round in the Green Mountains. Which is the real world, which is the better world, may be an open question; but for those homecoming men, and for those who welcome them, there must be, in the years immediately to come, the consciousness and the collision of two very different worlds in place of the former platitude of one world.

Willard L. Sperry   March 1919

traffic *TRA fik*
to trade in something illegal or improper

Most writers have more intelligence and knowledge of the world than to suppose it is wholly made up of nastiness, and they avoid or touch lightly the subjects in which Zola revels. Moreover, a number of them would hesitate to traffic on the morbid curiosity of the world about vice, and would be ashamed to pander to lickerish inquisitiveness. Zola has no such hesitation; he laughs at it, as the big boy laughs at the little boy who is averse to swearing, and he brands his opponents as milksops, the evident inference being that he is the only manly writer living.

Thomas Perry Sergeant   May 1880

tranche *trahnsh*
a portion; share; installment: French, a slice

In the early 1970s I was working at The New Statesman, in London, very near the Public Record Office, when a fresh tranche of Churchill's wartime papers was released. These covered the discussions between Churchill ("Premier," as the official papers called him) and Stalin about the future of postwar Eastern Europe.

Christopher Hitchens   April 2002

transfuse *tranz FYOO:Z*
to transfer, pass or pour from one thing into another; permeate

Personally, I believe that a composer, when creating a work, transfuses it not only with his musical power, but also with the entire meaning of his life — the essence of his being.

Serge Koussevitzky   August 1948

transitory *TRAN zuh taw ree*
having a brief life; temporary; fleeting; ephemeral

There is a new, profound reason why U.S. interests in Central America are permanent, not transitory: the United States is becoming a Caribbean nation. The character of American society is being subtly reshaped by the most enormous influx of migrants from a single region since the turn of the century, when nearly 9 million people arrived from Southern and Eastern Europe.

Robert A. Pastor   July 1982

transmute *tranz MYOO:T*
to change from one form into another

In a society like ours, where every man may transmute his private thought into history and destiny by dropping it into the ballot-box, a peculiar responsibility rests upon the individual. Nothing can absolve us from doing our best to look at all public questions as citizens, and therefore in some sort as administrators and rulers.

James Russell Lowell   October 1860

trifle *TRIGH fuhl*
to treat with a lack of due seriousness or respect

Owen Wister wrote *The Virginian* over fifty years ago, a romantic novel of the wild West which won instant success and skyrocketed its author to fame. For the first time, a cowboy was a gentleman and hero, but nobody realized then that it was the master design and that thousands of Westerns would be modeled on it. Before this, cowboys had been depicted as murderous thugs. The Virginian was utterly different from the heroes of his day; besides being handsome, he was humorous and human. He got drunk, played practical jokes, and showed you could not trifle with him — in that famous phrase, "When you call me that, *smile!*" Because of *The Virginian*, all the little boys wear ten-gallon hats and carry toy pistols. This one novel set the tradition of the West permanently.

Fanny Kemble Wister   May 1955

tripe *trighp*
something of no value; nonsense; rubbish

Of course most motion pictures are bad. Why wouldn't they be? Apart from its own intrinsic handicaps of excessive cost, hypercritical bluenosed censorship, and the lack of any single-minded controlling force in the making, the motion picture is bad because 90 per cent of its source material is tripe, and the other 10 per cent is a little too virile and plain-spoken for the putty-minded clerics, the elderly ingénues of the women's clubs, and the tender guardians of that godawful mixture of boredom and bad manners known more eloquently as the Impressionable Age.

Raymond Chandler   March 1948

✻ Tripe is the name given to the lining of the first and second stomachs of cattle, sheep and other ruminants when used as food. As a food name, tripe would seem to be more appetizing to the ear — and the mind's eye — than small intestines or stomach. The *Oxford English Dictionary* traces tripe and chitterlings (another term for small intestines as food) as far back as the 13th century, and sweetbreads (the thymus gland and pancreas) back to the 16th century, indications that innards by any other name are more appealing to ear, eye and mind, and have been for centuries. And yet, why are there no culinary euphemisms for brains, kidneys, tongue, heart and liver? In the butcher's trade, these organs, as well as the tails, feet and head of a slaughtered animal, are known as offal.

troglodyte   *TRAH gluh dight*
a caveman

In my youth a librarian was thought to be a guardian of books, a master of cataloging, a collector of petty fines, a troglodyte dwelling within grey Carnegie walls. The new generation of librarians believe that their primary function is to stimulate reading. The library today has been transformed into a cultural center, operating under a creed set forth by Lawrence Clark Powell as simply as this: "that books are basic and that people are good, and that to work with them is the best of all lives."

Edward Weeks   March 1959

trope   *trohp*
a figure of speech

The United States will never have a true national curriculum (besides *Jeopardy!*), and there will never again be a generation capable of replying "Polk," "Lillie Langtry," "2,005," "Rutherford B. Hayes's," and "Marseilles" to those questions from Go to the Head of the Class. But it probably makes sense to designate a dozen or so things that every American should know. I'm hardly an expert, but my short list would include: the difference between Theodore and Franklin, and between Joe and Eugene; the significance of Booth, Guiteau, Czolgosz, and Oswald; the meaning of the term "tax event"; the price of gasoline in other industrialized countries; the infield-fly rule; how to tell time on a nondigital watch; the custom that people be allowed off an elevator before others get on; the convention that when walking you keep to the right; the fact that a dozen specimens of a single species don't count as one item for Express Lane purposes; and the fact that the now universal linguistic trope "No problem" is not synonymous with "You're welcome."

Cullen Murphy   February 2001

truckle   *TRUH kuhl*
to yield to the wishes or the will of another; to act in a subservient manner
("truckler" is the noun)

Everybody talks well when he talks in the way he likes, the way he can't help, the way he never thinks of: the rest is effort and pretense. The man who says "trousers" because he likes to say it, and the man who says "pants" because he likes to say it, are both good fellows with whom a frank soul could fraternize; but the man who says "trousers" when he wants to say "pants" is a craven and a truckler, equally hateful to honest culture and wholesome ignorance. He belongs in the same sordid category with the man who wears tight shoes and high collars that are a torment to the flesh, who eats olives that he doesn't relish and drinks uncongenial clarets, in imitation of his genteel neighbor in the brown-stone front.

Contributors' Club: Oscar W. Firkins   February 1908

truculent   *TRUH kyuh luhnt*
disposed to fight; fierce; pugnacious

Ann Bonny was born in Cork. She was of a truculent disposition, and the murdering part of piracy was much to her taste. When her husband was led out to execution, the special favor was granted of an interview with her; but her only benediction was, — "I'm sorry to find ye in this state; if ye had fought like a man, ye would not be seein' yerself hung like a dog."

John Weiss   September 1862

trumpet   *TRUHM pit*
to proclaim proudly and widely

Upon its discovery, in 1930, scientists trumpeted that Pluto was about as large as Earth. By the 1960s textbooks were listing it as having a diameter about half that of Earth. In 1978 astronomers discovered that Pluto has a relatively large moon, whose brightness had been mistakenly lumped in with the planet's: when this was taken into account, Pluto was left with a diameter about a sixth that of Earth, or less than half that of Mercury — long considered the runt of the solar system. Seven moons in the solar system are bigger than Pluto.

David H. Freedman   February 1998

truncate   *TRUHN kayt*
to shorten or diminish by cutting off a part; mutilate

We are erotic and emotional animals, and when we react most fully to people, we react to them erotically and emotionally. We react this way to teachers and to students; to pop stars and to politicians; to interns, novelists, and waiters; to our elders and our juniors. It is a part of what allows us to relate to human beings across the social, political, and cultural spectrums. To demonize this responsiveness is to truncate our sensibility, our humanity.

Cristina Nehring   July/August 2005

tutelary   *TOO: tuh le ree*
watching over or safeguarding

Traditionally, Henry James has been placed slightly higher up the slope of Parnassus than Edith Wharton. But now that the prejudice against the female writer is on the wane, they look to be exactly what they are: giants, equals, the tutelary and benign gods of our American literature.

Gore Vidal   February 1978

twaddle   *TWAH duhl*
trivial, silly or tedious talk or writing; idle chatter; nonsense

I must say that the perpetual declaration on the 'woman's page' of modern periodicals that 'every woman should know how to cook a meal, and make her own clothes, and feed a baby' fills me with scorn unutterable. But then for that matter the mere fact of a 'woman's page' fills me with scorn. Why not a 'man's page,' with a miscellany of twaddle, labeled as exclusively, adapted to the masculine intellect?

Mary Leal Harkness   March 1914

tyro   *TIGH roh*
a beginner; novice

Reagan comes on stage moving his hands as if he were dribbling two basketballs simultaneously, apparently embarrassed by the applause. Then the shoulders come back, the chin rises, and the head bobbles as he speaks, habitual bits of body language learned at Warner Brothers that still translate into sincerity and good will. He is a professional political neophyte, the eternal tyro, and the best there is.

James Conaway   October 1980

unexpurgated

Even to-day there may be parents who would doubt the wisdom of
allowing a girl of fifteen the free run of a large and quite
unexpurgated library. But my father allowed it. There were certain
facts — very briefly, very shyly, he referred to them. Yet "read what
you like," he said, and all his books, "mangy and worthless," as he
called them, but certainly they were many and various, were to be
had without asking. To read what one liked because one liked it,
never to pretend to admire what one did not — that was his only
lesson in the art of reading.

Virginia Woolf   March 1950

see page 445

unaffected *uhn uh FEK tid*
not phoney or artificial; natural; sincere; genuine

Good writing owes its merit chiefly to little words, to light touches, to simple graces, to pungent idioms and a clean handling of the smaller parts of speech; lies in the set of a phrase, the hang of a sentence; belongs to those who have an unforced, unaffected way with language, a sensitive ear, a feeling for occasion.

Louis Kronenberger   September 1965

unalienable *uhn AY lee uh nuh buhl*
that which cannot be taken away: a still-current variation on "inalienable"

Perhaps the United States will emerge from the war on terrorism more powerful and influential than before. Perhaps it will continue the task that occupied it for so much of the twentieth century: spreading the gospel of the Declaration of Independence — the idea that all human beings (and not just a few lucky ones in North America and Western Europe) are born with certain unalienable rights.

David Brooks   April 2002

unassailable *uhn uh SAI luh buhl*
not open to adverse criticism

The Stoics, who proposed that men should practice virtue without compensation, were logically unassailable, but not persuasive to the average mind. It does not take much perspicuity to distinguish between an agreeable and a disagreeable happening, and once the difference is perceived, no argument can make them equally acceptable.

Agnes Repplier   June 1920

unbecoming   *uhn bee KUH ming*
not appropriate or suited to one's appearance or position, or what is expected of one; unseemly

> Hemingway was capable of great interest in and generosity toward younger writers and some older writers, but as he shows in *A Moveable Feast* (written in 1957-1959 and finished in the spring of 1961), he had a curious and **unbecoming** compulsion to poke and peck at the reputations of many of his literary contemporaries. Gertrude Stein, Sherwood Anderson, T. S. Eliot, not to mention Fitzgerald, Wolfe, Ford Madox Ford, James Gould Cozzens, and others, were invariably good for a jab or two if their names came up.

> Robert Manning   August 1965

uncanny   *uhn KA nee*
so remarkable as to seem to be supernatural or unexplainable; extraordinary ("uncannily" is the adverb)

> Fourteen years before the sinking of the *Titanic*, an obscure author published an **uncannily** prophetic novel entitled *Futility*. He invented a fabulous Atlantic liner, the *Titan*, almost identical in specifications with the *Titanic*; he loaded it with wealthy and complacent passengers; and he wrecked it on an iceberg on a cold night in April.

> Charles J. Rolo   January 1956

unconscionable   *uhn KAHN shuh nuh buhl*
not guided by conscience; unscrupulous; unjust; outrageously wrong

> Eighteen death-penalty states lack statewide public-defender organizations, and many of those that have them underfund them so seriously that lawyers end up handling huge caseloads that would be considered **unconscionable**, to say nothing of impractical, in the private sector. Most public defenders are so poorly paid that many talented lawyers tend to shy away from this sort of practice.

> Alan Berlow   November 1999

unctuous   *UHNK choo: is*
unpleasantly and excessively suave or ingratiating in manner or speech; showing affected, exaggerated or insincere earnestness

> It would be impossible to suffer acutely from boredom — we have here a contradiction in terms. True boredom causes a dull, grayish-hued misery that has nothing of pain's positive, colorful, capricious, anguished surprises. There are none of these in store for the genuinely bored person. He is like a man in a room with hermetically

sealed windows, breathing air that has been used over and over again. One doomed to listen endlessly to the unctuous, buttery voice of a radio announcer would know something of the same quality of hopeless despair.

James Norman Hall   March 1933

undertone   *UHN der tohn*
an underlying element; undercurrent

The bold, seemingly inexorable experiment that is Communist China, with all its strengths, has permanent undertones of weakness. The forced pace of economic expansion, falling most heavily on the sectors of agriculture and light industry, has prevented any considerable rise in individual living standards. Today, basic foods and clothing are still severely rationed, and the refugees that escape constantly into Hong Kong tell stories of chronic undernourishment, food queues, and general shortage of goods.

Tillman Durdin   December 1959

undulate   *UHN juh layt*
to have a wavy form or surface ("undulating" is the adjective)

Summer after summer we marveled at the miracle of our vineyard in Provence as the undulating slopes turned from grubby brown to a broadloom of tender green.

Mary Roblee Henry   May 1969

unexpurgated   *uhn EKS per gay tid*
having no objectionable material removed

Even to-day there may be parents who would doubt the wisdom of allowing a girl of fifteen the free run of a large and quite unexpurgated library. But my father allowed it. There were certain facts — very briefly, very shyly, he referred to them. Yet "read what you like," he said, and all his books, "mangy and worthless," as he called them, but certainly they were many and various, were to be had without asking. To read what one liked because one liked it, never to pretend to admire what one did not — that was his only lesson in the art of reading.

Virginia Woolf   March 1950

unfathomable   *uhn FA th:uhm uh buhl*
impossible to completely understand or penetrate; incomprehensible

Three things are as unfathomable as they are fascinating to the masculine mind: metaphysics; golf; and the feminine heart. The Germans, I believe, pretend to have solved some of the riddles of the first, and the French to have unraveled some of the intricacies of the last; will some one tell us wherein lies the extraordinary fascination of Golf?

Arnold Haultain   July 1904

unfettered   *uhn FE tuhrd*
free from restraint; unhampered or unhindered; not held back

It was by the merest chance that I fell into teaching. Possibly that is why, unfettered by pedagogic traditions and theories, I was able to throw myself unprejudiced into the life of the children and of the community, there to find adventure and happiness.

Benjamin Harrison Chaffee   October 1925

unflagging   *uhn FLA ging*
continuing at the same level; unfading; untiring; undiminished

A second marriage, as Samuel Johnson observed, represents "the triumph of hope over experience." The experience of marriage is one of conflict between ideals: the ideal of loving companionship and that of erotic intensity; the ideal of unflagging devotion to a single person and that of emotional responsiveness to many. And yet some of these ideals are not as irreconcilable — or as irreconcilable with marriage — as they appear. Unshakable loyalty to a central partner does not preclude passionate responses to other people. If it seems that way, it is only because of the puritanism, the pious emotional parsimony, of our American era.

Cristina Nehring   July/August 2005

unflinching   *uhn FLINCH ing*
not yielding or shrinking; resolute; steadfast; unwavering

Because of her unflinching candor and honesty Emily Dickinson was obliged to discard the conventions of Victorian verse and to search for ways of expressing aspects of truth that were not contemplated in the Victorian compromise. Hence she belongs with Emerson, Thoreau, Hawthorne, Melville, and Whitman, the group of nineteenth-century authors who carried on in this country bolder experiments in expressing "an original relation to the universe" than other writers in English were attempting.

George F. Whiche   February 1946

❊ The Victorian compromise was the attempt by poets, writers, philosophers and clergy in 19th-century England and America to express spirituality in ways that would keep religious values alive in the midst of a world where science and industry were making life easier, and society more materialistic.

unguarded   *uhn GAHR did*
open; natural; frank; vulnerable

Garland's concert performances were so intimate and **unguarded** that listeners believed she was singing for them individually.

Michael Joseph Gross   August 2000

unmindful   *uhn MIGHND fuhl*
ignorant or unaware of something one ought to know; failing to give due care or attention

Americans, traveled and untraveled, entertain to a remarkable degree a complacent view of their own country as contrasted with all others. With perfect equanimity they declaim against the wicked imperialism of European countries, **unmindful** of the fact that we have annexed territory more often and for less cause than any European nation.

H. H. Powers   February 1928

unregenerate   *uhn ruh JE nuh rit*
obstinate; unchangeable; unreformed; hopelessly bad

There may be inspired writers for whom the first draft is just right. But anyone who is not certifiably a Milton had better assume that the first draft is a very primitive thing. The reason is simple: Writing is difficult work. Ralph Paine, who managed *Fortune* in my time, used to say that anyone who said writing was easy was either a bad writer or an **unregenerate** liar.

John Kenneth Galbraith   March 1978

✳ John Kenneth Galbraith's original title for *The Affluent Society*, a book in which he urged the wiser use of America's wealth and the resetting of its economic and social priorities, was *Why People Are Poor*. In a May 1969 *Atlantic* article, Galbraith said he scrapped that title because it was "undescriptive," and a second title, *The Opulent Society*, because "opulence has a greasy, unattractive sound." He settled on *affluent* after finding it in his dictionary as a definition for *opulent*, but wondered "whether I could sell so dry a title to my publisher." In the book he also coined the term conventional wisdom, meaning ideas that are generally accepted by most people as true, though they may not be.

unrequited   *uhn ruh KWIGH tid*
not reciprocated or returned in kind

Robert Louis Stevenson is much admired by the French, not because he wrote *Treasure Island* or *Kidnapped*, or even *Dr. Jekyll and Mr. Hyde*, but because of a trip that resulted in his lesser-known work, *Travels With a Donkey*. In 1878, suffering from tuberculosis and unrequited love (the lady was married), Stevenson, then twenty-eight years old, spent twelve days trekking 125 miles through the mountainous regions of south central France. From the picturesque hills of the Velay, into the wilds of Gévaudan (only recently "deforested of wolves"), and across the Cévennes — 84,000 acres of sheer cliffs, gorges, waterfalls, rocky plateaus, and pine forests — he walked, his only companion a donkey named Modestine.

Jeanette Bruce   November 1978

unsettling   *uhn SET ling*
causing unease or insecurity; disturbing; upsetting; troubling

The burden of selling a book these days being on the author, a new and unsettling requirement is now added to the writer's already crowded identity. That is the need to be an entertainer. Novelists, biographers, historians, poets, and even those who prepare hardcover lists and dictionaries are endlessly crisscrossing the country in what has become known as the book promotion tour or, as it's called in the trade, the motor-mouth circuit

Caskie Stinnett   February 1978

unstinting   *uhn STIN ting*
with unhesitating generosity ("unstintingly" is the adverb)

Over seven thousand letters addressed to Chekov have been preserved. The Socio-Economic Publishing House has published excerpts from this mountain of mail and everywhere we meet that rarest of words: gratitude. "I am grateful for the money received." "I am grateful for helping me find work." "I am grateful for bothering about the passport." Nor could it have been otherwise. All Chekov's relations with people were like that: he took very little from them, usually nothing at all, but gave unstintingly and kept no record.

Kornei Chukovski   September 1947

unstrung   *uhn STRUHNG*
emotionally weakened or overwrought; unnerved

It is claimed that the nervous exhaustion produced by hours of sustained and monotonous labor sends the factory girl into the streets at night. She is too unstrung for rest. That this is in a measure true, no experienced worker will deny, because every experienced worker is familiar with the sensation. Every woman who has toiled for hours, whether with a sewing machine or a typewriter, whether with a needle or a pen, whether in an office or at home, has felt the nervous fatigue which does not crave rest but distraction, which makes her want to "go."

Agnes Repplier   September 1913

unsullied   *uhn SUH leed*
pure; pristine; untarnished

We need unsullied places. Somewhere in the mind's geography there must be a paradise, a place both beautiful and empty, where a man might dream of new beginnings. For the first Euopean explorer, all America was such a place; indeed, Columbus, coming to the mouth of the Orinoco, thought he had discovered one of the four rivers of Paradise and that the very Garden itself was upriver, an angel still standing at the gates, to be found by someone sufficiently bold.

Anthony Brandt   September 1981

untenable   *uhn TE nuh buhl*
incapable of being maintained or supported

Would we believe in Plath's poetry as much as we do had she not followed it with suicide? It's a distasteful question, and to answer it in the negative would seem to imply some untenable things: first, that she did well to kill herself, and second, that her poetry might not have made the grade without the violence in its history.

Cristina Nehring   April 2004

untrammeled   *uhn TRA muhld*
unconfined; unimpeded; unrestricted

The dominant spirit of the Enlightenment was one of skepticism toward all received truths and untrammeled free inquiry in the pursuit of knowledge. "Everything," Diderot enjoined in the great *Encyclopédie*, "must be examined, everything must be shaken up, without exception and without circumspection."

Merrill D. Peterson   December 1994

unwitting   *uhn WI ting*
unintentional; unaware

Artists and sculptors have collectively done a great, if unwitting, disservice to Winston Churchill. They have contrived to perpetuate a single aspect of his appearance and character, the "bulldog at bay," typifying a dogged and indomitable defiance in the face of heavy odds. But this aspect, characteristic as it is, is as incomplete as if he were always protrayed as Churchill the benign elder statesman, Churchill the painter, Churchill the humorist, Churchill the lover of children and animals.

John H. Peck   March 1965

upstage   *uhp STAYJ*
to draw attention to one person or event at the expense of another

We were preparing to boast quietly about the arrival of *The Atlantic*'s 115th birthday this month when the newspapers reported that Charlie Smith of Bartow, Florida, had just reached the age of 130. If an institution has to be upstaged on such an occasion, it may as well be upstaged by the likes of Mr. Smith. Born in Liberia and shanghaied aboard a slave ship, he was already fifteen and bound to a Texas slaveholder in November, 1857, when a group of abolition-minded New England literary men launched *The Atlantic Monthly*.

Robert Manning   November 1972

❋ Abducting men at seaports and forcing them to work aboard ships has no doubt existed worldwide since ancient times, but calling it being shanghaied began in the 1870s, when American sailors originated the term. Shanghai was a common destination for West Coast ships and about as far as one could be taken. Federal laws helped end the practice in the early years of the 20th century. So did the advent of the steamship, which required far less onboard labor than the sailing ship.

urchin   *ER chin*
a poor, ragged child

Before orphan asylums were common, orphaned, homeless, and neglected children, if they were not living, stealing, and begging on the streets, were housed, along with adults, primarily in almshouses, but also in workhouses and jails. The Victorian conviction that childhood was a time of innocence influenced attitudes toward destitute children. People came to believe that even street urchins could be rescued — removed to a better environment and turned into productive citizens.

Mary-Lou Weisman   July 1994

usurp   *yoo: SERP*
to seize or obtain power, property, position or rights in an unjust or illegal manner; to appropriate wrongfully

Stable government rests upon the confidence of the masses, and it follows that in America the masses must choose that government. The theory is that this Republic is "of the people, for the people, and by the people," and the practice should be made to conform to it. The prerogative, however, of naming the President has been usurped by nearly every convention, and the nominees rarely, if ever, represent the will of the parties. If the people can choose only between two men at an election, they have the right to say who those two men shall be. We have had a few able Presidents in the past, but it was in spite of, and not because of, the convention.

Oliver T. Morton   April 1884

utopia   *yoo: TOH pee uh*
a place where every aspect of life, society and government is ideal: from the imaginary island of Utopia in the book of that name by Sir Thomas More (1478-1535), who coined the name from the Greek ou, *not +* topos, *a place ("utopian" is the adjective)*

It is a cruel joke of history that in the twentieth century the passion for equality has been used to justify communist states in which everyone was reduced to an equality of poverty. Everyone, that is, except for a small number of politicians and celebrities and their families, who alone had access to good housing, good food, and good medicine. Egalitarianism is perhaps the aspect of utopian thinking that has been most discredited by the failure of communism.

Steven Weinberg   January 2000

uxorious   *uhk SAW ree uhs*
dotingly or submissively fond of a wife; devotedly attached to a wife

Mr. Wilson has always been an uxorious man. A more real partnership than that which exists between him and Mrs. Wilson it would be difficult to find. The President will not budge without his wife. In France, the trip to the devastated regions had to be postponed because Mrs. Wilson had sustained a slight injury to her foot and could not go.

Charles H. Grasty January 1920

vox populi

There is no democracy in culture and the
arts. In other words, the vox populi is
usually worth nothing. With rare
exceptions, the artists and cultural voices
that caught the public's fancy did not
survive. For the occasional genius

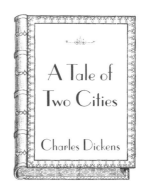

A Tale of
Two Cities

Charles Dickens

recognized in his lifetime, such as Dickens, there are always
scores who are ridiculed, if they are noticed at all.

John Simon   December 1978

see page 463

vacillate   *VA suh layt*
to show indecision; waver

Over the course of the past two hundred years Americans have vacillated between two great fears — fear of chaos and fear of conformity. During some periods we worried that individualistic energies would tear apart the bonds of community. During others we feared that our national élan was being enervated as we tamed our personalities in order to climb the corporate ladder and lead sensible, respectable lives.

David Brooks   March 2002

vacuous   *VA kyoo: is*
empty-minded; devoid of substance

The small-town "hick," the country "rube," are as rare as the city "slicker." None of them ever existed in a statistical sense. They are literary figures. They are states of mind which are found everywhere, in the big cities as well as the smallest hamlets, exactly as the shrewd man-of-the-world type is found everywhere. There are vacuous bumpkins living in New York, Boston, and San Francisco, and there are men in small towns whose dress is urban, whose manners are urbane, who have culture, worldly wisdom, savoire-faire, polish — whatever it is that bumping against one's fellows in big cities is supposed to impart.

Earnest Elmo Calkins   February 1936

vade mecum   *VAY dee MEE kuhm*
a book for ready reference; manual; handbook: Latin, go with me

Roget's Thesaurus, which had come into being as a linguistic example of the Platonic ideal, became instead a vade mecum for the crossword cheat. It already had other, more insidious shortcomings. By eschewing definitions altogether, and thus suggesting no choices, it fostered poor writing. It offered facile answers to complex linguistic questions. It appealed to a growing desire for snap solutions to tricky verbal situations. It enabled students to appear learned without ever helping to make them so. It encouraged a malaprop society. It made for literary window dressing. It was meretricious.

Simon Winchester   May 2002

vanguard   *VAN gahrd*
the leading positions or persons in a movement: originally, the part of an army that advances ahead of the main body

Of the thirty-odd species of oceanic dolphins, none makes a more striking entrance than *Stenella attenuata*, the spotted dolphin. Under water spotted dolphins first appear as white dots against the blue. The beaks of the adults are white-tipped, and that distinctive blaze, viewed head-on, makes a perfect circle. When the vanguard of the school is "echolocating" on you — examining you sonically — the beaks all swing your way, and each circular blaze reflects light before any of the rest of the animal does. You see spots before your eyes.

Kenneth Brower   July 1989

It is chiefly because the United States has long been in the vanguard of much scientific and technological research, of course, that English is so widely used in these fields. If the United States were for the most part French-speaking, surely French would be the language of science and technology; there is nothing inherent in English to tie it to these fields. And if something as earthshaking as the Internet had been developed in, say, Japan, perhaps English would not now be dominant to the extent that it is.

Barbara Wallraff   November 2000

vapid   *VA pid*
dull; flat; trite ("vapidity" is the noun)

Of Thomas E. Dewey's vapidity in 1948 the Louisville *Courier-Journal* observed, "No presidential candidate in the future will be so inept that four of his major speeches can be boiled down to these four historic sentences: Agriculture is important. Our rivers are full of fish. You cannot have freedom without liberty. The future lies ahead."

Jack Beatty   September 1996

vascular   *VAS kyuh luhr*
spirited; passionate; vigorous

What made Elizabethan poetry great, above all, was the fearlessness with which it plunged into the problems of consciousness itself. No item of man's awareness was too trivial to be noted, too terrifying to be plumbed. Shakespeare's poetry is everywhere **vascular** with this rich consciousness of self, thought being carried boldly into the realm of feeling, and feeling as boldly carried into the realm of thought.

Conrad Aiken   October 1964

venal   *VEE nuhl*
able to be bribed or corrupted ("venality" is the noun)

Lauren Weisberger has produced a work of trash fiction of such unimpeachable quality — I enjoyed every page — that the golden girls of the form can hang up their spurs. *The Devil Wears Prada*, which is apparently based on its author's tenure as the *Vogue* editor in chief Anna Wintour's assistant, takes for its plot the old story handed down through the ages: young lovely from good family moves to Manhattan, takes job in glamorous industry, encounters dissipation and human **venality** of every stripe, and emerges either tarnished or triumphant (in this case — being chick lit — the latter).

Caitlin Flanagan   July/August 2003

Modern political history in the United States dates from 1868, when the extreme conservatives, the railroad entrepreneurs, the extreme Eastern socialists, and the established manufacturers of the East seized control of the Republican Party, ousted the fervid abolitionists, dismissed the remaining Whigs to the status of innocuous elder statesmen, and entered into an era of corruption that even the more dishonorable of the early Federalists or the more **venal** of the leaders of the party sponsored by the Bank in Jacksonian days would have gagged at.

Ellis G. Arnall   October 1948

✳ The Bank referred to in the passage was the federally owned Second Bank of the United States. It stored the Government's money, paid its bills, made its loans and payments, and otherwise managed its finances. Believing that the doctrine of states' rights meant that a central bank was unconstitutional, President Andrew Jackson vetoed Congress's rechartering of the bank. It was, he said, a "hydra of corruption."

venial   *VEEN yuhl*
excusable; minor

Walking for walking's sake I do not like. The diversion appears to me one of the most factitious of modern enjoyments; and I cannot help looking upon those who pace their five miles in the teeth of a north wind, and profess to come home all the livelier and better for it, as guilty of a **venial** hypocrisy.

William Dean Howells   November 1869

veracity   *vuh RA suh tee*
adherence to the truth

Giants in the Earth is a moving narrative of pioneer hardship and heroism, told with such obvious veracity that it makes almost all other tales of the Western frontier seem cheap. At times, as in the description of the storm of locusts, of the blizzard, of the coming to the little settlement of a lone pioneer whose wife has gone mad with grief, it rises to great power. And the background of the boundless Dakota prairie, with its mysterious distances and its capacity for evil, is painted with alternating beauty and grimness.

Robert M. Gay   September 1927

verbatim   *vuhr BAY tuhm*
word for word

The famous description in *Antony and Cleopatra* of Cleopatra on her royal barge is taken almost verbatim from a translation of Plutarch's life of Mark Antony: "on either side of her, pretty, fair boys apparelled as painters do set forth the god Cupid, with little fans in their hands, with which they fanned wind upon her" becomes "on each side her / Stood pretty dimpled boys, like smiling Cupids, / With divers-colour'd fans, whose wind did seem / To glow the delicate cheeks which they did cool." (Notice how Shakespeare improved upon the original.)

Richard A. Posner   April 2002

verbose   *ver BOHS*
wordy; long-winded

A lawyer who grows verbose arguing a motion may be prodded by the court, but I have never heard of an attorney being hurried when asking mercy for his client. Respect for the dignity of the individual demands that the attorney be heard fully.

Judge Irving R. Kaufman   January 1960

verboten   *ver BOH tuhn*
forbidden; prohibited

On July 20 thirty years ago my family — like millions of other South African families — was huddled around a crackling radio, listening to the moonwalk. Nobody in the entire country could watch it on TV. Television was verboten — a criminal technology under apartheid. Not until 1976 did South Africa's first TV sets flicker into life.

Rob Nixon   July 1999

verdant   *VER dint*
covered with vegetation; green

Verdant, rife with swimmable lakes, scenic panoramas, lovely unspoiled villages, and mounded hills friendly to the middle-aged hiker, the Berkshires are also one of the preeminent arts places in the country. The vacationer who craves concerts, plays, dance performances, uncrowded art museums, architectural shrines, and stop-the-car New England houses at seemingly every turn in the road will find in the Berkshire Hills what my wife and I found on a recent trip — a cultural dreamscape.

Jack Beatty   May 1993

veritable   *VE ri tuh buhl*
being truly or very much so; practically or in effect

Hospitality was a **veritable** passion with Anton Pavolvich Chekov. No sooner had he settled down in a village than he began inviting throngs of guests to visit him. He filled his house to overflowing with guests whom he dined and wined and doctored. He once rented a summer house in an out-of-the-way Ukrainian provincial hole, and before he even saw it, he invited all sorts of guests from Moscow, from St. Petersburg, from Nizhni-Novgorod. And when he made his home outside Moscow, his residence resembled a hotel. "They slept on the divans, several people in each room," his brother Mikhail recalls. "They even spent the night in the hallway. Writers, young women, local land department officials, local doctors, distant relatives" would crowd his home for weeks at a time.

Kornei Chukovski   September 1947

vex   *veks*
to trouble or distress ("vexing" is the adjective)

How could the man who wrote that "all men are created equal" own slaves? This, in essence, is the question most persistently asked of those who write about Thomas Jefferson, and by all indications it is the thing that contemporary Americans find most **vexing** about him. In a recent series of some two dozen radio talk shows, I was asked this question on virtually every program, either by the host or by a caller. Most often, those who point to this problem admire Jefferson, and they appear as reluctant to give up their admiration as they would be to give up the principle of equality itself. But they are genuinely baffled by the seeming contradiction.

Douglas L. Wilson   November 1992

vigor   *VI guhr*
active physical or mental strength; vitality

I first made acquaintance with Whitman's writings when a newspaper notice of the earliest edition of *Leaves of Grass* reached me, in Paris, in the autumn of 1855. It was the most exhilarating piece of news I had received from America during the six months of my absence abroad. Such vigor, such graphic force, such human sympathy, such scope and audacity in the choice and treatment of themes, found in me an eagerly interested reader of the copious extracts which the notice contained. When I came to see the volume itself, — the thin, small quarto of 1855, — I found in it much that impressed me as formless and needlessly offensive; and these faults were carried to extremes in the second and enlarged edition of 1856. Yet the tremendous original power of this new bard, and the freshness, as of nature itself, which breathed through the best of his songs or sayings, continued to hold their spell over me, and inspired me with intense curiosity as to the man himself.

John Townsend Trowbridge   February 1902

vile   *vighl*

highly offensive to the senses or sensibilities; repulsive; disgusting

Whoever first brought the ailanthus to Cleveland, I do not know. It is a pithy, rapidly growing tree, with great compound leaves sometimes three feel long — a sort of glorified sumac. The ailanthus adopted downtown Cleveland. It spread by self-seeding, and with incredible rapidity. The thicker the tenements and the population, the thicker the ailanthus. Where smoke and dust and grime and gases seem most vile, there the ailanthus flourishes prodigiously.

Don Knowlton   July 1926

✳ Taking root and flourishing in places inhospitable to other trees, the ailanthus tree symbolizes the Nolan family's poverty-ridden yet vibrant tenement life in Betty Smith's 1943 novel *A Tree Grows in Brooklyn*. Like the ailanthus growing in their yard, the Nolans thrive in bleak surroundings as their daughter Francie develops into a strong, optimistic, life-loving young woman. The ailanthus, still abundant in Brooklyn's empty lots and unkempt yards (as well as across the United States), is also known as the Tree of Heaven, a translation of *aylanto*, the name of the tree in its native Indonesia.

vilify   *VI luh figh*

to use abusive or slanderous language about; revile; defame; slander
("vilification" is the noun)

Sauk Centre, Minnesota, advertises itself as the birthplace of Sinclair Lewis, whose 1920 novel *Main Street* used Sauk Centre as a model for the pettiness and meanness of small-town life. It also earned Lewis the vilification of family and friends for what seemed like life ever after.

Richard Manning   May 1979

vis-à-vis   *vee zuh VEE*
concerning; with regard to: French, face to face

Every other mode of transportation within France has limitations and disadvantages vis-à-vis barging. If you restrict yourself to planes and taxis, you are in effect turning your back on the lovely countryside. If you travel by train, you'll have to keep shlepping your bags from the station to the hotel and back. Rent a car and you'll not only have to keep packing and unpacking but also have to drive.

Barbara Wallraff   February 1996

viscous   *VIS kuhs*
thick; syrupy; slow-flowing

True balsamic vinegar is viscous, with a mahogany sheen that makes it seem more a glaze than a common vinegar. The flavor is mellow, deep, rounded, and of such concentrated sweetness that the acid serves only to accentuate the herbal notes conferred by the various aromatic woods in which the vinegar has aged for at least twelve years and often for decades.

Corby Kummer   September 1994

vitiate   *VI shee ayt*
to impair the quality or value of; make impure; spoil

To my ear the brown thrush in the wild state is a sweeter singer than any caged mocking-bird; but when both are free, the latter is infinitely superior at every point. There is a wide variety of pure flute notes expressed by the wild mocking-bird. These notes become vitiated in captivity and their tone degraded to the level of mere mellow piping.

Maurice Thompson   November 1884

vituperation   *vigh too: puh RAY shuhn*
violent denunciation or condemnation

Neither great fame nor great friendships could curb Pope's resentment when ridiculed or attacked; he became, indeed, so touchy as to magnify small slights, so suspicious as to manufacture them, so rancorous as to remember them for life. This is a matter of far more than biographical interest, seeing that Pope was endowed with the greatest genius for rhymed vituperation in English literature.

Louis Kronenberger   May 1969

* Alexander Pope (1688-1744), England's greatest 18th-century poet, chose as the target of frequent vituperation possibly England's worst poet, Colley Cibber, with whom he had an ongoing feud. Despite being a joke among his contemporaries, Cibber was appointed England's poet laureate in 1730, to which Pope responded with this verse:

> In merry Old England, it once was the Rule,
> The King had his Poet, and also his Fool.
> But now we're so frugal, I'd have you to know it,
> That Cibber can serve both for Fool and for Poet.

vivify   *VI vuh figh*
to make more lively or intense; give energy to

Walking has the best value as gymnastics for the mind. "You shall never break down in a speech," said Sydney Smith, "on the day on which you have walked twelve miles." In the English universities, the reading men are daily performing their punctual training in the boat-clubs, or a long gallop of many miles in the saddle, or taking their famed "constitutionals," walks of eight and ten miles. "Walking," said Rousseau, "has something which animates and vivifies my ideas." And Plato said of exercise, that, "it would almost cure a guilty conscience." "For the living out of doors, and simple fare, and gymnastic exercises, and the morals of companions, produce the greatest effect on the way of virtue and of vice."

Ralph Waldo Emerson   November 1904

voluble   *VAHL yuh buhl*
characterized by a ready and continuous flow of words

Reformers, being lovers of publicity, ignore none of the recognized advertising channels and love to lecture and to write. Their clamorous egotism finds expression in such spots as Hyde Park, where on every Sunday morning voluble orators declaim hopefully on vivisection, birth control, pacifism, the single tax, vegetarianism, spiritualism, and anarchy.

Claude M. Fuess   June 1931

vortex   *VAWR teks*
a place or situation regarded as drawing into its powerful center all that surrounds it; a whirlpool

The lives of French men of letters, at least during the last two centuries, have never been isolated or obscure. Had Rousseau been born on the borders of Loch Lomond, he might have proved in his own person, and without interruption, the superiority of the savage state; and after his death the information in regard to him would have been fragmentary and uncertain. But born on the shores of Lake Leman, centralization laid its grasp upon him, drew him into the vortex of the "great world," and caused his name to figure in all the questions, the quarrels, and the scandals of his day.

John Foster Kirk   April 1866

votary   *VOH tuh ree*
a devoted follower or admirer

Nearly thirty years after his death Winston Churchill remains a curiously problematic figure. To his hagiographers and to votaries of the Churchillian cultus he was the greatest man of his age (in extreme versions, of all time), and he is still an icon venerated by British politicians and American columnists. But that only makes it harder than ever to come to terms with him. He overshadowed more than half of a century, his career taking on that eerie quality that extreme longevity brings. A man who entered politics under Queen Victoria retired as Prime Minister under Queen Elizabeth II, fifty-five years later. Churchhill was elected to the House of Commons the year before President William McKinley was assassinated, in 1901, and was still sitting there the year after President John F. Kennedy was assassinated, in 1963.

Geoffrey Wheatcroft   February 1994

vouchsafe   *vowch SAYF*
to grant; give; allow

Little more than a year has elapsed since the greatest disaster in maritime history upset all our accepted theories of the unsinkability of modern liners. The wild paths of imagination along which we were willingly led by naval architects, launched us into a disaster such as the world hopes never again to witness. Some very practical test of the unsinkability of liners will have to be vouchsafed the public before its old confidence in the safety of ocean travel can be restored.

Alexander G. McLellan (under the pseudonym of Atlanticus)   August 1913

vox populi   *VAHKS PAH pyuh ligh*
the voice of the people; popular opinion or sentiment

There is no democracy in culture and the arts. In other words, the vox populi is usually worth nothing. With rare exceptions, the artists and cultural voices that caught the public's fancy did not survive. For the occasional genius recognized in his lifetime, such as Dickens, there are always scores who are ridiculed, if they are noticed at all.

John Simon   December 1978

W·Y·Z

wheedle

From the first, I delighted in stories that I contrived to wheedle out

of my nurses. Of these early stories, I liked best the chain-stories: —

"The fire began to burn the stick,
The stick began to beat the dog,
The dog began to bite the pig,
The little pig got over the stile…"

and the famous poem of *The House that*

Jack Built, as illustrated by Randolph Caldecott.

John Masefield   March 1951

see page 470

465

waif   *wayf*
a homeless, uncared for or neglected child; a child of the streets

Our unique contribution to the progress of the world is not so much liberty as it is equality. It is the easy, natural, confraternal mingling of our people. Poverty or riches, education or ignorance, may impede it here or there; but at bottom we take it so much as a matter of course that if we find an individual or a social set where it is not, our instinctive response to its absence is ridicule. Huckleberry Finn is our perfect symbol. Our imaginations accept him as a completely natural boy. And the presuppositions of that barely literate waif were all humane and equalitarian because Mark Twain put into him the feelings which are common to our people.

Lucien Price   August 1943

warren   *WAH ruhn*
an area of living or office space characterized as a mass of passages and small rooms

Ever since the invention of statistics, at the turn of the nineteenth century, heads of nations have paid particular attention to the procreational habits of their citizens. Censuses have been taken, and marriage and birth certificates filed, so that statisticians in their bureaucratic warrens, tallying and manipulating the data in dozens of arcane ways, can sketch profiles of given populations.

Gina Maranto   June 1995

watchword   *WACH werd*
a word or phrase embodying a guiding principle or rule of action

In a balancing world, modesty in actions and aspirations should be America's foreign-policy watchword. Because few external events pose an immediate danger to the

United States, it can usually afford to react deliberately to events — to wait and see if a potential threat becomes a real one.

Christopher Layne   July 1991

watershed   *WAH tuhr shed*
a crucial turning point between two phases

The first great watershed in the development of toys as we know them was the end of the Second World War. The Great Depression had made it impossible for most people to buy a lot of toys. The war had the same effect. When prosperity returned and the people now known as Yuppies began to be born, the modern toy industry was born as well. Propelling it toward maturity were the two great engines of post-war American culture: television and plastic.

David Owen   October 1986

wax   *waks*
to grow gradually larger

The population of the United States has multiplied itself nearly tenfold, while its wealth has increased in a still greater proportion, since the peace of 'Eighty-Three. Have the Representative Men of the nation been made or maintained great and magnanimous, too? Or is that other anomaly, which has so perplexed the curious foreigner, an admitted fact, that in proportion as the country has waxed great and powerful, its public men have dwindled from giants in the last century to dwarfs in this? Alas, to ask the question is to answer it.

Edmund Quincy   December 1857

wearing   *WAI ring*
tiring; wearisome; exhausting

I have never come across an autobiography in which the writer drew attention to the fact that his friends often found him a little wearing.

Samuel McChord Crothers   March 1923

wellspring   *WEL spring*
a source of abundant and continuous supply

When their living standards are rising, people do not view themselves, their fellow citizens, and their society as a whole the way they do when those standards are stagnant or falling. They are more trusting, more inclusive, and more open to change when they view their future prospects and their children's with confidence rather than anxiety or fear. Economic growth is not merely the enabler of higher consumption; it is in many ways the wellspring from which democracy and civil society flow. We should be fully cognizant of the risks to our values and liberties if that nourishing source runs dry.

Benjamin M. Friedman   July/August 2005

Weltanschauung   *VELT ahn showng*
the overall perspective from which one sees and interprets the world: German, world view

News coverage revolves around strong personas: in the Weltanschauung of the Washington press corps, the President must be the focus of events.

Steven Stark   April 1993

welter   *WEL ter*
a mass or multitude of things to contend with

The quest of every artist is to impose order upon chaos. There is Life to begin with: life in all its obvious multiplicity and muddle; the welter and variety of human experience, the passions of the human heart, the triviality of daily existence, the forces of the elements, the beauty and ugliness of nature, the conflicting values which man incessantly pursues. And there is the artist: observing, sorting, selecting; finding maybe a pattern within the flux, a meaning in the muddle, but concerned primarily with the shaping of a vision into a work of art, the embodiment of perceptions into concrete and harmonious forms.

Elizabeth Drew   October 1941

Weltschmerz   *VELT shmerts*
a weary or pessimistic feeling about life; a melancholy feeling about the state of the world: German, welt, *world* + schmerz, *pain*

William Dean Howells is quite the most American thing we have produced. Almost all that one can profitably say of him distributes itself about this central magnetizing fact. Of the lessons he has taught us, no other seems half so important as the supreme value of having a home, a definitely local habitation, not to tear one's self away from, to sigh for, to idealize through a mist of melancholy and *Weltschmerz*, but simply and solely to live in, to live for. This part of his doctrine, more than any other, has the noble force of an eternal verity preached with striking timeliness. It is in itself the special crown of Mr. Howells, the open secret of his democratic grandeur; and it wins double emphasis because it had to be urged against the sterile aesthetic cosmopolitanism of the eighteen-eighties.

Helen Thomas Follett and Wilson Follett   March 1917

wheedle *WEE duhl*
to influence or persuade by flattery, soothing words or coaxing; cajole

From the first, I delighted in stories that I contrived to wheedle out of my nurses. Of these early stories, I liked best the chain-stories: —

> "The fire began to burn the stick,
> The stick began to beat the dog,
> The dog began to bite the pig,
> The little pig got over the stile…"

and the famous poem of *The House that Jack Built*, as illustrated by Randolph Caldecott.

John Masefield   March 1951

wheel *weel*
to turn in a sweeping, circular motion ("wheeling" is the adjective)

Birds are creatures of the sun. No day in the country is really complete without sight or sound of their presence. To have seen a hummingbird in his nuptial flight, a dancing jewel in the sun, as his consort watches demurely from some exposed twig; to watch the wheeling mock battle of pairing eagles high in the sky as they dive and threaten and sail gracefully away, their screams floating down like sudden grace notes to their lovemaking — those experiences are marked in your memory book forever.

Clark C. Van Fleet   July 1963

whimsical *WIM suh kuhl*
subject to sudden change; unpredictable; capricious

Almost all the famous men and women of the day posed before Lewis Carroll's camera in the studio he erected on the Christ Church leads; but, with the whimsical contrariness which was characteristic of him, as soon as the wet plate with all its attendant difficulties and messiness went out and the clean, convenient dry plate came in, he abandoned photography, and not one photograph did he ever take by the new and infinitely simplified process.

Edith M. Arnold   June 1929

> ✳ A lead (pronounced leed) is a path or an alley. A blind lead, or a blind alley, is a path closed at one end. In its figurative sense it is an attempt that leads to nothing.

willful   *WIL fuhl*

determined to have one's own way against opposition; doing as one pleases;
strongly purposeful

When Isabella Stewart Gardner left her well-to-do family in Manhattan to marry a wealthy Bostonian, John Gardner, she carried with her an impulsive love for painting and sculpture, a zest for entertainment, a style that would have set her apart anywhere, and an aggressiveness that grew with the years. She was not beautiful, but her animation and her independence, her insatiable curiosity, and her sympathy made her powerfully attractive to men. She was hostess of the most spectacular salon Boston has known, and although conservatives never ceased to resent her as a willful outsider, they came in the end to acknowledge her unique contribution to the city.

Edward Weeks   January 1966

wily   *WIGH lee*

crafty; canny; cunning

I had read of people in East Africa approaching to within a few feet of perfectly wild lions at the midday siesta, — in fact, my own father was one of the first to show that this was possible provided one moved slowly enough, — but I never suspected that these tactics were applicable to such wily and arrogant animals as the red river hog of the forests. Nevertheless, I soon found myself right in the centre of the herd, noticed but unfeared by them. Perhaps the fact that I carried nothing smelling strange, like a gun or camera or other oily metal instrument, reassured them. Gently they moved around me, as we were all drifting in the same direction; sometimes all would vanish amid the foliage so that I knew of their presence only by their ceaseless, moaning grunts.

Ivan Sanderson   September 1937

winnow   *WI noh*

to separate or eliminate; sift

I recently watched a scene of ancient beauty in the Andean highlands of Ecuador: women reaching skyward to pour just-threshed quinoa from shallow baskets onto blankets, so that the wind would winnow the wide streams of falling grain. They knelt to gather up the grain back into their baskets, and then let it fall once more before they set it aside in a pile.

Corby Kummer   November 2002

wither WI th:uhr
to lose vigor or freshness; shrivel; fade; decay

In Germany, "the individual withers," and the world of State and Society, with its multifarious demands upon him, 'is more and more.' This is, of course, a socialistic tendency, but the substitute that the Germans are finding for unlimited competition is not radical Socialism, but organization. It is astonishing to what an extent the Germans have gone in organizing life in all its activities. The individual is everywhere learning that his independent strivings are ineffective both for himself and society, that as a unit he counts for little.

William C. Dreher   July 1911

wont *wahnt*
accustomed

A recent visitor from Singapore, an able and well-informed reporter from the Straits Times, wanted me to know that the people of East Asia were uneasy about what they perceived as a crisis in Chinese-American relations and that they expected the United States to back off. Didn't we realize that the Chinese had never been an aggressive or expansionist power? As academics are wont to do, and despite my own misgivings about America's China policy or lack thereof, I took a few minutes to lecture him on the history of the Chinese empire, on thousands of years of attacks on China's neighbors — Vietnamese, Tibetans, Uighers, Mongols, Koreans, and countless minority peoples who had the misfortune to get in the way.

Warren I. Cohen   March 1997

wooden *WOO din*
lifeless

The Adventures of Pinocchio, which Carlo Collodi first published, in serialized form, in 1881, has spawned hundreds of translations — many of them in appropriately wooden prose — and countless versions for the theater and the screen.

James Marcus   December 2002

woolgathering *WOOL ga thuh ring*
engaging in aimless or idle daydreaming or purposeless thinking; in a dreamy or absent-minded state

More than to his university or to any formal institution, Berenson believes that he owes his deepest obligation to his own roving curiosity. "The fruit of my life," he insists, "was my loafing, not my work — when I was woolgathering and satisfying useless curiosities. I didn't prepare myself for anything but my voracious appetites for the useless, such as reading anthologies of Greek and Provençal poets. I never feared wasting time."

Francis Henry Taylor   November 1957

✳ In his day, Bernard Berenson (1865-1959), an American art critic, connoiseur and writer, was considered the greatest authority on Italian art of the 13th to 17th centuries.

wrought   *rawt*
worked into shape; formed; fashioned; crafted

We take Mr. Kipling very seriously, for he is the greatest creative mind that we now have: he has the devouring eye and the portraying hand. And *Captains Courageous* is badly wrought and is less than the measure of his power. It may be when he sent it out some words of his own had been forgotten — words with which he dedicated one of his earliest books, —

> "For I have wrought them for Thy sake
> And breathed in them mine agonies."

It seems to us to lack this sort of inspiration.

W. B. Parker   December 1897

✳ Written by Henry Wadsworth Longfellow (1807-1882), this was the first poem published in the first issue of *The Atlantic Monthly*, November 1857:

> Whene'er a noble deed is wrought,
> Whene'er is spoken a noble thought,
>   Our hearts, in glad surprise,
>   To higher levels rise.
>
> The tidal wave of deeper souls
> Into our inmost being rolls,
>   And lifts us unawares
>   Out of all meaner cares.
>
> Honor to those whose words or deeds
> Thus help us in our daily needs,
>   And by their overflow
>   Raise us from what is low!

Other poems in that issue were by Ralph Waldo Emerson, John Greenleaf Whittier and James Russell Lowell.

yoke *yohk*
a condition of servitude, subjection or oppression

The war with Spain, which President McKinley did everything in his power to prevent, gave him the great opportunity of his life, and the one that he best improved. In it he lifted his administration to the plane of those of Washington and Lincoln, and linked his name with theirs for our time, if not for all time, as the liberator of millions from the yoke of Spain.

Henry B. F. Macfarland   March 1901

Zeitgeist *TSIGHT gighst*
the spirit of the time; the trend of thought or feeling characteristic of an age or generation: German, Zeit, time + Geist, spirit

Contemporary civilization is largely built upon the basic idea that the world may become any man's oyster. It is the *Zeitgeist* which impels our students to a profound reverence for acquisitiveness.

Bernard Iddings Bell   September 1932

zest *zest*
enthusiastic enjoyment

The most sensationally successful of all jazz derivatives was swing, which thrived in the late thirties. Here was a music that could be danced to with zest and listened to with pleasure.

Arnold Sundgaard   July 1955

Appendix

The Editors of *The Atlantic* in Boston, 1857-2005

James Russell Lowell   1857-1861

Before becoming *The Atlantic's* first editor, James Russell Lowell (1819-1891) founded a magazine of his own, the *Pioneer*, in 1843. Its mission was to provide readers with articles by American authors of merit, a substitute for "the enormous quantity of thrice-diluted trash, in the shape of namby-pamby love tales and sketches," as he described it, inundating them from popular magazines. It failed after three monthly issues, but Lowell's literary ideals and antislavery sentiments did not. In April 1857, publisher Moses Phillips, urged on by his assistant Francis Underwood, who had conceived the idea of *The Atlantic*, convened a group of Boston writers including Lowell, Ralph Waldo Emerson, Henry Wadsworth Longfellow and Oliver Wendell Holmes, to found a magazine with a similar high-culture and abolitionist mission. Lowell was chosen as editor for his literary and antislavery credentials. Emerson and others encouraged him to "defy the public" by printing only work of high quality and by unequivocally advocating the abolition of slavery.

James T. Fields   1861-1871

James T. Fields (1817-1881) became *The Atlantic's* second editor a few years after his publishing company, Ticknor & Fields, bought the magazine from Phillips, Sampson and Company. As a businessman concerned with *The Atlantic's* profitability as well as its quality, he recruited new writers whose lively essays, accessible poetry, realistic short stories and serialized novels added new readers while maintaining the magazine's intellectual and literary standards. Knowing that illustrations in other magazines had increased their popularity, Fields nevertheless refused to add them, feeling they would lower the magazine's stature.

William Dean Howells   1871-1881

William Dean Howells (1837-1920) became editor at the age of 34 after spending five years assisting his predecessor. Raised in Ohio and self-educated, he arrived in Boston when he was 23, wrote a campaign biography of Lincoln, and was appointed consul to Venice a year later. The first *Atlantic* editor from outside New England — a "westerner" — he expanded *The Atlantic's* constellation of writers beyond New England and into the West and Midwest, most notably with Mark Twain and Bret Harte. He discovered Sara Orne Jewett, Edith Wharton and Henry James, and nurtured their careers. He encouraged poetry and fiction that was realistic rather than romantic and sentimental. And he helped readers to see Mark Twain as not just a humorist, but a writer with a deep understanding of human nature. The *Atlantic* audience, Twain wrote to Howells, "is the only audience that I sit down before with perfect serenity (for the simple reason that it don't require a 'humorist' to paint himself stripèd and stand on his head every fifteen minutes." Howells' own novels, *The Rise of Silas Lapham* and *A Hazard of New Fortunes*, are considered among the best American fiction of the 19th century.

Thomas Bailey Aldrich   1881-1890

Thomas Baily Aldrich (1836-1907) was largely self-educated, having attended only elementary school. Before and after his editorship he was a well-known novelist, poet and short-story writer. At *The Atlantic* he wielded a merciless editorial pen among even the most experienced writers. While some of them praised Aldrich's substantial cuts, word changes and grammatical corrections as helpful, others strongly resented them as intrusions on their liberties. Aldrich responded to Richard Grant White, a steady contributor, by writing: "You are wrong, Dear Mr. White, in assuming that I have no responsibility because an article is signed. I am responsible for every word that appears in *The Atlantic*."

Horace Elisha Scudder   1890-1898

When Horace Elisha Scudder (1838-1902) became *The Atlantic's* fifth editor he remained editor in chief of the trade book division of Houghton Mifflin and Company. The publisher, Henry Oscar Houghton, had purchased the magazine in 1873 as a means of drawing both recognized and new American writers to the publishing house. Scudder was an idealist who brought to both editorial positions a sense of high culture and moral mission. In addition to his two full-time jobs, he wrote dozens of brief book reviews each month in the magazine, and looked at every submission. While Scudder's sometimes negative reviews of his own company's books brought complaints from Henry Houghton, he maintained his independent opinions.

Walter Hines Page   1898-1899

Walter Hines Page (1855-1918) was the first editor from a southern state, North Carolina. His passionate interest in current affairs and the nation's development led him to increase the number of *Atlantic* articles on America's social, economic and political issues, often in first-person accounts. Within a year of leaving *The Atlantic*, Page became a founding partner in Doubleday, Page and Company, publishing his own magazine, *The World's Work*, which he edited until 1913. That year one of his former contributors, Woodrow Wilson, appointed him ambassador to Great Britain.

Bliss Perry   1899-1909

Bliss Perry (1860-1954) became editor after 15 years of teaching English and American literature at Williams College and Princeton. In 1902 he added the job of editor in chief of Houghton Mifflin's trade books, and from 1906 through 1909 taught half-time at Harvard as well. His continual absence from the magazine required Perry to have assistants. The first was William B. Parker, who wrote to Jack London suggesting he use the name "John," as it was "better suited than Jack to literary purposes."

Ellery Sedgwick   1909-1938

Ellery Sedgwick (1872-1960) bought *The Atlantic* from Houghton Mifflin in 1908, kept Bliss Perry as editor for a year, and then became its editor. Sedgwick increased the emphasis on contemporary affairs, particularly coverage of World War I, decreased fiction and literary comment, and stimulated controversy on such issues as the Sacco-Vanzetti trial and the generational revolt of the 1920s. As a result, *The Atlantic's* circulation rose from 15,000 in 1908 to 137,000 in 1928. Sedgwick has the distinction of both rejecting poems by Robert Frost in 1912 ("We are sorry that we have no place in *The Atlantic Monthly* for your vigorous verse") and, in 1915 — after Frost had spent two and a half years in England where his work was acclaimed — eagerly accepting three as yet unpublished poems directly from Frost's hand, without even reading them first. They were "Birches," "The Road Not Taken" and "The Sound of Trees." Frost received $55 for the poems.

Edward Weeks   1938-1966

Edward Weeks (1898-1989) was a book salesman for the publisher Boni & Liveright in New York when in December of 1923 he received an offer to join the editorial staff of *The Atlantic Monthly* in Boston as an assistant editor. "Don't touch it," his father told him when he showed him the letter. "New York will always pay you better. And if you lose a job in Boston, you're out in the cold." Weeks began at *The Atlantic* the next month. He headed the magazine's book division, The Atlantic Monthly Press, beginning in 1927 and was appointed the magazine's editor in chief in 1938. During his editorship *The Atlantic's* circulation doubled to 265,000, due partly to the high profile he achieved through two weekly radio shows on the ABC and NBC networks. After the death of his first wife in 1970, he married *The Atlantic's* prolific book reviewer, Phoebe-Lou Adams. After retiring as editor in chief, Weeks continued as a book reviewer and consultant to the magazine and book division until 1987. Among his memoirs are *Writers and Friends, In Friendly Candor* and *The Open Heart*. He read manuscripts for *The Atlantic* until a few days before he died, at 91.

Robert Manning   1966-1980

Robert Manning (b. 1919), the tenth editor of *The Atlantic*, began his journalism career as a copy boy for the Binghamton Press, in New York. After serving as Washington bureau chief for the United Press and London bureau chief for *Time*, *Sports Illustrated* and *Fortune* magazines, he was invited to join the Kennedy Administration as assistant secretary of state for public affairs. Manning brought to *The Atlantic* a new journalistic immediacy. Articles on Vietnam, for example, were placed in forthcoming issues within weeks rather than months of their assignment. "There was still a need for the long-view and ivory-tower thinkers, and we continued to publish them," Manning wrote in his biography *The Swamp Root Chronicle* (1992). "But the flow of events called more and more for articles by writers who were fast on their feet, to whom 'Thou shalt meet thy deadline' was as sacred as any commandment Moses brought down from the Mount." Following his *Atlantic* years, Manning was editor in chief of the 25-volume *The American Experience in Vietnam* (1998).

William Whitworth   1980-1999

William Whitworth (b. 1937) began his journalism career reporting for *The Arkansas Gazette* and *The New York Herald Tribune*, and was a staff writer and then associate editor of *The New Yorker.* During his 19-year editorship, Whitworth never wrote an article for *The Atlantic*. (The passage for the word seer is actually an excerpt from his introduction to an article that the statesman George Kennan wrote.) He did, however, commission every article, talking frequently with the authors, and approve every short story and poem the fiction and poetry editors selected. His influence on the *Atlantic* writers and editors he nurtured has lived on long after his tenure. Known for his sharp-eyed and humorous comments in the margins of articles being prepared for publication, he once circled the first name in a byline that read "Jeff Tayler" and wrote: "Ernie Hemingway, Bob Penn Warren, Bill Faulkner, and Jim Joyce all advise against this."

Michael Kelly   1999-2002

When David Bradley became *The Atlantic Monthly's* new owner in 1999, he appointed Michael Kelly (1957-2003) its new editor. Kelly left that position in 2002 to complete a book, but remained editor at large, and in March 2003 began covering the Iraq war for *The Atlantic* and the *Washington Post*, embedded with the Army's 3rd Infantry Division. He had covered the 1991 Gulf War as a freelance correspondent for the *Boston Globe* and *New Republic*, traveling on his own in the war zone and winning a National Magazine Award and an Overseas Press Club Award for his dispatches. Afterwards he wrote a book about the conflict, *Martyrs' Day: Chronicle of a Small War*. Between the wars, Kelly was editor of *The New Republic* and the *National Journal*, and had earlier written for *The New York Times*, the *Boston Globe*, the *Baltimore Sun, Esquire* and *The New Yorker*. On April 4, 2003, while riding in an Army Humvee outside of Baghdad that fell into a canal while evading enemy fire, Kelly became the first American journalist killed in the Iraq war.

Cullen Murphy   2002-2005

Under Cullen Murphy's direction, *The Atlantic* continuously published incisive and insightful articles on national and global issues that made the magazine itself a newsmaker and a greater presence on the newsstand. Murphy sent writers to places for longer periods of time and ran lengthy articles that were submitted and edited closer to publication time, thus giving *The Atlantic* greater immediacy. His own, often offbeat articles were reminiscent of the light essays *The Atlantic* published in earlier times and served as counterpoint to the magazine's weightier pieces. Dozens of them appear in his book *Just Curious*. Before working at *The Atlantic*, Murphy wrote for *Harper's* magazine and was an editor at the *Wilson Quarterly*. Between 1979 and 2004, he wrote the script for the comic strip *Prince Valiant*, which his father, John Cullen Murphy (1919-2004), had drawn since 1970. (His sister, Mairead Nash, colored in the drawings and did the lettering.) Murphy concluded his tenure at *The Atlantic* at the end of 2005, when the magazine moved from Boston to Washington, D.C., and became editor at large of *Vanity Fair* magazine.

Contributors

Acheson, Dean
atavism

Ackerman, Bruce
faction

Ackworth, Marion Whiteford
censure

Adams, J. Donald
sophistry, specious

Adams, James Truslow
antics

Adams, Phoebe-Lou
ad infinitum, blather, diatribe,
poltroon, revere

Adenauer, Konrad
hegemony

Aiken, Conrad
vascular

Aldrich, Thomas Bailey
eidolon

Alger, George W.
animadversion, improvident

Allen, Arthur
febrile

Allen, Brooke
rapacious

Allen, Charlotte
frieze, resonate

Alper, Joseph
exponential

Alsop, Stewart
bonhomie, intimate, nest egg, pigeon

Anderson, Perry
cicerone

Andrews, John F.
grievous, inscrutable

Arnall, Ellis G.
venal

Arnold, Edith M.
whimsical

Aron, William
oxymoron

Atlantic Editors
adventurism, inexorable,
insurmountable

Atlanticus *See* McLellan, Alexander G.

Atlas, James
curt, discrepancy, disparage,
encomium, rail

Bacon, Martha
consummation

Badeau, Adam
sedulous

Baker, Harry T.
reductio ad absurdum

Ball, George W.
cumbersome, lodestone

Bancroft, George
obsequies

Barber, David
despondent

Barrett, Michael J.
flounder, pragmatic

Barrett, William
cavil, gossamer, seedy

Bartolucci, Marisa
mephitic, nurture

Barzun, Jacques
bugbear, reductive

Bass, Rick
monochromatic

Beam, Alex
painstaking

Beatty, Jack
balm, chestnut, decadent, lubricable,
nemesis, vapid, verdant

Beazell, William Preston
aspersion

Beebe, William
arboreal, catspaw, rent

Bell, Bernard Iddings
Zeitgeist

Bellow, Adam
meritocracy, nepotism

Beloff, Nora
inner sanctum

Benjamin, Samuel Green Wheeler
exigency

Benson, E. F.
jostle

Benson, Eugene
rankle

Benson, Michael
acrid

Berkeley, Bill
kleptocracy, totem

Berlow, Alan
hortatory, prima facie, unconscionable

Bettelheim, Bruno
buttress, inculcate

Bingham, Robert
contumely

Blaine, Graham B. Jr., M.D.
dispassionate, feign

Bloom, Paul
mealy-mouthed, secular

Blount, Roy Jr.
implicit

Boas, George
sluggard

Boewe, Charles
acumen

Bogan, Louise
rarefied

Bolick, Kate
malaise

Bonn, Moritz J.
inane

Bourne, Randolph S.
reproach, stultifying

Bowden, Mark
capitulate, high-water mark, quirk

Bowen, Catherine Drinker
loom, prodigal, spangle

Boyle, James E.
mitigate

Boyne, Daniel
hybrid

Bradford, Gamaliel
acme, obsequious, quibble, remote,
revel, solicitous, surmise

Brandt, Anthony
unsullied

Brauer, Carl
careerist

Broder, David S.
hobbyhorse

Bronowski, Jacob
backwater

Brooks, David
amalgam, grapple, highminded,
parameters, unalienable, vacillate

Brooks, John Graham
fleece

Brooks, Paul
chicanery

Brooks, Sydney
fusillade

Brosnan, Jim
scurrilous

Brower, Kenneth
abnegate, asperity, constituency,
despoil, vanguard

Brown, Michael H.
cascade

Brubach, Holly
allegorical, connive, fortissimo,
headlong

Bruce, Jeanette
unrequited

Brucker, Herbert
glut

Budiansky, Stephen
morphology

Bugby, James Mokeller
ingenuous

Burke, William T.
oxymoron

Burnhardt, Ken
coup

Burr, Chandler
embroil

Burroughs, John
commodious, paean

Bush, Douglas
risqué

Bush, Vannevar
coin, foolhardy

Cabot, James Eliot
parrot

Calder, Ellen M.
incorrigible, stickler

Calkins, Earnest Elmo
blazon, disconsolate, engross,
jaundiced, pastoral, vacuous

Cameron, Charles S., M. D.
complicity

Campany, Richard
backslide

Candler, Edmund
imputation

Cannon, Cornelia James
crank, disputatious, penumbra,
recrudescence, remuneration

Carmichael, Stokely
rift

Carson, Tom
preoccupy

Case, Elizabeth
apostasy

Castle, Terry
scabrous, sententious

Catapano, Fred
analgesic

Cate, Curtis
pillory

Cecil, David
ignoble

Chaffee, Benjamin Harrison
unfettered

Chamberlin, William Henry
nominal

Chandler, Raymond
huckster, tawdry, tripe

Cheever, David William
adulterate, peccadillo

Chen, Edwin
scathing

Chiang Kai-Shek, Madam
lip service

Chu, Lynn
apologia, fiefdom, torpedo

Chukovski, Kornei
unstinting, veritable

Chun, Rene
oeuvre

Cipes, Robert
browbeat

Clarke, Thomas Curtis
effect

Codman, Charles R.
oenologist

Cohen, Gary
audacious

Cohen, Warren I.
wont

Cohn, David L.
apathy, reel

Cole, John N.
catchall, indolence

Colvin, Ian
buoyancy

Conaway, James
tyro

Conly, John M.
frangible, gusto, incandescent, leonine, tintinnabulation

Cooper, Lady Diana
efface, elegy

Corbett, Patricia
conversant

Corbett, Scott
conjure up

Corson, Trevor
calculus, extrude, molt, opportunist

Cortes, Don
simile

Cory, Daniel
entertain

Cox, Harvey
auspicious

Cramer, Deborah
mainstay

Crankshaw, Edward
satrap

Crawford, John
svelte

Crease, Robert P.
anemic, broadside

Croffut, William A.
cadaverous, pertinacity

Crosby, John
scrofulous

Crothers, Samuel McChord
bunk, collocation, contemplative,
coxcomb, delusive, wearing

Cummings, E. E.
pall

Curtis, George William
decree

Curtis, Wayne
craggy, discomfited, obeisance, parlous,
prototype

Cyrus, Della D.
self-abnegation

Dallek, Robert
accrue, exculpate, figurehead,
prosthesis

Davis, Francis
bravura, distance, husk, je ne sais quoi,
nonentity, nuanced, protégé, shrinking
violet

Davison, Peter
beggar, bromide, bumper crop,
construe, eddy, epigraph, germinate,
immolate, lament, quip, sage, template,
tentative

Dawes, Henry Laurens
arrant

Dawson, Mitchell
salutary

Dayan, Moshe
studied

Deland, Lorin F.
anarchism

Delaney, Charles Terry
founder

De Mille, Agnes
languid

Denby, David
epigone

Denny, George V. Jr.
rabid

Derr, Mark
moratorium

Devlin, Lord Patrick
ex officio

DeVoto, Bernard
fixation

Dickens, Charles
proffer

Divakaruni, Chitra
counterpart, problematic

Dobie, J. Frank
categorically

Donatich, John
signature

Douglass, Frederick
supplant

Drabelle, Dennis
composite

Drake, Francis Vivian
blandishments

Dreher, William C.
wither

Drew, Elizabeth
welter

Drew, Elizabeth Brenner
canard

Drinker, Henry S. Jr.
infra dig

Drucker, Peter F.
congeries, incunabula, sentinel

Du Bois, W. E. B.
shibboleth

Duce, James Terry
cachinnate

Duncan, David Ewing
marginalize

Durdin, Tillman
undertone

Dwight, John Sullivan
solace

Easterbrook, Gregg
corporeal, depose, firmament,
incontestable, incubator, onerous,
supplicant

Eaton, Walter Prichard
befuddled, bulwark, elucidate,
erstwhile, odoriferous

Edman, Irwin
rebuke

Egan, Maurice Francis
deference

Eliot, Alexander
convivial

Eliot, Charles W.
contraband

Ellis, Havelock
extemporize, nubile, resuscitate

Emanuel, Ezekiel
enjoin

Emerson, Ralph Waldo
annals, articulate, augment, bon mot,
capital, captious, civility, coeval, dupe,
duplicity, flout, reproof, vivify

Emmerich, André
promontory

Engel, Carl
anodyne, multifarious, noxious

Epstein, Jacob
acute, inexplicable

Epstein, Joseph
modus operandi

Erard, Michael
gadfly

Essary, J. Frederick
maverick

Evans, Bergen
avarice, clairvoyance, degenerate,
delectation, engender, ignoramus,
obviate, pitfall, sullen

Evans, David
backslide

Evans, Elizabeth Glendower
discursive

Fadiman, Clifton
disjunction, emolument, palimpsest,
purblind

Fairbank, John K.
authoritarian

Fairfield, Faith
hamper

Fairlie, Henry
locus classicus

Fallows, James
askew, atavism, bumble, chameleon,
corollary, cul-de-sac, fiat, freight,
howler, miffed, passé, pussyfoot

Farrell, James T.
germane, oscillate

Fenton, Charles A.
dictum

Fernald, James Champlin
ipso facto

Field, Kate
minister, retiring

Fields, James T.
ameliorate, bumpkin, delineate, florid

Finletter, Gretchen
cad

Firkins, Oscar W.
truckle

Fiske, John
exultation, munificent, omniscient,
sinecure

Flagg, Wilson
controvert, devolve, notwithstanding,
propensity, sagacity, skirt

Flanagan, Caitlin
dismissive, humdrum, stricture, venal

Flexner, Abraham
deplore

Follett, Helen Thomas
mawkish, nexus, Weltschmerz

Follett, Wilson
mawkish, neologism, nexus,
redoubtable, Weltschmerz

Fontaine, Robert
sacred cow

Fontana, David
faction

Ford, Gerald
superfluous

Frankfurter, Felix
chafe

Fraser, Caroline
coy

Freedman, David H.
trumpet

Freeland, Richard M.
paradigm

Freeman, Milton
oxymoron

Friedman, Benjamin M.
wellspring

Fuess, Claude M.
ardor, artless, aversion, castigate,
convulsive, noncommittal,
supercilious, voluble

Fumento, Michael
alliteration

Furlaud, Alice
slapdash

Gaddis, John Lewis
determinism

Galbraith, John Kenneth
pecuniary, Promethean, unregenerate

Galsworthy, John
impasse

Gannett, Lewis
permutation, racy

Garber, Marjorie
avatar, messianic

Gardner, Erle Stanley
indifferent

Gardner, Mona
pandemic

Gaulin, A.
inquisitorial

Gay, Robert M.
efface, etymology, hauteur, impalpable, veracity

Geer, Cornelia Throop
catchword

Gellhorn, Martha
plump

Glassman, James K.
disseminate

Goddard, Harold
prosaic

Godwin, Park
scurvy

Gold, Herbert
converse, derogatory

Goodheart, Adam
hapless

Goodman, George Jerome
colloquialism

Gordon, George A.
immanent, magnanimous

Gordon, James S.
refractory

Gould, Gerald
prudery

Grant, Neil Forbes
highbrow

Grasty, Charles H.
uxorious

Graves, Robert
inveterate

Gray, Asa
hypothesis

Gray, George W.
puissant

Green, Joshua
assail, calibrate, hew, strident

Green, Julian
perspicacity

Green, Lee
enduring, skew

Green, Stanley
burgeon

Griffith, Thomas
base, begrudge, cocooned, depredation, lugubrious, makeweight, perquisite

Gross, Michael Joseph
artifice, unguarded

Gupte, Pranay
loquacious

Gurewitsch, Matthew
abound, ex nihilo, flag, font

Halberstam, David
querulous

Hall, James Norman
husband, unctuous

Hall, Leland
sojourn

Hamilton, Charles V.
rift

Handlin, Oscar
extirpate

Hannay, James
relish, sui generis

Harkness, Mary Leal
imperative, plume, reprehensible, twaddle

Harman, Carter
keen

Harper, Timothy
disaffected

Harriman, Averell
spearhead

Harrison, George R.
accede

Harrison, Lawrence E.
benighted

Hart, Captain B. H. Liddell
nonce

Hart, Rollin Lynde
mum

Haskins, Caryl P.
admixture, horde

Hassett, Kevin A.
disseminate

Haultain, Arnold
infinitesimal, unfathomable

Hawthorne, Nathaniel
preponderance

Hazewell, Charles Creighton
autochthon, cashier, homogeneous

Henderson, Archibald
ex post facto

Henry, Mary Roblee
undulate

Hensher, Phillip
gothic

Hepner, Arthur W.
approbation

Herring, Hal
aphrodisiac

Higginson, Thomas Wentworth
brood, demeanor, disenfranchise, effete,
foray, prelude, raiment, savant, tonic

Hill, Adams Sherman
dishabille, slipshod

Hilton, James
bait

Hiss, Tony
hard-boiled

Hitchens, Christopher
convoluted, coup de grace, debauchery,
desiccated, doppelgänger, exalt,
jingoistic, mote, plaudits, rebuff,
revenant, tranche

Hoberman, Barry
ambiguous

Holden, Arthur C.
hew

Holden, Edward S.
acquiesce

Holden, Stephen
finite

Holmes, Oliver Wendell
deliquesce, efflorescence, impecunious,
poetaster

House, Edward Howard
impertinent

Howard, Jane
kvell

Howe, Ben Ryder
harrowing, insurgency

Howe, Julia Ward
jocose

Howells, William Dean
privation, venial

Hubert, Philip G. Jr.
outstrip, ridicule

Huddleston, Sisley
annihilate, respite

Huffington, Arianna Stassinopoulos
propitious

Humphrey, Hubert H.
integrated, legacy

Humphrey, Seth K.
doddering, insensate

Hunt, Thornton
ramble

Hutton, John E.
laconic

Inge, W. R.
Machiavellian

Jacks, L. P.
contrivance, discordant, precarious

Jackson, George Anson
spoliation

James, Henry Jr.
badinage, measure

James, Jamie
bas-relief, haj, kitsch, nefarious,
salubrious

James, William
bellicose

Janeway, Elizabeth
confidante

Janos, Leo
actuary

Johnson, Burges
sotto voce

Johnson, Gerald W.
bullheaded, steeped

Johnson, Josephine
loathe

Johnson, Nora
bogey

Johnston, George Alexander
simulacrum

Jones, Edgar L.
benevolent

Jones, Howard Mumford
adventitious, per se

Jones, Leonard Augustus
compass

Josephy, Alvin M. Jr.
detriment

Judson, Horace Freeland
equitable

Jung, Carl
ratiocination

Kalich, Timothy
hoary

Kaminer, Wendy
bask, denigrate, harbor, prerogative,
puerile

Kaplan, Justin
comminuted

Kaplan, Robert D.
bleak, bracing, calcified, fiat, littoral,
riven, sallow, searing, servile, signal,
stagy, sycophant

Kapur, Akash
demure

Karnow, Stanley
implacable

Kaufman, Judge Irving R.
sedition, verbose

Kazin, Alfred
mellifluous, proletarian

Keegan, John
obtain, stalemate

Keeler, Lucy Elliot
resolution, sham, simulate

Keith, Agnes Newton
inspissate

Keller, Helen
admonition

Kellogg, Vernon
abasement

Kelly, Michael
paramount, quell, quotient, stanch

Kemble, Francis Anne
emendation

Kennedy, David M.
modus vivendi, posture, rejoinder

Kennedy, John Fitzgerald
disinterested, touchstone

Keyes, Frances Parkinson
carp, irrefutable

Killen, Mary
self-deprecation

Kilpatrick, Carroll
carp, rash

King, Clarence
corrugations

King, Robert D.
crucible

Kino, Carol
rash

Kipen, David
bleak, persiflage

Kirk, John Foster
vortex

Kirn, Walter
patrician

Knapp, Arthur May
glib

Knopf, Alfred A.
singular

Knowlton, Don
vile

Knox, Bernard
appropriate

Koltun, Frances
amalgam

Koning, Hans
obtuse

Koussevitzky, Serge
transfuse

Kronenberger, Louis
condign, garlanded, unaffected,
vituperation

Krutch, Joseph Wood
coextensive, terra firma

Kummer, Corby
apotheosis, apt, codify, creditable, dark
horse, flummox, indecorous, lustrous,
marry, monkey, nexus, pretentious,
repugnant, savory, viscous, winnow

Kunitz, Stanley
prosody

Kunstler, James Howard
antipathy

Kupferberg, Herbert
chary, currency, granitic, impresario,
kinship, nil, pithy, pointed, taut

Landry, Robert J.
soothsayer

Langdon, Philip
abut, robber baron, spur

McGill, Ralph
harangue

McGovern, George
dastardly

McLellan, Alexander G.
vouchsafe

McPherson, Harry
simplistic

McPherson, James M.
persuasion

Mearsheimer, John J.
construct, counterintuitive

Mehta, Ved
all-encompassing

Mellett, Lowell
crux

Mencken, H. L.
dross

Menon, Narayana
hidebound

Merwin, Henry Childs
bestir, curry favor, sloth

Meyer, Cord Jr.
doctrinaire

Miller, Arthur R.
keystone

Miller, Matthew
jurisprudence

Mills, Harriet C.
edict, prostrate

Milne, A. A.
inordinate

Mitsukuri, Kakichi
ascetic

Mizener, Arthur
dogma

More, Paul Elmer
militate

Morgan, Arthur E.
panacea

Morgan, L. D.
sway

Morison, Samuel Eliot
intersperse

Morris, Charles R.
lion's share

Morton, Charles W.
dispensation

Morton, Oliver T.
usurp

Moses, Robert
apace, carpetbagger, diadem, intact, jeremiad

Moskos, Charles
bellicose

Motley, John Lothrop
filigree

Moulton, John Fletcher
timorous

Mueller, Tom
necropolis

Muir, Edwin
fructify

Muir, John
conifer, invincible, physiognomy, plunder, ravage

Mumford, Lewis
latterday

Münsterberg, Hugo
repose

Murphy, Cait
accoutrements, lurid

Murphy, Cullen
ascribe, avenue, awry, congeal,
consequential, continuum, conundrum,
curmudgeon, declivity, dolt,
extrapolate, founder, guarded, heyday,
iconic, inane, ineradicable, laissez-faire,
leach, leverage, mint, overarching,
presage, repository, riposte, riverine,
secular, solace, taxonomy, tender, trope

Mursell, James L.
nugatory

Myers, B. R.
patronize

Nehring, Cristina
adventurism, loath, resoundingly,
truncate, unflagging, untenable

Neon *See* Ackworth, Marion Whiteford

Newton, A. Edward
afford, farce, frequent, hardened,
lubricate, quietus, recherché, smug

Nichols, William I.
adroit

Niebuhr, Reinhold
circumspect, cursory, flush,
obscurantist, suasion

Nixon, Rob
verboten

Nock, Albert Jay
ex parte

Norman, Henderson Daingerfield
amplitude

Norton, A. B.
laity

Norton, Charles Eliot
hotbed, labyrinth

Nunberg, Geoffrey
doomsayer, ineluctable

O'Brien, Conor Cruise
ancien régime

Olson, Steve
evince

Origo, Iris
insidious

O'Rourke, P. J.
agglomeration, byword, jejune,
pertinent, Sisyphean

Ortega Y Gasset, José
demagogue

Orth, Samuel P.
casuistry, disgruntled

Orton, William
hierophant

Owen, David
aesthetic, apoplectic, minuscule,
reflexive, watershed

Ozick, Cynthia
polemical

Packard, Vance
pretentious

Page, Walter Hines
antebellum

Pappu, Sridhar
barb

Park, J. Edgar
beseech

Parker, W. B.
wrought

Pastor, Robert A.
transitory

Pattee, Richard
diffusion

Patton, Carl S.
perversity

Peabody, Andrew Preston
dullard

Peattie, Donald Culross
embattled, familiar, sesquipedalian

Peattie, Elia W.
depreciate, filch, momentum

Peck, John H.
unwitting

Peirce, Zina Fay
misnomer

Perkins, Samuel Cony
boon

Perry, Bliss
buttonhole, fallow, inverse, palliate

Peterson, Merrill D.
untrammeled

Peterson, Peter G.
beleaguered, pander, sustain

Pike, Robert E.
flirt, presentiment

Pinkerton, James P.
nostrum

Plissner, Martin
platitude

Plummer, Mark L.
cheeky

Poore, Ben Perley
cordial, preface

Posner, Richard A.
parody, verbatim

Powell, E. Alexander
crystallize

Powers, H. H.
unmindful

Powers, Thomas
pall

Powers, William
baleful, ne plus ultra

Press, Eyal
constraint, orbit

Preston, Harriet Waters
facile

Prévost, Jean
pretext, skinflint

Price, Lucien
waif

Prittie, Terence
hitherto

Prokofiev, Sergei
indignant

Purdy, Ken W.
diffident

Putnam, Eleanor
eldritch

Putnam, George W.
broach

Quammen, David
fulsome

Quincy, Edmund
anomaly, wax

Raines, Howell
lofty

Rathje, William
defray

Rauch, Jonathan
imponderables, polarized

Reich, Robert B.
conciliate

Reid, Alastair
remove

Rembar, Charles
plutocracy

Repplier, Agnes
dejected, prattle, unassailable, unstrung

Rich, Louise Dickinson
malign

Richardson, Elliot
aggrandize

Rideing, William Henry
fillip

Riis, Jacob
sepulchral

Ritter, Friedrich
enervate

Robinson, James Harvey
slacker

Rocca, Francis X.
fait accompli

Rogers, Anna A.
phlegmatic

Rolland, Romain
syzygy

Rolo, Charles J.
aficionado, blue-nose, cartographer,
claptrap, confute, romanticize, uncanny

Ronald, Malcolm B.
bête noire

Roosevelt, Eleanor
indisposition

Roosevelt, Theodore
concession, expedient, impracticable,
peremptory

Rose, Lloyd
cocky

Rose, Phyllis
forensic, staccato

Rosenberg, Tina
calculus

Rossetti, William M.
comport

Roth, Philip
charlatan, piquant

Rothenberg, Randall
aggregate, minion

Rubin, Richard
chastened

Russell, Bertrand
countenance, impious

Russell, Elizabeth H.
dictates

Rybczynski, Witold
bare-bones, blight, grandiloquence,
provenance

Sacher, H.
apothegm

Sage, Abby
enamored

Sagoff, Mark
cartel

Sanborn, Alvan F.
apotheosis, askance, coherent,
disconcerting, extenuation,
irretrievable, noisome, pied-à-terre

Sanborn, Franklin Benjamin
reproach

Sandburg, Carl
acclamation

Sandel, Michael J.
agrarian, republican

Sanderson, Ivan
protuberant, wily

Santayana, George
chattel, hobnob

Satel, Sally
hard-nosed

Scarf, Maggie
imbibe

Schauffler, Robert Haven
raison d'être

Schell, Jonathan
tandem

Scherman, Tony
diaspora, gulf, prismatic

Schiff, David
apocalyptic, avocation, consign,
inimitable, pigeonhole, quick study,
rake, schmaltz

Schlefer, Jonathan
foist

Schlesinger, Arthur M. Jr.
chagrin, condign, decimate, illimitable,
prelapsarian, revisionism

Schlosser, Eric
carnage, elude, revile, swath

Schneider, William
fealty

Schoenfeld, Gabriel
etiology

Schouler, James
redound

Schulberg, Budd
histrionic, lavish, splice

Schuman, Frederick L.
lackey

Schwarz, Benjamin
ad nauseam, attendant, autarky,
conflate, excoriate, historiography, lout,
magisterial, manumission, myopia,
obdurate, recondite, sardonic, stance

Scudder, Horace Elisha
jaunty, legerdemain, piecemeal, recur,
scrupulous

Scully, William Charles
disembowel

Sedgwick, Arthur George
desideratum, incidental music, satiated

Sedgwick, Ellery
equilibrium, ferret, gesticulate,
palisade, parsimonious, punctilio

Sedgwick, John
NIMBY

Sedgwick, Ora Gannett
calumny

See, Thomas Jefferson Jackson
conjecture

Sergeant, Thomas Perry
traffic

Shackford, Martha Hale
penuriousness

Shahn, Ben
blasphemy, rout

Shaler, N. S.
presage

Shand, John
dramatis personae

Shanly, Charles Dawson
appreciable, din, lark

Shell, Ellen Ruppel
cagey

Shenk, Joshua Wolf
euphoria

Siegel, Lee
arch, astringent, contested,
hagiography, repartee

Sikorsky, Igor
recoil

Simmons, Ernest J.
irrefutable

Simon, John
vox populi

Simonson, Lee
fresco, induce, jeer

Sitwell, Dame Edith
incipient

Sitwell, Sir Osbert
dunderhead, hosannahs

Sitwell, Sacheverell
connoisseur

Slocum, William Frederic Jr.
prig

Smith, Adam *See* Goodman, George
Jerome

Smith, Bradford
temporize

Smith, Daniel
philippic

Smith, Glanville
pacific

Smith, Logan Pearsall
avowal

Smith, Moses
inertia

Sokolov, Raymond A.
foist

Sokolsky, George E.
codify, cupidity, mulct

Sorel, Nancy Caldwell
lachrymose

Soros, George
epistemology, laissez-faire, postulate

Spaulding, Martha
rue

Sperry, Willard L.
touchstone

Spier, Leslie
protrude

Spock, Benjamin, M. D.
namby-pamby

Sprague, Charles James
immutable, obloquy, promulgate

Stanley, Herbert Wilton
enormity

Stark, Steven
atomize, fop, Weltanschauung

Starobin, Paul
spare

Stegner, Wallace
expurgate, glean

Steinberg, Rabbi Milton
rara avis

Steiner, George
discern

Stephenson, Wen
austere, resurgence

Stern, Jane and Michael
barnstorm, embodiment, flaunt

Stewart, Charles D.
jovial

Stewart, R. S.
animus

Steyn, Mark
injunction

Stiglitz, Joseph
gull

Stille, Alexander
esoterica

Stillman, William James
atelier

Stinnett, Caskie
unsettling

Stirling, Monica
felicity

Stolberg, Benjamin
sacred cow

Storey, Moorfield
prurient

Stossel, Scott
degrade, demur, spawn

Stowe, Harriet Beecher
droll

Stravinsky, Igor
homogeneous

Strickland, Edward
stellar

Strunsky, Simeon
petulant

Sullivan, Lawrence
pro forma

Sundgaard, Arnold
bridle, soporific, zest

Talbot, Margaret
litmus test, lubricious, sashay

Tallmadge, Thomas E.
corollary, grandiose

Tayler, Jeffrey
absolutism, churlish, devolve, entrepôt,
farrago, fastness, hurly-burly,
perdurable, sanctum sanctorum,
tatterdemalion

Taylor, Francis Henry
woolgathering

Taylor, Stuart Jr.
quotidian

Teale, Edwin Way
evidence

Teller (of Penn & Teller)
sleight of hand

Terkel, Studs
doggerel

Thittila, Bhikkhu U
conducive

Thomas, Benjamin B.
antagonism, bespeak, fervid, ludicrous

Thomas, Caitlin
enfant terrible

Thompson, Maurice
appellation, deluge, vitiate

Thoreau, Henry David
compunction, propagate, rank, saunter,
sedentary

Thurow, Lester C.
disequilibrium

Tinder, Glenn
dichotomy

Todd, Richard
addle, paradigm

Tonelson, Alan
defang

Toperoff, Sam
minuscule

Torrey, Bradford
hag-ridden

Toynton, Evelyn
nefarious

Traquair, Ramsay
spur

Treaster, Joseph B.
indignant

Trowbridge, John Townsend
vigor

Trueheart, Charles
lacuna, naif, opprobrium

Tuckerman, Henry Theodore
irrevocable

Tunis, John R.
descant, en masse, scuttle

Tunney, Gene
bristle, rancor

Turow, Scott
maxim

Twain, Mark
alluring, bankrupt

Ungar, Sanford J.
crusty, staunch

Van Fleet, Clark C.
pellucid, wheel

Vidal, Gore
dim, tutelary

Viereck, Peter
confute

Vigeland, Carl
register

Villard, Henry
dextrous

Vincent, Leon H.
expatiate

Walker, Francis A.
arable

Wallraff, Barbara
heady, louche, retrofit, vanguard,
vis-à-vis

Walter, William E.
itinerant

Warner, Charles Dudley
desultory, importunity

Washburn, Jennifer
constraint, orbit

Waters, Ethel
apparition

Waterston, Anna Morton
intercourse

Wattenberg, Martin P.
abysmal, inviolable

Webster, Samuel Charles
plum

Wechter, Dixon
bumptious, impertinent

Weeks, Edward
beneficent, camaraderie, expostulate,
maelstrom, prescient, sally,
skulduggery, troglodyte, willful

Weinberg, Steven
utopia

Weisman, Mary-Lou
Dickensian, urchin

Weiss, John
truculent

Welles, Sumner
envisage

Wells, H. G.
adumbrate

Wentworth, Philip E.
reconcile

Wertenbaker, T. J.
sap

Wharton, Edith
métier, polity

Wheatcroft, Geoffrey
bemuse, ennui, factitious, mutatis
mutandis, replicate, votary

Whicher, George F.
cardinal, unflinching

Whipple, Edwin Percy
disapprobation, heat, judicious,
nebulous, preeminent, slovenly

Whitaker, Jennifer Seymour
counterpoint

Whitcomb, Robert
agog

White, Merry I.
bawdy

White, Richard Grant
frivolous, pettifoggery

White, William Allen
clamor

Whitman, David
testament

Whitman, Walt
capacious, sinewy

Whitworth, William
seer

Wilber, Rhona Ryan
morass

Wilkins, Roy
forgo

Willert, Sir Arthur
salient

Williams, Alexander W.
humbug

Williams, Keith
effervescence

Wills, Garry
ameliorate, banter, interregnum,
preternatural, sangfroid

Wilson, Angus
squalor

Wilson, Douglas L.
abate, affinity, multiplicity, vex

Wilson, Edward O.
empiricism, prefigure

Wilson, Woodrow
organic

Winchester, Simon
vade mecum

Winthrop, Theodore
buffet, excrescence, plaint

Wise, David
conduit, cow, quagmire

Wise, Michael Z.
indemnify, recede

Wister, Fanny Kemble
trifle

Woglom, William H.
barefaced

Woolf, Virginia
analogous, fetter, unexpurgated

Worth, Andrew Dickson
cant

Worth, Nicholas *See* Page, Walter
Hines

Wright, Claudia
jar

Yardley, Jonathan
éclat

Yin, Xiao-huang
perturb

Young, Alexander
prognosticate

Zak, Steven
outlandish

Bibliography

Print Resources

Allen, Frederick Lewis. *The City in Slang: New York Life and Popular Speech*. New York: Oxford University Press, 1993.

American Heritage Dictionary. Edited by William Morris. Boston: Houghton Mifflin, 1978.

Axelrod, Alan, and Harry Oster. *The Penguin Dictionary of American Folklore*. New York: Penguin, 2000.

Ayto, John. *20th Century Words*. New York: Oxford University Press, 1999.

Bartlett, John. *Familiar Quotations*. Boston: Little, Brown, 1955.

Beckson, Karl, and Arthur Ganz. *A Reader's Guide to Literary Terms*. New York: Noon Day Press, 1962.

Bernstein, Theodore M. *The Careful Writer*. New York: Atheneum, 1966.

Bierce, Ambrose. *The Devil's Dictionary*. N.p.: Albert & Charles Boni, 1935.

———. *Write It Right*. New York: Charles L. Bowman, 1934.

Bliss, A. J. *A Dictionary of Foreign Words and Phrases*. New York: E. P. Dutton, 1966.

Botkin, B. A. *Sidewalks of America*. Indianapolis: Bobbs-Merrill, 1954.

Brewer, Ebenezer Cobham. *Brewer's Dictionary of Phrase and Fable*. New York: Harper & Row, 1970.

Brinton, Crane. *The Shaping of Modern Thought*. Englewood Cliffs, N. J.: Prentice-Hall, 1963.

Bryson, Bill. *Made in America: An Informal History of the English Language in the United States*. New York: William Morrow, 1994.

Bullock, Alan, and Oliver Stallybrass. *The Harper Dictionary of Modern Thought*. New York: Harper & Row, 1977.

Burgess, Gilett. *Burgess Unabridged*. Hamden, Conn.: The Shoe String Press, 1986.

Chapman, Robert L., ed. *Dictionary of American Slang*. New York: HarperCollins, 1995.

Chicago Manual of Style. 15th ed. Chicago: University of Chicago Press, 2003.

Clark, Thomas L. *Western Lore and Language*. Salt Lake City: University of Utah Press, 1996.

Crowell, Thomas Lee Jr. *NBC Handbook of Pronunciation*. New York: Thomas Y. Crowell, 1964.

Cuddon, J. A. *A Dictionary of Literary Terms*. London: Penguin Books, 1982.

Davidson, Alan. *The Oxford Companion to Food*. Oxford: Oxford University Press, 1999.

Desaulniers, Louise, ed. *119 Years of The Atlantic*. Boston: Little, Brown, 1977.

Dickson, Paul. *Slang*. New York: Pocket Books, 1998.

Dillard, J. L. *American Talk*. New York: Random House, 1976.

Duberman, Martin. *James Russell Lowell*. Boston: Houghton Mifflin, 1966.

Ehrlich, Eugene. *Amo, Amas, Amat and More*. New York: Harper & Row, 1985.

Eppard, Philip B., and George Monteiro. *A Guide to the Atlantic Monthly Contributors' Club*. Boston: G. K. Hall, 1983.

Evans, Bergen, and Cornelia Evans. *A Dictionary of Contemporary American Usage*. New York: Random House, 1957.

Evans, Toshie M. *A Dictionary of Japanese Loan Words*. Westport, Conn.: Greenwood Press, 1997.

Flexner, Stuart Berg, ed. *I Hear America Talking*. New York: Touchstone, 1979.

Flexner, Stuart Berg, and Anne H. Soukhanov. *Speaking Freely*. New York: Oxford University Press, 1997.

Follett, Wilson. *Modern American Usage*. New York: Avenel Books, 1980.

Fowler, H.W. *A Dictionary of Modern Usage*. New York: Oxford University Press, 1950.

Funk, Charles Earle. *2107 Curious Word Origins, Sayings & Expressions*. New York: Galahad Books, 1993.

Gilman, E. Ward, ed. *Merriam-Webster Dictionary of English Usage*. Springfield, Mass.: Merriam-Webster, 1989.

Goodman, Susan, and Carl Dawson. *William Dean Howells: A Writer's Life*. Berkeley: University of California Press, 2005.

Grambs, David. *Literary Companion Dictionary*. London: Routledge & Kegan Paul, 1984.

Hardwick, Michael and Mollie. *The Sherlock Holmes Companion*. New York: Bramhall House, 1962.

Harvey, Paul. *The Oxford Companion to English Literature*. Oxford: Oxford University Press, 1967.

Hastings, James, ed. *Dictionary of the Bible*. New York: Charles Scribner's Sons. 1963.

Hayakawa, S. I. *Use the Right Word*. N.p.: The Reader's Digest Association, 1968.

Hendrickson, Robert. *The Literary Life and Other Curiosities*. New York: Viking, 1981.

Holy Bible. Philadelphia: A. J. Holman, n.d.

Hopkin, Daniel J., ed. *Merriam-Webster's Geographical Dictionary*. Springfield, Mass.: Merriam-Webster, 1995.

Hopkins, Joseph G. E. *Concise Dictionary of American Biography*. New York: Charles Scribner's Sons, 1964.

Ives, George B. *Text, Type and Style: A Compendium of Atlantic Usage*. Boston: The Atlantic Monthly Press, 1921.

Jones, Barry, and M. V. Dixon. *The Rutledge Dictionary of People*. New York: Rutledge Press, 1981.

Knowles, Elizabeth, ed. *The Oxford Dictionary of New Words*. New York: Oxford University Press, 1998.

Kohl, Herbert. *From Archetype to Zeitgeist*. Boston: Little, Brown, 1992.

Kostelanetz, Richard. *Dictionary of the Avant-Gardes*. Pennington, N.J.: Chicago Review Press, 1993.

Labensky, Steven, Gaye G. Ingram, and Sarah R. Labensky. *Webster's New World Dictionary of Culinary Arts*. Upper Saddle River, N.J.: Prentice Hall, 1997.

Laird, Pamela W. *Advertising Progress: American Business and the Rise of Consumer Marketing*. Baltimore: Johns Hopkins University Press, 1998.

Longfellow, Ernest Wadsworth. *Random Memories*. Boston: Houghton Mifflin, 1922.

Manning, Robert. *The Swamp Root Chronicle: Adventures in the Word Trade*. New York: W. W. Norton, 1992.

Marckwardt, Albert H. *American English*. New York: Oxford University Press, 1958.

Matthews, Mitford M. *Americanisms*. Chicago: University of Chicago Press, 1966.

McArthur, Tom, ed. *The Oxford Companion to the English Language*. Oxford: Oxford University Press, 1992.

McPherson, James M. *How Lincoln Won the War with Metaphors*. Fort Wayne, Ind.: Louis A. Warren Lincoln Library and Museum, 1985.

Mencken, H. L. *The American Language*. New York: Alfred A. Knopf, 1962.

——. *The American Language, Supplements I and II*. New York: Alfred A. Knopf, 1962.

Merriam-Webster's Biographical Dictionary. Edited by Robert McHenry. Springfield, Mass.: Merriam-Webster, 1995.

Merriam-Webster's Dictionary of American Writers. Springfield, Mass.: Merriam-Webster, 2001.

Metcalf, Allan A., and David K. Barnhart. *America in So Many Words*. Boston: Houghton Mifflin, 1997.

Mugglestone, Lynda. *Lost for Words: The Hidden History of the Oxford English Dictionary*. New Haven: Yale University Press, 2005.

Nicholson, Margaret. *American-English Usage*. New York: Oxford University Press, 1957.

Ostler, Rosemarie. *Dewdroppers, Waldos, and Slackers*. New York: Oxford University Press, 2003.

Partridge, Eric. *A Dictionary of Clichés*. London: Routledge & Kegan Paul, 1985.

——. *A Dictionary of Slang and Unconventional Usage*. New York: Macmillan, 1970.

Perrin, Noel. *Dr. Bowdler's Legacy*. Boston: David R. Godine, 1992.

Polley, Jane, ed. *Stories Behind Everyday Things*. Pleasantville, N.Y.: The Reader's Digest Association, 1980.

Quinion, Michael. *Ballyhoo, Buckaroo and Spuds*. Washington, D.C.: Smithsonian Books, 2004.

Random House Dictionary of the English Language. Edited by Stuart Berg Flexner. New York: Random House, 1987.

Rawson, Hugh. *Devious Derivations*. Edison, N.J.: Castle Books, 2002.

Reader's Digest. *Family Word Finder*. New York: The Reader's Digest Association, 1975.

——. *Success with Words*. New York: The Reader's Digest Association, 1983.

Riley, Dick, and Pam McAllister. *The Bedside, Bathtub & Armchair Companion to Sherlock Holmes*. New York: Continuum, 1999.

Rodale, J. I. *The Synonym Finder*. Emmaus, Pa.: Rodale Books, 1961.

Rohman, Chris. *A World of Ideas*. New York: Ballantine Books, 1999.

Rosten, Leo. *The Joys of Yiddish*. New York: McGraw-Hill, 1968.

——. *The Joys of Yinglish*. New York: McGraw-Hill, 1989.

Scholes, Percy A., *The Concise Oxford Dictionary of Music*. London: Oxford University Press, 1964.

Sedgwick, Ellery. *The Atlantic Monthly, 1857-1909*. Amherst: University of Massachusetts Press, 1994.

Segell, Michael. *The Devil's Horn: The Story of the Saxophone, from Noisy Novelty to King of Cool*. New York: Farrar, Straus and Giroux, 2005.

Serjeantson, Mary S. *A History of Foreign Words in English*. London: Routledge & Kegan Paul, 1935.

Siegel, Allan M., and William G. Connolly. *The New York Times Manual of Style and Usage*. New York: Times Books, 1999.

Strunk, William Jr., and E. B. White. *The Elements of Style*. New York: Macmillan, 1979.

Super, R. H. "Truth and Fiction in Trollope's Autobiography." *Nineteenth-Century Literature* 48, no. 1 (June 1993): 74-88.

Train, Arthur Jr. *The Story of Everyday Things*. New York: Harper & Brothers, 1941.

Tulloch, Sara. *The Oxford Dictionary of New Words*. Oxford: Oxford University Press, 1991.

Unger, Harlow Giles. *Noah Webster: The Life and Times of an American Patriot*. New York: John Wiley & Sons, 1998.

Webster, Noah. *An American Dictionary of the English Language*. Springfield, Mass.: G. & C. Merriam, 1875.

Webster's New World College Dictionary. 4th ed. Edited by Michael Agnes. New York: Macmillan, 1999.

Webster's New World Encyclopedia. Edited by Stephen P. Elliot, Martha Goldstein, and Michael Upshall. New York: Prentice Hall, 1992.

Webster's Ninth New Collegiate Dictionary. Edited by Frederick C. Mish. Springfield, Mass.: Merriam-Webster, 1985.

Webster's Third New International Dictionary. Edited by Philip P. Gove. Springfield, Mass.: G. & C. Merriam, 1976.

Weeks, Edward, and Emily Flint, eds. *Jubilee: One Hundred Years of the Atlantic*. Boston: Little, Brown, 1958.

Wentworth, Harold, and Stuart Berg Flexner. *Dictionary of American Slang.* New York: Thomas Y. Crowell, 1975.

Wilton, David. *Word Myths: Debunking Linguistic Urban Legends.* Oxford: Oxford University Press, 2004.

Winchester, Simon. *The Meaning of Everything: The Story of the Oxford English Dictionary.* Oxford: Oxford University Press, 2003.

Wright, William Aldis, ed. *The Complete Works of William Shakespeare.* New York: Garden City Books, 1936.

Internet Resources

The Atlantic Monthly. Edited by Sage Stossel. www.theatlantic.com.

Encyclopedia Britannica. Edited by Dale H. Hoiberg. www.britannica.com.

Making of America Digital Collection. Cornell University Library. http://cdl.library.cornell.edu/moa.

The New York Times. Edited by Jim Roberts. www.nytimes.com.

OneLook Dictionaries. www.onelook.com.

Oxford English Dictionary. Edited by John Simpson. www.oed.com.

World Wide Words. Edited by Michael Quinion. www.worldwidewords.org.

Permissions

The authors wish to acknowledge the assistance of those listed below in granting permission to reprint from the works cited:

Bruno Bettelheim: "Punishment Versus Discipline," by Bruno Bettelheim, in *The Atlantic Monthly*, November 1985. From A GOOD ENOUGH PARENT (Knopf), copyright ©1987 by Bruno Bettleheim. Reprinted by permission of the author's agents, Raines & Raines.

Catherine Drinker Bowen: "The Nature of the Artist," by Catherine Drinker Bowen, in *The Atlantic Monthly*, November 1961. "The Search for Francis Bacon," by Catherine Drinker Bowen, in *The Atlantic Monthly*, January 1966. Reprinted by permission of Harold Ober Associates Incorporated. David S. Broder: "The Democrats' Dilemma," by David Broder, in *The Atlantic Monthly*, March 1974. ©1974 by The Washington Post. Reprinted with permission. Stokely Carmichael and Charles V. Hamilton: "Dynamite," by Stokely Carmichael and Charles V. Hamilton, in *The Atlantic Monthly*. From BLACK POWER, copyright ©1967. Courtesy of Random House and Charles V. Hamilton. Raymond Chandler: "Oscar Night in Hollywood," by Raymond Chandler, featured in *The Atlantic Monthly*; ©1948 Raymond Chandler Limited, a Chorion company. "Writers in Hollywood," by Raymond Chandler, featured in *The Atlantic Monthly*; ©1945 Raymond Chandler Limited, a Chorion company. All rights reserved. Diana Cooper: "The Lion's Heart," by Diana Cooper, in *The Atlantic Monthly*, March 1965. Copyright ©1965. Reprinted by permission of the Estate of Diana Cooper, courtesy of Artemis Cooper.

E. E. Cummings: "I & My Parents' Son," by E. E. Cummings, in *The Atlantic Monthly*, April 1953. From I: SIX NONLECTURES by E. E. Cummings, ©1953. ©1981 by the Trustees for the E. E. Cummings Trust. Used by permission of Liveright Publishing Corporation. Moshe Dayan: "Encounters," by Moshe Dayan, *The Atlantic Monthly*, June 1981. From BREAKTHROUGH, Alfred A. Knopf, copyright ©1981. Courtesy of Knopf Publishing Group. Clifton Fadiman: "The Ghost of Napoleon," by Clifton Fadiman, in *The Atlantic Monthly*, May 1942. With permission of Lescher & Lescher, Ltd. "Herman Melville," by Clifton Fadiman, in *The Atlantic Monthly*, October 1943. With permission of Lescher & Lescher, Ltd. "Pickwick Lives Forever," in *The Atlantic Monthly*, December 1949. With permission of Lescher & Lescher, Ltd. Robert Graves: "Homer's Winks and Nods," by Robert Graves, in *The Atlantic Monthly*, November 1959. With permission of Carcanet Press Limited. George R. Harrison: "Albert Einstein," by George R. Harrison, in *The Atlantic Monthly*, June 1955, from WHAT MAN MAY BE, by George R. Harrison, copyright ©1953, 1954, 1956 by George R. Harrison. With permission of HarperCollins Publishers.

Horace Freeland Judson: "The Rage to Know," by Horace Freeland Judson, in *The Atlantic Monthly*. From THE SEARCH FOR SOLUTIONS, by Horace Freeland Judson, ©1987 by Playback Associates. Reprinted by permission of Henry Holt and Company. Carl Jung: "Jung's View of Christianity," by Carl Jung. From MEMORIES, DREAMS,

REFLECTIONS, copyright ©1963. Courtesy of Pantheon Books. Alfred Kazin: "Hemingway as His Own Fable." First published in the June 1964 issue of *The Atlantic Monthly;* ©1964 by Alfred Kazin, permission of the Wylie Agency. "The Bitter 30's: From a Personal History." First published in the May 1962 issue of *The Atlantic Monthly;* ©1962 by Alfred Kazin, permission of The Wylie Agency. John Keegan: "Shedding Light on Lebanon," by John Keegan, in *The Atlantic Monthly*, April 1984, copyright ©John Keegan 1984. "The Ordeal of Afghanistan," by John Keegan, in *The Atlantic Monthly*, November 1985. Copyright ©John Keegan 1985. With permission of Gillon Aitken Associates, Ltd. Helen Keller: "Three Days to Live," by Helen Keller, in *The Atlantic Monthly*, January 1933. Copyright ©1933 Helen Keller, used with permission of the American Foundation for the Blind. Bernard Knox: "Home Sweet Home," by Bernard Knox. Copyright ©1987 by Bernard Knox. Originally appeared in *The Atlantic Monthly* (May 1987). Reprinted by permission of Georges Borchardt, Inc., on behalf of the author. Thomas Mann: "The Making of 'The Magic Mountain,'" by Thomas Mann, in *The Atlantic Monthly*, January 1953. In "Einführung in den Zauberberg. Für Studenten der Universität Princeton." From: Thomas Mann, *Gesammelte Werke in Dreizehn Bänden. Band XI. Reden und Aufsätze.* ©1960, 1974 by S. Fischer Verlag GmbH, Frankfort am Main. "The Joseph Novels," by Thomas Mann, in *The Atlantic Monthly*, February 1943. In "Joseph und seine Brüder. Ein Vortrag." From: Thomas Mann, *Gesammelte Werke in Dreizehn Bänden. Band XI. Reden und Aufsätze.* ©1960, 1974 by S. Fischer Verlag GmbH, Frankfort am Main.

John Masefield: "The Joy of Story-Telling," by John Masefield, in *The Atlantic Monthly*, March 1951. Reprinted with permission of the Society of Authors as the Literary Representative of the Estate of John Masefield. Ved Mehta: "A Donkey in a World of Horses," by Ved Mehta. Copyright ©1957 by Ved Mehta. Originally appeared in *The Atlantic Monthly* July 1957. Reprinted by permission of George Borchardt, Inc., on behalf of the author. Elliot Richardson: "The Saturday Night Massacre," by Elliot Richardson, in *The Atlantic Monthly*, March 1976. From THE CREATIVE BALANCE, by Elliot Richardson, ©1976 by Elliot Richardson. Reprinted by permission of Henry Holt and Company, LLC. Philip Roth: "Joe College," by Philip Roth, in *The Atlantic Monthly*, December 1987. ©1987 by Philip Roth, with permission of the Wylie Agency. "On Satirizing Presidents — An Interview With Philip Roth, in *The Atlantic Monthly*, December 1971. ©1971 by Philip Roth, with permission of the Wylie Agency. Bertrand Russell: "The Exceptional Man," by Bertrand Russell, in *The Atlantic Monthly*, November 1949. From AUTHORITY AND THE INDIVIDUAL. With permission of The Bertrand Russell Peace Foundation Ltd. "Authority and the Individual," by Bertrand Russell, in *The Atlantic Monthly*, September 1951. With permission of Thomson Publishing Services.

Carl Sandburg: "Those Who Make Poems," by Carl Sandburg, copyright ©1942 by Carl Sandburg, in *The Atlantic Monthly*, March 1942. Copyright 1942 by Carl Sandburg, reprinted by permission of the Carl Sandburg Family Trust. Edith Sitwell: "When I Was Young and Uneasy," by Edith Sitwell, in *The Atlantic Monthly*, March 1965. With permission of David Higham Associates. Osbert Sitwell: "The Happiest Time of One's Life," by Osbert Sitwell, in *The Atlantic Monthly*, April 1946. From THE SCARLET TREE, 1946. With permission of David Higham Associates. "New York in the Twenties," by Osbert Sitwell, in

The Atlantic Monthly, February 1962. With permission of David Highham Associates. Sacheverell Sitwell: "The Artistic Genius of Holland," by Sacheverell Sitwell, in *The Atlantic Monthly*, April 1954. With permission of David Higham Associates. Ethel Waters: "Mamba's Daughter," by Ethel Waters and Charles Samuels, in *The Atlantic Monthly*, March 1951. From HIS EYE IS ON THE SPARROW, copyright ©1951. Courtesy of Random House, Inc. Edith Wharton: "Confessions of a Novelist," by Edith Wharton, in *The Atlantic Monthly*, April 1933. Copyright ©1933. Reprinted by permission of the estate of Edith Wharton and the Watkins/Loomis Agency. Virginia Woolf: "The Art of Biography" from THE DEATH OF THE MOTH AND OTHER ESSAYS by Virginia Woolf, copyright 1942 by Harcourt, Inc. and renewed 1970 by Marjorie T. Parsons, Executrix, reprinted by permission of the publisher. "My Father: Leslie Stephen" from THE CAPTAIN'S DEATH BED AND OTHER ESSAYS by Virginia Woolf, copyright 1950 and renewed 1978 by Harcourt, Inc., reprinted by permission of the publisher.

In addition, the authors wish to thank the individuals who granted permission to reprint from the works of the following contributors: Conrad Aiken, Stewart Alsop, Martha Bacon, George W. Ball, William Barrett, Nora Beloff, Robert Bingham, Jacob Bronowski, John N. Cole, Scott Corbett, Lord Patrick Devlin, Bergen Evans, John K. Fairbank, Henry Fairlie, Erle Stanley Gardner, Martha Gellhorn, Thomas Griffith, James Norman Hall, Hubert H. Humphrey, Burges Johnson, Gerald W. Johnson, Howard Mumford Jones, Alvin M. Josephy Jr., Irving R. Kaufman, Louis Kronenberger, Herbert Kupferberg, Walter Lippmann, Charles McDowell Jr., Arthur Mizener, Cord Meyer Jr., Vance Packard, Donald Culross Peattie, Charles Rembar, George Santayana, Ben Shahn, Benjamin J. Spock, Wallace Stegner, Caskie Stinnett, Caitlin Thomas, Angus Wilson and Fanny Kemble Wister.

The authors also wish to acknowledge the following contributors for granting permission to reprint from their works: Bruce Ackerman, Arthur Allen, Brooke Allen, Charlotte Allen, Perry Anderson, John F. Andrews, William Aron, James Atlas, David Barber, Michael J. Barrett, Marisa Bartolucci, Alex Beam, Jack Beatty, Adam Bellow, Michael Benson, Bill Berkeley, Alan Berlow, Paul Bloom, Roy Blount Jr., Charles Boewe, Kate Bolick, Mark Bowden, Daniel Boyne, Anthony Brandt, David Brooks, Kenneth Brower, Michael H. Brown, Holly Brubach, Stephen Budiansky, William T. Burke, Chandler Burr, Tom Carson, Terry Castle, Fred Catapano, Curtis Cate, Edwin Chen, Lynn Chu, Rene Chun, Robert Cipes, Gary Cohen, Warren I. Cohen, James Conaway, Trevor Corson, Harvey Cox, Deborah Cramer, Robert P. Crease, Wayne Curtis, Robert Dallek, Francis Davis, David Denby, Mark Derr, Chitra Divakaruni, John Donatich, Dennis Drabelle, Elizabeth Brenner Drew, Peter F. Drucker, David Ewing Duncan, Gregg Easterbrook, Alexander Eliot, Ezekiel Emanuel, André Emmerich, Joseph Epstein, Michael Erard, James Fallows, Caitlin Flanagan, David Fontana, Gerald Ford, Caroline Fraser, David H. Freedman, Richard M. Freeland, Milton Freeman, Benjamin M. Friedman, Michael Fumento, Alice Furland, John Lewis Gaddis, John Kenneth Galbraith, Marjorie Garber, James K. Glassman, Herbert Gold, Adam Goodheart, George Jerome Goodman, Joshua Green, Lee Green, Michael Joseph Gross, Pranay Gupte, Matthew Gurewitsch.

David Halberstam, Oscar Handlin, Timothy Harper, Lawrence E. Harrison, Kevin A. Hassett, Phillip Hensher, Arthur W. Hepner, Hal Herring, Tony Hiss, Christopher Hitchens, Stephen Holden, Ben Ryder Howe, Arianna Stassinopoulos Huffington, Jamie James, Leo Janos, Wendy Kaminer, Justin Kaplan, Robert D. Kaplan, Akash Kapur, Stanley Karnow, David M. Kennedy, Robert D. King, Carol Kino, David Kipen, Walter Kirn, Frances Koltun, Hans Koning, Corby Kummer, Stanley Kunitz, Philip Langdon, William Langewiesche, Eve LaPlante, Christopher Layne, Christopher B. Leinberger, Brad Leithauser, Nicholas Lemann, Toby Lester, Bernard Lewis, James Lieber, Joseph Lieberman, J. E. Lighter, Leon F. Litwack, Margot Livesey, Ann Wilson Lloyd, Charles Lockwood, David Lodge, Sandra Tsing Loh, Ralph Lombreglia, Michael Lydon, Thomas Mallon, Charles C. Mann, James Mann, Robert Manning, Gina Maranto, David Marc, James Marcus, Gordon D. Marino, Jonathan Maslow, Kathleen McAuliffe, George McGovern, James M. McPherson, John J. Mearsheimer, Arthur R. Miller, Matthew Miller, Harriet C. Mills, Charles R. Morris, Charles Moskos, Tom Mueller, Cait Murphy, Cullen Murphy, B. R. Myers, Cristina Nehring, Rob Nixon, Geoffrey Nunberg, Conor Cruise O'Brien, Steve Olson, P. J. O'Rourke, David Owen, Cynthia Ozick.

Sridhar Pappu, Robert A. Pastor, Peter G. Peterson, James P. Pinkerton, Mark Plummer, Richard A. Posner, Thomas Powers, William Powers, Eyal Press, David Quammen, Howell Raines, Jonathan Rauch, Robert B. Reich, Francis X. Rocca, Phyllis Rose, Tina Rosenberg, Randall Rothenberg, Richard Rubin, Witold Rybczynski, Mark Sagoff, Michael J. Sandel, Sally Satel, Maggie Scarf, Jonathan Schell, Tony Scherman, David Schiff, Arthur M. Schlesinger Jr., Eric Schlosser, William Schneider, Gabriel Schoenfeld, Benjamin Schwarz, Ellen Ruppel Shell, Joshua Wolf Shenk, Lee Siegel, John Simon, Daniel Smith, Raymond A. Sokolov, Nancy Caldwell Sorel, George Soros, Martha Spaulding, Steven Stark, Paul Starobin, George Steiner, Wen Stephenson, Jane and Michael Stern, Mark Steyn, Joseph Stiglitz, Alexander Stille, Scott Stossel, Arnold Sundgaard, Margaret Talbot, Jeffrey Tayler, Stuart Taylor Jr., Teller, Studs Terkel, Lester C. Thurow, Glenn Tinder, Richard Todd, Alan Tonelson, Evelyn Toynton, Joseph B. Treaster, Charles Trueheart, Scott Turow, Sanford J. Ungar, Gore Vidal, Carl Vigeland, Barbara Wallraff, Jennifer Washburn, Martin P. Wattenberg, Steven Weinberg, Mary-Lou Weisman, Geoffrey Wheatcroft, Merry I. White, David Whitman, William Whitworth, Garry Wills, Douglas L. Wilson, Edward O. Wilson, Simon Winchester, David Wise, Michael Z. Wise, Jonathan Yardley, Xiao-huang Yin and Steven Zak.

While we have made every attempt to acknowledge all copyright holders, we will gladly address any unintended omissions in future printings.

Acknowledgments

Toby Lester, a deputy managing editor at *The Atlantic*, opened the door to this project, responding enthusiastically to our proposal and setting us on the road to a great personal and intellectual adventure. We are indebted to him.

What began as our semi-solitary task of drawing memorable passages from 148 years of *The Atlantic Monthly* ended as an endeavor involving the help and generosity of hundreds. We spent ten months reading through back issues and doing associated research at *The Atlantic's* offices in Boston where, at one point or another, every member of the staff was helpful to us. And so we thank Katie Bacon, David Barber, Nell Beram, Ken Berard, Leslie Cauldwell, Lee Caulfield, C. Michael Curtis, Jennifer Farmer, Benjamin Healy, Emerson Hilton, Gillian Kahn, John Kefferstan, Corby Kummer, Julia Livshin, Linda Lowenthal, Robert Moeller, Bessmarie Moll, Muriel Montiero, Mary Parsons, Lucie Prinz, Yvonne Rolzhausen, Benjamin Schwarz, Martha Spaulding, Scott Stossel, Elizabeth Shelburne, Amy Swan, Barbara Wallraff, Eric Westby and Jon Zobenica. Our thanks, too, to Alfred Carfagna, whose hearty "Good morning!" at the entrance to 77 North Washington Street greeted us hundreds of times.

David Bradley's blessing for this project was heartening. We thank *The Atlantic's* chairman for his encouragement and enthusiasm.

Managing editor Cullen Murphy welcomed us into the staff's monthly editorial meetings, Web site editor Sage Stossel started us on the road to contacting hundreds of *Atlantic* authors, and office manager Michael Kubit settled us in and brought us into the *Atlantic* fold. His warm friendship was a highlight of our Atlantic experience.

Several of *The Atlantic's* indispensable interns proved valuable to us, too, and we thank Zaina Arafat, Michael Gibson, Eva Hoffman, Ryder Kessler, Elizabeth Pantazelos, Jennifer Percy and Shwan Ziad.

We are deeply grateful to the many family members, executors, literary agents, publishers' staff members and others who gave permission for the use of a writer's work, or who helped us to reach the party who could.

For their contributions to this book in a variety of ways we thank Enid Anker, Robert Anker, John J. Annese, John Cooney, Avril Cornell, Ofer Egber, Jean Evans, Janet Ewell, Francisco Fazio, Bruce Feffer, Norman Friedman, Elyse and Mel Glenn, Joan Goody, Diane Graham, Richard Grayson, Lisa Greenman, Sara Greenman, Martha Guson, Don Harlow, Anita Israel, Nancy K. Jones, Madelyn Kelly, Pamela W. Laird, Paul Leder, John Losey, Dina and Roman Losovsky, Jack Lynch, Joan Mann, Robert Manning, Mary Naughton, Steve O'Donoghue, Svetla Olsson, Merrill Perlman, Robert Plotkin, Jeff and Sally Redmond, Claire Regan, Nancy Hall Rutgers, Hillina Seife, Michael Simms, Richard Smith, Annie Sokolov-Uris, Rachel and Michael Weiss, William Whitworth and Howard Zaharoff.

During our ten months at *The Atlantic* we lived in several different homes in the Boston area, and are grateful for the help and hospitality extended to us by Luise Erdmann, Lucie Prinze and Richard Edelman, and Nancy, Ryke and Eleanor Spence. Special thanks to Massachusetts Congressman Bill Delahunt, who not only transported our possessions from one apartment to the next but carried them up five flights of stairs to a new apartment, assisted by his daughters Kirstin and Kara. Ruth Goodman, our guardian angel in Boston, found places for us to live, supplied her own home in between, and was our companion, our refuge and our social director.

Thanks to Philip B. Eppard for the names of the once anonymous members of *The Atlantic*'s Contributor's Club; and to Ellery Sedgwick, whose vast knowledge of *Atlantic* history enhanced the editors' biographies in this book's appendix.

Our thanks to the Levenger Press gang — Danielle Furci, Ray Moore, Vicki Ehrenman, Tim Barbini, Tina St. Pierre, Sherdean Rhule and Megan Gordon — for their craftsmanship and the loving care they took in turning manuscript into book. Thank you, Steve and Lori Leveen, founders of Levenger, for believing in the power of words. We are proud to once again be a part of a company devoted to serving an audience for whom reading and writing are not only pleasurable, but essential.

Our editor, Mim Harrison, helped to shape this book's format, contents and spirit. It is a wonderful thing for authors to know that their book is in the best of hands.

To our daughters, our sons-in-law and our grandchildren, our thanks for their support and for patiently enduring our cloistered lives. And our thanks to each other for the undiminished pleasure we had working together on this book.

Finally, our thanks to the editors whose minds, hearts and souls since 1857 helped to guide and ennoble *The Atlantic Monthly*, which in turn has helped to shape the principles, progress and direction of America. We are privileged to have been a part of *The Atlantic* for a brief while, to have known its admirable staff, and to have created this book.

About the Authors

Robert Greenman is a consultant to *The New York Times's* Newspaper in Education program and the author of many of its curriculum guides. He is a frequent workshop presenter on the topic of newspapers as a teaching tool, addressing conferences of the Journalism Education Association and the Columbia Scholastic Press Association. His previous book published by Levenger Press, the first *Words That Make a Difference*, is based on passages from the *Times*.

A graduate of Emerson College, Mr. Greenman has taught more than 10,000 high school and college students the value, power and pleasure of using language effectively. Among the national awards he has received for contributions to journalism education is the *Times's* Charles R. O'Malley Award for Excellence.

Mr. Greenman serves on the executive council of the New York City chapter of the Society of Professional Journalists. He is a member of the American Dialect Society, the Dictionary Society of North America and the American Name Society.

Carol Greenman provided research services for the first *Words That Make a Difference*. This book marks her first full collaboration with her husband. The Greenmans live in Brooklyn.

Enjoy more of this enduring American tradition

We hope these pages have whetted your appetite for reading more of *The Atlantic*. We invite you to sample the magazine online at **www.theatlantic.com**.

Uncommon Books for Serious Readers

Boston
Henry Cabot Lodge

A Boy at the Hogarth Press
Written and illustrated by
Richard Kennedy

Delight
J. B. Priestley

The Dream
Sir Winston Churchill

Feeding the Mind
Lewis Carroll

A Fortnight in the Wilderness
Alexis de Tocqueville

**The Little Guide to
Your Well-Read Life**
Steve Leveen

The Making of The Finest Hour
Speech by Winston S. Churchill
Introduction by Richard M. Langworth

New York
Theodore Roosevelt

On a Life Well Spent
Cicero
Preface by Benjamin Franklin

Rare Words
Jan Leighton
and Hallie Leighton

Samuel Johnson's Dictionary
**Selections from the 1755 work
that defined the English language**
Edited by Jack Lynch

Samuel Johnson's Insults
Edited by Jack Lynch

The Silverado Squatters
Six selected chapters
Robert Louis Stevenson

Words That Make a Difference
with passages from *The New York Times*
Robert Greenman

Levenger Press is the publishing arm of

L E V E N G E R®
TOOLS FOR SERIOUS READERS

www.Levenger.com   800.544.0880